BRITAIN – VEGETAI

There are over 100 vegetarian
Cornwall, Cumbria, Scotland and
But you'll never find most of th

C000023783

Vegetarian Britain features:

500 restaurants and take-aways across the country.
Detailed reviews with prices, hours, sample dishes,
plus what's on the menu for vegans.
200 veggie friendly places to stay.
Ethnic restaurants with huge veggie menus.
Hundreds of health food and wholefood stores.

New in this edition:

250 extra pages – biggest guide ever!
Hugely **expanded** guest house listings, with real prices and
what to do in the area so you won't need to send for brochures.
Features on Top Ten Veggie Destinations.
Munchie maps of Brighton, Edinburgh, Liverpool, central London.
New **London accommodation map**.
Maps of England, Scotland, Wales, Cornwall and Cumbria.
Veggie and veggie-friendly **hostels** for budget travellers.
Dozens of fabulous **new restaurants and guest houses**.
New chapters for Ireland, Isle of Man and Channel Islands.
Bursting with yummy veggie goodness!

Over 20,000 copies in print !

Vegetarian Guides is the world's first international vegetarian guidebook
company, mapping the world for veggies, vegans and those who love delicious,
healthy, animal-free nosh.

Alex Bourke went vegetarian at fourteen and didn't meet another for five years.
Having been "the software guy" at a guidebook company in the eighties, he spent
two years doing time in France, and a year as Campaigns Coordinator at Viva! All
these experiences came together in the co-production of *Vegetarian Britain*,
Vegetaran France, Vegetarian Europe and four editions of *Vegetarian London*.

Australian born **Katrina Holland** became vegan at the age of seventeen without
having ever met another vegan. A couple of years later she started a vegan social
group and newsletter. At the age of twenty-one she moved to England. She has
travelled extensively around Western Europe, Turkey and several other countries
and she wrote three sections of *Vegetarian Europe*.

Alex and Katrina contribute travel articles to magazines and write a monthly page
for the American newspaper *VegNews*. They have helped countless journalists
and researchers, and appeared on radio and tv in several countries.

Praise for the first edition of *Vegetarian Britain*

"From Penzance to Peebles, everywhere you need to know for a perfect night out, weekend or holiday." – **The Vegetarian Society**

"This guide to Vegetarian Britain is one of the brightest ideas we've come across in a long time. It's a little cracker of a book which tells you where to find really good vegetarian food – from a snack to a slap up gourmet meal." – **Paul & Linda McCartney**

Praise for previous editions of Vegetarian London

"For people living in or visiting the capital, this book is more important Society

"A thorough run down of health and food shops, restaurants serving vegetarian food, green shops and places to buy cruelty-free cosmetics and clothes." – **Time Out**

"You'll have no trouble finding nosh with this remarkably thorough guide to everything vegetarian in London." – **Tony Banks MP**

"From Wood Green to Wimbledon, the book is a comprehensive catalogue of the best restaurants, shops and tourist attractions in the capital." – **The Big Issue**

"The most striking thing about this hand-sized guide to all things animal friendly is its appeal to non-vegetarians." – **The Big Issue**

"This well laid out guide ... tells you where to buy cruelty-free cosmetics, leather-free clothing and even lists dozens of organisations where you can meet people who want to enjoy a fun lifestyle that is not at the expense of animals." – **Traveller Magazine**

"A feast of food for under six pounds." – **BBC Vegetarian Good Food**

Vegetarian
Britain

By Alex Bourke and Katrina Holland

700 places to eat and sleep

published by
Vegetarian Guides

VEGETARIAN BRITAIN (2nd edition)
By Alex Bourke & Katrina Holland

ISBN 1-902259-041
Published October 2002 by Vegetarian Guides Ltd,
PO Box 2284, London W1A 5UH, England
www.vegetarianguides.com
info@vegetarianguides.com
Fax (+44) (0) 870-121 4721

UK and worldwide distribution: Portfolio Books
Unit 5, Perivale Industrial Park, Horsenden Lane South,
Greenford, Middlesex UB6 7RL, England
Tel: (+44) 020-8997 9000, Fax: (+44) 020-8997 9097
sales@portfoliobooks.com
Also available from Gardners, Bertrams and Suma

Distributed in USA and Canada by
Casemate, Havertown, NJ
Tel 610-853 9131, Fax -610 853 9146
casemate@casematepublishing.com

Vegetarian Guides available worldwide mail order at
www.vegetarianguides.com

**Printed and bound in Great Britain by
Ebenezer Baylis, Worcester**

We spent eight months of our lives compiling this. Please don't rip this book off by photo-
copying big chunks of it or sticking it on your website. We figure if people can afford to eat out
and go to hotels, they can afford a little book like this, which will enable us to produce more.
If you want to buy a few copies of our books to give or sell to your friends or customers, we will
do you a good deal.

Credits

Cover design and photos by Mickaël Charbonnel and Marion Gillet
Layout and maps by Mickaël Charbonnel
Vegetarian Guides logo design: Marion Gillet
Inside photos by Marion Gillet, Mickaël Charbonnel and Mike Bourke
Contact: mickael.marion@btopenworld.com
and mikebourke@vegetarianguides.com

Contributors: Maresa Bosano, Sam Calvert, Vanessa Clarke, John Curtis, Peter Despard, Sophie Fenwick, Paul Gaynor, Dr Michael Grill, Carol Hart, Brian Jacobs, Laurence and Christine Klein, Läyne Kuirk-Schwarz-Waad, P. Lennox, everyone at London Vegans, Nana Luke, Laurence Main, Harry Mather, Joy Olver, Karin Ridgers, Beverly Riley, George Rodger, Julie Rosenfield, Bani Sethi, Peter Simpson, Patrick Smith, Patricia Tricker, Bryony Whipp, Ronny Worsey Richards and everyone else ... **THANK YOU!!**

Also published by Vegetarian Guides:

- *Vegetarian France*, 150 places to eat and sleep
- *Vegetarian London*, 400 places to eat and shop
- *Vegetarian Europe*, 300 places to eat in Europe's top destinations
- *other guides in preparation*

For veggie travel guides to other countries, and to print off a list of updates to this book, visit

www.vegetarianguides.com

About Veggie Guides

Alex Bourke gave up a career as a software engineer to set up Vegetarian Guides to map the world for vegetarians and vegans. His aim was to make it easy to eat cruelty free anywhere in the world. Since 1991 he's travelled widely on four continents, working with the world's leading veggie and vegan activists and creating an unrivalled research network. As well as publishing our own guides, Vegetarian Guides buys in great veggie travel guides from other publishers to sell mail order and can provide info on eating pretty much anywhere in the world. We just haven't gotten around to writing it all down yet. That's where we hope you'll come in.

We don't do the usual naff reviews by a person who's tasted one dish at 1,000 restaurants in 3 months. Instead we list all the nice looking vegan dishes with prices, and get as much info as we can from local veggies who eat there all the time. We don't judge. If a place isn't up to standard we leave it out. We figure if it's still open someone likes it, so we give enough info for the students to pick the cheapie places, the couples to spot the ones with candles, and the business types to know where to go to impress. Of course if a place delights everyone we might rave about it.

Vegetarianism is growing explosively. Veganism is growing even faster within vegetarianism. The veggie market is bigger than the gay market, yet hardly addressed at all by the media and travel guides beyond a few token listings. We are building the first truly comprehensive series of guides, in partnership with the people best placed to write them, the coordinators of local and national vegetarian organisations in each country.

We are doing for veggies what Lonely Planet, Rough Guides, Let's Go and Moon have done for independent travellers, making full use of the opportunities provided by the internet, cheap international phone calls and travel.

When there's a veggie guide to every city and country, it will be easy for everyone in the world to eat veggie, and we will retire.

If you'd like to help us to map the rest of the world and fill in the gaps, write (or publish - we'll tell you how) a guide for your town or a section of one of our guides, or you have some suggestions or recommendations, we'd love to hear from you.

Happy travels!

www.vegetarianguides.co.uk, info@vegetarianguides.co.uk
Vegetarian Guides Ltd, PO Box 2284, London W1A 5UH, UK

England

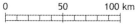

Table of contents

Introduction

How To Use This Guide

England

Ronny's Top Tips For Restaurateurs 515

Indexes 519

Maps

The Vegetarian Society's
°CORDON VERT Cookery School

The **original** home of vegetarian cuisine.

Learn to cook French, Turkish, Mediterranean, Coast to Coast USA and much more.

Relaxed and friendly atmosphere.

Day, weekend, leisure, professional and diploma courses all year round.

Expert tuition in small groups.

En-suite accommodation.

Gift vouchers available.

Call **0161 925 2014** for a brochure, or visit **www.vegsoc.org/cordonvert**

The Vegetarian Society
Altrincham Cheshire WA14 4QG

Registered Charity No. 259358

Introduction
Top 10 Destinations

Romantic dinners, birthday and anniversary celebrations don't have to be limited to your county. Why not whisk your loved one, or just yourself, off to the veggie hotspots of Britain and Ireland? Each has its own character and there are enough here to keep you coming back every month for years.

1. Brighton p.137
Veggie capital of the south with a dozen great vegetarian eateries between the central station and the sea, Brighton is the ideal day out as a side trip from London. The area around the Laines is packed with lovely little shops, veggie cafes and even a veggie pub. There are clubs galore and beaches too. Don't miss Vegetarian Shoes in Gardner Street (closed Sunday). To make a long weekend of it, we've given you half a dozen places to stay, but make sure you book ahead.

2. Cornwall p.59
At the far south-west corner of England, Cornwall has sandy beaches, surfing, sailing, coastal walks, the fabulous Eden Project and Heligan Gardens, arty St Ives, and lots of gorgeous guest houses. The top place to relax for a week in summer, or come for a quiet recharge weekend out of season.

3. Cumbria p.74
One of Britain's top walking destination, the Lake District National Park in the north-west of England offers stunning scenery and a huge concentration of veggie guest houses.

4. Devon p.105
Next door to Cornwall, yet totally different, Devon is much more hilly, with wild and windswept moors, cute coastal towns, and many lovely veggie retreats.

5. Edinburgh p.461
Veggie capital of Scotland and the north, packed with history, a castle, lovely parks and squares, tremendous bars and nightlife and a dozen yummy veggie restaurants.

6. Glastonbury p.333
The town, not the huge hippy festival nearby in the last weekend of June, with its magical Tor, several veggie guest houses and cafes, and a New Age spirit, combine to make this the best little place in Britain for a spiritual makeover.

7. Dublin p.512

The friendliest city in Europe, a cheap flight away by Ryanair. Fantastic pubs and nightlife, plenty to see and buy, and heaps of veggie places to dine. This young, fashionable, trendy capital is very popular for weekends away, hen and stag nights, for example at Bono and the Edge's nightclub the Grafton on the river Liffey, close to the Temple Bar area where young folks go to party and dance away Friday and Saturday night. Everything is within walking distance including some very nice shops.

8. London p.237

With one hundred vegetarian restaurants, a dozen of them vegan, London veggies are the envy of the world. When not on a veggie cafe crawl around the West End, there is fantastic fashion shopping in the mile long Oxford Street, the cutest boutiques in Covent Garden, outstanding theatre and nightlife around Soho, and heaps of attractions from the ancient relics of the British Museum to the brand new London Eye. We've found some veggie guest houses, a luxury hotel with superb cuisine for our rock and movie star readers, and added London campsites and friendly central backpacker hostels with kitchens for our budget travellers.

9. Scottish Highlands p.425

To truly get away from it all, you can't beat a highland guest house. Like the couples who leave the city to start a new life running these wonderful places, you too can wake up to birdsong with not a car in sight. Walk amongst the glens, sit by a loch, enjoy the beautiful wilderness, soak up the history of a ruined castle or whisky distillery, and stuff yourself silly on yummy Scottish veggie grub.

10. Wales p.475

Britain's other great unspoiled natural escape, north and west Wales offer walking, mountains, peace and relaxation. And stacks of vegetarian guest houses.

VEGETARIAN TRAVELLERS' CHECKS

Every week we help hundreds of our members with their travel plans, offering them advice on where to stay and where to eat both at home and abroad.

Our members are also entitled to discounts at over 800 establishments worldwide and their exclusive hotline provides useful translations and phrases and lists of guest houses, restaurants and health food stores.

Our activities range from major promotions such as National Vegetarian Week to working with the food and catering industry, health professionals, caterers and school children. We also teach the best of vegetarian cookery at our **Cordon Vert Cookery School** in the heart of Cheshire.

We are an independent voice when it comes to issues such as BSE and vegetarian nutrition. To let that voice be heard we need your support.

For a free starter pack and membership details call today on 0161 925 2000 or email your request to info@vegsoc.org

Vegetarian
SOCIETY

Parkdale Dunham Road Altrincham
Cheshire WA14 4QG
Tel: 0161 925 2000 email: info@vegsoc.org
www.vegsoc.org
REGISTERED CHARITY NO. 259358

Kat's Top Ten Restaurants In Britain

1. The George – Brighton – East Sussex
The best local pub ever! They serve delicious veggie and vegan grub, high in quality but at reasonable prices.

2. Manna – Primrose Hill – London
Top class cuisine and very friendly service. Ideal for a romantic dinner. Walk up Primrose Hill afterwards for a great view of London.

3. Krakatoa – Brighton – East Sussex
Excellent Oriental cuisine at reasonable prices. You sit on cushions at low tables. Unfortunately they also serve fish, but I had to include them, because I love this place so much!

4. Quince and Medlar – Cockermouth – Cumbria
This place is truly unique. It's formal in an old fashioned traditional sense, but is still very friendly. We were served by the owner's young daughter who was doing her best to be a Silver Service waitress! The food was delicious.

5. Herbivore – Inverness – Scotland
An oasis in a veggie desert, where you can try vegetarian haggis if you dare.

6. Terre a Terre – Brighton – East Sussex
Top class innovative cuisine, always beautifully presented.

7. Country Life – Central London
I was truly amazed when I first came to this place for lunch. It took me a while to grasp that everything in the gorgeous looking buffet was actually vegan!

8. Rainbow Cafe – Cambridge – Cambridgeshire
The only veggie cafe in Cambridge. They fed my ravenous stomach well the night I was there. They have good vegan cakes too.

9. Black Bo's – Edinburgh – Scotland
Imaginative and flavoursome dishes. It's the perfect place to dine while on a romantic night out in Edinburgh.

10. Red Veg – London and Brighton
I think that Red Veg are doing something really important for vegetarianism by finally offering us late night, greasy, fast food.

The Good Island Guide

Veggie eateries may be few in these places, but if you're well supplied, nothing beats a good island break.

Isle of Wight
Enjoy a slower pace of life just below Southampton off the south coast of England. Perfect for sailing or just watching. There's even a vegan guest house.

Isle of Man
Get away to where no one will ever find you on this big island in the Irish Sea. Open an offshore bank account and relax in complete tranquility. (except during the annual TT motorcycle races)

Jersey
Of the two main Channel Islands, close to the coast of France, Jersey is the fun island for a self-catering holiday with sunbathing, surfing, swimming, country walking and a couple of great places to eat out. It's no wonder bronzed Aussie lifeguards come over in droves during their winter to work the beaches. For an altogether quieter time head for Guernsey.

Scottish Islands
To truly get away from it all, watching seabirds, seals and beautiful sunsets on a windswept, deserted beach, head for Orkney, Shetland or the outer Hebrides.

"One of the simplest and most powerful ways to rekindle passion is to get out of the house on a romantic getaway.... Try to get away at least one night a month."

John Gray, *Mars and Venus In The Bedroom*

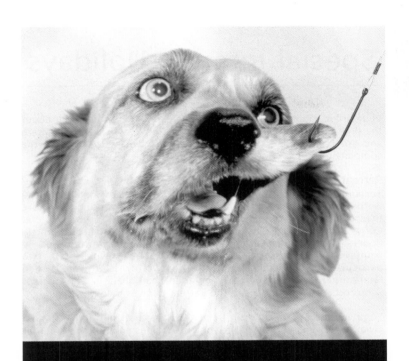

If you **wouldn't**
do this to a **dog,**
why do it to a **fish?**
G O V E G A N

PEOPLE FOR THE ETHICAL TREATMENT OF ANIMALS
For a free vegetarian starter kit,
call 020 8870 3966 or visit PETAEurope.org.uk

Special Interest Holidays

Vegetarian Britain gives you places to sleep and eat. But what about the time in between meals? How about a holiday or weekend where you are pampered or provided with fun activities to enjoy in the company of other veggies?

Retreat Centres

Throughout the accommodation listings, you'll occasionally see the words Retreat Centre, indicating that this is a place offering a lot more than bed and breakfast. Burn out is a constant risk of modern life. Come and rejuvenate at guest houses run by holistic health practitioners, healers and assorted New Age and personal growth gurus. Be pampered with massage, Reiki, yoga and other revitalisers. Two particularly well recommended retreat centres are the vegan Heartspring in Wales and the vegetarian Shambhala in Glastonbury, Somerset. You'll find more in the Retreat Centres index.

Yoga centres are usually run by vegetarians and the food is almost always veggie. Find them in the yoga magazines in WH Smith or larger health food stores.

Veggie Festivals in Britain

You could synchronise your holiday or weekend to coincide with a vegetarian festival. The annual Christmas Without Cruelty Fair is organised by Animal Aid on the closest Sunday to 1st December at Kensington Town Hall, London. See www.animalaid.org.uk. The perfect place to do all your Christmas shopping. They also organise a one week festival of vegetarianism in south Devon in late May.

The one day National Vegan Festival takes place at Conway Hall, Holborn, London at the end of September.
See www.veganfestival.freeserve.co.uk

Music and Arts festivals

The Edinburgh Festival throughout August is heaven for theatre and music fans. Make sure you book accommodation well ahead. There are plenty of other festivals all over Britain throughout the year, which you can find listed in music magazines and via tourist offices.

For a bargain weekend away, pack a tent for festivals such as Glastonbury, on the solstice weekend at the end of June, where there are heaps of veggie cafes in the Green Fields area. At other events such as Reading Festival and the Big Green Gathering, you'll also find specialist veggie caterers like Leon Lewis (see Essex). For all these events it's best to buy tickets in advance or you probably won't get in!

Veggie Holidays Abroad

The International Vegetarian Union (IVU) and European Vegetarian Union (EVU) organise week long World and European Vegetarian Congresses, based around a hotel with talks, cookery demos and excursions. You can come to learn all about activism, or just hang out and socialise with veggie voyagers from all over the world. Check out the latest events at www.ivu.org. Coming soon are a vegetarian food festival in Moscow in May 2003, European Vegetarian Festival in Turkey June 2003, and a vegan congress in Brazil in September 2003.

Vegi Ventures offer guided vegetarian holidays for small groups from Peru to Turkey. For keen cyclists, Bicycle Beano tour around the UK and you don't have to be a hardened expert rider to join in.

If you've scoffed your way right through a now frazzled and dog-eared copy of this guide and fancy a city break further afield in Paris, Amsterdam or Barcelona, make a romantic investment in a copy of our *Vegetarian Europe* guide. It contains all the capitals and tourist hotspots from Seville to St Petersburg. Guaranteed to get your loved one in the mood for veggie love.

Vegetarian Heaven

Alex Bourke, founder of Vegetarian Guides, reveals an explosion of demand for vegetarian food in Britain and assesses the trends in eating out, ethnic dining and desserts.

In 1945 there were 100,000 vegetarians in Britain, all considered eccentric. By 1975 there were one million. Cranks restaurants served thick crust pasties and macrobiotic eateries required you to chew every worthy mouthful thirty times. At least that's how the world perceived us. As 1984 dawned, vegetarianism's most popular advocate was windy hippy Neil in *The Young Ones* TV series.

Just as we seemed doomed to lentil jokes for eternity, Linda McCartney and a funky new Vegetarian Society laid the bearded, beaded, spaced out New Age stereotype to rest. Suddenly we were cool and veggie celebs 'came out' in droves. Pizza, pasta and salad bars took over the high street. The veggie-lution stormed on through the nineties until today there are over four million of us. According to the Vegetarian Society, 250,000 take the plunge each year, but a new survey reveals that a hundred times as many are veggie at least two days a week. Now that I've got your attention, let's look at how and why.

British meat eaters consume a third less than the French and half as much as Americans. A survey in summer 2000 for the RSPCA revealed that only 38% of meat eaters eat it daily, 21% four or five times a week, 33% two or three times and 8% just once a week or less. In other words, an incredible 60% of people have become demi-vegetarian, a trend that is tremendously benefiting the best veggie restaurants. Country Life vegan restaurant in London surveyed their lunchtime customers and found that 70% are omnivores, proving that vegetarian is as much a mainstream cuisine in its own right as Indian.

Some vegetarian restaurants have been going out of business as customers drift off to non-veggie places that have started to copy veggie dishes. With even Burger King and McDonald's doing veggieburgers, is there still enough demand for vegetarian restaurants to survive in the ubiquiveg noughties? Oh yes, but only if they stay on the innovative leading edge.

Compiling *Vegetarian London* and *Vegetarian Britain* since 1994, it's clear that traditional cheese and egg *cooking* is losing ground to grain and bean based world *cuisine*. In ten years veggiedom expanded steadily from three to four million, but vegans have surged meteorically from 80,000 in 1993 to a quarter of a million in 2000 (RealEat survey). Every fourth group of four veggie diners now includes a vegan. Many veggies too are fed up to the back teeth with cheese toppings on every dish and are going for vegan food in droves. Far from limiting your choices by removing cheese and eggs, eating modern international vegan opens up the richest and most diverse cuisine of all, with hundreds of new ingredients, a riotously colourful, multi-textured, aromatic, herby-spicy, melt in your mouth fusion of African, south-east Asian, Japanese, Indian and middle Eastern dishes plus heaps of raw and steamed veg. The invention of vegan chocolate cake, apple pie, soya cream, ice-cream and custard means no more fuming over a boring sorbet or fruit salad while your mates tuck into something sinful. We've nobly tried them all and in this guide we tell you where they are.

If you want a taste of the future, there are legendary vegetarian restaurants throughout this book that attract regulars from all over

Britain, setting the trail with ethnic and new vegan cuisine of quite astonishing breadth and deliciousness. Examples include **Wild Ginger** in Harrogate and **Hitchcocks** in Hull, Yorkshire; **The Gate** in London; **Black Bo's** in Edinburgh; **West 13th** in Glasgow and countless more. To further whet your appetite for gastonomic galavanting, see Kat's Top 10 Restaurants in Britain.

Getting away is no longer a problem for us. Every month brings a new addition to the UK's 100 vegetarian guesthouses, many competing to serve the biggest and most extensive cooked breakfast. For example Hugh Wilson and Suzanne Allen's Edinburgh **Greenhouse Guesthouse** offers rashers, sausages, mushrooms, baked beans, hashbrowns, tomatoes, scrambled tofu, bagels with Tofutti cream cheese, croissants, pancakes with maple syrup, juices, cereals, fruit salad and vegan yoghurt.

What to do when there's nowhere veggie in town, or the veggie place is closed on Sunday night? Your best bet is to avoid British and American style places, especially if you're a vegan, and head for an Indian or Middle Eastern restaurant where as much as half the menu could be veggie. In cities with few or no veggie eateries, we've included ethnic places that local veggies and vegans have told us they love.

The number of veggies in Britain has increased forty fold in 55 years. Despite massive subsidies, the meat and dairy industries continue to decline and indeed pork, lamb and beef would collapse without state intervention. Whereas without any support, our kind of food is showing strong growth both in restaurants and retailers. This is just the beginning. One day I expect to see a vegetarian restaurant on every street, as in India. The future has never looked brighter, healthier, or more profitable for Britain's four million vegetarians, 400 vegetarian restaurants and guest houses, and the thousands of shops, supermarkets and eateries that have been extending their vegetarian range. Vegetarianism, and especially veganism, truly are the food of the future, and we will continue to direct you to the very best there is in the vegetarian paradise that is Britain.

Animal Aid
Campaigning for all animals

Animal Aid is Britain's leading animal rights group, campaigning against vivisection, factory farming and all other animal abuse. We also promote vegetarianism and cruelty-free living, and have an active educational wing offering free school speakers, campaign literature and videos for teachers.

We urgently need more members if we are to continue with and expand our vital work. Please use the form on this page or send your details on a piece of paper with a cheque made payble to Animal Aid. For more information or to join by credit card see our website or phone number.

We need you to help us to help animals.

Please Join Animal Aid Today

Your details (please use block capitals)

Surname: .... First name:............................... Title: ....

Address: ....

.... Post code: ....

What it costs (please tick appropriate boxes)

Annual membership: ☐ £14 waged ☐ £9 Unwaged ☐ £6 Youth (17 or under) ☐ £240 Life

I enclose a donation of £ .... I enclose a cheque for a total of £ ....

Please return this form to:

Animal Aid, The Old Chapel, Bradford St, Tonbridge, Kent TN9 1AW

Tel: (01732) 364546 ● Fax: (01732) 366533
email: info@animalaid.org.uk ● web: www.animalaid.org.uk

New in this edition

The first edition of Vegetarian Britain contained 500 places to stay and sleep. This one has over 700, plus hundreds more shops. For those of you who've been patiently waiting, we apologise for the delay. We had no idea just how much could happen in four years and that our planned extra 70 pages would turn into another 200 – our biggest guide ever!

We've added **veggie munchie maps** of Brighton, Edinburgh, central London and Liverpool, a map showing places to stay in Greater London and maps of Cornwall, Cumbria, England, Scotland and Wales. There are around **100 fabulous new vegetarian cafes, restaurants and guest houses.** This book is bursting with yummy veggie goodness and here are some of the highlights.

Many readers told us it could take time to locate suitable places in the first edition of Vegetarian Britain. We listened. We've now arranged the book by county, added side tabs for rapid browsing, and indexes.

Five years ago you could count London's vegan restaurants on one hand. Now you need to take your shoes off. Reflecting the trend in the veggie world away from eggs and dairy, vegan restaurants have mushroomed in the capital. Nationwide there are several new vegan guest houses and restaurants, a new vegan pub in Glasgow, even an all vegan sandwich bar in Edinburgh, and so for the first time in any of our guides we've now added an **index of vegan places**.

Our **Top Ten** guides help you to choose where to start exploring, parts of Britain with an especially high concentration of vegetarian delights.

Also new in this edition is a selection of places to visit in **Ireland**. We plan to considerably expand this section in future editions.

We've added hundreds of **health food and wholefood shops** in city centre or tourist locations, where you can pick up snacks and picnic supplies. When travelling around, we won't always be able or even want to eat out twice a day. Many wholefood stores are run by veggies or vegans and sell sandwiches, pasties and dairy-free ice-cream. The ubiquitous **Holland & Barrett** chain has 400 branches conveniently located in high streets, perfect for picking up flapjacks, nuts, dried fruit and trail mix. For a wider range with less packaging, we've also

THEY CALL IT TESTING. TO HER IT'S TORTURE

You could help end animal testing forever

In the UK nearly three million animals suffer in laboratories every year. The BUAV opposes all animal experiments and campaigns peacefully and effectively to end them. Visit www.buav.org to find out more.

Call the BUAV on 020 7619 6963 or email fundraising@buav.org

- To support the BUAV with a donation
- To sign up to our supporter scheme as a BUAV *Campaigner*

British Union for the Abolition of Vivisection, 16a Crane Grove, London, N7 8NN

included many independently run wholefood stores recommended by guest house owners and readers and we'd love to hear about any more that you come across.

We've recently set up national distribution of Vegetarian Guides into independently owned wholefood stores. If your local shop would like to be included in the next edition, or to sell our current books, please ask them to contact us at info@veggieguides.com.

What to do late at night when the vegetarian restaurant is closed? We've included **omnivorous restaurants with big veggie menus** where we recognised that many vegetarians eat there, either through choice, or when in a group of friends who don't want to go where we do. Top of the list of handy places for when your mates veto a veggie venue are of course Indian restaurants, some of which have more dishes for us than most vegetarian eateries. Lebanese, Italian, south-east Asian, Greek and Mexican restaurants aren't far behind, and we've picked off some cracking places all over the country. Chains like Pizza Express have been a veggie standby for years, and now Pizza Express tell us for the benefit of vegan readers that their pizza bases are vegan and they can make pizzas without cheese.

Join the Veggie Guides Team!

We hope you enjoy eating your way around this book as much as we enjoyed compiling it. Please send us your plaudits, brickbats and especially updates and new addresses. We can't always answer every letter, but we do add every comment to our database, and the best letters will receive a free copy of the next edition or any of the guides we publish ourselves. You can contact us by email (ideally) at info@veggieguides.com or write to:

PO Box 2284
London
W1A 5UH
England

Happy eating!

Getting Around

TRAVELLING IN BRITAIN

For **cheap flights** within the British Isles try www.easyjet.com, ryanair.com, go-fly.com, buzzaway.com.

Train times can be found at thetrainline.com, though this site can be tricky for locating the cheapest ticket on a particular date, so you could follow up with a phone call to national rail enquiries 0845-7484950. You can get 1/3 off travel if you have an under-26 or senior citizen's railcard.

For the cheapest travel if you're not in a hurry, you can't beat National Express **coaches**, gobycoach.com

We discovered you can **hire cars** for as little as £9 a day at www.easycar.com. To figure out your route, at multimap.com you can type in your origin and destination and it gives you a map and written instructions. Excellent service!

TOURIST INFORMATION

The easy way to find out what's happening in Britain is to contact a local **tourist information centre** (TIC) in every town, who can give you stacks of free brochures and maybe a map. They can also help with booking accommodation not listed in this guide, where you should at least be able to get a basic breakfast which you could supplement with munchies from the local health food shop.

Many people nowadays are researching their trips on the **internet**. You may even be one of the thousands of people who discovered Vegetarian Guides by searching for vegetarian restaurants at google.com. Some of our favourite websites for finding things to do in new places are the online versions of bestselling guidebook series such as lonelyplanet.com, roughguides.com, letsgo.com. For what's happening in individual counties, try the "thisis" websites, e.g. thisisessex.co.uk or thisislondon.co.uk.

For our overseas visitors, the number for **Directory Enquiries** is 192, though be warned it isn't free. But yell.com is.

IF KILLING FOR MEAT MAKES YOU SICK...

...DON'T LET HIM BE HUNTED AND KILLED JUST FOR FUN!

How to use this guide

We've arranged this guide by county, so that wherever you are, you'll find all the guest houses then restaurants then shops together.

The core of this book are the big veggie English counties: **Cornwall, Cumbria, Devon, East Sussex, Somerset, London** and **Yorkshire**, plus Scotland – especially **Edinburgh** – and **Wales**. If you're planning a weekend away, these are the places to start.

Interspersed are the other counties of the British Isles, some rich in veggie places, others with leaner pickings. In towns with no vegetarian place, or for days when the local veggie is closed, we've listed ethnic restaurants with a big choice of vegetarian and vegan dishes. We've also added a few hundred health food stores where you can top up on high energy travellers' fare.

We've taken on board feedback from the last edition, and added **tabs** down the sides of the pages to help you locate areas quickly, plus **indexes** at the end of the book and additional ones at the start of big sections. Our **Top Ten** listings at the front will help you get started if you're bamboozled by such an awesome choice of eateries.

At the end of the guide is **Ronny's Top Tips for Restaurateurs**, ideal to photocopy and hand to places where they want to do more for veggies and vegans but aren't sure how to get started.

How we write the listings

We sent detailed questionnaires to several hundred guest houses and restaurants, following up with phone calls. Those that replied have extensive full page and half page entries. Others we took details for on the phone and these listings are shorter.

As well as opening times, address, phone and whether they accept credit cards, allow smoking or serve alcohol, we list sample dishes with prices. Normally the examples chosen are vegan, not just because a high proportion of our readers are vegan or cutting back on dairy and eggs, but also because vegan dishes are the "lowest common denominator" of vegetarian cuisine, suitable for just about everyone, healthier than cheese and egg based vegetarian dishes like lasagne or quiche, and often much more delicious as they don't rely

Name of the place

Type of place

Detailed
description

Lancrigg

Lancrigg is set in 30 acres of idyllic gardens overlooking the serenity of Easedale. You will appreciate the total absence of traffic noise and the sound of nearby waterfalls and birds. There is excellent walking right from the doorstep.

There are 13 rooms, with singles, doubles, twins and families, all with ensuite bathrooms. Most have special features such as gorgeous views and whirlpool spa baths. Prices range from £50–£99 per person per night and include a four course dinner. Cheaper rates for stays of three nights or more. Deduct £20 if you don't want dinner.

In the morning help yourself to fruit juices, fruit salads and natural cereals. This is followed by a continental or full cooked breakfast of basil tomatoes, vegetarian burgers, baked beans, mushrooms and toast. Vegan margarine, soya milk, soya yoghurt, vegan muesli, veggie sausages and vegan croissants are all available.

Dinner could be roasted aubergine and tomato torte with a romesco sauce, followed by carrot and fennel soup. Your main might be provençal mushroom, leek and pinekernel stuffed pepper, with a tomato and olive sauce and new potaotes, roasted in lemon and fresh herbs, served with salad. For dessert, chocolate and walnut cake. Finish off with fresh ground coffee and chocolates. Organic wine available. Special diets catered for. Food is organic where possible and free from artificial additives.

Champagne and luxury chocolates may be ordered to be in your room on arrival. Tea & coffee making and TV in rooms.

122

Accomodation CUMBRIA England

Location finder

Type of place finder

Vegetarian
Country House Hotel

Easedale
Grasmere
Cumbria LA22 9QN
England

Tel: 015394 35317

Fax: 015394 35058

www.lancrigg.co.uk

Email: info@lancrigg.co.uk

Train Station:
Windermere 8 miles
then taxi

Open: all year

Directions: From the M6,
take the A591 to
Grasmere. In the centre
of the village, turn left up
Easedale Road. The
entrance is 1/2 mile on
the right.

Parking: available

Children and pets
welcome. They have cots
and high chairs.

Smoking in rooms only

Breakfast can be served in
rooms if requested

10% discount to members
of the Vegetarian Society,
Vegan Society, Viva! and
people presenting this
book.

Practical info
(such as location,
opening time and
contact details.)

on fat to be tasty. We tell you if a guesthouse serves soya yoghurt, veggie sausages, veggie rashers, scrambled tofu etc – dishes that appeal to both veggies and vegans, as well as meat eaters and meat reducers. In restaurants we list the most exciting dishes from around the world, such as Mexican, Asian, Lebanese, African or Mediterranean.

It is clearly marked in the book if a place is veggie, vegan or omnivorous. All guest houses and restaurants cater for vegans unless otherwise stated. The core of die-hard vegans who prefer not to dine with people consuming meat or dairy products at the next table can avail themselves of our new vegan index, which whilst not long is twice as long as it would have been in the previous edition.

Bedfordshire

The Sky's Buffet

Omnivorous Oriental restaurant

9 The Broadway
Bedford
Open: Every day 12–14.30, 18–23.30

Tel: 01234 219 180

Oriental restaurant with a buffet, 40% vegetarian and vegan. £5.50 lunch, £8.90 evening. Also take–away. 3 doors from Kwik–Fit.

Green Cuisine

Vegetarian catering company

10 Ribble Way
Bedford

Tel: 01234–305 080

Previously a vegetarian restaurant by the same name, now do outside catering for any function from dinner parties to wedding receptions for up to 200 people. Can do entirely vegan catering including cakes.

Golden Dragon

Omnivorous Chinese restaurant

1 Tring Road
Dunstable, Bedfordshire LU6 2PX
Open: Mon–Sun 12.00–14.00, 16.00–23.00

Tel: 01582–661 485
www.nebsweb.co.uk/gol dendragon

Omnivorous restaurant, with extensive separate vegetarian and vegan menu. Several mock meat dishes, starters £2.70–£6.50; mains £3.20–£6 and desserts from £2.50. Separate smoking section. Visa, MC.

The Lotus

Vegan Chinese restaurant

43 Cheapside, Luton LU1 2HN
Mon–Sat 12–14.30, 17.30–23.00, Sun 12.00–22.00

Tel: 01582–721 116
Fax: 020–8200 9313

New vegan Chinese restaurant with a variety of vegetable and mock meat dishes. Starters from £2 and mains £3.80–£4.80. Vegan ice creams available. Separate smoking section. Visa, MC.

Nature's Harvest

Wholefood shop

2 North Street
Leighton Buzzard, Bedfordshire

Wide range of homemade savouries and cakes.

Holland & Barrett

Health food shop

10 Horne Lane, Harpur Centre, Bedford MK40 1TP

Tel: 01234 352866

158 Arndale Centre Luton LU1 2TG

Tel: 01582 482574

Berkshire

You're most likely to end up in Berkshire through work, education or visiting people. But some people do come here for its own sake.

The big tourist attractions are Windsor Castle, Legoland (take a veggie picnic), and the River Thames. But there is more: some excellent and very accessible walking and cycling country lies around here. For the leisurely, there is gentle walking (and sometimes cycling) all along the Thames as well as the Kennet and Avon Canal, and boats to hire at the main towns.

Bracknell Forest is perfect for mountain-biking, with an extensive network of tracks from family to highly technical. You can hire bikes at the Lookout, opposite Coral Reef leisure pool (great to play and sauna in afterwards), both of which are well sign-posted in Bracknell. Either pack a picnic, or cycle all the way through the forest to Bagshot, where there are a couple of curry houses, a chip shop, and an excellent Indian take-away, as well as a small supermarket.

North of Reading are the Chiltern Hills with their extensive network of woodland footpaths and bridleways. The Crooked Billet (listed) in Stoke Row is in a prime position as a refuelling stop for hungry people on a gentle walk or epic on- or off-road cycle. Another good lunch-stop is the pub on the green at the centre of Warborough. This is officially Oxfordshire, but you are likely to access it from Berks, especially if you plan to get there by train. For a one-way cycle, try planning a route between train stations, such as Oxford, Goring, Pangbourne (tasty things at Garlands Organic shop) and Reading, with the help of the odd Ordnance Survey map.

Sophie Fenwick
Vegan Society Local Contact
Berkshire

Cafe Iguana

Vegetarian restaurant

Reading's only vegetarian restaurant with an internationally influenced, vegan friendly menu and a cocktail bar upstairs.

Starters from £3 such as vegetable samosa or bruschetta.

Mains, £5.50–£7, including Thai pumpkin and coconut curry and spinach and mushroom risotto.

They try to source locally and organically as much as possible and everything is freshly cooked on premises Fair trade coffees and teas available.
Can cater for special diets. Separate smoking section. Visa, MC.

11 St Marys Butts
Reading
Berkshire
RG1 2LN

Tel: 0118-9581 357

Open:
Mon–Sat 11.00–23.00,
soon to be opening
Sundays.

Cocktail bar upstairs
Mon–Sat 17.00–23.00

Global Café

**Omnivorous cafe
and bar**

Omnivorous global café-style restaurant and bar (with 30 kinds of beer including unusual foreign ones) close to the Oracle shopping centre. 75% of the main menu is vegetarian, around half the hot dishes vegan. They use as much fair trade and organic produce as possible, and sell it in the adjoining shop. Average price for a meal £5–6.

Different specials every day, eg falafel platter or Mexican chilli. Sandwiches £1.95–2.50. Desserts £3–4 including vegan ones. Soya cappucinos. Smoke free area during day, gets a bit smokey at night. After 10pm Fri–Sat £2 cover charge. Booking advised Thu–Sat night if you want a particular table. Parties can be arranged. No credit cards. Children welcome before 8pm, wheelchair/pram access to whole dining area.

35–39 London Street
Reading RG1 4PS

www.risc.org.uk
theglobalcafe@risc.org.uk

Tel: 0118 958 3555
Fax: 0118-9594357

Open:
Mon 12–14.30,
Tue –Thu 12–23.00,
Fri 11–Sat 01.00;
stop serving food at 9pm
then it's a bar

Himalayan Hotspot

Omnivorous Indian restaurant

1 School Road
Tilehurst, Reading
Open: 18–23.00 every day (23.30 Fri–Sat),
also Sun 12–14.00

Tel: 0118 945 1681

Indian restaurant, basic café–like, not for a posh meal. Very nice food, easily the best quality curry we've had in Reading. A good place to go to if you're visiting friends in Reading, or to get a take–away. Off the road towards Pangbourne.

Le Shanghai

Omnivorous Oriental restaurant

32 Church Street
Caversham, Reading
Open: every day 18–23.30, 12–14.30

Tel: 0118 947 2097

Omnivorous Thai, Cantonese, Szechuan and Singapore, spicy and non–spicy Asian omnivorous restaurant in the north part of Reading, with a comprehensive vegetarian menu. You could spend £18 each on a bespoke feast where you just ask for "everything without eggs, dairy and MSG and make it spicy" or whatever. High chairs. Good place for a romantic meal or to take relatives to as it's smart. You wouldn't feel silly in jeans but it's a nice place to dress up for.

The Spice Oven

Omnivorous Indian restaurant

2–4 Church Street
Caversham, Reading RG4 8AT
Open: Mon–Sat 12–14.30, 18–23.00,
Sun 12–16.00, 18–22.00

Tel: 0118 948 1000

Omnivous Indian restaurant with a variety of Indian cuisines, including unusual ones like a smokey dish. They understand veganism, even prepared vegan naan bread on request. The buffet nights are more busy and service is slow then, also not great value for veggies so it's better to stick to the a la carte menu on non buffet nights.

Garland's Organic Shop

Wholefood shop

6 Reading Road
Pangbourne RG8 7LY
Open: Tue–Fri 9–17.30, Sat 9–17.00

Tel: 01189 844770
Fax: 01189 844220

People travel from Reading to this amazing shop which has a big range of hard to find vegan foods like tempeh, hemp pesto and hemp ice-cream. A brilliant place to stock up.

Holland & Barrett

Health food shop

22 High Street
Bracknell RG12 1LL

Tel: 01344 455313

69 High Street
Maidenhead SL6 1JX

Tel: 01628–789 622

105a North Brook Road
Newbury RG14 1AB

Tel: 01635–552 218

2 Union Street
Reading RG1 1EU

Tel: 0118–950 7825

58 The Broad Street Mall
Reading RG1 7QE

Tel: 0118–957 2787

Unit 2 Queensmere Centre
Slough SL1 1DB

Tel: 01753–694 355

Natural Childbirth

www.hurricanehub.com/childbirth

Any pregnant people wanting a satisfying drug-free birth, take a look at Sophie Fenwick's website. There's a veggie slant on nutritional guidance, animal-free and potentially pain-free birth and tips on setting up a vegan dairy farm.

City and County of
Bristol

Arches Hotel

Omnivorous Guest House with vegetarian proprietor. There are ten rooms; three singles at £24.50–£31.50 per night, one double at £43–£45, one double ensuite at £49–£51, one twin at £45, one twin ensuite at £51 and three family rooms at £58–£64 per night.

Breakfast could be veggie sausages, tomatoes, beans and fried bread. A continental breakfast is included in the room charge, however a cooked breakfast is £2.25–£2.75. Vegan muesli, vegan margarine, soya yoghurt, rice and oat milk are all available.

Dinner is not offered but there are several restaurants nearby serving veggie food. The owners can advise you of where to go. There are also health food shops where you can pick up snacks.

Attractions close by include Brunel's suspension bridge, two cathedrals, museums, several theatres and concert halls, as well as the waterfront and marina.

Children six years and over are welcome. Pets are welcome with prior notice. Tea and coffee making facilities, televisions and washbasins are in the rooms.

No smoking throughout.

Omnivorous Guest House

32 Cotham Brow
Cotham
Bristol BS6 6AE
England

Tel and Fax:
0117 9247398

www.arches-hotel.co.uk

Email:
ml@arches-hotel.co.uk

Train station: Bristol Temple Meads, 2km, then bus or taxi.

Open: all year, except Christmas and new year.

Directions: 1km north up A38 (from Broadmead) turn left at first mini roundabout. Hotel is 100m on left.

Parking: on street

Basca House

Elegant Victorian house retaining many original features. The house has a peaceful atmosphere and is situated in a quiet tree lined street in a residential area, but is only one mile from the city centre. There are two single rooms at £25–£35 per night, one single ensuite at £35 per night and two twin rooms at £45 per room per night.

There is an excellent veggie/vegan spread for breakfast including fresh fruit, fruit juice, cereal or muesli and soya yoghurt followed by veggie sausages, baked beans, mushrooms and herbed tomatoes with wholemeal bread and home made preserves. As one of the proprietors is Indian, a more adventurous breakfast is also offered which includes spicy potatoes and dal. Vegan muesli, vegan margarine and soya milk are available.

Dinner is not offered but there are numerous restaurants in town offering veggie food. Bristol offers a lively night life with many clubs, theatres, music venues and pubs. During the day, take a look at the famous Clifton Suspension Bridge, the symbol of Bristol and visit the Create Environment Centre, or one of the many cathedrals, museums or art galleries. You could explore further afield and visit the Cheddar Caves and Gorge or the Wookey Hole in Wells.

Basca House is about five minutes walk from two yoga centres and an interesting shop selling Indian clothing and artefacts. All rooms have televisions, radio alarms and tea and coffee making facilities. Children are welcome and they have high chairs. No smoking throughout.

Omnivorous
Bed and Breakfast

19 Broadway Road
Bishopston
Bristol
Somerset BS7 8ES
England

Tel: 0117 9422182

Train Station:
Bristol Temple Meads,
1.5 miles, then taxi or bus.

Open: all year, except Christmas to New Year period.

Directions:
At big roundabout by Debenhams, take A38 Stokes Croft, signposted Redland/Cotham (this road has a building over it, go under building). Continue on this road then go under railway arches, bear right at next junction and just before Texaco petrol station, turn left into Berkeley Road. Go up hill and take the first left into Broadway Road.

Parking: on street. No restrictions.

Café Maitreya

Vegetarian restaurant

New vegetarian restaurant off the M32, very much into organic and fair trade with no GM. This is the kind of place Bristol has needed for years.

Menu changes regularly. Here are some examples:

Breakfast/brunch till 3pm: full English cooked veggie or vegan breakfast £4.50–4.95; muesli with chopped fruit or (soya) yoghurt £1.95; toast £1.

Lunch till 3pm: soup £2.95, roasted stuffed pepper with potatoes £3.95, salad £3.60. See board for lunchtime specials. Maitreya mezze £4.50 served till 5.30pm, choose 3 from hummus, oven roasted veg, aubergine salad, dip, served with sourdough bread / olives / salad. Ciabatta or wholemeal sandwiches £2.95. Kids menu for under-5's.

Evening menu two courses £9.95, three £12.95, excluding service. 10% service charge added to tables of over 10 people. Start with soup, vegetable tempura, bruschetta, sweet pepper and tomato fritter, or a salad. Main courses inclue Thai stir fry with rice, Spanish tortilla, okra masala in a coriander and cumin pancake, warm salad. Several desserts and dairy free cream available.

Freshly squeezed juices £2.20 and smoothies £2.40-2.80. Other drinks 95p–£1.50, soya milk no problem.

You can bring your own wine, but not beer, corkage 50p goes to charity, or choose from their list. House vegan wine £8.25 bottle white, £8.75 red, glass 250ml £3.25. Most wines are vegan. Vegan beers and cider £2.45-2.75.

89 St Mark's Road
Easton
Bristol BS5 6HY

Tel: 0117 951 0100
Fax: 0117 951 0200

thesnug@
cafemaitreya.co.uk

Open:
Tue 10-18.00, Wed–Fri 10–23.00,
Sat 11–23.00,
Sun 11–18.00,
closed Mon

Directions:
Near to M32 Stapleton Road.
From centre go out along Old Market, head towards M32 but veer off onto Stapleton Road and cross over M32.
Bus 48 or 49 from town, get off on Stapleton Road and walk down Berwick Road.

No smoking.

No credit card, just cash or cheque.

Kids menu.

Reservations needed evenings.

Royce Rolls Wholefood Café

Vegetarian cafe

The Corn Exchange, St Nicholas Market,
Corn St, Bristol BS1 1JQ
Open: Mon–Fri 07.30–16.00, Sat 09.30–16.00.
Closed Sun.

Tel: 0117–982 4228
Fax: 0117–982 4228

Friendly central vegetarian take–away with café seating too. Rolls, savoury snacks, flapjacks, tea, coffee, flapjacks and cakes. Vegan and gluten free options available. Soya milk offered. No smoking. Cash only.

Holland & Barrett

Health food shop

83 The Horsefair
Bristol BS1 3JP

Tel: 0117–929 3170

21 Clifton Down, Shopping Centre
Whiteladies Road
Bristol BS8 2NN

Tel: 0117–973 8188

Unit 2 Odeon Dev.
Broadmead
Bristol BS1 3DN

Tel: 0117–926 0557

Buckinghamshire

Veggie World
Vegetarian Chinese restauarant

150–152 Queensway
Bletchley, MK2 2RS
Open: Tue–Sat 11.30–14.30, Tue–Sun 17.00–22.30

Tel: 01908–632 288
Fax: 0870–744 9978
www.veggie-world.com

Chinese vegetarian restaurant, predominantly vegan though some dishes contain egg, with lots of meat substitutes like fake chicken and pork, plus tofu, stir–fried veg etc. Big and complex menu. Starters and soups around £2. Chef's recommendation main course £3.60. Main courses £3.80. Rice from £1.50. Cheaper at lunchtime, about £3–4 to eat there. No alcohol. Non smoking. Visa, MC.

The Eating Point
Vegetarian restaurant

Christ Church, Stantonbury Campus
Stantonbury (Saxon St side), Milton Keynes
Open: Mon–Fri lunchtime, not at weekends

Tel: 01908 315627

Vegetarian wholefood restaurant, quite unlike the Chinese alternative place with no meat substitutes. Lots of beans, pasta, rice, vegetables and very cheap as they have a few volunteer staff. Off the V7 road that runs north–south through the centre, in north Milton Keynes.

Carlos
Omnivorous Portuguese restaurant

11 Temple Street, off Friar's Square Shopping
Complex, Aylesbury
Open: every day, closed Sunday night

Tel: 01296 421228

Portuguese restaurant with lots of veggie food.

Eat As Much As You Like
Omnivorous Chinese restaurant

35–37 New Street
Aylesbury

Tel: 01296 422191

Up–market buffet restaurant. Lunchtime around £5–6, evening £9–10. 30% suitable for veggies. Round the back of Sainsbury's.

Health Right
Health food shop

Friar's Square Shopping Centre
Aylesbury

There's another branch in Chesham

The Good & Plenty

Omnivorous take-away & cafe

17 Cambridge Street
Aylesbury

Tel: 01296 485258

Omnivorous take-away with café upstairs, owned by veggies. They have veggie sandwiches, baked potatoes, even veggie sausages. There's also a Portuguese restaurant with veggie dishes in Temple Street nearby, just off Friar's Square.

Back to Nature

Health food shop

14 The Cornwalls Centre, off the High Street
Buckingham
Open: Mon–Sat 9.15–17.30 (17.00 Sat)

Tel: 01280 812694

Alternatives

Health food shop

Burchard Crescent, Shenley Church End
Milton Keynes
Open: Mon–Fri 10–18.00, Sat 10–17.00

Health food shop and complementary health centre.

Holland & Barrett

Health food shop

in the Food Centre, near Sainsburys
Milton Keynes

There's another branch in Bletchley in the Brunel Centre.

Milton Keynes Vegetarians & Vegans

Peter Simpson
psimpson.vegcac@pgen.net

Tel: 01908 503919

Affiliated to the Vegetarian Society, they collect for national campaigning organisations and have monthly meals at Veggie World restaurant, currently on a Wednesday. Also stalls at local events.
Peter is the General Secretary of the Vegetarian Cycling & Athletic Club and represents the athletics side. See www.vegcac.co.uk

Cambridge

Cambridge is full of students in the winter, and tourists in the summer, who enjoy punting down the river, or chilling in one of the city's many open spaces. Cambridge has a lot of elegance, character and history, a great shopping centre and some excellent health food shops.

There are disappointingly few eating places that cater well for veggies and vegans, but these are usually packed as demand is high. The city could definitely do with more veggie restaurants....

... and the great news is that top veggie chef Bill Sewell, proprietor of The Place Below in London and The Cafe @ All Saints in Hereford, will be opening a big new 90-seat veggie restaurant slap bang in the middle of Cambridge, probably around November 2002 or early 2003, to be called Michael House. Check our updates page for Vegetarian Britain at www.vegetarianguides.co.uk for news.

By Ronny

Dykelands Guest House

Detached guest house on the south side of the city offering modern, spacious, well laid out accommodation. There are nine rooms; one single ensuite at £30 per night, one double and one twin at £38 per room per night, two double ensuites and one twin ensuite at £47 per room per night and three family rooms at £55–£68 per room per night.

For breakfast choose from a selection of cereals with juice, toast and preserves. A cooked veggie breakfast is available but there's not much on the menu for vegans unfortunately. They do have soya milk though.

There is no shortage of trendy cafes and restaurants in this university town, most offering veggie food. For a cheaper alternative you could take a picnic and enjoy it by the river. Make sure you try punting down the river, but try not to fall in!

Cambridge has loads of tourist attractions including National Trust sites Anglesey Abbey, Houghton Mill, Wicken Fen and Wimpole Hall as well as English Heritage sites Audley End, Bury St Edmunds Abbey and Denny Abbey. There's also the American Military Cemetry, Ely Cathedral, the Iron Age Fort on Gog Magog Hills, Mountfitchet Castle, Norman Village and an RSPB Nature Reserve all nearby.

Rooms have tea and coffee making facilites, televisions and radios. Children and dogs are welcome. (Dogs in ground floor rooms only). No smoking throughout.

Omnivorous
Guest House

157 Mowbray Road
Cambridge
Cambridgeshire CB1 7SP
England

Tel: 01223 244300

Fax: 01223 566746

www.dykelands.com

Email:
dykelands@fsbdial.co.uk

Train Station: Cambridge,
1 mile then taxi or bus.

Open: all year

Directions: From
A10/M11 junction 11
A1309. At seventh set of
traffic lights turn right
into Long Road. At next
roundabout first exit is
Mowbray Road.

Parking: available

Joan's B&B

Vegan bed and breakfast

74 Sturton Street, Cambridge CB1 2QA
Train Station: Cambridge, five minutes walk
Open: by arrangement

Tel: 01223 311828
Fax: 01223 300318

Two rooms, one double and one single £22 per person per night. Evening meal by arrangement, two courses, £8. No children or pets. No smoking throughout.

Stockyard Farm B&B

Omnivorous bed and breakfast

Wisbech Road, Welney,
Wisbech, Cambridgeshire, PE14 9RQ
Train Station: Littleport, 7 miles
Open: all year, except Christmas

Tel: 01354 610433
Fax: 01354 610422

Two rooms, one double and one twin £18–£20 per person per night. Children aged five and over welcome, pets welcome. No smoking throughout. Vegetarian owner. Near wildlife and wetlands centre. Between Ely and Wisbech on A1101, at north end of village.

Rainbow Vegetarian Bistro

Vegetarian restaurant

9A Kings Parade, Cambridge
Open: Mon–Sat 11am–22.30 last orders,
closed Sunday

Tel: 01223–321551
www.rainbowcafe.co.uk

Rainbow is totally vegetarian, using freshly made food without additives, colourings or flavourings. Vegan, gluten or nut free is clearly indicated, they even have soya garlic bread. Soupe du jour £2.95. Mains £6.95 such as tagliatelle or apricot tagine. Children's portions £2.95 such as mushroom pasta. All cakes home made, half vegan, £3.25. All ice cream is vegan, Swedish glace. All wine, beer and cider is vegan organic. Wine £11.95 bottle, £2.95 glass. Non smoking. Visa, MC.

Cambridge Blue

Omnivorous restaurant

85 Gwydir Street, Cambridge CB1 2LG
Open: Mon–Sat 12.00–14.30, 18.00–21.30

Tel: 01223–361 382

Always vegetarian options available with at least one hot dish, £4.75. Not much for vegans and can only cater for them on request with advance notice. Visa, MC.

Hobbs Pavilion Restaurant

Omnivorous restaurant

Parkers Piece, Cambridge CB1 1JH
Open: Mon–Sun 12.00–23.00

Tel: 01223 367480
www.hobbspavilion.co.uk

Omnivorous restaurant with separate vegetarian menu. Main dishes at £7.95 typically include Mediteranean risotto, Bombay spicy vegetables and vegetable chilli. Can cater for vegans with items suitable clearly marked as such on menu. Licensed with house wine from £9.95 for a bottle, £2.50 for a glass. Separate smoking section. Visa, MC. Offer 15% discount to Vegetarian and Vegan society members and 10% to students.

The Gardenia

Omnivorous Greek restaurant

2 Rose Crescent, Cambridge CB2 3LL
Open: every day 12.00–23.00

Tel: 01223–356 354

Omnivorous Greek café/take-away with lots of cheap vegetarian and vegan food. Most options under £5.

Holland & Barrett

Health food shop

Unit 7 Shopping Mall, Grafton Centre,
Cambridge CB1 1PS

Tel: 01223–314 544

Holland & Barrett

Health food shop

4 Bradwells Court, Cambridge CB1 1NH

Tel: 01223–368 914

Holland & Barrett

Health food shop

1 Coronation Parade, High Street
Ely CB7 4LB

Tel: 01353–662 330

Cambridge Stop Press!

Vegetarian cafe

The day we send the book to the printers, we've just been told about a new vegetarian cafe Madal Bal at 94 Mill Rd, Cambridge. In the same street is Arjuna Wholefood Cooperative at 74 and Koh-I-Noor omnivorous Indian restaurant which is very vegan friendly and has a special vegetarian night once a week.

Cheshire

The Greenhouse   Vegetarian restaurant

41/43 Oxford Rd   *Tel: 0161–929 4141*
Altrincham, Cheshire WA14 2ED
Open: Mon–Sat 08.30–17.30

Vegetarian restaurant near the headquarters of the Vegetarian Society. Always have vegan options available such as spicy African stew, £5.50. Non smoking. Visa, MC.

The Greenhouse   Health food shop

41/43 Oxford Road   *Tel: 0161 928 4399*
Altrincham, Cheshire WA14 2ED
Open: Mon–Sat 9.00–17.30

Adjoining health food shop to vegetarian restaurant of same name.

Holland & Barrett   Health food shop

7 Paddock Row, Grosvenor Precinct *Tel: 01244–348 153*
Chester, Cheshire CH1 1ED

Holland & Barrett   Health food shop

25 Victoria Street   *Tel: 01270–253 022*
Crewe, Cheshire CW2 2JE

Holland & Barrett   Health food shop

Mill Street Mall   *Tel: 01625–424 256*
Macclesfield, Cheshire SK11 8AJ

Holland & Barrett   Health food shop

39 High Street   *Tel: 01270–610 041*
Nantwich, Cheshire CW5 5DB

Cleveland

The Waiting Room

Vegetarian restaurant

Vegetarian restaurant, which caters for vegans if given advance notice.

Starters, £2.50–£3.50 include melon and sorbet; Indian savouries; and tomato and basil soup.

Main courses, £6.75–£7.45 include pepper stuffed with garlic mushrooms; and korma nutballs with curry sauce.

Desserts from £2.95, including treacle and apple tart; and fresh fruit crumble. Vegan ice cream is always available.

Tea and herbal tea, 85p; coffee, £1.20

House wine £2.30 glass, £8.50 bottle.

Cards accepted.

9 Station Road
Eaglescliffe
Stockton on Tees
Cleveland
TS16 0BU

Tel: 01642 780 465

Open:

Mon–Sat 11.00–14.30
& 19.00–22.00.

Closed Sunday

The Food Parcel

Vegetarian cafe

Stockton International Family Centre
66 Dovecot Street, Stockton on Tees
Open: Mon–Fri 12.15–13.30

Tel: 01642 612400
Fax: 01642 608432
www.sifc.org

Great value vegetarian café and takeaway. 20 entrees from 75p, soups including borsht, pakoras, falafel, daal. Salads and main meals from £2 such as stir fry veg, chickpea wellington, dansak, pancakes, lentil flan. Usually something vegan but can adapt items for vegans and gluten free diets with notice. Desserts 50–80p with vegan cakes. Tea 25p, coffee 30p. Menus and recipes on website. Disabled access. Non smoking. No credit cards.

Holland & Barrett

Health food shop

184 Middleton Grange Shopping Centre
Hartlepool TS24 7RG

Tel: 01429–860 810

Holland & Barrett

Health food shop

16 Castle Way
Stockton TS18 1BG

Tel: 01642–671 127

Cornwall

Places in Cornwall

Hotels and Guest Houses

Restaurants

Shops

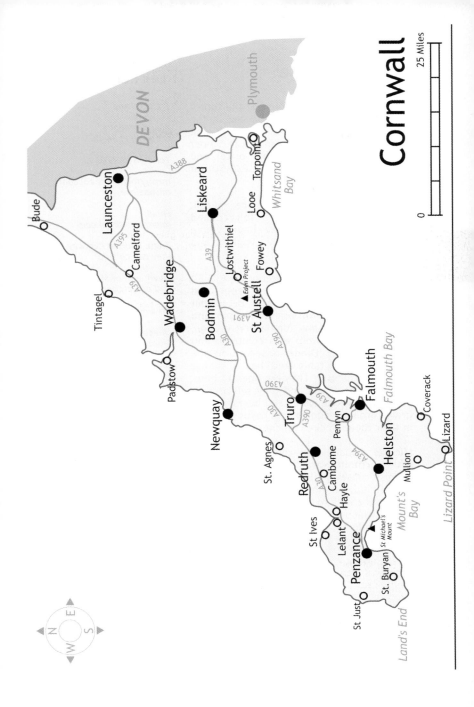

Cornwall

Michael House

Trelake Lane
Treknow
near Tintagel
Cornwall PL34 OEW

Tel: 01840 770592

http://members.aol.com/
michaelhse

Email:
michaelhse@aol.com

Train: Bodmin Parkway,
they can collect.

Open: end of March to the
end of October

No smoking throughout

One hundred year old house at the top of a valley looking down to the sea in the sleepy village of Treknow. There is one double and one family room at £21.50 per person per night (children half price), and two double ensuite rooms at £29.50 per person per night.

Breakfast comprises of fruit juice, muesli, home-baked bread and a full cooked English breakfast. They have vegan margarine, soya milk, soya yoghurt and vegan muesli.

A three course dinner is offered for £15.50 and could be leeks in mixed peppercorn vinaigrette to start, followed by walnut roulade served with braised fennel and tomato concasse and for dessert orange, apricot and tofu whip with cointreau and orange topping. Dinner is served on one long candle-lit table and has a dinner party atmosphere. They are open to non-residents for dinner and they sell organic veggie and vegan wines and beers. Home grown organic veggies and herbs are used in their food. Packed lunches available.

Directions:
From the A39, the village of Treknow is one mile south of Tintagel.
From the A39 Bude to Wadebridge Road, take the B3263 (Camelford to Tintagel) stretch until you reach Trewarmett.
As you go through the village on your left hand side is a small garden centre which is followed by a left hand bend. Immediately following this corner is an unmarked lane to the left. This is Trelake Lane and goes down into the village of Treknow. Michael House is on your right just before the church on the left.

Michael House is in the heart of King Arthur country and a walk along the Cornish coastal path to Tintagel castle and Merlin's Cave is not to be missed. It is a ten minute walk to the beach at Trebarwith Strand which is popular with both surfers and families. Surfing equipment and bicycles can be hired by the day.

Parking: plenty available

10% discount for Vegetarian Society members if staying 5 nights or more.

Further afield are the historic and mysterious Bodmin Moors and the National Trust maintained Old Harbour of Boscastle. The Eden project is a 45 minute drive away.

There is a TV lounge. Tea and coffee making facilities in the rooms.

Dolphin Cottage

Veggie B&B for women set in a 17th century traditional Cornish Cottage. The guest cottage sleeps five people with two doubles and one single room, available for B&B, or self-catering if you book the whole cottage, when mixed groups are welcome. B&B £18 per person per night, £17 for seven nights or more, or £24 if staying for one night only.

Breakfast could be fresh fruit salad and soya yoghurt, then mushrooms, tomatoes, baked beans, veggie sausages, toast and jam. Soya milk is available and vegan margarine and vegan muesli by request.

An evening meal is available if required for £10-15, such as dill and fennel soup, cashew nut, mushroom and parsnip loaf and raspberries and ice cream.

The cottage has a large living room with wood burning stove, piano, TV, books, games and tea and coffee making.

Dolphin Cottage lies on the slopes of the Lamorna valley and is half a mile from the sea. It is set in two acres of land with peaceful and secluded gardens. Within sight are two standing stones. The Merry Maidens stone circle is 5 minutes walk.

The Penwith district of Cornwall is famous for its magnificent coastline and wild rugged moorlands. There are hundreds of ancient sites including standing stones, holy wells, underground fogous and stone circles. The area has long attracted artists and there are many galleries nearby. Walking the coastal path is an ideal way to explore the Penwith Peninsula. There are chances to sight whales, dolphins, seals and rare birds. Wild flowers and sub tropical plants grow abundantly. The Eden Project is a fifty minute drive.

Newtown
St Buryan
Penzance
Cornwall TR19 6BQ

Tel : 01736 810394

Email:
dolphcot@globalnet.co.uk

Train station:
Penzance, 4 miles, then bus or taxi

Open: all year

Directions:
From Penzance take the B3315 passing through Newlyn and Sheffield. Follow this road past the turn for Lamorna Cove. Take a sharp left after Boleigh Farm sign posted 'to Menwinnon House'. Dolphin Cottage is a white cottage on the right of the lane.

Parking: plenty available

No smoking throughout.

England **CORNWALL** Accommodation

The Croft

Veggie B&B set in over half an acre of terraced gardens, bordered by a coastal path to the north, a stream to the east and a cliff edge and the sea to the south. It is only three minutes walk from the beach. There are three twin rooms from £18–£22.50 per person; two with ensuite bathrooms and one with access to private facilities. All rooms have sea views and one has a balcony.

Breakfast begins with a selection of fresh or stewed fruits followed by veggie bacon, veggie sausages, tomatoes, mushrooms, beans and home-made bread. Soya milk, vegan margarine and yoghurt available.

Dinner is offered by arrangement at £11.50 and could be soup, then nut roast and roast veg, and apple crumble with (vegan) cream.

Coverack has outstanding natural beauty and is of special geological interest. There are many delightful coves and beaches around the Lizard coast and there is a windsurfing school nearby. You can also visit Cornish villages, harbours and ancient churches. Further afield are stone circles, quoits, fogous, ruins of Iron Age villages, Celtic crosses and Celtic field patterns.

St Ives, Penzance and Truro are an hour's drive, the Eden Project and Lost Gardens of Heligan 75 minutes and there are several National Trust and private gardens within 30 to 40 minutes. There are also many potters, artists and craftworkers' studios which are open to visitors.

Well behaved dogs are welcome by arrangement. Tea and coffee making facilities in the rooms. No smoking throughout.

Vegetarian Bed & Breakfast

Coverack
Cornwall TR12 6TF
England

Tel and Fax:
01326 280387

www.cornwall-online.co.
uk/the-croft

Email:
chezebrown@m-b-t.co.uk

Train station: Redruth,
Truro or Penzance all
about 23 miles away, then
get a bus or taxi

Open: all year

Directions:
From Helston take the
A3083 Lizard Road, then
turn left at mini round-
about onto B3293 for St.
Keverne/Coverack. The
turn off for Coverack is on
the right, about a mile
past Zoar Garage. Go
past the car park at the
foot of the hill and when
the road turns right, turn
a sharp left into the lane.
The Croft is the third
house on the right.

Parking: plenty available

The Great Escape

Vegetarian
Bed & Breakfast

16 Park Avenue
St. Ives
Cornwall
TR26 2DN

Tel: 01736 794617

www.g-escape.freeuk.com

Train station:
St. Ives, 1/2 mile

Open: all year

Directions:
From St. Ives station turn right onto St. Andrews Street, then left onto Street-an-pol, right onto Treganna Place, then left onto Gabriel Street and left again onto Park Avenue.

Parking: on street

Veggie B&B run by two vegetarian women, five minutes walk from the harbour and the centre of St. Ives. There are four double ensuite rooms (two with harbour views) at £20–£25 per person per night.

Start the morning with a glass of freshly squeezed orange juice, cereal, fresh fruit and soya yoghurt. Follow with a cooked breakfast of hash browns, veggie sausages, grilled tomatoes, fried mushrooms, baked beans, home baked rolls, toast and preserves and tea or coffee.

No evening meal is offered but there is a veggie cafe and most of the restaurants in St. Ives serve plenty of veggie food.

The clean sandy beaches, artists and little cobbled streets of St. Ives combine to create an enticing Mediterranean stlye resort.

You can go swimming or surfing at one of the four beaches nearby, or for a scenic walk along the South West Coastal Path.

Other attractions include Hepworth Gardens and the Tate Gallery, which displays work by St. Ives based artists. There are several other galleries, studios and craftshops.

The Great Escape is a short walk from St. Ives Leisure Centre which has an ozone treated swimming pool and a fully equipped fitness suite.

Dogs are welcome by arrangement. Tea and coffee making facilities, televisions and CD players in the rooms. No smoking throughout.

Boswednack Manor

Spacious granite farmhouse on the north coast of the Land's End Peninsula, overlooking Gurnard's Head – one of the wildest promontories in Cornwall.

Boswednack Manor has five rooms. One single, one twin and one family at £18–£19 per person; two double ensuite rooms (one with sea views) £21–£22 per person. It is set in a three acre organic small holding and private nature reserve. There is a meditation barn for occasional meditation and yoga retreats.

Breakfast is juice, cereal and fresh fruit followed by potato waffles, mushrooms, tomatoes, toast and tea, coffee or herbal tea. Soya milk, vegan margarine and vegan muesli are available. Dinner is not offered but there are veggie restaurants in St. Ives and Penzance.

The lounge has a piano and a library, which includes local interest and history. Free walking maps. Tea and coffee making facilities in the rooms.

Treryn Dinas, one of Cornwall's ancient cliff castles, is here. There are many walks such as the South West Coast Path where you can enjoy the unspoilt scenery of the moors and the coast and see stone circles, standing stones and quoits. Near Zennor lies a unique cromlech which contains two sepulchres covered by one great stone.

There are all the attractions of nearby St. Ives, Penzance and Marazion which include sandy beaches, a windsurfing school, a surfing school, indoor pools, gardens, galleries, museums, nightclubs, restaurants, shops and summer festivals.

Zennor
St. Ives
Cornwall
TR26 3DD

Tel : 01736 794183

Train station:
Penzance or St. Ives,
6 miles, then bus or taxi.
Collection is sometimes
possible.

Open: Easter–October

Directions:
One mile west of Zennor
on the St. Ives to Land's
End coast road B3306.

Parking: available

5% discount to members
of the Vegetarian Society,
Vegan Society or people
presenting this book for
stays of three nights or
more.

Children are welcome and
there is a cot and high
chair.

No smoking throughout.

Mount Pleasant Farm

Omnivorous
Bed & Breakfast

Omnivorous B&B with veggie owners on an organic small holding. There are four rooms: one single, one double and one family at £17–£20 per person, and one double ensuite at £20–£23 per person.

Wake in the morning to porridge with sesame seeds and fruit compote or crispy tofu with mushrooms and tomatoes. Veggie sausages, vegan muesli, vegan margarine, soya milk and soya yoghurt are all available.

A substantial one course dinner is available by request three days a week for £8.50. Dinner is always veggie or vegan and could be a home made pie, pastie, burger or nut loaf with seasonal salad and home grown potatoes. All the food is local and organic where possible and most of their vegetables are home grown. Special diets are catered for with prior notice.

Mount Pleasant Farm is an excellent base for walks through beautiful scenery. It is on the eastern edge of the Roseland Peninsular and just a mile from the coastal footpath where wildlife abounds. There are three unspoilt beaches nearby, the closest is a mile away and ideal for children.

The famous Heligan gardens are three miles away and the Eden Project is nine miles away.

Alternative therapies are available. Bike hire offered.

Children are welcome and they have a cot and high chair. There are tea and coffee making facilities, televisions and washbasins in the rooms. No smoking throughout.

Gorran High Lanes
St. Austell
Cornwall
PL26 6LR

Tel: 01726 843918

www.vegetarian-cornwall.co.uk

Email:
jill@mpfarm.vispa.com

Train station:
St. Austell, 8 miles, then get a bus to Mevagissey where they will collect you.

Open:
end March–end October

Directions:
Take the road from St. Austell to Mevagissey. After ascending a steep hill past Pentwan beach, you come to a cross roads. Take the turning on your right, sign posted 'Gorran'. Follow this road. You will pass Heligan on your left and after three miles, at a phone box, you will see the Mount Pleasant Farm tourism sign on your right. Follow further signs from here. Please take care not to enter the drive of their neighbours at Mount Pleasant House.

Parking: plenty available

5% discount to members of the Vegetarian Society, Vegan Society and people presenting this book if staying for three nights or more.

Woodlands Hotel

Omnivorous hotel with a vegan proprietor one mile from Newquay centre. There are fifty four rooms: 11 singles, 23 doubles, 16 twins and 4 family rooms all with ensuite bathrooms. Rooms are £20–£40 per person and many have breathtaking views.

For breakfast you can choose from a selection of juices and cereals, followed by a full cooked English breakfast of veggie sausages, hash browns, tomatoes, mushrooms and beans with toast and preserves. Vegan margarine, soya milk and vegan muesli are all available.

A four course dinner is included in the nightly rate and they are open to non-residents. There is a separate vegetarian/vegan menu which changes daily and could start with vegetable pate served with hot toast and salad garnish followed by soup of the day. Then a main course of pasta pesto or a vegan cutlet with sesame battered mushrooms served with various salads, potatoes and fresh seasonal vegetables. Finish off with apricot crumble and soya cream.

Woodlands' grounds go down to the Gannel Estuary and the hotel has inspirational views over this and the open sea. It is close to beaches and has its own sauna, solarium and outdoor swimming pool. It also has an all weather, floodlit, four rink, full sized bowling green of which guests have exclusive use.

All rooms have telephones, televisions and tea and coffee making facilites. Guide dogs only accepted. Smoking is allowed in the bar and lounge only.

Pentire Crescent
Newquay
Cornwall
TR7 1PU

Tel: 01637 852229

Fax: 01637 852227

*www.
newquayaccommod ation
.co.uk/woodlands*

*Email:
woodlandshotel@
talk21.com*

*Train station:
Newquay, 2 miles*

*Open: 22 Feb 2002 to 2
Jan 2003. Possibly open
all year round in 2003.*

*Directions:
From the A392 Gannel
Link Road the town will be
on your right. When you
reach the end of this road
you will be at a round-
about. Turn left into
Pentire Road., then turn
left again into Trethellan
Hill. This road divides
and becomes Pentire
Crescent. Take the left
fork. Woodlands Hotel
will be on your left.*

Parking: available

Making Waves

Victorian terraced house in a quiet lane overlooking St. Ives Bay, just above semi-tropical gardens. There is one double room at £21 per person, one twin at £23 per person, and a double/family room with a view at £28.50 per person. Extra adults in family room £14, extra child under sixteen £12, under four years free.

Sit inside or out for your delicious vegan breakfast of muesli or cereal, fruit salad and soya yoghurt with freshly extracted juice or a milkshake, followed by a fry-up with toast and toppings and filter coffee.

A three course organic dinner can be provided by arrangement for £14.50. It could be warm tempeh and mung bean salad, followed by kebabs with peanut sauce, then chocolate and pecan brownies with ice cream. Food is free from hydro-genated fats and GM ingredients. Any special diets are catered for – let them know in advance.

The town centre and harbour are a two minute walk and all St. Ives' beaches are within a ten minute stroll. It is an artistic community and you will find many galleries around town. Other attractions including ancient Pagan monuments, St. Michael's Mount, Land's End, Seal Sanctuary or the Lost Gardens of Heligan. Activities include surfing, kite flying, diving, walking and cycling. Lots of pubs, night clubs and restaurants serve veggie/vegan food. Vibrant live music scene.

Making Waves has a small experimental veganic forest garden growing a variety of edible flowers, fruits and herbs. Guest lounge with TV, musical instruments, music system and books. Tea and coffee making facilites and washbasins in rooms. They have a cot and high chair.

3 Richmond Place
St. Ives
Cornwall
TR26 1JN

Tel: 01736 793895

www.making-waves.co.uk

Email:
simon@
making-waves.co.uk

Train Station: St. Ives, 1/2 mile, then taxi or collection is possible.

Open: March–October

Directions: Follow the A30 through Cornwall, then the signs to St. Ives. Descending into St. Ives from Carbis Bay, turn right at Porthminster Hotel downhill into St. Ives. Follow to the right at Barclays Bank, then first left into Market Place. Turn left again at New World Chinese. Making Waves is 50 metres up Richmond Place on the right.

Parking: available

5% discount to members of Vegan Society, Viva!, Animal Aid, PETA and Vegan Organic Network.

10% discount for stays of six nights or more (not June, July or August).

No pets and no smoking.

Secure bicycle storage.

Lanherne

Veggie and vegan B&B situated in the village of Mullion, on the west coast of the beautiful Lizard Peninsula. The views across the village towards Mount Bay are spectacular. There are three rooms, one double and two twin/family rooms. All cost £23 per person and have showers and washbasins. Two have panoramic views. Children 5-13 half price, under-5 free.

Help yourself to a breakfast buffet of cereals or porridge, juice and fruit, then tofu, onion, mushrooms and dill on toast. Or have a full cooked breakfast of veg sausages, nut rissoles or bean burgers with grilled tomatoes, baked beans, mushrooms and scrambled tofu with toast. Vegan margarine, soya milk, rice milk, vegan muesli and soya yoghurt available. Rice cakes and spelt bread for those with wheat allergies.

A two course meal is £10. The impressively long menu includes Shepherd's Beany Pie with fresh veg; Savoury Nut Roll with roast potatoes, fresh veg and gravy; Vegetable Pie with new potatoes and broccoli, amongst several more dishes. Dessert could be Kathy's pudding of the day or fresh fruit salad with soya cream or ice cream. Bring your own wine.

The Lizard Peninsula is an unspoiled area of outstanding natural beauty. It's full of wooded valleys, ancient hedgerows, rugged cliffs and sandy coves and has some of the best beaches in West Cornwall. Enjoy the tranquility and breathtaking views on the cliff tops. Take a boat trip from Mullion Cove. Guided birdwatching can be arranged.

Rooms have tea and coffee making, water filter, TV and clock radio. Guests are welcome to share lounge and gardens.

Vegetarian Bed and Breakfast

Meaver Road
Mullion
Helston
Cornwall
TR12 7DN

Tel: 01326 241381

Train Station: Redruth, 20 miles, then two buses or collection can be arranged

Open: all year

Directions: Head for the M5 and A30. Exit A30 at Scorrier/Helston. When you approach Helston, follow the Lizard sign, then sign to Mullion. The right hand turn to Mullion is Meaver Road.

Parking: available in grounds

Discounts on stays of five nights or more

No smoking

Cot available

Bike hire available

Special diets catered for

Woodcote Hotel

Vegetarian Hotel

The Saltings, Lelant,
St. Ives, Cornwall, TR26 3DL
Open: all year, except Christmas and New Year

Tel: 01736 753147
Train Station:
St. Erth, one mile

Double rooms £33–£35 and double ensuite rooms £38–£40. Prices are for dinner, bed and breakfast and are per person per night. Deduct £13 for just bed and breakfast.
Children over twelve welcome. No pets. No smoking throughout.

St Ives Self Catering

Self catering

2A Gabriel Street, Royal Square
St Ives, Cornwall TR26 2LU
martyn.jenkins1@btopenworld.com

Tel: 01736 795255
Fax: call first

Vegetarian owned self catering flat in St Ives, above a hair salon and tea rooms, overlooking St Ives Bay. For 2 to 6 people. 2 double bedrooms en suite with fitted kitchen, large lounge with two single bed-settees for children, small patio area. From £180 per week to £415 in peak season according to number of people and rooms used.

Archie Brown's Café

Vegetarian cafe

Brown's Gallery, Bread Street
Penzance, Cornwall TR18 2EQ
Open: Mon–Sat 10.00–16.00 last orders, closed Sun.
Also most Friday nights from 7pm, booking essential.

Tel: 01736–362 828

Vegetarian wholefood café and art galllery which caters well for vegans. Mains £3–£6 such as homity pie. Home made cakes, some of them vegan, and they also have vegan ice cream. House wine, £8. Non smoking inside. Visa, MC. 10% discount to Vegetarian Society members. Situated over Richard's Health Food Shop which you go through to get to the cafe.

The Cafe

Vegetarian restaurant

Island Square
St. Ives, Cornwall TR26 1NX
Open: Mar–Oct 18.30–22.00 every day

Tel: 01736 793621

Vegetarian restaurant just back from the harbour front. Six starters, at least half vegan, £3.20–£4.80. Six mains, £8.60–£9.50, at least two are or can be vegan, such as potato gnocchi on a bed of fresh spinach with tamarind and cranberry sauce. Desserts £3.95 include fruit crumble or treacle tart, plus soya ice cream. Wine £2.50 glass, £9.50–£12.50 bottle, including organic vegan. No smoking. Visa, MC.

The Feast
Vegetarian restaurant

15 Kenwyn Street
Truro, Cornwall TR1 3BU
Open: Mon–Sat 10–17.00, closed Sun.
Last weekend of month open for themed evening.

Tel: 01872 272546

Vegetarian world food restaurant with tea garden and good choice of Belgian fruit, white, blonde and chimay beers. Starters £2.50–£3.35, 4 vegan. Salads £3.30–£4.50, savoury and sweet pancakes which can be made vegan, jacket potatoes, sandwiches, dish of day etc. Desserts feature enticing (soya) ice creams, cakes made on premises and always something vegan. Can cater for diabetic and gluten free diets. Smoking section. No credit cards.

Terra Firma
Omnivorous restaurant

10 Lostwithiel Street
Fowey, Cornwall
Open: Wed–Sun 19–22.00 (last orders)

Tel: 01726 833023
terra-firma@talk21.com

Mainly vegetarian restaurant 20 minutes up the coast from St Austell. Five veggie dishes £7.95 and are spicy unless you ask, like stuffed pancakes with roquet salad, veg tikka masala, fajitas, 2 or 3 of them vegan.. Desserts £3.50 but none vegan. Non smoking. Visa, MC, Diners. Children welcome, high chair. Paying and free car parks nearby.

The Top House
Omnivorous restaurant

The Lizard
nr Helston, Cornwall TR12 7NQ

Tel: 01326 290974
Open: Mon–Sun 18.30–21.00

Omnivorous restaurant with vegetarian dishes from £5.95, but lean pickings for vegans. Licenced. Separate smoking section. Visa, MC.

The Granary

Wholefood & fruit and veg. shop

Causeway Head
Penzance

Richard's Health Food Shop

Health food shop

Brown's Gallery, Bread Street
Penzance, Cornwall TR18 2EQ
Open: Mon–Sat 9.00–17.30, closed Sunday

Tel: 01736–362 828

Wholefood and vitamins shop with take–away food that's made in the vegetarian cafe Archie Brown's upstairs.

Good Health

Wholefood shop

Tregenna Place
St Ives
Open: Mon–Sat 9–17.30, closed Sun

Tel: 01736–794726
Salad bar 799868

Central vegetarian wholefood shop opposite Spar, with a take–away salad bar (not vegetarian) at the front which can also cater to vegans. £1.85 for a three scoop salad, £2.50 for five; sandwiches and split big rolls also £1.85.

Holland & Barrett

Health food shop

48 Market Street
Falmouth

Tel: 01326–319 327

3 Market Place
Penzance

Tel: 01736–331 855

13/14 Aylemer Square
St Austell

Tel: 01726–73548

1 Francis Street
Truro

Tel: 01872–272 991

England CORNWALL Shops

The Lake District
Cumbria

The Lake District, in the heart of Cumbria, is the largest of England's National Parks and offers some of the best walking in Britain. It is an extremely beautiful area with high fells, rocky crags, lush green dales, huge peaceful lakes and busy villages. As a vegetarian, it is an excellent place to take a holiday, as there are veggie and veggie friendly guesthouses and restaurants in many of its villages.

The main bases for the Lakes are Keswick in the North and **Windermere and Bowness** in the South. Windermere and Bowness is the largest tourist centre and is full of B&B's, restaurants and attractions like The World of Beatrix Potter. It gets inundated by tourists and can feel like a seaside resort, so don't come if you're after peace and quiet. Two of its good qualities though are the veg guesthouse, Cambridge House and the veg friendly, Kirkwood Guesthouse. If the weather's not so great for walking, visit the Lake District Centre at Brockhole, by Lake Windermere. It has an adventure playground, interactive exhibitions, beautiful gardens, games' lawn and a gift shop.

Keswick, next to Derwent Water is particularly popular with walkers. It's still a busy town, but it feels more relaxed than Windermere. Take a boat trip or row a hired boat around the lake for a refreshing change from walking. A pleasant four mile circular walk from the town centre to the Castlerigg Stone Circle, believed to be around 3000 years old offers excellent views. Have lunch at the vibrant wholefood veggie café, Lakeland Peddlar, or take a tasty snack away with you.

Just north of Windermere and Bowness is **Ambleside**, a pretty town and a popular centre for walkers and climbers. It's a good base to explore the Southern Lake District, but although slightly less hectic than Windermere and Bowness, it is still regularly inundated. Beechmount Guesthouse caters well for veggies.

If you're into the poetry of Wordsworth, a visit to **Grasmere** is esssential. It is the home of Dove Cottage where he wrote many of his poems, and the Wordsworth Museum. It is a very pretty village but is often overrun with tourists, so it is best to visit out of season. The place to stay is Glenthorne Country Guesthouse.

Coniston Water and the town are both beautiful. There are some lovely walks in the area, particularly up the Old Man of Coniston. If it's a clear day, the view from the top is breathtaking.

Be sure to dine at least one evening at the Quince and Medlar in **Cockermouth**, one of the best veggie restaurants in Britain. If you're not staying in Cockermouth, it's worth the drive. Cockermouth is just outside the Lake District, which makes it quieter than many of the other villages. It's a great base to explore the North West, particularly Crummock Water and Buttermere.

Kendal, on the eastern outskirts of the Lakes is a busy market town with several interesting museums and galleries, but it's selling point for veggies and vegans would have to be Fox Hall Vegan Bed and Breakfast serving imaginative breakfasts and delicious three course dinners, or Lakeland Natural Vegetarian Guesthouse.

If you'd prefer to be out of the main hub of the Lake District, consider **Grange-over-Sands** on the southern edge of the park where you could stay at Fernhill Vegetarian Country House, or **Alston**, close to The Pennines, home to Nentholme Vegetarian Guesthouse.

The Lake District offers many opportunities for learning about the area. It is possible to do navigated walks and bike rides and learn to map read.

If you're tired of walking or it's just not your thing, most of the lakes have boat trips around them, which can be a relaxing way to still see some gorgeous scenery. There are also some great cycling routes around the Lake District, particularly the Cumbria Cycle Way which takes five to seven days. There are many books available on cycling in Cumbria.

A word of warning: try to avoid the Lake District on summer weekends as it is the second most visited area in Britain behind London. It's quite hard to enjoy nature when you have a crowd of strangers around you!

by Katrina Holland

Places in Cumbria

Hotels and Guest Houses

Beechmount, Sawrey, Hawkshead, Ambleside – omnivorous B&B	78
Yewfield, Hawkshead, Ambleside – vegetarian B&B	79
Nab Cottage, Rydal, Ambleside – omnivorous B&B	95
Nentholme, Alston – vegetarian guesthouse	80
Pumpkin House, Cockermouth – vegetarian B&B	95
Beech Tree, Coniston – vegetarian guest house	81
Fernhill, Witherslack, Grange-over-Sands – vegetarian B&B	82
Glenthorne, Grasmere – omnivorous guesthouse	83
How Beck, Grasmere – vegetarian B&B	95
Lancrigg, Grasmere – vegetarian hotel	84
Fox Hall, Sedgwick, Kendal – vegan B&B and self-catering	86
Lakeland Natural, Kendal – vegetarian guesthouse	88
32 Skiddaw Street, Keswick – vegetarian B&B	89
Eden Green, Keswick – omnivorous guest house	90
Edwardene Hotel, Keswick – omnivorous hotel	91
Honister House, Keswick – omnivorous guesthouse	92
Pickle Guest House, Kirkby Lonsdale – vegetarian guesthouse	93
Kirkwood Guest House, Windermere – omnivorous guesthouse	94

Restaurants

Zeffirellis, Ambleside – vegetarian Italian restaurant	97
Garden Room Café, Ambleside – vegetarian café	98
The Watermill Restaurant, Wigton – vegetarian restaurant	98
Quince and Medlar, Cockermouth – vegetarian restaurant	96
The Rowan Tree, Grasmere – vegetarian café	98
Dove Cottage Tea Rooms Restaurant, Grasmere – omnivorous	99
Waterside Wholefood, Kendal – vegetarian café & wholefood shop	98
Lakeland Pedlar, Keswick – vegetarian restaurant & bicycle centre	99
Maysons, Keswick – omnivorous restaurant	99
Little Salkeld Watermill, near Penrith – vegetarian tea room	97
Village Bakery, Melmerby, near Penrith – omnivorous organic cafe	100

Shops

The Granary, Cockermouth – health food shop	100
Kan Foods, Kendal – wholefood shop	100
Sundance Wholefoods, Keswick – wholefood shop	100
Living Well, Milnethorpe – wholefood shop	100
Nature's Health Store, Penrith – wholefood shop	100
Appleseeds, Ulverston – health food shop	100

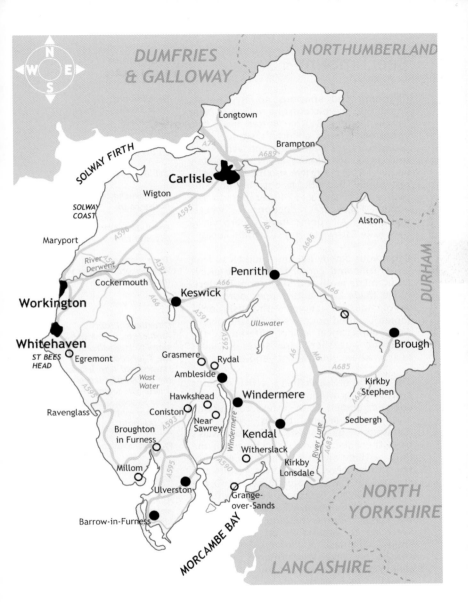

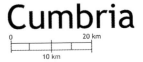

Cumbria

0   20 km

10 km

Beechmount

Charming and spacious country house, situated in the picturesque village of Near Sawrey, where Beatrix Potter lived and wrote her famous children's stories. The proprietors are vegetarian and vegan and breakfasts are almost always completely veggie. There are five rooms; one single, one family, two double ensuites and one twin ensuite all at £24 per person per night. There are reductions for weekly bookings. All rooms have superb views over Lake Esthwaite and Grizedale Forest.

Begin your day by helping yourself to fruit juice, fruit and cereal followed by either home made lentil and mushroom burgers, home made corn and pepper burgers or veggie sausages served with mushrooms, tomatoes, fried potatoes and baked beans. An evening meal is not offered at the moment but there are several places nearby where you can get veggie food.

The village of Hawkshead is five minutes away with its winding narrow streets and cobbled ginnels with cafes, restaurants and shops selling books, gifts and paintings by local artists. There are walks from the door and you can be up in the hills within minutes where there are spectacular views, tarns, lakes, woods and streams. Or you could go across to the 9,000 acres of Grizedale Forest with its fascinating sculpture trails and Theatre in the Forest. For something a little more lively go to Ambleside or Bowness for shops, cinemas, restaurants, nghtclubs, cruises on Lake Windermere, canoeing, sailing or winsurfing. Or you could hire a mountain bike for the day.

The guest lounge has a TV and there are TV's in the rooms. Tea and coffee making facilities in rooms.

Omnivorous
Guest House

Beechmount
Near Sawrey
Hawkshead
Ambleside
Cumbria LA22 OJZ
England

Tel: 015394 36356

www.beechmountcountry house.co.uk

Email: beechmount@ supanet.com

Train Station: Windermere, 4 miles via the car ferry.

Open: all year

Directions: From Ambleside, follow the signs to Hawkshead. At the T junction in Hawkshead turn left on the B5285 and travel two miles. On seeing the Near Sawrey sign, Beechmount is opposite on the right.

Parking: available

Smoking allowed in some areas.

Animals and children welcome. They have a high chair

Yewfield Vegetarian B&B

Vegetarian B&B
and Self Catering

Impressive Gothic Victorian house with panoramic views over the Vale of Esthwaite, Lake Winderemere and the fells beyond. There are two double ensuites and one twin ensuite for £22.50–£37 per person per night. Single person supplement £5.

Begin the day with a wholefood continental buffet including fresh fruits, vegan muesli, cereals and home baked bread with preserves, followed by a full cooked breakfast. Vegan margarine and soya milk available. Dinner is not offered but Ambleside's veggie restaurant, Zeffirellis is only four miles away.

Yewfield is ideally situated for walking and enjoying this region of rare natural beauty. A ten minute stroll takes you to a magnificant viewpoint overlooking Tarn Hows and the rugged fells of the central Lakes. The house stands in over thirty acres of private grounds, which include native woodland, rough fell pasture and a small tarn and stream. Areas closer to the house include organic veggie gardens, orchards, a herb patio and a mixed border. A nature trail through the land and gardens is there to guide you.

If you prefer self catering, there are four self contained holiday apartments in the former coach house and stables, set 150 yards away from the main house. Please contact Heart of the Lakes on 015394 32321 with enquiries.

Tea and coffee making facilities, radios and televisions in the rooms. Lounge and library area available for guests' use. Children over nine welcome. Pets accepted by arrangement in the self catering apartments only.

Hawkshead Hill
Ambleside
Cumbria LA22 0PR
England

Tel: 015394 36765

Fax: 0154394 36096

www.yewfield.co.uk

Email: derek.yewfield@ btinternet.com

Train Station: Windermere, 6 miles, then taxi

Open: Feb–mid Nov

Directions: from Ambleside take the A593 Coniston Road and at Clappersgate (1/2 mile), turn a sharp left at junction signposted B5286 Hawkshead. Proceed for just over one mile, then on the brow of a hill, turn right into an unclassified road signposted Tarn Hows. Follow this road for 2.4 miles (passing the Drunken Duck Inn), before reaching the drive up to Yewfield on the right.

Parking: available

No smoking throughout.

Nentholme Vegetarian Guest House

Nineteenth Century house standing in its own one acre grounds with views of the surrounding fells. There are three rooms, all with good views; one double ensuite and one family ensuite for £25 per person per night and one twin room with private bathroom for £20 per person per night.

Breakfast comprises of cereal followed by a full cooked breakfast which could include lentil and mushroom burgers and bean croquettes. Vegan margarine, soya milk, vegan muesli and veggie sausages are all available. Packed lunches are £4.

A three course evening meal with wine is offered for £15. It could be carrot and coriander soup to start, followed by a main course of Shepherd's lentil pie with mixed veggies and for dessert, apple crumble, all finished off with coffee and mints. Organic produce used whenever possible.

Nentholme offers a tranquil environment but is only a few minutes walk from the centre of the quaint town of Alston, with it's cobbled streets and 17th and 18th Century buildings. It is situated in a designated Area of Outstanding Natural Beauty, surrounded by the unspoilt fells and High Pennines. It is close to the Coast to Coast Cycle Route. The area has something to interest almost everyone with a passion for the outdoors. Activities you could partake in include, walking, cycling, bird watching, golf and canoeing. Alston is an ideal base for touring Northern England, Southern Scotland, the Lake District and Northumbria.

Relax in the guest lounge by the open fire. Rooms have tea and coffee making facilites, televisions and radio alarms.

The Butts
Alston
Cumbria CA9 3JQ
England

Tel and Fax:
01434 381523

www.nentholme.co.uk

Email: bob@green
halgh90.freeserve.co.uk

Train Station: Penrith, 20 miles, then bus or taxi.

Open: all year

Directions: From the motorway/train station at Penrith, take junction 40 exit from M6 at Penrith. Follow signs for Alston (A686). They are in the centre of Alston. Turn into The Butts at the Market Cross.

Parking: free and ample

Children and pets are welcome.

No smoking throughout.

Beech Tree Guest House

Vegetarian
Guest House

Beech Tree Guest House is set in its own grounds, at the foot of the Old Man of Coniston, 150 yards from the centre of the village. There are six double rooms, three with ensuites and two twin rooms, one with an ensuite. Rooms with ensuites are £25–£26 per person per night and those without are £19–£22 per person per night.

Begin the day with fruit juice, cereals and grapefruit followed by a sesame burger or vegetarian sausages, mushrooms, beans, tomatoes and toast. Vegan margarine, soy milk and vegan muesli are available. Special diets catered for. Let them know your requirements when you book. No evening meal is offered, but there is a wide range of restaurants and pubs in Coniston and the surrounding villages.

There are walks right from the house to local waterfalls, the lower valleys or to Coniston Old Man and the high fells. Some of the most beautiful scenery in the Lake District is nearby, as well as many famous houses and attractions.

Coniston is an ideal stopover on the Cumbria Way. It is an excellent centre for many activities. There is much to do for people of all interests and abilities, such as walks ranging from gentle strolls to difficult climbs, sailing and canoeing, and of course just sightseeing and relaxing. Coniston makes a good base to explore the Langdale Valleys, Wastwater and the Southern Fells.

Guests are welcome to enjoy the small but interesting garden. Drying facilities are available. Tea and coffee making facilites in rooms. Guest lounge with television.

Yewdale Road
Coniston
Cumbria LA21 8DX
England

Tel: 015394 41717

Train Station:
Windermere, 12 miles,
then bus

Open: all year

Directions: phone for
details and map

Parking: ample private
parking

Children over 10 only.

No pets.

No smoking throughout.

England CUMBRIA Accommodation

Fernhill Vegetarian Country House

Vegetarian guest house at the southern edge of the Lake District National Park with views over the Winster valley. There are three rooms; one single, one double and one double ensuite all at £30 per person per night. 10% discount on stays of three nights or more.

There is plenty to choose from for breakfast including fruit juice, cereals, fresh fruit and toast with home made preserves, followed by potato cakes, mushrooms, tomatoes and veggie sausages. Soya milk, vegan muesli and vegan margarine are available. Bread is organic and home made.

A three course dinner is offered in the dining room for £20, or you could opt for a less formal one course dinner to be taken in the kitchen with the proprietors. In summer you could dine under the apple trees in their organic vegetable garden. Picnic lunches are available on request. There are also a number of restaurants and pubs within a short drive that serve vegetarian and vegan meals.

Take walks in the hills and woods watching for red squirrels, deers and badgers with the central fells spread out before you. The proprietors know the area well and can provide guided walking, scrambling and mountain biking. Climbing and other activities can be arranged.

Please be aware that although all the food served is vegetarian, meat is cooked in the house as one of the proprietors is not veggie.

Vegetarian
Guest House

*Witherslack
Grange–over–Sands
Cumbria LA11 6RX
England*

Tel: 015395 52237

Fax: 015395 52185

*Email:
alibramall@lineone.net*

Train station: Oxenholme, 10 miles or Grange–over–Sands, 5 miles, then taxi.

Open: all year

Directions: From M6, junction 36, take A590 to turning for Grange/ Barrow. After approximately 5 miles, turn right into Witherslack. Follow signs for Halecat nursery. Fernhill is 1/3 mile further on the left.

Parking: available

Animals and children are welcome and there are a cot and high chair.

Fax and internet facilities.

Laundry service and drying room.

No smoking throughout.

Glenthorne Country Guest House

Victorian country house set in one of the most peaceful locations in Grasmere. It's as large as a hotel but not as formal. There is accommodation to suit everyone including self catering apartments and three simple bunk style rooms for walkers and cyclists. Single, double and twin rooms are £26–£44 per person per night without ensuite facilities and £33–£49 with ensuite facilities. Family rooms are £26–£49 per person per night.

Cereal and a full cooked veggie breakfast are offered. There's not so much for vegans although they do have soya milk.

A three course dinner is available for £12 and the restaurant is open to non residents too. There is always a veggie option which could be melon cocktail, followed by nut roast with provençale sauce and for dessert, fresh fruit salad. If you are vegan or have any other dietary requirements, let them know in advance.

Glenthorne is surrounded by fells and beautiful scenery. Take strolls around Grasmere village and lake, or set out for the day with a packed lunch provided by the guest house for a more challenging walk.

Alternatively, have a lazy day relaxing in the lounges or gardens with a book.

There is a conference room which seats up to 45 people. Tea and coffee making facilities in the rooms.

Omnivorous Guest House & Restaurant

Easedale Road
Grasmere
Cumbria LA22 9QH
England

Tel and Fax:
015394 35389

www.glenthorne.org

Email:
info@glenthorne.org

Train Station:
Windermere, 10 miles,
then bus or taxi.

Open:
February–November

Directions: from junction 36 on the M6 take the A591 to Grasmere. Turn left into the village, then go past the Red Lion Hotel and Heaton Cooper Studio. Turn left onto Easedale Road. Glenthorne is at the top of the hill on the left.

Parking: available

Conference room

Clothes drying and bike storage facilities..

No smoking throughout.

Children are welcome and they have cots and high chairs.

England **CUMBRIA** Accommodation

Lancrigg

Lancrigg is set in 30 acres of idyllic gardens overlooking the serenity of Easedale. You will appreciate the total absence of traffic noise and the sound of nearby waterfalls and birds. There is excellent walking right from the doorstep.

There are 13 rooms, with singles, doubles, twins and families, all with ensuite bathrooms. Most have special features such as gorgeous views and whirlpool spa baths. Prices range from £50–£99 per person per night and include a four course dinner. Cheaper rates for stays of three nights or more. Deduct £20 if you don't want dinner.

In the morning help yourself to fruit juices, fruit salads and natural cereals. This is followed by a continental or full cooked breakfast of basil tomatoes, vegetarian burgers, baked beans, mushrooms and toast. Vegan margarine, soya milk, soya yoghurt, vegan muesli, veggie sausages and vegan croissants are all available.

Dinner could be roasted aubergine and tomato torte with a romesco sauce, followed by carrot and fennel soup. Your main might be provençal mushroom, leek and pinekernel stuffed pepper, with a tomato and olive sauce and new potaotes, roasted in lemon and fresh herbs, served with salad. For dessert, chocolate and walnut cake. Finish off with fresh ground coffee and chocolates. Organic wine available. Special diets catered for. Food is organic where possible and free from artificial additives.

Champagne and luxury chocolates may be ordered to be in your room on arrival. Tea & coffee making and TV in rooms.

Vegetarian
Country House Hotel

Easedale
Grasmere
Cumbria LA22 9QN
England

Tel: 015394 35317

Fax: 015394 35058

www.lancrigg.co.uk

Email: info@lancrigg.co.uk

Train Station:
Windermere 8 miles
then taxi

Open: all year

Directions: From the M6, take the A591 to Grasmere. In the centre of the village, turn left up Easedale Road. The entrance is 1/2 mile on the right.

Parking: available

Children and pets welcome. They have cots and high chairs.

Smoking in rooms only

Breakfast can be served in rooms if requested

10% discount to members of the Vegetarian Society, Vegan Society, Viva! and people presenting this book.

Lancrigg

VEGETARIAN
COUNTRY HOUSE HOTEL

THE LAKE DISTRICT

GRASMERE

"Where time stands still"

**Idyllic mountain setting, whirlpool baths,
4 posters, fresh air, pure food and fine wine
provides inspiration for Lakeland lovers.**

✱✱✱✱✱✱

*L*ancrigg's timeless charm comes from it's unrivalled
position overlooking the serenity of Easedale.
Whether on foot, car or local transport, you are but
half a mile away from the Lakeland village of Grasmere.

*O*ne aspect you will really appreciate is the total absence
of traffic noise - the silence puctuated only by the sound
of nearby waterfalls and birdsong.

*E*njoy the relaxed atmosphere of the
elegant Georgian dining room
where meals are served overlooking
Easedale valley. Soft music and
candlelit tables add to the setting.

**Special
Breaks**

Tel: 015934 35317
Email: info@lancrigg.co.uk
www.lancrigg.co.uk

Fox Hall Vegan B&B

Seventeenth century converted barn in the rural village of Sedgwick, four miles south of Kendal. There is a double and a single room available in the house for £18 per person per night. Children aged five to sixteen stay for £10 and those under five are free. There is an adjoining self-catering holiday cottage which can sleep 5 people and costs £200-£295 for a week.

Breakfast is entirely vegan and is a selection of cereals or porridge with soya milk, soya yoghurt and fresh fruit followed by a choice from several dishes including creamed mushrooms on toast; tofu, onion, mushrooms and dill on toast; home made lemon and sultana pancakes or the Big One-two nut rissoles or bean burgers with scrambled tofu, mushrooms, onions and plum tomatoes. Organic and GMO free foods are used where possible.

A three course home cooked meal is £12. There is an extensive menu from which you could choose leek and potato soup, wholemeal pancakes layered with fennel, spinach and tomato and for dessert, chocolate and orange gateau. A child's meal is £3.50. Packed lunches are available for £3.

From Sedgwick, there are good local walks along the disused Lancaster to Kendal Canal towpath, the banks of the River Kent and into Leven Park. Levens Hall and Sizergh Castle are within walking distance. The town is ideally situated for exploring the lakes and mountains of Cumbria and the North West coast. It's only twenty drive minutes to Windermere.

Guests are welcome to use the family lounge. Tea and coffee making and TVs in the rooms.

Vegan B&B
and Self Catering

Sedgwick
Kendal
Cumbria LA8 0JP
England

Tel and Fax:
015395 61241

www.fox.hall@
btinternet.co.uk

Email:
fox.hall@btinternet.com

Train Station: Oxenholme,
3 miles, then bus or taxi.

Open: all year

Directions: From junction 36 on M6, follow A590 to Barrow-in-Furness. Drop down to roundabout for A590/A591. Follow Sedgwick one mile. Go under canal bridge. Fox Hall is the first house on the left.

Parking: three spaces

Travel cot and high chair.

No smoking throughout.

FOX HALL VEGAN B&B
& FOX COTTAGE SELF-CATERING

Sedgwick, Kendal, Cumbria, LA8 0JP

Come and stay with a vegan family who care about your holiday in our 17th century converted barn 4 miles south of Kendal, South Lakes. Extensive menu - all vegan. Comfortable, well-equipped cottage and happy family home. Children very welcome, travel cot and high chair available. Sorry, no smoking or pets. Good local walks. Ideal base for exploring the English Lake District.

**Tel/Fax: Sylvia or Chris on 015395 61241
E-mail: Fox.Hall@btinternet.com or
Visit our Website: fox.hall.btinternet.co.uk
for more info and pictures.**

Lakeland Natural

Victorian home with stunning views over looking Kendal and the surrounding fells. Only five minutes from the town centre. Their large garden adjoins Serpentine Woods with its sculpture trail and woodland walks. There is one single room at £34 and two doubles and two twins at £29 per person per night. Also two family rooms, (cost depends on the age of the child). All have ensuite bathrooms. Self-catering studio apartment also available.

Start the day with fruit juice and cereal, fruit salad, soya yoghurt and home made vegan muffins. Then move on to veggie sausages, tomatoes and mushrooms served on home baked toasted bread with preserves. Vegan margarine, soya milk and vegan muesli are available.

A three course dinner is £15.95 and could be soup and a roll, veggie goulash and rice with a side salad finished with fruit tart with soya cream or ice cream. Organic beer and wine available.

Kendal is a vibrant historic market town with a range of shops and restaurants (including Waterside Wholefood Restaurant and Shop owned by the same people). It is an ideal base to explore the Lake District. Walk from the front door over Scout Scar with its magnificent panorama of the Lakeland Fells and Morecambe Bay. The Cumbrian coastline is a short drive away. As well as walking, you can windsurf, sail, go hot air ballooning, cycling, orienteering and kayaking to playing golf and visiting museums.

Ask about their vegetarian cookery and bread baking courses. Tea and coffee making facilities, TV's and hairdryers in rooms.

Vegetarian Guest House

*Low Slack
Queen's Road
Kendal
Cumria LA9 4PH
England*

*Tel and Fax:
01539 733011*

*www.lakelandnatural.
co.uk*

*Email: relax@lakeland
natural.co.uk*

Train station: Kendal or Oxenholme, 2 miles, then taxi.

Open: all year

Directions: Ten minutes from M6 junctions 36 and 37, whch give easy access to Kendal.

Parking: off street parking available.

*Children welcome.
hey have a cot, high chair and outdoor play facilites.*

Pets by arrangement.

Laundry and drying facil-ities.

No smoking throughout.

32 Skiddaw Street

Veggie B&B set in the popular Lake District town of Keswick. There are one double and one family room at £20 per person per night.

Breakfast can be vegan by arrangement and consists of a selection of cereals, followed by veggie sausages or burgers, tomatoes, beans, mushrooms and toast. Vegan margarine and soy milk are available.

Dinner is not offered, but veggie food is easily available in Keswick. For lunch, try the Lakeland Pedlar Cafe.

Keswick is an excellent centre for exploring the fells, walking and climbing. There are many museums, galleries and country houses to visit nearby. See entertainment at Keswick's Theatre by the Lake, open throughout the year. It hosts a wide range of visiting drama, music, dance, talks, comedy and film.

The Keswick Museum and Art Gallery reveal Keswick's past, from an industrial mining centre to home of the Lakeland Poets.

If you need a day off walking, but still want to take in fresh air and magnificant scenery, take a boat trip around Derwentwater. You can spend all day hopping on and off at any of the seven landings.

Tea and coffee making facilities and televisions in the rooms.

32 Skiddaw Street
Keswick
Cumbria CA12 4BY
England

Tel: 017687 72752

Train Station: Penrith, then get a bus

Open: all year, except Christmas and New Year

Directions: A66 from Penrith, left hand slip road to Keswick. Right at Chestnut Hill, past BP petrol station, under bridge, past fire station, then second left into Blencathra Street. Follow to right, then turn left into Skiddaw Street.

Parking: on street

Children aged five and over welcome.

House trained pets welcome.

No smoking throughout.

England CUMBRIA Accommodation

Eden Green

Eden Green is in an old Victorian house two minutes walk from Keswick town centre. Relax and enjoy your stay in the friendly atmosphere. There are six rooms; one single at £19 per person per night, and one single ensuite, three double ensuites and one family ensuite at £22 per person.

Breakfast begins with a buffet of cereals, fruit salad and fruit juice, followed by veggie sausages, mushrooms, tomatoes, hash browns, baked beans, fried bread and toast. Herbal tea, soy milk and vegan margarine are available.

There is no evening meal but there are plenty of veggie friendly cafes, restaurants and pubs in Keswick. If you can fit lunch in after the huge breakfast, go to the vegetarian cafe, Lakeland Pedlar. A packed lunch is available by prior arrangement for a small charge. They will fill up your thermos flask with tea, coffee or hot water free of charge.

Lake Derwentwater is five minutes walk away and the fells are also easily accessible. Keswick and the Northern Lakes is a region of spectacular scenery, and there is much to do. You can experience the mountains, valleys and lakes, visit museums and galleries, do some gift shopping, and go to the theatre.

Eden Green is an ideal base for a walking or cycling holiday as they have a separate drying room and cycle storage. Be sure to walk to the Castlerigg Stone Circle while you are here.

Each room has a television, hairdryer, radio alarm and tea and coffee making facilities.

Omnivorous Guest House

20 Blencathra Street
Keswick
Cumbria CA12 4HP
England

Tel: 017687 72077

Fax: 017687 80870

www.edengreenguest house.com

Train Station: Penrith, 18 miles, then take bus X4, X5 or X50 which runs every half hour.

Open: all year, except Christmas

Directions: from the M6 at junction 40 to Penrith, take the A66 to Keswick, then take the A591 onto Penrith Road. Turn left into Greta Street then right into Blencathra Street.

Parking: on street parking available

Drying room

Cycle storage

Pets and children by prior arrangement only.

No smoking throughout.

Edwardene Hotel

Omnivorous hotel with a veggie proprietor, in an 1885 traditional grey slate, three storey building. There are eleven rooms, all with ensuite bathrooms; two singles at £28–£31 per night, and six doubles, two twins and one family all at £26–£29 per person.

Veggie and vegan breakfasts are not a problem. You could have Morning Glory – oats and fruit steeped in maple syrup and soya milk, or a full cooked veggie breakfast. Vegan muesli, vegan margarine, soya milk and veggie sausages are all available.

Dinner is £15.50. The main course could be Fruity Bean Casserole with savoury rice, served with naan bread. They are open to non-residents for dinner too. Visit the veggie cafe in town for lunch.

The hotel is in a quiet position, but is only two minutes walk from the town centre and all attractions. Keswick has shops, restaurants, numerous pubs, a theatre, a cinema, as well as galleries and museums. Keswick is set amidst spectacular scenery and is paradise for walkers. The town is overlooked by Skiddaw, the fourth highest mountain in England. It is an excellent base from which to explore the Central and Northern Lake District.

Co-proprietor, Margaret is a qualified Chiropodist and Reiki Therapist, and is happy to attend to your needs.

There is a guest lounge with a fireplace, television, video player and hi-fi. There is no bar, but they are licensed to sell alcohol. All rooms have a direct dial telephone, alarm clock and radio, television, hairdryer and tea and coffee making facilities.

Omnivorous
Hotel

26 Southey Street
Keswick
Cumbria CA12 4EB
England

Tel: 017687 73586

Fax: 017687 73824

www.edwardenehotel.com

*Email: info@edwardene
hotel.com*

*Train Station: Penrith,
16 miles, then bus or taxi*

Open: all year

*Directions: From the M6
junction 40, follow the
A66 west towards
Keswick. Turn left on the
A591 and follow signs to
town centre. Just before
pedestrian traffic lights
turn left, then sharp left
again into Southey Street.
They are 150 yards on the
right.*

Parking: limited

*Children of any ages are
welcome and they have
facilities like high chairs.*

*Pets in special circum-
stances.*

No smoking throughout.

Honister House

Centrally located 18th century home in the lovely market town of Keswick. There are seven rooms all with ensuite bathrooms; three doubles, two twins and two families all at £20-£30 per person per night.

A breakfast of fruit juice, fresh fruit and cereal or porridge is offered followed by hash browns, veggie sausages, mushrooms, tomatoes, baked beans, toast and preserves. Soya milk and vegan margarine are available.

Dinner is not offered but there are plenty of restaurants and pubs which have veggie food. There is a veggie cafe in town but that unfortunately is closed in the evening. After dinner you could take in a movie at the cinema or go the the 'Theatre by the Lake'.

Keswick is surrounded by beautiful mountains and lake Derwentwater. There is unlimited walking for all abilities, as well as cycle routes.

If you want to take it easy, go for a cruise on Derwentwater and take in the magnificent views from a different angle.

There are many places of historical and cultural interest within easy reach such as the 4,000 year old Castlerigg Stone Circle and William Wordsworth's home.

Children are welcome. They have a cot and a high chair and can do baby sitting by arrangement. Packed lunches on request. They have bicycle storage, boot storage and a drying area. Tea and coffee making facilities in the rooms.

Omnivorous Guest House

*1 Borrowdale Road
Keswick
Cumbria CA12 5DD
England*

Tel: 017687 73181

Fax: 0870 120 2948

www.honisterhouse.co.uk

*Email:
philandsueh@aol.com*

*Train station:
Penrith, 20 miles, then bus or taxi.*

Open: all year

*Directions:
From the town centre and tourist information follow the right hand fork, Lake Road. After one minute walk you will find them on the left hand side.*

Parking: available

Discounts given to Viva! members.

*Children welcome.
Cot and high chair.
Baby sitting.*

Drying area.

Bicycle storage.

No smoking throughout.

Pickle Country House

Eighteenth century farmhouse in a secluded location with panoramic views over the surrounding countryside. There are three rooms: two double ensuites with balconies and one twin ensuite for £28–£34 per person per night.

Breakfast is whatever you would like. It could be fresh and dried fruits, home made muesli and granola, followed by a variety of cooked foods and home made breads and preserves. Veggie sausages, vegan muesli, vegan margarine, soya milk and soya yoghurt are all available.

A three course dinner is offered from Thursday to Saturday for £18 and includes a pre-dinner drink. A light supper for guests arriving late on their first night is also available for £10. There are many restaurants in and around Kirkby Lonsdale where veggie food can be found.

Pickle is located in the Lune Valley between the Yorkshire Dales and the Lake District. Walk from the door to the climbing spot of Hutton Roof Crags and to the Rakes, a spectacular limestone pavement. A few minutes drive away is the nature reserve and bird sanctuary at Leighton Moss. Kirkby Lonsdale is walking distance where you could visit Devil's Bridge, Ruskin's View and the many interesting shops. Ingleton is a short drive away for waterfalls and caves or for serious walking go to the Three Peaks of Whernside, Ingleborough and Pen y Ghent. You could also visit the market towns of Dent, Settle and Skipton. In the other direction is the Lake District famous for its scenery and fell walking.

At night, relax in the sitting room in front of the wood-burning stove. Tea and coffee making facilities in the rooms.

Pickle Farm
Hutton Roof
Kirkby Lonsdale
Cumbria LA6 2PH
England

Tel: 015242 72104

www.picklefarm.co.uk

Email:
stay@picklefarm.co.uk

Train station: Carnforth, 10 miles.

Open: all year

Directions: From Kirkby Lonsdale Tourist Information Centre, take New Road out of town to mini roundabout. Turn left and pass Booths Supermarket. Turn right at roundabout onto A65 towards Kendal, then take the first left, signposted Hutton Roof 3 miles. At the T junction turn right. After another mile turn right into Hutton Roof. Proceed through village to the church on the left. Pickle gateway is on the right 200 yards past the church.

Parking: plenty available

Exclusively for adults.

No smoking throughout.

England CUMBRIA Accommodation

Kirkwood Guest House

Omnivorous guest house that's been trading for seventeen years, with vegetarian proprietors.

There are seven rooms: five double ensuites (three with four poster beds) and two twin ensuites at £22–£26 per person per night.

Breakfast could be fruit, juice and cereal or muesli followed by beans, tomatoes, mushrooms, hash browns and veggie sausages. They sometimes have pancakes. Soya milk, vegan muesli and soya yoghurt are available, but it is best to let them know in advance if you are vegan.

Windermere is a very popular base to explore the Lake District and at times can feel like a seaside resort. If you are wanting a lively stay in the Lakes, this is the town to come to. There are lots of restaurants and bars, many offering veggie food.

There are cruises around Lake Windermere or you could hire your own rowing boat. For rainy days, there are museums including the Steamboat Museum and the World of Beatrix Potter.

Orrest Head is a one and a half mile climb from the train station and offers great Lakeland views. Another good viewpoint is Brant Fell. Beatrix Potter's cottage at Hill Top and the village of Hawkshead are walking distance away.

There is a guest lounge. Rooms have tea and coffee making facilities, radio, hairdryer and TV.

Omnivorous
Guest House

Princes Road
Windermere
Cumbria LA23 2DD
England

Tel and Fax:
015394 43907

www.kirkwood51.co.uk

Email:
info@kirkwood51.co.uk

Train Station:
Windermere, 1/2 mile,
then walk or get a taxi for
£2.

Open: all year

Directions: Please phone
or see map on website for
directions

Parking: available

No smoking

Children welcome

Animals welcome

Nab Cottage

Omnivorous Guest House

Rydal, Ambleside, Cumbria, LA22 9SD
Train Station: Windermere, 8–9 miles
Open: all year

Tel: 015394 35311
www.kencomp.com/nab
ell@nab.dial.lakesnet.co.uk

Seven rooms, one single and two twin/doubles at £22 per person per night and four twin/double ensuites at £24 per person. Vegans and those on special diets catered for with advance notice. Children of all ages welcome at a discounted price. Pets by arrangement. Smoking in the sitting room only.

Pumpkin House

Vegetarian Bed and Breakfast

3 Challoner Street, Cockermouth, CA13 9QS
www.lakesnw.co.uk/pumpkinhouse
Train Station: Penrith or Carlisle, 25 miles

Tel: 01900 828269
Open: all year,
except Christmas

Two rooms, one double and one family, £16–£18 per person per night. Evening meal available by request. Children of all ages are welcome. No pets. No smoking throughout.

How Beck

Vegetarian Bed and Breakfast

Grasmere, Cumbria, LA22 9RH
Email: trevor.eastes@btinternet.com
Open all year, except Christmas and New Year

Tel: 015394 35732

Two double ensuite rooms £26–£29 per person per night. Evening meal available. No children or pets. No smoking throughout.

England CUMBRIA Accommodation

Quince and Medlar

Gourmet vegetarian food, twice winner of 'vegetarian restaurant of the year' and three times runner up. Situated in a listed Georgian building with a wood panelled candlelit dining room featuring work by local artists. Very swish, recommended for a special occasion.

Starters £3.75–£5.50 such as soup, roast aubergine and sundried tomato pate, and baked french onion tart.

Main courses £11.50 include parsnip, fennel and basmati rice discs with white truffle oil and Madeira sauce; lentil and apricot strudel in filo pastry on a bed of wilted spinach leaves with tomato and red wine sauce; spiced Moroccan vegetable cone with creamed coconut, lemongrass and tumeric, with a ring of wild rice and chutney.

Home-made garlic bread £1.30.

Desserts £4.45 include chocolate orange pie, lemon tart, and coffee and Tia Maria parfait. Vegan ice cream is available.

The menu changes every 6–8 weeks. Vegan options are available but not marked on the menu. About half the ingredients used are organic.

House wine £9 a bottle, £2.50 glass, other wines up to £30.

They appreciate advance notice of special diets.

The owners take great pride in their restaurant and have even won 'loo of the year' award!

13 Castlegate
Cockermouth
Cumbria CA13 9EU

Tel: 01900 823 579

Open:
Tue–Sun from 19.00

Booking advisable

Licensed

Non smoking

Visa, MC

Restaurants CUMBRIA England

Little Salkeld Watermill

Organic vegetarian cafe using flour from the next door traditional 18th century water-powered mill, which is open to visitors for £3.50 adult, £1.50 child.

The cafe sells organic tea and coffee, along with soups, quiches, scones, biscuits and fruit pies, all made from their own flour.

Soup £2.50, £3.50 with a plate of today's breads. Ploughman's style lunch £5 though our sample menu did not have a vegan option. Special diets by arrangement in advance. Cakes, scones and flapjacks. Fruit juices 75p-£1.40, squash 45p. Soya milk is available.

High chairs and children's portions. Breadmaking and advanced courses, write or phone for brochure. Evening visits for groups. Mill shop with flours, cereals and wide range of organic foods.

Vegetarian Organic Wholefood Tea Room

Little Salkeld
6 miles NE of Penrith
Cumbria CA10 1NN

01768 881 523

www.organicmill.co.uk

Langwathby or Penrith stations.
7 miles from M6 exit 40.
C2C cycle route.

Open: 5th Feb-21st Dec,
Mon-Fri 10.30-17.00

Not licensed - bring your own to mnothly candlelit suppers

No smoking

Disabled access to cafe, toilet and lower floor of mill.

Visa, MC

Zeffirellis

Italian vegetarian restaurant in complex with 2 screen cinema, shopping gallery and vegetarian pizzeria.

Starters and side dishes from £2.50, pizzas £5.50-£7.45 including Mexican red bean chilli and Mediterranean pizza.
Several pasta dishes, £5.95-£6.75, such as Pomodoro - classic Italian tomato sauce with spaghetti. Desserts from £2.95. Can cater for special diets including gluten-free, wheat-free and vegans.

House wine, £9.95 for a bottle, £2.25 for a glass.

Recorded film programme information: 015394-31771

Italian Vegetarian Restaurant

Compston Road
Ambleside
Cumbria LA22 9AN

Tel: 015394-33845
Fax: 015394-32986

Open:
Mon-Fri 18.00-21.45,
Sat-Sun 17.00-21.45.

Non smoking.

Visa, MC

Garden Room Cafe

Vegetarian cafe

Zeffirellis Complex, Compston Road
Ambleside, Cumbria LA22 9DP
Open: Mon-Fri 10-17.00, Weekend 10-17.30

Tel: 015394 31612

Vegetarian café in lovely Lakeland. Homemade soups, pates £2.25. Salads £2.75-£4.25. Daily specials, e.g. polenta with sun dried tomatoes, hot filled baguettes, vegan chilli, jacket potatoes. Usual desserts and an abundance of homemade cakes, slices and buns including vegan options such as date or apricot slices. Licensed. Non smoking. No credit cards

The Watermill Restaurant

Vegetarian restaurant

Priest's Mill
Caldbeck, Wigton, Cumbria CA7 8DR
Open: Mon 11-16.00, Tue-Sun 10-17.00,
closed annually Jan 6th until mid Feb

Tel: 016974-78267
www.watermillrestaurant.co.uk
joeshort@
watermillrestaurant.co.uk

Vegetarian restaurant using freshly made local produce, light refreshments to full meals. Some tables overlook the river or you can sit outside on the grassy terrace overlooking the village cricket pitch. Starters from £2.75, mains £6. Always something available for vegans. Non smoking. No credit cards. Evening parties and outside catering by arrangement.

The Rowan Tree

Vegetarian cafe

Church Bridge, Grasmere, Cumbria LA22 9SN
Open: Spring-Autumn Mon-Sun 10-17.00, 18-21.00;
Winter till Xmas day and evening Fri-Sun;
Jan-Feb just weekends daytime

Tel: 01539 435 528

Highly recommended vegetarian café. Always have vegan dishes available. Non smoking. Visa, MC.

Waterside Wholefoods

Vegetarian cafe & wholefood shop

Kent View, Off Lowther Street, Waterside
Kendal, Cumbria LA9 4PH
Open: Mon-Sat 08.30-16.00

Tel: 01539-729 743
www.lakelandnatural.co.uk
relax@lakelandnatural.co.uk

Vegetarian café and wholefood shop. Starters £2.10, normally three with at least one vegan. Salads £1 a portion or £3.50 as main course. Mains £2.20-£4.40 from choice of three casseroles, pies, bobbotie, roulade etc. Choice of desserts including vegan ice cream. House wine £6.99 bottle. Non smoking. Visa, MC.

Dove Cottage Tea Rooms Restaurant Omnivorous tea room

Town End, Grasmere, Cumbria LA22 9SH
Open: every day 10.00–17.00,
also June–Sept Wed–Sun 18.30–21.00

Tel: 015394 35268
Fax: 015394 35268

Tea room in exquisite Grasmere. 25% of menu vegetarian including 2–3 main courses for £8.75, though lean pickings if any for vegans. Non smoking. Visa, MC.

The Lakeland Pedlar Vegetarian cafe & bicycle centre

Bell Close Car Park, Hendersons Yard
Keswick
Open: Mon–Sun 9.00–17.00

Tel: 017687-74492
www.lakelandpedlar.co.uk
lakeland.pedlar@btclick.com

Wholefood vegetarian restaurant with bicycle shop upstairs. Serve breakfast until 11am, full vegetarian or vegan for £5.45. Sandwiches, £3.50, and mains such as burritos, nachos, falafel from £5. Plenty for vegans including ice cream and fruit crumble from £1.25. Some outside tables. Fully licensed. Non smoking. Visa, MC. Offer 10% discount to Vegetarian Society members.

Mayson's Wholesome Food Restaurant Omnivorous restaurant

33 Lake Road
Keswick, Cumbria CA12 5DQ
www.maysonsrestaurant.btinternet.co.uk
Open 7 days, summer 10–21.00, winter 10.30–16.00

Tel: 017687-74104
maysons@btinternet.com

Omnivorous restaurant with about 30% of meals veggie such as vegan biryani curry £5.65. All salads vegetarian. Desserts around £1.95, but only flapjacks 95p for vegans.

House wine £1.90 glass, half carafe £4.80, litre carafe £9.50. Lots of bottled and draft beers. Pot of tea 85p, coffee 95p, but no soya milk. No smoking. No credit cards, cash or cheque only. Half portions for children, and they have high chairs.

They own a take-away called Mayson's directly opposite which does veggie and vegan sandwiches, around £2.65, that you can bring into the restaurant.

The Village Bakery

Omnivorous organic cafe

Melmerby, 9 miles north-east of Penrith on A686
Open: Mon–Sat 08.30–17.00, Sun 09.30–17.00,
special evening meals on certain Saturdays

Tel: 01768 881515
www.village-bakery.com
info@village-bakery.com

Omnivorous restaurant using local organic ingredients and organic salad and herbs from the smallholding behind the bakery, plus breads from their wood-fired oven. Light snacks, meals, coffee and tea. Wheat, gluten and dairy free catered for, see website for full list. Bakery shop sells organic bread, cakes (apricot and date flapjacks are vegan), organic groceries, baking books and equipment. Upstairs, the Made In Cumbria Interiors gallery displays the work of local crafts-people plus books and pamphlets on organic gardening and agriculture. Baking courses.

The Granary

Health food shop

24 Market Place
Cockermouth, Cumbria

Tel: 01900 822633
Open: Mon–Sat 9–17.00

Kan Foods

Wholefood shop

9 New Shambles
Kendal, Cumbria

Tel: 01539 721190
Open: Mon–Sat 9–17.00

Sundance Wholefoods

Wholefood shop

33 Main Street
Keswick
Open: 7 days a week 09.00–17.00

Tel: 017687–74712

Living Well

Wholefood shop

26 The Square
Milnthorpe, Cumbria

Tel: 015395 63870
Open: Mon–Sat 9–17.00

Nature's Health Store

Wholefood shop

1 King Street
Penrith, Cumbria
Open: Mon–Sat 9–17.00 (16.30 Wed)

Tel: 01768 899262

Appleseeds

Health food shop

59 Market Street
Ulverston, Cumbria

Tel: 01229 583394

Derbyshire

No.3 Organic Vegan B&B

Vegan Bed and Breakfast in a Victorian town house built in 1877, located in St. Leonard's, one of Chesterfield's quiet and unspoilt parishes. There are two double rooms: one ensuite at £25 per person and one without, £22.50.

Vegans can relax and eat what they like here as all the food is vegan. Breakfast is fresh organic fruit with a choice of cereals or muesli and soy yoghurt to begin, followed by veg sausages, tempeh, baked beans, tomatoes, mushrooms and toast with home made preserves. Obviously soy milk and vegan marg are available. Dinner is £15 and could be nut stuffed giant mushrooms to begin, then bean and vegetable enchiladas with a crisp green salad and spicy potato wedges, finished with a dessert of home made chocolate cake and ice cream. Packed lunches £5. All the food is non GM and most is organic with some home grown. Special diets may be catered for with advanced notice.

Chesterfield is a lively and bustling market town. The town is surrounded by many sites of natural and historical interest including numerous stately homes. Creswell Crags, Sherwood Forest and The Peak District National Park are all nearby. Derbyshire is a popular area for those seeking adventure activities. It has some of the country's best walking, climbing and cycling.

Children are welcome. Tea and coffee making facilites and televisions in the rooms. Dining room is also the guest lounge and contains a wide range of books, maps and local information. No smoking throughout.

3 Hartington Road
Chesterfield
Derbyshire
S41 0HE

Tel: 01246 203727

http://homepage.ntlworld
.com/no3veg

Email:
no3veg@ntlworld.com

Train Station:
Chesterfield, less than a mileaway, then walk or get a taxi.

Open: all year

Directions: From the M1 take the A617 (junction 29) to Chesterfield. Double back at the large roundabout (Frankie and Benny's on left) and take the immediate slip road towards Hasland. Turn left onto Spital Lane before crossing the bridge, then take second right and then immediate left onto Hartington Road. It is the second house on the right, adjacent to the old corner shop.

Parking:
available on street

The Cottage Tea Room

Vegetarian tea rooms

3 Fennel Street, Ashford-in-the-Water
Bakewell DE45 1QF
Open: every day except Tue and Fri, 14.30-17.00 in
summer, earlier in winter

Tel: 01629 812488

Vegetarian traditional tea rooms on the old Roman road. Accent on home cooking with traditional English cakes, hand kneaded breads and scones. 6 variations of afternoon tea or just a pot and a slice of cake. Set tea from £2.50, £4.75 for full afternoon tea. Big selection of teas and herbals. Can cater for gluten free and diabetic.
Unspoilt conservation area, in exquisite Peak District village. The cottage is 2 miles north of Bakewell and 8 miles south of Buxton Spa, just above the ford by the sheepwash bridge.

The Natural Choice Cafe

Vegetarian cafe and shop

5 Long Shambles
Chesterfield S40 1PX
Open: Mon-Sat 9.00-17.00 closed Sunday.

Tel: 01246-558 550
Fax: 01246-558 550

Vegetarian café and health food shop in Chesterfield, famous for its twisted church spire. Cooked breakfast £1.99 Mon-Fri only. Afternoon tea £1.45 with scone, cookie or toasted teacake. Soup, pate from £1.95. Salads up to £4.50. Mains £2.15-£5 include vegan pasties, pies, casserole, savoury roasts. Sandwiches and jacket potatoes. Many cakes and desserts suitable for diabetics, gluten free and vegans. Menu changes daily. No smoking. Visa, MC.

Good For You!

Vegetarian cafe

23 Firs Parade
Matlock DE4 3AS
Open: Tue-Sat 10.00-15.30. Open in evenings for
special bookings of parties of 10 or more.

Tel: 01629-584 304
r.litchfield@virgin.net

World food. 100% vegetarian café and shop (upstairs) in the beautiful Peak District. Starters such as vegan channa daal soup with roll, £2.50; mains £4-£4.50 such as Spanish fried rice. Always vegan and gluten free options available. Vegan desserts include tofu cheesecake £1.90 and ice-cream. Child friendly with rocking horses and toys. Non smoking. Has Vegetarian Society information point.

Caudwell's Country Parlour

Vegetarian restaurant

Caudwell's Mill Craft Centre
Rowsley, nr Bakewell DE4 2EB
Open: summer 10–17.30, winter 10–16.30

Tel: 01629–733 185

Vegetarian restaurant with snacks and starters from £1.95 and mains at £4.95. Non smoking. No credit cards.

The Wild Carrot

Vegetarian shop

5 Bridge Street
Buxton SK17 7AD
Open: Mon–Sat 09.30–17.30

Tel: 01298 22843
www.wildcarrot.freeserve.co.uk
shop@wildcarrot.freeserve.co.uk

Vegetarian and predominantly vegan wholefood and organic shop with a take–away selection of Indian, Italian and Mexican snacks, 45p to £1.66. Operate an organic VegBox scheme, where they prepare organic vegetable boxes for collection or delivery. Stock vegan ice cream and other vegan sweet items. 10% discount to Vegetarian and Vegan Society members.

Holland & Barrett

Health food shop

Unit 18, Crown Walk, Eagle Centre
Derby

Tel: 01332–360 664

Devon

Fern Tor

Vegetarian & Vegan Guest House

Relax in our 12 acres,
or explore
Exmoor, North & Mid-Devon.

En-suite, non-smoking rooms.
Children & pets welcome.
Cordon Vert host.

Meshaw,
South Molton, Devon, EX36 4NA

Tel/Fax 01769 550339
email: veg@ferntor.co.uk
http://www.ferntor.co.uk

Places in Devon

Hotels and Guest Houses

Restaurants

Shops

Fern Tor Vegetarian and Vegan Guest House

Vegetarian
Guest House

Veggie and vegan guest house set in over twelve acres of grounds. There is one double room with a door opening onto the patio garden and a twin room, £19 per person per night, plus one double with private lounge, £25 per person. All have ensuite bathrooms. (picture page 105)

You will be well looked after by the vegan proprietors, one of whom is Cordon Vert trained. Breakfast starts with a selection of stewed or fresh fruit with cereal, home made granola or porridge, followed by a full cooked breakfast of vegan sausages, veg bacon, tomatoes, mushrooms, beans, potatoes and home made bread. Eggs are from their rescued hens. Soya milk, soya yoghurt and vegan margarine are available. A two course dinner is offered for £10 and a three course dinner for £13. It could be garlic mushrooms, followed by cabbage parcels on a bed of red peppers, then for dessert FernBocker Glory. Organic veg and their own produce is used whenever possible. Special diets are catered for with advanced notice. Packed lunches available.

You could have a holiday just relaxing in their five acres of grassland along the Little Silver River which is rich with wildflowers. The remaining land is used for their rescued animals and for growing organic fruit and veg. There are many tourist attractions nearby such as castles and museums, as well as walks for both the serious and the recreational walker.

Explore the beaches, moors and other attractions of the North Devon Coast, Exmoor and Mid Devon. Exmoor National Park is a 20 minute drive and Dartmoor National Park is within an hour's drive.

Meshaw
South Molton
Devon EX36 4NA

Picture page 105

Tel and Fax:
01769 550339

www.ferntor.co.uk
Email: veg@ferntor.co.uk

Train Station: Kings Nympton, 6 miles, then they will collect you.

Open: all year

Directions: on B3137, 4 miles south of South Molton, between villages of Alswear and Meshaw. Look out for a large stone wall.

Parking: available

Children welcome
Cot and high chair

Pets welcome

No smoking

Cycle hire available locally

Lounge with log fire. Rooms have TV, radio and tea and coffee making facilities.

10% discount to members of Viva! and League Against Cruel Sports.

10% discount on stays of five nights or more and bargain breaks available Nov–March.

England **DEVON** Accommodation

Berry Cottage B&B

Charming seventeenth century detached cottage set in the idyllic old village of Lympstone, well situated for exploring Devon. There is a single room for £25 per night and two double rooms from £22–£27 per person per night.

Start the day with a fresh fruit platter and cereal followed by a cooked breakfast of veggie sausages, mushrooms, tomatoes and toast with Marmite or hummous. Organic herbal teas and dandelion coffee are available as well as regular tea and coffee, also soya milk. Let them know if you have any dietary requirements. Organic produce is used where possible. Evening meal is available on request.

Berry Cottage is set in attractive gardens with a wide range of shrubs and flowers such as rosemary, passionflower, bay and wisteria. Lympstone is a past winner of Britain in Bloom and has stunning views across the water. It has some cobbled streets, a tower, an old Parish church and a few pubs. There are magnificent beaches in Exmouth to explore where there are pleasure boat trips, windsurfing hire, scuba diving, sailing instruction and much more.

Exeter, the nearest city, is home to one of the finest medieval cathedrals in the region (www.thisisexeter.co.uk) and is worth a visit, as are the coastal villages of Budleigh Salterton, Sidmouth, Beer and Seaton, all with safe clean beaches. The wild countryside of Dartmoor National Park is a must visit while in Devon.

Tea and coffee making devices in the rooms and one of the double rooms has a TV.

Longmeadow Road
Lympstone
Devon EX8 5LW
England

Tel: 01395 264944

Email: philippe.g.young @ex.ac.uk

Train Station: Lympstone Village, 1/2 mile then bus, or collection is sometimes possible.

Open: all year

Directions: Located off the Exeter to Exmouth Road (A376) in the part of Lympstone Village known as Upper Lympstone.

Parking: available

Children welcome and they have facilities for babies

No smoking throughout

10% discount given to members of the Vegetarian Society, Vegan Society, Viva!, PETA, Animal Aid and people presenting this book.

Accommodation **DEVON** England

⑤

16TH CENTURY

Berry Cottage, Upper Lympstone

Ansteys Cove Hotel

Omnivorous hotel owned by a lifetime vegetarian, set in one of the warmest climates in Britain. There are nine rooms, all with ensuite bathrooms. Single rooms £29–£35 per night, doubles and twins £52–£64 per room, or treat yourself to the special double room £58–£70 per night. Ask about the arrival gifts that can be added to your room surprise your partner.

At breakfast help yourself to fruit juice, cereals, fruit, toast and preserves, tea and coffee. Follow with a full cooked breakfast of veggie sausages, smoked sliced tofu, baked beans, tomato, mushrooms, hash browns and fried bread. Soya milk, vegan muesli and vegan margarine available.

A two course meal is offered for £12 or three courses for £15. You must book in advance. Starters include soup of the day and mixed pepper pudding with a spicy tomato sauce, both served with home made bread. A sorbet is then served to cleanse your palate before the main course which could be baked aubergine, veggie mock fillet of 'sole' stuffed with chives and celery, vegetable curry with rice and pickle, or Cornish Starry Gazy pie. Desserts include Helston Pudding and spicy apple pie served with soya cream. Proprietor/Chef is Cordon Vert trained, so expect something delicious.

Set amidst spectacular unspoilt scenery and within walking distance of award winning beaches. Good public transport to all attractions in Torquay, as well as South Devon and Dartmoor National Park. Beautiful coastal walks in the area.

All rooms have satellite TV, direct dial phone, hairdryer, alarm clock radio and tea and coffee making facilities. They also run certified courses in food hygiene.

327 Babbacombe Road
Torquay
Devon TQ1 3TB

Tel: 01803 200900
Freephone:
0800 0284953

Fax: 01803 211150

www.ansteyscove.co.uk
www.torquayengland.com

Email:
info@torquayengland.com

Train Station: Torquay, 1.5 miles, then bus or taxi.

Open: December–September (inclusive)

Directions: Take the A3022 Riviera Way. Go straight on at roundabout. Go left at the traffic lights by Courts Store into Hele Road B3199. At the roundabout, turn left for Teignmouth Road. At the next roundabout turn right for St Marychurch B3199. Head towards Babbacombe going straight on through the next roundabout. Follow road through St Marychurch Village. The hotel is one mile on the right just pass Babbacombe Pottery.

Veggie and vegan wines

No pets

No smoking

Parking: available

TV lounge and two bars

Cuddyford

Veggie B&B in a rural setting within Dartmoor National Park. There are two rooms, one double room (which can be converted into a family room) and one twin room for £17.50–£19 per person per night. The twin room has views of the Woodland River Valley with Dartmoor on the horizon.

Breakfast begins with cereal and juice and is followed by veggie sausages, veggie rashers, beans, tomatoes and pancakes. Vegan margarine, soya milk and soya yoghurt are available.

Dinner is offered for £12 and begins with soup or salad, then a curry or pasta, and a dessert usually made from honey, like honey cakes, but vegan desserts aren't a problem. There is a kitchenette for the use of guests where you can make a packed lunch. Organic fruit and veg are grown on the property.

Cuddyford is well situated for exploring Dartmoor with its mysterious stone circles, the Dart Valley and the South Devon coast line. There are white water sports on the River Dart, beaches with sailing and coastal footpaths.

Nearby there are steam trains, a sports hall with a gym and shops selling arts and crafts.

Alternative therapies available locally.

Tea and coffee making facilities in rooms . Television in one of the rooms.

Vegetarian Bed and Breakfast

Rew Road
Broadpark
Ashburton
Devon TQ13 7EN
England

Tel: 01364 653325

Train Station:
Newton Abbott, then 20 minute bus or taxi ride.

Open:
all year, except Christmas

Directions: Follow the A38 from Exeter or Plymouth. Turn off into Ashburton. Continue down the main street until you reach the Golden Lion. Opposite the hotel you will see Roborough Lane. After half a mile turn left at a cross roads into Rew Road. Cuddyford is the fourth house on the right.

Parking: off street parking

No smoking throughout

Children welcome
High chairs

Pets welcome with advance notice

England DEVON Accommodation

Enstone Guest House

Small friendly guest house with a vegetarian proprietor. It's situated in a peaceful garden at the end of a residential cul-de-sac, adjacent to the River Sed, with the park beyond.

There are six rooms: one single, one twin and one family at £16 per person per night, plus three doubles at £15 per person. Cheaper weekly and child rates available.

Breakfast begins with fruit, fruit juice and cereal with soya yoghurt followed by veggie sausages, baked beans, tomatoes, mushrooms and hash browns. Soya milk and vegan margarine are available.

Dinner is £7 and could be spaghetti veg bolognaise, vegetable and soy protein pie with three veggies or risotto, followed by fresh fruit or stewed fruit with soya ice cream. Special diets are catered for with advance notice.

Enstone Guest House is only a few minutes walk to the centre of Sidmouth, a charming and tranquil resort town. It offers a cinema and a theatre. There are lots of nice walks by the river and along the cliffs and it's a ten minute walk to the beach. There's a donkey sanctuary nearby.

Guest lounge with television. There are tea and coffee making facilites in the rooms. Children aged three and over are welcome and they have a cot and high chair. No smoking throughout.

Omnivorous Guest House

Lennox Avenue
Sidmouth
Devon EX10 8TX
England

Tel: 01395 514444

Train Station: Honiton, 8 miles, then bus or taxi or collection is possible.

Open: April–September (inclusive)

Directions:14 miles from Exeter off the A3052.

Parking: available on site

10% discount given to members of the Vegetarian Society and people presenting this book.

Children aged three and over welcome, they have a cot and high chair

No smoking throughout

Little Burrows Organic Accommodation

Vegetarian
Bed and Breakfast and
S/C Retreat Centre

Shilstone Lane
Throwleigh
Devon EX20 2HX
England

Tel: 01647 231305

www.organicaccommo
dation.com
www.sacredartstudio.com

Email: kristin@organic
accommodation.com

Train Station: Exeter St.
Davids, 15 miles, then
bus, pony and trap pick
up or car pick up.

Open: all year

Directions: From Exeter
take A30 towards
Okehampton. At first
roundabout take left exit
into Whiddon Down, then
second left signposted
Throwleigh. Then
immediately turn right
into road signposted
Throwleigh 2 miles. Take
the second left in the
centre of the village (at
Church steps). After 200
metres, park next to the
house on the left in lay-
by. Little Burrows is 20
metres down drive at the
side of this house.

No smoking throughout.

Parking: available

Animals welcome
Children welcome

10% discount on stays of
seven days or more

Veggie organic bed and breakfast and self catering creative retreat centre, set in a large garden in a secluded corner of Dartmoor, the largest area of wilderness in the South of England. There is one double room in the house for £22–£24, or stay in one of their self contained wooden cabins for £22–£24 for B&B or £18–£20 self catering. (Prices are per person per night). There is also a caravan which can sleep four people for £12 per person.

Begin the day with fruit juice, fresh organic fruit and home made muesli or cereal followed a cooked veggie breakfast. They have soya yoghurt, soya milk, vegan margarine, veggie sausages and a wide selection of dry and fresh herb teas. Dinner is available for £12 and could be home made spicy lentil pie with leafy green veggies, baked root veg, fresh mixed salad and herb sauce, followed by Swedish soya ice cream with fresh raspberries. All food is organic. Special diets catered for.

Both proprietors are artists and enjoy making improvised music. There are an art studio and a music studio and tuition is available. Little Burrows is a peaceful haven overlooking the moors. The surrounding area is full of rock strewn rivers, stone circles, wild ponies and woodland walks. A truly magical place to explore. Chagford is three miles away and has interesting shops, pubs, a pool and an organic community cafe. South Zeal is two miles away and has a shop selling organic produce, pubs and a cyber cafe.

Meditation hut on property. Bike hire and tent hire available. Massage and healing by arrangement. Lounge with TV. Tea and coffee making and TV's in the rooms.

Lower Norris House

Lower Norris House is built on an ancient site, set in beautiful countryside overlooking a tranquil valley with streams and woodland. There are three rooms, one double ensuite at £30 per person per night, one double/twin and one single both £25 per person. Both doubles can become family rooms.

Breakfast begins with fruit, fruit juice and cereal and is followed by veggie sausages, beans, tomatoes, mushrooms and toast.

An evening meal is £12.50 and might be a nut loaf, stuffed peppers, vegetable crumble or a vegetable curry. Special diets are catered for. Organic produce is used where possible. The house is supplied by natural spring water.

There are many local attractions and walks within wasy reach. The village of South Brent is nearby, also Shipley Bridge with waterfalls and wildlife. Dartmoor National Park is ten minutes drive. Walkers, cyclists, birdwatchers and artists will love it here. Buckfastleigh is a short drive east, where you can make a tour of the historic Benedictine Abbey, famous for its tonic wine. Visit the Butterfly Farm and Otter Sanctuary, or take a steam train to Totnes.

The house has a spacious lounge with a TV and a large dining room with a log fire. Stunning views of the valley can be enjoyed from here. Relax and unwind in the friendly surroundings. Aromatherapy massage, reflexology and spiritual healing are available by request.

Tea and coffee making in the rooms.

Vegetarian Guest House

North Huish
Totnes
Devon TQ10 9NJ
England

Tel and Fax:
01548 821180

Train Station: Totnes,
7 miles, then collection is
possible

Open: all year

Directions: From the A38, take the South Brent/ Avonwick exit (B3210) and follow signs to Avonwick. Pass under the A38 and turn left. After a mile turn right just before garage, then take first turning on left by phone box. Drive for about one mile. After entering North Huish take second turn on right, following signs for Coombe House. Pass the cottages on the left, then take first right. Lower Norris House is at the bottom of the hill on the left just before the bridge. Cross cattle grid, keep right at the top of the drive.

Parking: plenty available

Children welcome and they have high chairs

Well behaved pets accepted by arrangement.

Smoking in garden only

10% discount to people presenting this book

The Old Forge at Totnes

Omnivorous
Bed and Breakfast

Bed and Breakfast in an ancient stone creeper clad building within easy walk of the river and town centre. There are ten rooms: five double ensuites, one double with private bathroom and two twin ensuites at £27–£31 per person per night, plus two family rooms for around £112 per room per night for four people. (Price depends on the age of children)

Start the day with a choice of fruit juices, fruit and cereal, followed by veggie sausages, tomatoes, mushrooms, baked beans, potato waffles and wholemeal toast with a variety of teas and coffees. Soya milk and vegan margarine are available. Breakfast can be served in rooms by arrangement. Dinner is offered by prior arrangement and they will cook to your requirements and price accordingly. Dave, the co-proprietor, is apparently an excellent chef.

There is a blacksmith's prison cell on the property which is now a listed building, and a coach arch which leads to a walled garden.

In Totnes there are markets on Friday and Saturday, many interesting shops, a steam train, castle, museum and cruises on the river.

Attractions in the area include Dartmoor National Park, English Riviera beaches, many castles, National Trust properties and beautiful gardens. There is good night life in Torquay. Dartmouth, Kingsbridge and Salcombe are all within easy reach. The Eden Project is 1 1/2 hours drive away.

Guest lounge has television. Whirlpool spa in conservatory. Tea and coffee making facilities and televisions in the rooms.

Seymour Place
Totnes
Devon TQ9 5AY
England

Tel: 01803 862174

Fax: 01803 865385

www.oldforgetotnes.com

Email: enq@oldforge totnes.com

Train Station: Totnes, 1/2 mile, then taxi.

Open: all year

Directions: M5 to Exeter, A38 to Buckfastleigh/ Staverton/Totnes exit A384. Follow signs to Totnes town centre. Turn right at big roundabout (at Safeway petrol station). At mini round-about by Seven Stars Hotel, turn left over town bridge, then second on left. See brown tourist board sign. Go straight on down hill into Totnes. Turn left.

Children of all ages are welcome and they have cots and high chairs

Parking: available

Limited disabled access

No smoking throughout

England **DEVON** Accommodation

Riverbank Hotel

Attractive seventeenth century hotel situated on the bank of the River Lowman, with garden seating overlooking the river. There are one twin, one double and one family room, all ensuite, at £36 per room per night or £20 for single occupancy.

For breakfast choose from a selection of cereals and fruit followed by cooked tomatoes, beans, veggie sausages, fried potatoes and garlic mushrooms. Vegan margarine and soya milk are available. You can have breakfast in your room if you feel like being spoilt.

Dinner is offered in the cafe for £4–£5 and could be risotto, pasta, spicy pumpkin and coconut curry with rice, or polenta with Mediterranean roasted veggies. All food and cakes are freshly made. They have vegan ice-cream and vegan cakes. House wine £2 per glass or £7.50 for a bottle. Beer £1.20.

The cafe is sometimes open to non-residents in the evenings, quite often on Friday and Saturday nights.

Tiverton is a historic market town on the rivers Exe and Lowman. There are a swimming pool, castle, cinema and markets. The town is not far from Exmoor and Dartmoor where there are plenty of attractions.

Riverbank Hotel offers massage, reflexology and aromatherapy.

There is internet access to check your emails and a locked shed to store bicycles.

Rooms have tea and coffee making facilities and televisions.

45 Gold Street
Tiverton
Devon EX16 6QB
England

Tel: 01884 254911

www.riverbankhotel.co.uk

Email:
shirleyfield@talk21.com

Train Station: Tiverton Parkway, 7 miles.

Open: all year

Restaurant open:
Tue–Sat 10.00–18.00
Sun–Mon closed

Directions: M5 to A361 to first turning for Tiverton. Follow signs for town centre and go past Esso garage on left.

Parking: limited

Children welcome, they have a cot and high chair

Smoking in garden only

The Sanctuary

Vegan basic self-catering accommodation in the Dartmoor national park, 10 miles from Okehampton. The house is used as Vegfam (see page 109) headquarters, all profits go to the charity. The house has 6.5 acres (2.7 ha) private nature sanctuary. Very peaceful location with Dartmoor and all its delights on the doorstep. 25 miles from Plants for a Future.

Self-catering small single £7–10 per night; double or twin (king size double or two divans, with French doors to verandah) £8–13 per person.
There is a well stocked health food shop Kilworthy Kapers, 8 miles by bus or car in Tavistock. For visitors travelling light, pre-paid basic foodstuffs could be provided.
You need to book so check directions then.

Plants for a Future

Vegan education centre, a resource centre for rare and unusual plants. They practice vegan-organic permaculture with an emphasis on creating an ecologically sustainable environment and accept volunteers here and at their Cornish site.

Five camping pitches. Self catering, only vegan food allowed on site. Health food shops in Holsworthy and Launceston and much "grazing" can be done in the kitchen garden. Very basic facilities, so may not be suitable for children. They can provide contact for nearby B&B or self-catering.
Directions: Take A388 north from Launceston to Holsworthy. Get to Clawton, turn around and head south again. First left after 1 mile, next left, they are 200m on left.

Vegan self-catering

The Sanctuary
Nr Lydford
Okehampton
Devon EX20 4AL

Tel: 01822 820203
Fax: 01822 820203
Open: most of the year

10 miles from Okehampton. 25 miles from Plants for a Future. Between the turn to Lydford Village and Beardon Farm on A386 where road crosses the river Lyd, in middle of S bend.

No stairs, bungalow. Children welcome. Dogs on lead as sheep in next field.

Education Centre and Camping Ground

Blagdon Cross,
Ashwater, Beaworthy,
Devon, EX21 5DF

Tel: 01208 872963
0845 4584719

Open: phone to check

www.pfaf.org
www.scs.leeds.ac.uk/pfaf
Email:
webmaster@pfaf.org

Train Station:
Plymouth/Exeter, 40 miles
Bus X9 to Holsworthy,
they can collect you

Pets welcome

Southcliffe

Omnivorous guesthouse with veggie owners, in the village of Lynton, a short distance from the picturesque harbour of Lynmouth. There are nine rooms all with ensuite bathrooms: one single and two twins at £21–£23 per person per night and six doubles at £21–£25 per person. Two of the doubles have balconies.

There is a full cooked veggie or vegan breakfast. Soya milk, vegan margarine, soya yoghurt and veggie sausages are available.

Dinner is offered for £14 and could be cashew and mushroom layer bake, mushroom risotto or rigatoni and asparagus au gratin. There is also a good selection of local pubs and restaurants with veggie options nearby.

Southcliffe is set in some of the finest coastal scenery in the country. Lynton and Lynmouth have been known for many years as 'England's little Switzerland'. There is an incredible variety of scenery and interest within a few square miles. A five minute walk from Southcliffe will take you to an unusual furnicular railway which links the twin villages.

Take a boat cruise along the Heritage Coast with its nesting colony of seabirds. Drive only a short way and you will be in the heart of Exmoor. Spot the wild red deer roaming in the heathered hills and wooded valleys. Visit the Doone Valley, setting for the novel *Lorna Doone* by R.D Blackmore.

TV lounge. Tea and coffee making facilities. TV's and hairdryers in the rooms.

Omnivorous Guest House

Lee Road
Lynton
North Devon EX35 6BS
England

Tel: 01598 753328

www.southcliffe.co.uk

Email:
info@southcliffe.co.uk

Train Station: Barnstaple, 20 miles, then bus

Open: all year

Directions: the house is opposite the post office on Lee Road

Parking: available

No children

Dogs welcome by arrangement

No smoking throughout

Sparrowhawk Backpackers

Newly established vegetarian backpackers hostel, independently run by experienced travellers. Sparrowhawk is situated in a small Dartmoor town, fourteen miles uphill and west of Exeter. Private room available for £30 shared. Fourteen dorm beds upstairs for £11 per person, dorm can be divided by curtains. Children £6 per night.

There is a fully equipped strictly vegetarian kitchen to make your meals in. An organic veggie box is available with a couple of days notice. Tea and coffee are provided free and if the mood takes them, the veggie proprietors Alison and Darren might make cakes and flapjacks. They can also provide wholesome stews or soups for weary walkers. Local shops sell organic and wholefood supplies. Vegetarian meals are available in nearby pubs and cafes.

Situated within the Dartmoor National Park, with open moorland nearby, it is a great place to walk and cycle. There are Magnificent Tors, stone circles and burial sites of ancient civilisations to be explored. You'll see wild ponies and buzzards in your explorations. There are year round guided walks and talks organised by the National Park.
More info at www.dartmoor-npa.gov.uk

Moretonhampstead is a small town and has a few shops, cafes, pubs, a solar heated outdoor pool, recreation fields and footpaths leading to the moors. Bike hire is available. The third week in August is carnival week. The Eden Project is 1–2 hours drive away, or visit the Steward Community Woodland to see sustainable living in practice – dedicated vegan eco-warriors living in 32 acres of woodland. (www.stewardwood.org)

45 Ford Street
Moretonhampstead
Devon TQ13 8LN
England

Tel and Fax:
01647 440318

**www.
sparrowhawkbackpackers
.co.uk**
under construction

Train Station: Exeter, Okehampton or Newton Abbot, 12 miles, then get a direct bus.

Open: all year

Directions:
From Exeter, take B3212 signposted on the one way system at the bottom end of Fore Street. From M5, take J31 to A30 Okehampton. Moretonhampstead is signposted a couple of miles on. Moretonhampstead is on cross roads of A382 and B3212. Sparrowhawk is on Ford Street going towards Chagford. Park in the car park and walk down.

Parking: available nearby

Facilities for babies

Secure bicycle storage

Smoking outside only

England **DEVON** Accommodation

The Whiteleaf

Omnivous hotel in a comfortable 1930's house standing in its own gardens near the North Devon Coastal Path. Croyde Bay is a couple of minutes walk across the dunes. There are five rooms: three doubles, two twins and one family all with their own private facilites. The doubles and twins cost £28-£34 per person per night and the family is £84-£96 for the room. Cheaper rates for longer stays.

A veggie breakfast could be cereal followed by tomatoes, mushrooms, baked beans and veggie sausages with toast.

Dinner is £18 for residents and is cooked by the co-proprietor and qualified chef, David. There are a few veggie options on the menu but nothing for vegans, though almost anything can be done by request or prior arrangement. Fresh local produce is used. The restaurant is licensed and open to non residents. House wine is £2.60 per glass or £9.75 per bottle. Beer is £2.20.

Croyde village is two minutes away with its thatched cottages, inns and tea rooms. A stream runs along the main street. The town of Georgeham is nearby with its 13th century church as well as the bustling village of Braunton, reputedly England's largest village.

The area has many natural attractions such as the beach, forests and remote moorlands. Golf, surfing, walking, bird watching and sea trips are some of the activities that could keep you amused during your stay.

All rooms have radios, televisions, tea and coffee making, fridge/bar and hair dryers. Guest lounge. Dogs welcome with well behaved owners at £3 per day.

Croyde
Braunton
North Devon EX33 1PN
England

Tel: 01271 890266

www.thewhiteleaf.co.uk

Train station: Barnstaple, 12 miles, then bus or taxi.

Open: all year (except 25-27 December)

Directions: from junction 27 on the M5, take the A361 North Devon Link Road through Barnstaple to Braunton. Turn left at traffic lights in Braunton. Keep straight on through Faunton into Croyde. Whiteleaf is on the left hand side opposite Bayview Farm

Parking: available

Dogs welcome

Children welcome

Smoking in some areas

Herbies

Relaxed, unpretentious bistro–style veggie restaurant.

Starters £1.50–£3.50 include dhal with chapatis, soup of the day, provençal mushrooms, paté, hummous, various types of bread. Snacks £1.95–£4.25, such as nut & beanburgers, pizza, stir–fry, jacket potatoes and wraps.
Main courses £5.25–£6.50 such as homity pie, vegan spinach and mushroom lasagne, or courgette, mushroom and polenta flan. Items marked V on the menu *may* be vegan, you need to ask. Cakes, desserts and ilces listed on blackboards.
Drinks 90p–£2.25 such as mineral water, juices, organic cola and ginger cordial. Coffee 80–90p. Organic wine £2.50 a glass or £11.50 for litre bottle. Lagers and beers from £2.15, alcohol-free beer £1.85.

15 North Street
Exeter
Devon EX4 3QS

Tel: 01392 258473

Open:
Mon–Fri 11–14.30,
Sat 10.30–16.00.
Tue–Sat 18–21.30.
Closed Sun.
(end times are for last orders)

Children's portions
High chairs

Non–smoking area

Switch, Visa, MC

England DEVON Restaurants

Plymouth Arts Centre

Vegetarian
Restaurant

Long established vegetarian restaurant close to historic Barbican, and based in arts centre which also houses gallery spaces and an independent cinema. Serve light refreshments all day, lunch from 12–14.00 daily and evening meal 17–20.00 Mon–Wed, 17–20.30 Thu–Sun. Baked potato from £1.50, variety of filled wraps (Mexican, Satay veg), £2.75, and chilli with rice, £3.80. Vegans always have plenty to choose from. World cooking night once a month such as Caribbean, Indian, African, Spanish, Italian and French. Fully licensed and will shortly be stocking vegetarian wine.
Takeaways available, parties catered for and outside catering also offered. Separate smoking section. Credit cards accepted if no other means of payment available. 20% student discount on Tuesday evenings.

Plymouth Arts Centre
38 Looe Street
Plymouth
Devon PL4 0EB

Tel: 01752-202 616

www.plymouthac.org.uk
arts@plymouthac.org.uk

Open: Mon 10.00–17.00,
Tue–Wed 10.00–20.00,
Thur–Sat 10.00–20.30

Willow Vegetarian Restaurant

Vegetarian wholefood restaurant using organic produce where available. Relaxed and informal though it is very busy at peak times. Counter service daytimes and table service in the evenings. Indian menu Wednesday night, live music on Friday evening.

Menu changes daily. Lunch: soup such as spicy lentil £2.75. Salads £1.90, £2.75, £5.40. At least four mains, one or two of them vegan, such as blackeye bean bake or savoury tofu flan £3.75-£4, with mixed salads £5.95. Light lunch of small soup, mixed salad and roll £4.60. Baked potato with filling £2.95. Vegan dip with hot pitta £3. Filled roll £2.20. Desserts £1.50-3.50 such as fruit slices, flapjacks, both vegan and sugar free, brownies, carrot cake, chocolate and vanilla Swedish Glace vegan ice cream. Vegan, wheat free and gluten free dishes clearly marked.

Sample dinners: Indonesian vegetable soup £1.95. Sundried tomato and tofu dip plus tomato and avocado dip with warm pitta £3.30. Main courses £5.70-7.00 such as creamy mushroom and tofu flan with salad, or Sunny Islands Casserole of coloured peppers, courgettes, mange-tout and sweet potatoes in coconut sauce with rice and baked marinated tofu. Or have a mixture of salads with today's dips and a roll. On Indian night you can compose your own thali for £6.50 or £7.95 though vegans should check how many of the curries are ok. Take-away curry £3.80, organic rice £1.40, dal £1.10, 2 curries and rice £4.20.

Organic beers, lager & cider. 8 vegan wines from £7.95 a bottle, £1.65 a glass. Beer from £2. Coffee £1. All coffees, teas and fruit juices are organic.

Vegetarian Restaurant and take-away

87 High Street
Totnes
Devon TQ9 5PB

Tel: 01803-862 605

Open:
Mon-Sat 10.00-17.00
(Fri from 9.00)

also Wed, Fri-Sat
19.00-22.00

closed Sun

Licensed

Cash or cheque, no credit cards.

Booking recommended evening

Veggie Perrin's

Gujarati vegetarian (80% vegan) restaurant and takeaway.

Starters £1.50–£2.40 samosa, bhaji, kachori, stuffed puri etc. Lots of veg curries £2.90–£4.95, even "korma sutra" on request. Rice from £1.50 and all those scrummy breads, also that English ethnic delicacy, chips.

Various desserts (only one vegan, carrot halva). Big selection of Indian and world beers. Glass of house wine £1.80, bottle £7.95 and up.

Take–away, 20% off a la carte prices. Also catering for events and summer festivals.

97 Mayflower Street
Plymouth
Devon

Tel: 01752–252 888
Fax: 01752–220 808

www.veggieperrin.com

Open: Mon–Sat 12.00–14.00, 18.00–22.00, closed Sun except for private functions

One high chair

Non smoking

Visa, MC

England **DEVON** Restaurants – Accommodation – Shops

A few sites to help you plan

www.devon.gov.uk

www.dartmoor-npa.gov.uk

www.thisisexeter.co.uk

www.thisisplymouth.co.uk

www.devonwebpages.co.uk

Animal Aid holds a south–west festival of vegetarianism in late May. See www.animalaid.org.uk

The Garret Café

Vegetarian cafe

Beach approach, The Strand
Brixham, Devon TQ5 8JL
Open: Mon–Sun 08.30–17.30,
some nights later, phone to check

Tel: 01803–882 610

Vegetarian and vegan café. Home cooked food, locally produced. Soups all vegan, £1.95 with roll. Mains such as veggie stir fry with noodles or potato skins with chilli, both vegan, £3.25. Always a vegan dessert, such as banana fritters, £1.75 and sorbets. Visa, MC.

The Courtyard Café

Vegetarian cafe

76 The Square
Chagford, Devon TQ13
Open: all year Mon–Sat 9–17.00, closed Sunday

Tel: 01647–432571

Vegetarian café, nearly all organic, and they sell vegetables and wholefoods, tofu, yofu etc. About 3 miles from Sparrowhawk Backpackers hostel. Soup and bread £2.60. salads. Cappucinno £1.25, lots of cakes. Different dishes daily including one or two vegan meals and wheat free, pasties and pies. Pot of tea £1.20 for one, £2.30 for two, mug of tea £1, all kinds of herbal and Rooibosch. Capuccino £1.25. Big bulletin board with what's going on in the area and they double as the Tourist Information Centre. Newspapers to read with your coffee.

Cranks

Vegetarian cafe

Cider Press Centre, Shinners Bridge
Dartington, Devon TQ9 6JB
Open: Mon–Sat 9.30–17.00,
also Sundays Easter–December

Tel: 01803 862 388
www.cranks.co.uk

Sole surviving branch of the famous veggie chain of restaurants set in crafts centre within grounds of Dartington Hall. Open for breakfast, always have vegan and gluten free dishes, soups £2.75, main dishes range from £4.75–£5.95 such as thai curry and various homemade burgers. Have a garden for al fresco dining. Non smoking.

Bistro 67

Omnivorous bistro

67 Fore Street
Totnes, Devon TQ9 5NJ
Open: Mon–Sat 12.00–late

Tel: 01803–862 604

Omnivorous bistro with 1/3 menu vegetarian. Can adapt items for vegans. Non smoking. Visa, MC.

Coolings

Omnivorous bistro & wine bar

11 Gandhi Street
Exeter, Devon EX4 3LS
Open: 10 for coffees, alcohol from 11,
lunch Mon–Sat from 12 till 23.00, Sun till 22.30

Tel: 01392-434184

Bistro/wine bar in the city centre. Always a hot veggie dish £6.50 and four salads, £5.60 for a big bowl. Vegan food available, though not every day but if you call ahead they'll do it.

The Country Table

99% vegetarian restaurant

12 Bank Street
Newton Abbot, Devon
Open: Mon–Sat 9.00–16.30. Closed Sunday.

Tel: 01626 202 120

Wholefood café, restaurant and take–away. Breakfasts fry–up £3.65 9–11a.m. Soups £2.65, salads £2.50–£3.30, Italian paninis from £3.45. Mains £4.50 such as spicy parsnip & lentil pie, bean & tomato bake. Always something vegan or gluten free. Desserts from £1.30 with vegan apricot or date slices, and Tofutti ice cream £2.30. Soya milkshakes. Non smoking. No credit cards. 10% discount to Vegetarian & Vegan Society members.

Tooleys

Omnivorous Chinese take–away

The Ridgeway
Plympton, Plymouth
Open: Mon–Sat 17.30–22.30, closed Sun

Tel: 01752-342211

Chinese take–away. They used to have a huge separate vegetarian menu, but now they've combined it with the meat menu which leads to the meat–eaters choosing more veggie dishes, £3.20–£4.40. The cook is a pure Buddhist. During the day it's an ordinary English café run by other people.

Alternate

Omnivorous cafe & wholefood shop

South Devon College, Newton Road
Torquay, Devon TQ2 5BY
Open: Mon–Fri 10–14.00

Tel: 01803 406393
College 01803 400700

Small omnivorous café and wholefood shop, about 50% vegetarian, mostly organic, in a community college. The people making the food are on a course. Quiche and salad £2, home made soup £1.50 with roll, baked potatoes with fillings. Cup of tea 50p, coffee 60p. No smoking. No credit cards. Children welcome but no high chair.

Reapers

Health food shop & take-away

18 Bampton Street
Tiverton
Open: Mon–Sat 8.30–17.00

Tel: 01884 255310

Central health food shop in the former Corn Exchange, one of the oldest buildings in Tiverton where John Wesley preached. Strong on organics with fresh fruit and veg. Chiller and freezer, tofu, vegan cheese and vegan ice-cream. Locally made take-aways, sandwiches, pasties, savouries, flapjacks, cakes (including vegan). Baby section with environmentally friendly nappies, Ecover refills, supplements. A homeopath and a herbalist operate from the shop by appointment.

Holland & Barrett

Health food shop

North Cotes, 92 High Street
Barnstaple

Tel: 01271 328295

16 Waterbeer Street, Guildhall
Exeter

Tel: 01392–277 494

16–18 Princesshay, Exeter

Tel: 01392–251 590

58 Cornwall Street, Plymouth

Tel: 01752–661 822

Unit 2, 36 Royal Parade
Plymouth

Tel: 01752–661 076

35 Fore Street, Tiverton

Tel: 01884–256 690

28 Union Street, Torquay

Tel: 01803–212 215

Dorset

Places in Dorset

Hotels and Guest Houses

Restaurants

Shops

St. Antoine Guest House

St. Antoine is set on a quiet road only a few minutes walk from the beach. There are seven rooms: one single, two doubles, two twins and two family ensuites at £19–£21 per person per night.

Start your day with cereal and fruit juice followed by veggie sausages, mushrooms, tomatoes and toast with home made preserves. Soya milk and vegan margarine are available.

A three course dinner is offered for £8 and could be soup followed by stuffed mushrooms or vegetable bean pie and finished with apple blackberry pie. Everything is home made. If you fancy going out for dinner there is a veggie restaurant in nearby Boscombe.

On St. Antoine's doorstep is the local park which has tennis courts, bowling greens and croquet lawns. There is a golf course ten minutes walk away. It is a five minute stroll to The River Stour where there are interesting walks and lots of opportunities for bird watching. The New Forest is within easy driving distance.

Nearby Christchurch is a historic town with a nine hundred year old Priory.

A warm friendly welcome is promised. Rooms are well furnished and comfortable. All have washbasins and tea and coffee making facilities. There is a guest lounge with a television.

Children are welcome and they have facilities such as high chairs. No smoking throughout.

Omnivorous
Guest House

2 Guildhill Road
Southbourne
Bournemouth
Dorset BH6 3E7
England

Tel: 01202 433043

Email:
kathden@kathden.fsnet.
co.uk

Train station:
Christchurch, 2.5 miles,
then bus or taxi

Open: Easter–October

Directions: Southbourne is to the eastern side of Bournemouth between Boscombe and Christchurch.

Parking: available

Children welcome
High chairs

No smoking throughout

England DORSET Accommodation

Cowden House

Cowden House is set in its own three acres of land in the beautiful Cerne Valley and offers spacious accommodation for up to six guests. There are four rooms; one double and one twin at £22 per person per night, one double ensuite at £25 per person, and one twin ensuite at £24 per person. All rooms have lovely views.

Breakfast is a choice of cereals, fruit salad and fruit juice followed by a full cooked veggie breakfast if desired, or simply toast or bread with various spreads and jams. Soya milk, vegan muesli, vegan margarine and veggie sausages are available.

Dinner is offered for £13.50 and could be bruschetta followed by Moroccan tofu and aubergine casserole with cous cous salad, then a dessert of fruit crumble and vegan ice cream. They are open to non residents for dinner.

Cowden House is on the edge of Godmanstone, a tiny unspoilt village. You can walk up a farm lane and off into the hills and go for miles away from roads.

The house is ideal for individuals or for small groups who wish to stay for a period with a particular theme, such as a painting weekend or personal growth work.

Dorset has dozens of picturesque villages to explore, beautiful gardens and historic houses to visit, plus a spectacular coastline. The west of the county is completely rural and to the east are Poole and Bournemouth, great centres for shopping, night life and clean sandy beaches.

Tea and coffee making facilities in the rooms and television in the lounge.

**Vegetarian
Bed and Breakfast**

*Frys Lane
Godmanstone
Dorchester
Dorset DT2 7AG
England*

Tel: 01300 341377

www.cowdenhouse.co.uk

Train station: Dorchester, 5 miles, then bus ot taxi or collection is possible.

Open: all year, except Christmas.

Directions: Cowden House is five miles north of Dorchester, just off the A352. Frys Lane is the first left on entering Godmanstone.

Parking: available

One dog is welcome

Children welcome and they have a high chair

No smoking throughout

Firleas

Vegetarian
Bed and Breakfast

Veggie bed and breakfast with two rooms;:one double and one family room at £17.50–£20 per person per night or £110 per person per week. One of the rooms overlooks the garden and the distant sea.

Breakfast is fruit juice, fresh grapefruit or oranges, cereal or home made muesli with chopped apples and nuts followed by toast and home made preserves. Alternatively you could have a cooked breakfast of veggie burgers or sausages, tomatoes and mushrooms with toast. Vegan margarine, soya milk and rice milk are available.

Dinner is offered by arrangement and is £10 for two courses or £12.50 for three courses. It could be soup or pate on toast to begin, followed by home made nut roast or rissoles with potatoes done how you like and organic vegetables with sauce or gravy. Finish with fruit or pudding.

Veggie meals are available at most hotels and Inns in the area. There are health food shops in Bridport and Axminster.

There is a park five minutes walk away. The town is fifteen minutes walk along the river and offers museums, a cinema, shops and the beach, where there is a cobb (natural stone wall) going out into the sea. Walk to the town of Charmouth along the beach when the tide permits, or to Seaton through the woods.

Talks on psyshic and spiritual studies are held in Lyme Regis on the second Tuesday of every month.

There are tea and coffee making facilities in the rooms and a television in the double room.

8 Colway Close
Lyme Regis
Dorset DT7 3BE
England

Tel: 01297 443528

Train station: Axminster, 5 miles

Open: February to November (inclusive)

Directions: Go down A35 to Hunter's Lodge in Lyme Regis. Turn left, cross straight down into town. Turn left at 'Black Dog' then pass over bridge. Turn left at Talbot Road, then first right into Colway Close.

Parking: available

5% discount to members of the Vegetarian Society, Vegan Society and people presenting this book.

Children aged seven and over are welcome

No smoking throughout

England DORSET Accommodation

Wessex Tales

Vegan restaurant

20 Ashley Road, Boscombe
Bournemouth
www.geocities.com/vegetarian_restaurant
Open: Tue–Sat 11.30–15.00,
Fri, Sat evenings 19–22.00

Tel: 01202-309 869
wessextales@onetel.net.uk

Vegan restaurant with world food menu. Starters £1.50–£2.00 such as garlic mushrooms on onion and herb bread. Mains include nut roast, and the ever popular masala dosa, £5, £7 in evenings. Desserts include Swedish glace vegan ice cream and cakes £2–£3, chocolate cake daily and others vary such as orange and lemon. Wine £9 bottle, £1.90 for a glass. Most of the food is organic. Non smoking. No credit cards.

Walnut Grove

Omnivorous restaurant

25 Durngate Street
Dorchester, Dorset DT1 1JP
Open: Mon–Sat 9.30–17.00

Tel: 01305-268 882

Omnivorous restaurant with a third of menu vegetarian. Friendly and will try and adapt items for special diet needs. Non smoking. No credit cards.

Clipper Restaurant

Omnivorous restaurant

The Dolphin Centre
Poole, Dorset
Open: Mon–Fri 9.30–17.00, Sat 9.00–17.15

Tel: 01202-683 334

At the top of the shopping centre, this omnivorous restaurant offers an extensive vegetarian choice. Big salad bar with salads from £1.85, many without dressings and suitable for vegans. Jacket potatoes with fillings from £2.95. Separate smoking section. Visa, MC.

Flossies

Vegetarian restaurant

73 Seamoor Road
Westbourne, Dorset
Open: Mon–Sat 9.00–17.00

Tel: 01202-769 959
www.flossies.co.uk

Vegetarian restaurant with fresh home made food. Lunch from £5. Vegan items available such as nut and herb rissoles and some pasta dishes. Non smoking. No credit cards.

Café 21

Vegetarian restaurant

21 East Street
Weymouth, Dorset DT4 8BN
Open: Mon–Sun midday–late, bookings taken

Tel: 01305–767 848
cafe2021@hotmail.com

Vegetarian restaurant. Starters from £2.45, lunch from £5 and evening meal from £7. Main dishes such as sweet potato African stew and spicy nut roast. Desserts from £2.95 including ginger and rhubarb crumble. Non smoking. No credit cards. Offer 10% discount to Vegetarian and Vegan Society members and also to members of Greenpeace and Friends of the Earth.

Earthfoods

Organic wholefood shop

75 Southbourne Grove
Southbourne, Bournemouth
Open: Mon–Sat 9.00–18.00

Tel: 01202–422 465

Organic wholefood shop. Widely and well stocked shop of 35 years, 80% organic and all vegetarian or vegan and GM free. Fresh fruit and vegetables; pulses and beans; nuts, seeds and herbs. Range of takeaway foods including raw food items. Also stock chemical and cruelty free products from cosmetics and toiletries to household products such as paints and brushes, hemp tiles, wall paper and glue; all vegan and environmentally friendly.

Holland & Barrett

Health food shop

23 The Arcade
Bournemouth

Tel: 01202 297713

54 South Street
Dorchester

Tel: 01305–251 857

25 Kingland Terrace
Poole

Tel: 01202–649 291

33 St Mary's Street
Weymouth

Tel: 01305–766 485

County Durham

33 Newgate B&B

Omnivorous Bed and Breakfast

33 Newgate, Barnard Castle, Co. Durham, DL12 8NJ
Email: peter.whittaker@tinyworld.co.uk
Train Station: Darlington

Tel: 01833 690208
Open: all year

One family room with private facilities £20–£25 per person per night.
Evening meal £10. Children welcome. No pets. No smoking
throughout.

The Alms Houses

Omnivorous cafe

Castle Green
Durham

Right outside the cathedral and caste. Lots for veggies and vegan
offerings improving all the time.

Health Warehouse

Health food shop

Post House Wynd
Darlington, County Durham
Open: Mon–Sat 9–17.30 (17.00 Wed & Sat)

Tel: 01325 468570

Health food shop with lots of take-away food like pasties and
flapjacks, very handy as Darlingotn does not have a veggie café,
though you can get veggie food in many places.

Holland & Barrett

Health food shop

5 Queen Street
Darlington

Tel: 01325–365 656

Holland & Barrett

Health food shop

13 Milburngate
Durham DH1

Tel: 01913–842 374

Brighton

Brighton rivals London and Edinburgh as being the best city in the UK for veggies and vegans. However, Brighton's small centre means you'll never be more than five minutes walk from a veggie restaurant. It offers the city excitement of clubs, pubs, restaurants and theatres but it's by the sea and only a short cycle ride to the countryside. There is a thriving arts scene and a vibrant student, veggie and gay population.

Brighton is an ideal day trip from London, but everyone knows it, so to avoid the crowds come on a weekday. You'll find restaurant and bar staff friendlier and there'll be no need to fight for a table. There are vegetarian restaurants for all budgets, from cafés and take-aways and the wicked **veggie pub**, The George, to the decadence of Trogs Restaurant or Terre à Terre.

To really chill out, come for a few days. There is a good range of accommodation from hostels to B&B's to the luxury of the Granville Hotel. If you do come on a weekend, book your accommodation well in advance. Most guesthouses in Brighton cater for veggies and vegans. Almost every vegan delight available can be obtained at the local wholefood co-op, Infinity Foods, so if you ask nicely, your guesthouse should be able to get you whatever you need.

You could spend hours getting lost in the winding alleys of **The Lanes** exploring the shops and drinking in the bars. North of Church Street is the slightly less touristy bohemian quarter, North Laine. You'll find plenty of second hand clothing, New Age and record shops in amongst trendy cafés, expensive clothes stores and gadget shops. A visit to **Vegetarian Shoes**, the animal friendly shoe shop and the interesting collectables shop, Snooper's Paradise, is a must. Don't bypass the **Peace and Environment Centre** if you're after a book on an environmental or animal rights issue, or an eco-friendly gift. If you're dying for a soyaccino and can't find your way to the nearest veggie gaff, rest assured that most cafés in Brighton have soya milk.

It's almost impossible to walk through Brighton without seeing the distinctive Oriental inspired **Royal Pavilion**. It was built between 1815 and 1822 as a villa for Prince George (future George IV) to have lavish parties. It's well worth a visit and is open daily from 9:30am–5pm. Entry is £5.35 or £3.85 for seniors, students and unemployed with relevant ID. Family tickets £8.65 (one adult) or £14 (two adults). Brighton's **Museum and Art Gallery** on Church Street has a fascinating collection of paintings, furniture and ceramics, which includes some valuable Art Deco and Art Nouveau items. Some people come just to see Salvador Dali's famous 'Lip Sofa'. Entry is free and it's open Tuesday to Saturday 10am–5pm, Sunday 2pm–5pm and closed on Mondays.

If you fancy a spot of exercise and some breathtaking scenery, cycle along the coast to the town of **Rottingdean**, or a bit further to **Saltdean**, stopping for a quick bevvie in one of the pubs on the seafront before heading back.

There are also water sports, ten pin bowling and an ice skating rink to keep you amused. Kids love Brighton for the beach with its paddling pools and play equipment and the Palace Pier with its funfair rides and candyfloss. Further down the beach towards Hove is the disused listed West Pier.

Be sure to go to the **Brighton Festival** in May when for three weeks there is even more music, theatre and comedy than usual. The Fringe events are worth seeing too and often feature local talent.

Getting there: From London's Victoria Station, Brighton is a fifty minute train ride. There is a fast train every half an hour every day, except for peak times and Sundays when it takes about one and a half hours. There's also a train that goes through King's Cross, Blackfriars and London Bridge but it's slow. Phone National Rail Enquiries for information and times on 08457 484950. Most guesthouses are a walk or short taxi ride from the station. Once you're in Brighton you don't need a car. It's much better to leave it at home, as parking is hard to find and expensive.

by Katrina Holland

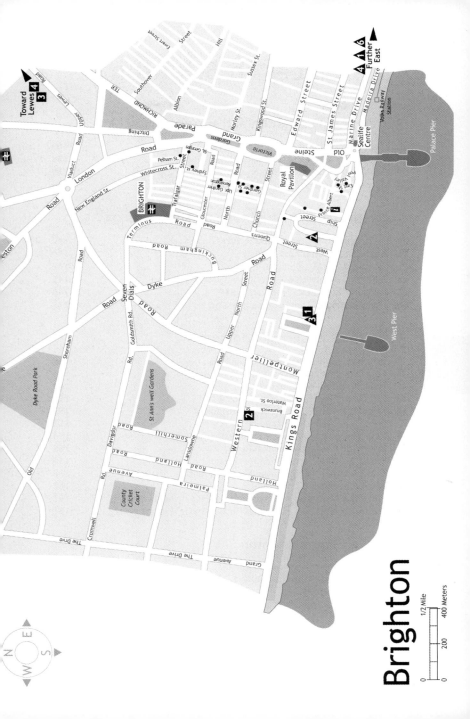

Brighton

N W E S

1/2 Mile
0 | 200 | 400 Meters

County Cricket Court

Dyke Road Park

St Ann's well Gardens

BRIGHTON

Royal Pavilion

Victoria Gardens

Sealife Centre

Volks Railway Station

Palace Pier

West Pier

Toward Lewes 3 4

Further East 4 4 6

Places in Brighton

Restaurants in Brighton and surroundings

Accommodation in Brighton and surroundings

Restaurants in Central Brighton

Shops in Central Brighton

EAST SUSSEX England

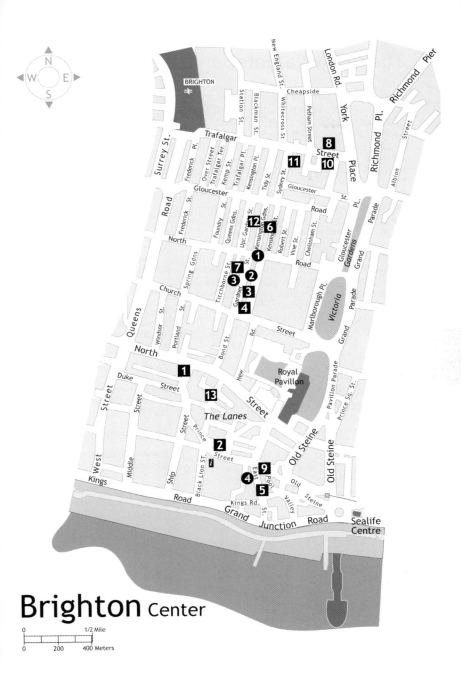

The Granville Hotel

Treat yourself to luxury and comfort at the Granville Hotel, set on Brighton's sea front opposite the Grade A listed West Pier. Each of the twenty four ensuite rooms are decorated in their own distinctive style and offer a choice between sea views and tranquil north facing accommodation. Doubles are £37.50–£77.50, twins £37.50–£57.50 and family rooms, £30–£50 per person per night. Some rooms have jacuzzis and four poster beds. One room has a water bed.

Begin your day with a delicious veggie breakfast in bed which could consist of cereal and organic fruit juice followed by veggie sausages, veggie rashers, organic baked beans and tomatoes with toast. Soya milk, soya yoghurt, vegan margarine and vegan muesli are all available. The food is guaranteed to be free of GM content and additives and they use organic produce.

You won't have far to walk for dinner as Trogs vegetarian restaurant and cafe/bar is downstairs. See the Brighton restaurant section for details.

The beach is just across the road where there is a basketball court, climbing areas, paddling pools and several bars and night-clubs. The working pier with its fun fair rides is a ten minute stroll and a six screen cinema is only five minutes walk away.

There are loads of veggie restaurants and cafes in Brighton, as well as many bars, pubs and nightclubs.

There are televisions and tea and coffee making faciities in the rooms.

124 Kings Road
Brighton
East Sussex BN1 2FA
England

Tel: 01273 326302

Fax: 01273 728294

www.granvillehotel.co.uk

Email:
granville@brighton.co.uk

Train station: Brighton,
1/2 mile, then walk or get
a bus or taxi.

Open: all year

Directions:
The Granville is on the
sea front opposite the
West Pier.

Parking: limited

Children welcome and
they have facilities like
high chairs.

Pets welcome.

Smoking in designated
areas only.

THE
GRANVILLE HOTEL
BRIGHTON

From the moment you step through the door, you will sense the difference that will make your stay at The Granville a memorable one and help to explain why more than half our guests are repeat bookings. Elegance, style and comfort combined with friendly personal service and a central location with magnificent sea views makes The Granville the perfect place to stay in Brighton.

TROGS
VEGETARIAN RESTAURANT AND CAFE BAR

A jewel in The Granville's crown, by night Trog's vegetarian organic restaurant offers you not simply a feast of the most exquisite cuisine in town, but a wonderful evening in an atmosphere that is as friendly as it is charming. Before you dine, why not take a few minutes to relax in the intimate surroundings of the fully licensed Trogs Cafe Bar?

124 Kings Road, Brighton BN1 2FA
Tel: 01273 326 302 Fax: 01273 728 294
www.granvillehotel.co.uk   e-mail: granville@brighton.co.uk

Brighton Backpackers

A fun packed crazy place for international travellers and students. Brighton Backpackers is located right in the centre of town and has a relaxed and friendly atmosphere. It is the only hostel in Brighton with sea views.

There are four to eight beds in each room costing £11–£12 per person per night. (£12–13 in summer) Weekly rate is £60. Dorms are mixed and single sex.

Two or three double rooms with ensuite bathrooms are also available for £30 per night and are located right on the sea front. Most of the rooms directly overlook King's Beach.

No meals are offered, but there is a kitchen for you to cook your own stuff. Pick up your supplies from Infinity Foods. There are also many veggie restaurants, clubs and bars within walking distance.

In front of the hostel, there are water sports facilities, including windsurfing and sea canoes.

The hostel is located close to the North Laine with its many interesting shops selling ethnic clothing and second hand records. The Royal Pavillion and the Art Gallery are also close by.

There is a social area with a hi-fi, satellite television, bar and a pool table.

Internet access for contacting your friends.

Lockers to keep your valuables safe.

24 hour access to hostel.

Backpackers Hostel

*76 Middle Street
Brighton
East Sussex BN11AL
England*

Tel: 01273 777717

www.brightonback packers.com

Email: stay@brighton backpackers.com

Train Station: Brighton, ten minutes walk

Open: all year

Directions: from train station, walk down Queen's Street and North Street to the seafront, then turn left onto Kings Road.

Parking: none available

10% discount to people presenting this book

No children or pets.

Smoking allowed in some areas.

24 hour access

Paskins Town House

Omnivorous
Hotel

Omnivorous hotel with a vegetarian proprietor in a grade 2 listed building. Paskins promises you a stay that will evoke memories of a more gracious past. There are eighteen rooms, most with ensuite facilities; seven singles, nine doubles and two twins all priced £35–£45 per person per night. They pride themselves on their individually styled 'Laura Ashley' bedrooms, particularly the added luxury of the four poster beds in the premier double rooms and the Victorian room.

For breakfast there is a choice of fruits, spiced dried fruit compote, muesli, bran, cereals and toast and preserves. Then choose from an impressive menu which includes a full veggie cooked breakfast of home-made sundried tomato, paprika and tarragon sausages, fritters, corn sauce, tomatoes, mushrooms and fried bread. Or you could go for organic porridge made with oats, malted wheat, barley and raisins. There are also croissants, New York bagels, apple crepes and more. Most of the food is organic and comes from local Sussex farms. None contains genetically modified ingredients. Soya milk, vegan margarine and vegan muesli are available.

All that Brighton has to offer including the beach and lots of veggie restaurants is within walking distance.

Each room is equipped with television, direct dial telephone and tea and coffee making facilities. Tea and coffee is Fair Trade and none of the toiletries are tested on animals. Lounge bar.

18/19 Charlotte Street
Brighton
East Sussex BN2 1AG
England

Tel: 01273 601203

Fax: 01273 621973

www.paskins.co.uk

Email:
welcome@paskins.co.uk

Train station:
Brighton, then bus or £3 taxi ride.

Open: all year

Directions:
Arrive at the Palace Pier and proceed with the sea on your right towards Newhaven. They are ten minutes walk from the pier.

Parking: on street

10% discount to members of the Vegetarian Society, Vegan Society and people presenting this book.

Children welcome and they have facilities including high chairs. Children up to 11 get 25% discount if sharing with two adults.

Pets welcome.

Smoking permitted in rooms and some other areas.

England **EAST SUSSEX** Accomodation – Brighton

Rozanne Mendick B&B

Vegetarian bed and breakfast in a large family home close to the centre of Brighton. There are three rooms; one single, one double and one twin all costing £20 per person per night.

Wake in the morning to a delicious veggie or vegan breakfast which could consist of fresh and dried fruit, fruit juice, cereal or muesli and soya yoghurt followed by soya sausages, mushrooms, tomatoes, baked beans, toast and more if requested. Vegan margarine, soya milk and vegan muesli are all available.

No evening meal is offered but you certainly won't go hungry in Brighton! There are lots of veggie cafes and restaurants and even a veggie pub in town. Just take a look at the Brighton restaurant section in this book. If you fancy going on a picnic, there are several health food shops around town where you can get tasty snacks. See the Brighton health food section in this book.

The town centre is a fifteen minute walk away with its many shops, pubs and clubs. It's a twenty minute walk to the seafront.

The sea front is a twenty minute walk where you can enjoy strolls on the beach watching the sunset, or go on the fun fair rides on the pier.

Tea and coffee making facilities and televisions in the rooms.

Vegetarian Bed and Breakfast

14 Chatsworth Road
Brighton
East Sussex BN1 5DB
England

Tel: 01273 556584

Email:
r_mendick@yahoo.co.uk

Train station:
10 minute walk north of Brighton station, near Seven Dials,
bus or taxi

Open: all year

Directions: Ten minutes walk north of station, near Seven Dials.

Parking: on street

Children of any ages are welcome, but no baby facilities

No pets

No smoking throughout

Beynon House

Omnivorous Guest House

24 St. George's Terrace,
Brighton, East Sussex, BN2 1JJ
www.brightonpages.co.uk/beynonhouse.co.uk
Email: beynonhouse@hotmail.com
Train Station: Brighton, 20 minutes walk

Tel: 01273 681014
Open: all year

Seven rooms; five doubles and two double ensuites £22–£27 per person per night. Some rooms can be converted to twin or family rooms. Vegans catered for with advanced notice. No children or pets. No smoking throughout.

The Silverdale

Omnivorous Guest House

21 Sutton Park Road,
Seaford, East Sussex, BN25 1RH
www.histral.co.uk/silverdale/silver.htm
Email: silverdale@histral.co.uk
Train Station: Seaford, four minutes walk

Eight rooms; two doubles at £13–£19 per person per night, four double ensuites at £15–£30 per person per night and two family rooms at £12–£22 per person per night. Three course evening meal £12. Coeliacs catered for. Disabled access, category three. Children and pets welcome. Smoking allowed in some rooms and the bar.

England **EAST SUSSEX** Accommodation – Brighton

Bombay Aloo

Eat as much as you like at Bombay Aloo for only £4.95. It's open late on Friday and Saturday nights so it's the place to head for those post pub munchies. Monday to Friday 3.15–5.15pm are happy hours when you can stuff yourself for only £3.50.

There is heaps to choose from and it's all delicious. There are always six curries, like Tarka Dal, Swede and Mushrooms, Vegetable Dhansak, Chickpeas Aloo, Saag Aloo and Mixed Vegetable Curry. There are many accompaniments including pakoras, onion bhajees, naan bread, pappadums, samosas, pilau rice, mixed salad, onion salad, as well as dips and pickles. Vegans won't have a problem here as there are usually at least four vegan curries. Just ask one of the friendly staff to show you what's suitable.

You don't have to pay any extra for a dessert as they always have a fruit salad and a pudding as part of the buffet. If you want a dessert from the menu, it's £2.50.

There is a separate menu with cooked to order items, but it hardly seems worth it when the buffet is such good value. If you have any special requests, they can sometimes make something for you if they've got time.

House wine is £1.80 per glass or £7.95 per bottle. Beer is £1.40 for a half pint or £2.60 for a pint. Coffee is £1.20.

For kids they have high chairs and the buffet costs £3.95.

When the restaurant is busy, they open the upstairs, which has lots of extra seating and a second buffet. They can take large group bookings.

39 Ship Street
Brighton
East Sussex BN1 1AB
England

Tel: *01273 776038*
      01273 771089

Train Station: Brighton, 15 minutes walk

Open: every day
Sun–Thu 12.00–23.00
Fri–Sat 12.00–24.00

People presenting this book pay £4.45 instead of £4.95 for buffet

Licensed

Credit Cards accepted (not Amex)

No smoking, except in smoking area

Infinity Foods Cafe

Veggie Co-op devoted to the cause of organic and natural food and drink. They are committed to offering food with 95% organic content and free of GMO's. All their fruit, vegetables, grains and pulses are 100% organic.

Choose what you want by looking in the display counter. Soup of the Day (always vegan) is £2.95, or £2.35 take away and is served with an organic bread roll. Their most popular soups include Pumpkin, Coconut and Coriander, Fennel and Roasted Pepper, and Tomato, Lentil and Fresh Basil. There is a choice of five fresh salads every day and they are all vegan. They could include Chinese marinated tofu salad, leafy greens, rice, pasta, potato, cous cous or bulghur salad, coleslaw, and watercress, beetroot and red pepper salad. A side salad is £2.75 eat in or £1.75 take away. As a main meal, it is £4.95 eat in or £3.75 take away. There is a different main meal every day and it's often vegan, £5.50 eat in and £4 take away. It could be Polenta with roasted vegetables and tomato and herb sauce or Vegetable Curry and Dahl with rice. Pasties £1.75/£1.55, Millet Slice £1.55/£1.35 Falafel 95p/70p and a variety of filled baps £3.44/£2.85.

Most of their desserts are vegan, sugar free, wheat free and gluten free, and include date and apricot flapjacks £1.30/£1.10; pumpkin, lemon and coconut tart, vegan chocolate cake and a variety of tofu cheesecakes, all £2.50/£2.

Most special diets are catered for. Vegan margarine, soya milk and soya cappuccinos are available. All food is freshly prepared on premises. Most products are Fair Trade. Eco friendly products used and they recycle.

Vegetarian Co-operative Cafe

50 Gardner Street
Brighton
East Sussex BN1 1UN
England

Tel and Fax:
01273 670743

www.infinityfoods.co.uk

Train Station: Brighton, ten minutes walk

Open: six days
Mon–Sat 9.30–17.00
Sun closed

Global cuisine

Not licensed
They hope to get a licence for alcohol in the near future.

No cards, cheques over £5 only

High chairs for kids.

Smoking outside only

Kai Organic Cafe

Kai is the only organic cafe in Brighton we know of to be certified by the Soil Association. They offer a wide selection of vegetarian, vegan and wheat free dishes. There are a few table downstairs, but if you can get a table upstairs by the window, it's a great place to watch the world go by from above.

Choose a freshly made sandwich or salad from the fridge. All items are clearly marked by colour coding whether they are vegetarian, vegan or wheat-free. You can eat in or take away.

Otherwise, order something from the menu. The Mezze Plate is light but satisfying. It is made up of houmous, cous cous and roasted vegetable salad, Greek salad, marinated olives and warm pitta bread and costs £4.95. If you're vegan, ask for it without the fetta. There is always an Eastern Mediterannean Daily Special, see the blackboard for details. The Calzone is £4.80 and is made in their own pizza oven. It is classic pizza dough filled with sundried tomatoes, kalamata olives, courgette, aubergine, onions and garlic. Soup of the Day served with bread is £3.25, or if you're really hungry get a large bowl with extra bread for £3.75.

Wine is £2.60 for a glass. Beer is also £2.60. Cappuccino £1.70. Soy milk is available. Vegan organic wine and vegan margarine are available.

There are a couple of outside tables, but on Saturday the street is pedestrianised and the cafe can seat as many as twenty people outside.

52 Gardner Street
Brighton
East Sussex BN1 1UN
England

Tel: 01273 684921

Fax: 01273 620104

Email: kaiorganic@btinternet.com

Open: every day
Mon–Sat 9.00–17.30
Sun 10.30–17.00

Mediterranean and modern British cuisine

High chairs for kids.

Fully licensed

Most cards accepted

No smoking

Krakatoa

Tucked away in Pool Valley, you'll find Krakatoa, an oriental restaurant serving delicious oriental food. Veggie dishes are clearly marked and most of these are either vegan or can be made vegan on request. For the best experience, ask to sit upstairs where there is Asian style seating with cushions and low tables. It's perfect for either a party or a cosy intimate dinner.

To begin, choose from Binte, a Sulawesian coconut and corn soup with tofu and bean sprouts £4.50, Lumpia – Indonesian spring rolls with sweet chilli sauce £3.75, Kakiage – crispy vegetable and sweet potato fritters £3.95, Vegetable Gyoza – steamed or grilled Japanese vegetable dumplings £3.95, or our reviewer's favourite, Hanoi Rice Paper Rolls £3.95.

Main courses include the delicious Nasi Campur Special – an Indonesian dish of yellow rice served with tofu and sweet potato curry, pergedel, tempeh goreng and spicy stir fried vegetables £8.50. The popular noodle dish, Pad Thai is £5.95 as is Gado Gado. Krakatoa Bento Box £8.95, is a selection of Japanese Treats: Miso soup, Japanese rice, noodles, tempura, teriyaki marinated tofu and Java curry. Yasai Udon £5.95 is stir fried Udon noodles with wakami seaweed, tofu and bean sprouts. Sayur Tumis, also £5.95 is Asian green vegetables stir fried with tofu, fragrant spices and garnished with basil. Massaman Curry is a southern Thai dish, a combination of tofu, potato and peanuts in a rich coconut milk sauce, £5.95.

The chefs take care to cook the fish separately from the vegetarian food. Vegetarian owned. Organic wine available. House wine is £2.50 for a glass or £10.75 for a bottle. Beer is £2.50–£2.75. Gluten and wheat free diets catered for.

Vegetarian & Fish Restaurant

7 Pool Valley
Brighton
East Sussex BN1 1NJ
England

Tel: 01273 719009

www.krakatoarestaurant.co.uk

Train Station: Brighton, 10 minutes walk

Open: every day 12.00–23.00

Oriental cuisine

Fully licensed

Most cards accepted

Smoking allowed, except in smoke free room

10% service charge

Pulp

It's hard to miss the bright blue facade of Pulp as you walk through the North Laine. The standard of food is high and the staff are friendly. There's a casual but efficient vibe to the place, the music is chilled and the decor is pleasant. Oak benches line the walls providing extra seating and paintings by local artists hang on the cream coloured walls.

At first glance the menu doesn't appear very vegan friendly and dishes aren't marked, however this is deceptive as most items can be made vegan. One of our reviewer's favourites is the Corn Bread filled with Roast Vegetables and Houmous served with salad at £3.95. Mexican Parcels £5.95 (bean and vegetable chilli filled tortillas) can be made vegan and are served with corn chips, guacamole and salad. Falafels with pitta bread, houmous and salad are £5.95 and House Salad with bread is £4.50. Soup of the Day £2.95, is always vegan and always delicious. Check the board above the counter for daily specials. Cheaper prices for take-away. There is only one non-veggie item on the menu with tuna.

They have a good selection of cakes, like Banana and Walnut Cake and Carrot and Orange Cake both £2.50 and both vegan. These are to die for! There is a wide choice of Fresh Organic Juices and Smoothies, £2.25 small, £2.75 medium and £3.25 large, like Vitalizer (carrot, apple, beetroot, ginger and lemon) or Superjuice (carrot, apple, celery and greens) or try a wicked Chocolate Bliss Smoothie (choc soya milk, strawberries and banana). Fresh Wheatgrass is £1.50 for a shot. Fair trade organic coffee costs £1.20, Cappuccino £1.40, Hot Chocolate £1.50, Tea £1.00. Soya milk and vegan margarine available.

Vegetarian and Fish Cafe and Juice Bar

Kensington Gardens
Brighton
East Sussex BN1 4AL
England

Tel: 07990515358

Train Station: Brighton, 10 minute walk.

Open: every day
Mon–Sat 9.30–18.00
Sun 10.00–17.30

Organic Juices
Fresh Wheatgrass
Toasted Sandwiches,
Falafels, Soups and Salads
Eat in or take away

Not Licensed

No Credit Cards

No smoking

Two outside tables.

Red Veg

The first and only veggie fast food restaurant in Brighton is situated in the North Laine, a few shops up from Vegetarian Shoes. It's perfect for a quick meal on the run, but it's also a great place to sit and relax, as the decor and furniture are much more comfortable than most fast food outlets.

They say: 'No lentils and no meat, no pain and no suffering, no hassle, no exploitation and no competition. More people are concerned with health, more people care about the world and about what they eat, meat is less and less popular, we need an alternative, we need an alternative tasty food fast. Red Veg provides vegetarian fast food. It's different and affordable with a global menu from independently created recipes.'

Try a Red Veg or Chilli Veg Burger for £2.85 (very tasty and 'meaty'), a Jamaican Roll or No Name Nuggets for £2.95. Falafels are £3.25, as are the Oriental Noodles. Friest 95p for a medium serving and £1.15 for a large. Plantain Chips £1.55. Carrot and Coriander Goujons, Crispy courgette and Breaded Mushrooms are all £1.35. All items can be made vegan.

They sell a range of soft drinks, beers, wines and spirits. £2.25 for a glass of house wine or £10.55 for a bottle, £2.90 for a beer, £1.50 for coffee. Soya milk available. Veggie and vegan organic wines.

No GM ingredients used. They develop all their own products. Veggie proprietor.

Check out the other branch next time you're in London, 95 Dean Street, Soho, just off Oxford Street near Virgin Megastore.

21 Gardner Street
Brighton
East Sussex BN1 1UP
England

Tel: 01273 679910

www.redveg.com

Train Station: Brighton, 10 minutes walk.

Open: every day
Mon–Sun 10.00–22.00

Global Cusine
Fast food to eat in or takeaway.

Licensed

High chairs for kids.

No Credit Cards

Smoking allowed, except in smoke free area.

Room 101

Funky New York style veggie restaurant down the bottom of Trafalgar Street, only five minutes walk from the station. Established just two years ago as a veggie/vegan cafe bar, it has grown into much more of a restaurant, but retains the look and relaxed feeling of a cafe bar.

Starters £3.50 to £5.25 include Herb Gnocci. Two are always vegan.

Salads from £4.95 to £6.95 include avocado and cherry tomato salad with croutons.

There are three vegan mains £6.95 to £7.95, including Sweet Potato and Broad Bean Curry.

Desserts are £4.95 and two are vegan, including Chocolate Fudge Cake with fudge sauce and ice cream.

Soya milk for soyaccinos and soya milkshakes and smoothies. Vegan margarine, vegan ice cream and veggie/vegan wine are all available.

House wine £2.80 per glass or £10 per bottle. Beer £2.45. Coffee £1.50.

Gluten and wheat free diets are catered for. Separate lunch and dinner menu.

Seats 40 inside. Outside seating coming soon.

Come on a Friday evening and chill to the sounds of soul and funk played by live DJ's.

Available for private hire as a bar.

101 Trafalgar Street
Brighton
East Sussex BN1 4ER
England

Tel: 01273 687064

Train Station: Brighton, 5 minutes walk.

Open: every day
Mon: 12.00–17.00
Tue–Sat: 12.00–23.00
Sun: 12.00–22.30

Global Cuisine

Licensed

Credit cards accepted

Smoking allowed everywhere

Children's portions available

12.5% service charge to large tables

England **EAST SUSSEX** Restaurants – Brighton

Terre a Terre

Terre a Terre is known throughout Brighton and beyond for its innovative cuisine. You'll feel truly spoilt dining here. Come for the evening, relax and enjoy the friendly efficient service and fabulous food. The restaurant is large and spacious, seating over a hundred people. It has a vibrant, modern feel and is perfect for either a large party or a cosy candlelit dinner for two.

Starters include Soup of the Day with bread for £4.75, Channa Chaat, a coriander and mustard seed muffin with black salt smashed potato salad in minted coconut lime, layered with fried chaat spice channa and poori and tamarind jelly £6.40, or the gorgeous Terre a Tapas for £14 (enough for two). There are six salads, including Smoked Sakuri Soba Salad and Chefs Salad which contains dressed legumes, blanched haricot vert minted cucumber, basil tomatoes, griddled peppers, cracked olives and focaccia croutons with mixed leaf bundles, seeds and hoi sin tofu, both £6.20 as a starter or £10.80 as a main. There are eight main courses from £10.80–£11.80, including Cha Cha Bindi Kichadia–a South Indian dish, Sumac Scented Aubergine and Squeeky Rostibrown. Three of the nine desserts are vegan and include Cherry Apple Eccles–fried Eccles with Calvados ice cream and cinnamon cherry apples £5.50 and vegan Truffles £4.50, which are also available in take home boxes. There are several side dishes, breads and nibbles to choose from.

Soya milk, vegan margarine, vegan ice cream, vegan cheese, soya cappuccinos are available.

Good organic veggie and vegan wine list.

Vegetarian
Restaurant

71 East Street
Brighton
East Sussex BN1 1HQ
England

Tel: 01273 72905

Fax: 01273 327561

www.terreaterre.co.uk

Train Station: Brighton, 15 minutes walk.

Open: every day
Mon 18.00–22.30
Tue–Thu 12.00–22.30
Fri–Sat 12.00–23.00
Sun 12.00–22.30

Global cuisine

Licensed

High chairs
Kid's portions.

Credit cards accepted

No smoking, except in smoking area.

Book early for evening meals, especially at weekends.

Outside catering for weddings and parties.

The Guarana Bar

Juice
Bar

36 Sydney Street
Brighton
East Sussex BN1 4EP
England

Tel: 01273 621406

Fax: 01273 621415

www.goguarana.com

Email:
ejk@guarana.demon.co.uk

Train Station: Brighton,
10 minutes walk

Open: every day
Mon–Sat: 10.30–18.30
Sun: 12.00–18.00

10% discount to people
presenting this book

Non alcoholic juice bar
with New Age retail

Not licensed

Most credit/debit cards
accepted, except Amex.

Smoking allowed

Two tables outside.

Europe's only Guarana Bar is in Brighton's North Laine. Based on Brazilian guarana bars and Dutch coffee shops, it's the place to find natural energy drinks, safe and legal herbal highs, power nutrients and aphrodisiacs. It's a small and cosy place with a chilled out vibe. If you are a guarana novice, ask for advice on the products as the staff are well informed and happy to help.

Guarana is made from sun dried seeds of a Brazilian bush, Paullinia Cupana, and is a natural pick-me-up and aphrodisiac. It gives you a natural high.

Choose from a wide range of freshly made hot and cold drinks like Hot Guarana Punch £2 or Guarana Vitamin Shake – your favourite juice mixed with guarana powder and crushed ice £2. All slushies are available with wheatgrass or spirulina. Amazon Crush for £1.60 is guarana syrup mixed with crushed ice, sparkling water and guarana powder. There are lots of drinks to choose from in the fridge too, including Gusto Original with Chinese herbs, Brazilian guarana, ginseng and kolanut £1.80, Guarana Brahma – the national soft drink of Brazil £1, or Black Booster, an energy drink from Holland with a refreshing cola taste £1.50. Drinks can be made to your specifications.

You can purchase supplements and herbs to take home with you, like guarana in capsule, powder or tincture, herbal viagra, St. Johns wort, kava kava, echinacea and a wide range of Rainforest Botanicals and herbal highs. They also sell chill out CD's, gifts, smoking paraphernalia and Vegetarian Guides' books.

Soya milk available for soyaccinos and soya smoothies.

The George

Don't expect your usual pub grub at the George, one of the best places to eat in Brighton. It's at the bottom of Trafalgar Street, only five minutes walk from the station. The cosy interior is filled with chunky dark wooden tables and chairs. Dramatic abstract paintings adorn the walls. Order drinks and food from the bar, then sit in the busy area nearby or at a quieter table in one of the many nooks. In summer relax in the beer garden, which is covered and heated during the colder months. In winter they have open fires.

Light meals include Soup of the Day £3.25, Mushroom Pate and Pickled Cucumber Ciabatta £4.95 and Nachos £5.45. Salads £5.55. Side Salad £1.95. Main meals include Pasta of the Day £5.45, Falafel Platter £5.85, Marinated Kebab Platter £6.95 and George Tapas (enough for two) £8.50. The menu changes seasonally but they always keep a few favourites like Bangers and Mash £5.45, Homemade Nut Burger £4.95 and Hot Sausage Baguette £4.45. Check the blackboards for daily specials which include a dessert of the day for £2.95. On Sundays there is a different menu each week, but always a Nut Roast. Sunday evenings from 18:30 Tapas are served to chilled out tunes from live DJ's.

The draught cider and several draught lagers are vegan, but not beers. Pint of lager £2.55–£2.70. House wine £2.50 for 175ml glass, £3.50 for 250ml, £10.25 for a bottle. Fair Trade organic coffee £1.25, cappucino £1.40, hot chocolate £1.30, pot of tea £1.10. Drinks with soya milk 5p cheaper.

Most of the menu is vegan or can be made vegan with soya milk, vegan margarine, mayonnaise, ice cream and cheese available.

5 Trafalgar Street
Brighton
East Sussex BN1 4EQ

Tel: 01273 681055
Fax: 01273 696752

Train Station: Brighton, then five minute walk.

Open: every day
Mon–Thu 12.00–23.00, last food orders 21.30.
Fri–Sat 12.00–23.00, last food orders 20.30.
Sun 12.00–22.30, food served 12.30–18.00 then tapas 18.30–21.30

Children welcome until 7pm. There are high chairs and kiddy sized food portions available.

Dog friendly

Credit cards accepted

Smoking allowed, except in no smoking area

Special diets catered for. All the food is completely home made. No GM ingredients used.

25% discount on food to members of Viva!
10% discount on food to members of the Vegetarian Society, Vegan Society, Animal Aid, PETA and people presenting this book.

Purchase Vegetarian Guides' books here.

Vegan manager and some veggie and vegan staff.

Brighton's only vegan & vegetarian pub

the george

the george

5 trafalgar street, brighton
01273-681 055

Trogs

Unique restaurant under the Granville Hotel, across the road from Brighton's seafront and West Pier. Trogs has both a gourmet restaurant for special occasions and a relaxed cafe bar for casual dining.

A four course inclusive meal in the restaurant costs £20, otherwise you can order courses separately. Starters include Soup of the day with crusty bread £4.50, Trogs Vegan Antipasto £6 and Sweet Potato and Sultana Madras Timbale with Exotic Fruits and Pear and Lime Raita £6. Main courses include Warm Moroccan Cous Cous, Spinach, Apricot and Almond Salad, topped with Orange, Mint and Cinnamon marinated Tofu and Aubergine Rolls £12 and Sumatan Risotto balls drizzled with Gado Gado Sauce, with a Noodlesque Yum-Yum Soup and Exotic Fruit Salad £12. If you've still got room for dessert, try the Blue Moon Brulee, oozing with Blueberries and Blue Caracao, served with Strawberry Wine, or Pear Cheesecake accompanied by Pear Jelly, a poached Pear and Pear Sorbet both £6 and both vegan!

If you're here for a more casual meal, eat in the cafe bar where you'll find the food cheaper but still of a high standard. Starters £2.50-£5 include Garlic Bread or Soup of the Day. Mains £4.50-£7 include Thai Green Curry with Basmati Rice, Veggie Burger with Salad and Chips and Ratatouille with Dumplings. Heavenly desserts £3.50-£5, such as Gooseberry Fool or Fruit Crumble with Soya Ice Cream. Some of the best vegan puds in Britain!

Sit outside if you're there on a nice day. All food is organic. Soya milk, vegan margarine, vegan cheese, organic and vegan wine available. House wine £3.20 per glass, £8.50 per bottle. Beer £2.80. Coffee £1.50.

124 Kings Road
Brighton
East Sussex BN1 2FA
England

Tel: 01273 204655

Fax: 01273 728294

www.trogs.co.uk

Email:
granville@brighton.co.uk

Train Station: Brighton

Open: every day
Mon–Thu: 12.00–23.00
Fri–Sun: 10.00–23.00

10% discount to members of the Vegetarian Society, Vegan Society, Viva!, PETA, Animal Aid and people presenting this book.

Global cuisine

Licensed

Credit Cards accepted

Separate smoking area

High chairs for children

Dog friendly

Food For Friends

Vegetarian Restaurant

17-18 Prince Albert Street,
Brighton, East Sussex, BN1 1HF
Open: every day, Mon-Sat 8.15-22.00
and Sun 9.15-22.00

Tel: 01273 202310
Cuisine: Global Vegetarian
Train Station: Brighton, 10
minutes walk

Soup and bread £2.35, medium salad £3.90, hot dishes £3.95-£6.95. Nice ambience and chilled out vibe. Fully licensed. No smoking except in designated area. Gluten free and nut free diets catered for. All major cards accepted if spending over £5. 20% discount off eat-in for members of Vegetarian Society, Vegan Society and Viva! Vegans beware, most hot dishes are covered in cheese and recently a vegan couple we know got served a meal that contained cheese by mistake and ate it, though hopefully they will have fixed that by now.

Wai Kika Moo Kau

Vegetarian Cafe

11a Kensington Gardens,
Brighton, East Sussex, BN14AL
Train Station: Brighton, 5 minutes walk
Open: Mon-Fri & Sun 9.00-18.00, Sat 9.00-19.00

Vegetarian Cafe
Cuisine: Global Vegetarian

Starters £1.50-£3.75, mains £4.95-£7.25, desserts £1.20-£2.95. The menu is extensive but not too good for vegans. Smoking allowed everywhere. Fully licensed. All major cards accepted except Amex.

Wai Kika Moo Kau

Vegetarian Cafe

42 Meeting House Lane,
Brighton, East Sussex, BN1 1HB
Train Station: Brighton, 10 minutes walk
Open: Mon-Fri 11-23.00, Sat 10-23.00, Sun 10-18.00

Tel: 01273 323824
Cuisine: Global Vegetarian

Starters £3.50, mains £6, desserts £3 (including vegan cakes). Smoking allowed everywhere. Fully licensed. All major cards accepted except Amex.

Infinity Foods Co-operative

Wholefood shop

25 North Road, Brighton, East Sussex, BN1 1YA
Open: Mon-Thu & Sat 9.30-17.30,
Fri 9.30-18.00, Sun closed

Tel: 01273 603563
www.infinityfoods.co.uk

Vegetarian and vegan shopping heaven! This excellent wholefood shop has almost every veggie and vegan delight you could think of, like vegan fetta, loads of different veggie sausages and burgers, fishless fish cakes, and a good selection of vegan and organic ice creams and chocolates. Buy those to die for Booja Booja chocolates here. They also stock organic fruit and vegetables, freshly baked bread (from their bakery) and all sorts of eco friendly cleaning products and toiletries. If you've got enough dosh, you could do all your shopping here. Is this what meat eaters feel like in Sainsbury's?

Lush

Cruelty-free cosmetics

41 East Street, Brighton
Open: Mon-Sat 9.00-18.00, Sun 11.00-17.00

Tel: 01273 774700
www.lush.co.uk

You can smell Lush before you even walk through the door. It's full of gorgeous hand made body products made with natural ingredients. Many of the products are vegan. You'll find soaps, bath bombs, shampoos, conditioners, hair treatments, moisturisers, massage bars and more.

Holland & Barrett

Health food shop

105 London Road, Brighton

Tel: 01424-696209

Another branch at 66–68 North Street, Town Centre. Tel 746343.

Peace and Environment Centre

Ethical shop

43 Gardner Street, Brighton BN1 1UN
www.bpec.org
Open: Mon–Sat 10.00–17.30, Sun closed

Tel: 01273 692880
Fax: 01273 689444
bripeace@pavilion.co.uk

Ethical trade shop selling goods from organisations promoting peace, justice, and environmental issues, as well as from Fair Trade importers. Great place to pick up a gift for a friend. They stock stationery, greeting cards, books, journals, tea, coffee and crafts. If you join the Peace and Environment Centre, you can borrow books from their comprehensive library and use their computer services for a small charge.

Vegetarian Shoes

Veggie shoes & accessories

12 Gardner Street, Brighton, East Sussex, BN1 1UP
Open: Mon–Sat 10.00–17.30,
Sun and public holidays closed

Tel: 01273 691913
www.vegetarianshoes.com
info@vegetarianshoes.com

You may have ordered your shoes from them already by mail order, but while you're in Brighton, make sure you check out the shop. They don't just sell shoes and boots either. You can also get belts, jackets, bags, T-shirts and wallets.

Check out their web site before coming or call for a catalogue. If they're down to the last pair of what you want, you can try them on and they'll send you your shoes as soon as they're ready.

See display ad at the start of this chapter.

Why vegetarian shoes?

I don't eat the inside and I won't wear the outside.

Leather is just fur with the hair scraped off.

The skin is a large part of the value of an animal. Without it, the meat industry would not be viable.

The strong chemicals used in tanning, to get the last of the flesh off the skin, cause water pollution.

The material used to make veggie shoes is superior. It breathes like leather, letting perspiration out, but it doesn't let water in. Great news if you've just stepped in a deep puddle.

For these reasons, at Veggie Guides we don't wear leather.

A trip to Brighton is an opportunity to investigate the alternatives.

For more information on leather and the alternatives:

www.vegansociety.com and search on "leather"

www.petaeurope.org/cmp/leth.html

www.cowsarecool.com

www.vegetarian-shoes.com

www.freerangers.co.uk

www.ethicalwares.com

East Sussex
Other places

The Sanctuary Cafe

Relax and be sanctified in this unique cafe spanning three floors of a distinctive Brunswick building. It's arty, eclectic, comfortable and friendly.

Order your meal from the counter, while drooling over the wide selection of gorgeous cakes, of which about half are vegan. Their menu includes Toasted Bagels £2.25 and Freshly Baked Baguettes £2.95, with houmous and a salad garnish. Jaket Potatoes with sweetcorn are £4.10, with beans £3.95 and with houmous £4.15 All served with a selection of salad. The salads are delicious and can be a meal in themselves. A regular Salad is £4.25 and an extra large Salad is £5.50. Houmous and warm pitta with salad, and Pate of the Week, such as aubergine, tarragon and lime, with warm bread and salad are £4.50. Soup of the Day served with bread is £3.50 and could be carrot, parsnip, lentil and mushroom. Daily specials could include Mixed Vegetable Curry served with sticky rice, mango chutney and salad garnish for £5.50, Wraps with courgette, aubergine and mushroom in a garlic and basil tomato sauce served with salad are also £5.50. A delicious veggie/vegan roast is served on Sundays. House wine is £2.70 per glass or £10.50 per bottle. Beer £2.30 and coffee £1.50. A huge slice of delicious vegan cake is £2.50 and could be Carrot and Orange, Lemon and Poppyseed or Coffee and Walnut.

Downstairs is The Cella, a funky and intimate venue for regular live music, poetry, performance and creative innovations. Also available to hire for parties.

For table service add 10%. Deduct 10% for take-away. Organic and vegan wine available. Soya milk for soyaccinos and smoothies.

Vegetarian and Fish Cafe

51-55 Brunswick St East Hove
East Sussex BN3 1AU
England

Tel: 01273 770002

Cella enquiries/Fax: 01273 770006

www.thesanctuarycafe.co.uk

Email: info@thesanctuarycafe.co.uk

Train Station: Brighton or Hove

Open: every day 9.00-23.00

Global Cuisine

High chairs Children's portions

Licensed

Credit cards accepted

Smoking allowed, except in smoke free area

England **EAST SUSSEX** Restaurants

The Snowdrop Inn

Friendly pub in a quiet street on the outskirts of Lewes, which offers an almost totally vegetarian range of snacks and meals. Around half the food is vegan. 40% organic, 100% GM free.

Starters £1.75–£4 include sweet potato and coconut soup, garlic mushrooms, pesto or garlic pizza bread.

Mixed salad £2.60, Avocado avalanche salad £5.50. They include bulgar, quinoa, barley and puy lentils in all salads.

Main courses £4.95–£6.50 such as pizzas (can be vegan), Tuscan puff pastry parcels, thali with organic rice, and three bean pie.

Extensive specials board which changes every day. Lots of sandwiches and wraps.

Desserts £2–2.50 include chocolate cake, strawberry cheesecake and fruit/apple crumble, all of these vegan, and (soya) ice cream.

Gluten, wheat and nut-free options.

House wine £1.80 glass, £7.50 bottle. Beer from £2. Organic and vegan wine available.

Coffee from £1.10, including organic Fair Trade. Soya milk available.

Non-smoking area, plus tables in the garden.

Sometimes hosts live music.

The women's toilets feature an unusual collage made from old comic strips.

119 South Street
Lewes
East Sussex

Tel: 01273 471018

Pub open:
Mon–Sat 11–23.00,
Sun 12–22.30

Food served:
Mon–Sat
12–15.00 & 18–21.00,
Sun 12.30–15.00
& 19–21.00

15 minutes walk from Lewes train station

Children's portions

Smoke free area

No credit cards

Vegan proprietor

Restaurants EAST SUSSEX England

Wealden Wholefoods Café

Vegetarian organic wholefood café with take-away soup and sandwiches too. Run by a cooperative with an emphasis on organic, fair traded, locally produced foods.

Savoury dishes like Homity pie, spinach pie, lentil and buckwheat slice, nut loaf croquettes, vegetarian Kiev. Salads £1 small, £2 large. Homemade cakes and (vegan) ice cream.

Coffee £1.50 for a cafetiere that holds two cups. Soya milk available. Organic house wine £2.50 glass, £5 bottle; beer £3 pint.

Small outside seating area for 4-6 people.

High Street
Wadhurst
East Sussex TN5 6AA

Tel: 01892 783 065
Fax: 01842-783351

www.
wealdenwholefoods.co.uk
barbara@
wealdenwholefoods.co.uk

Open:
Mon-Sat 09.00-16.45
Sun closed

England EAST SUSSEX Restaurants

Heaven and Earth

Vegetarian cafe

37e Robertson St
Hastings, East Sussex
Open: Mon–Sun 10.00–18.00; Fri, Sat evenings
April–Oct. Closed some Sundays in mid–winter.

Tel: 01424 712 206

Café and bakery with counter service. Always vegan options and salad bar is entirely vegan. Also do vegan pizza, £1.60, and vegan cakes, £1.30–£1.50.

East 2 West

Vegetarian restaurant

50 George Street, Old Town
Hastings, East Sussex TN34 3EA
Open: Mon closed. Tue 11–14.30, evening closed
unless you want to book for a group; Wed 19–22.00;
Thu–Sat 11–14.30 or later if busy and 19–22.00;
Sun 11–14.30 or later, can be as late as 5 or 6pm.

01424 429092

New vegetarian restaurant. Indian, Mexican, Italian, Chinese and African dishes home cooked on the premises. Starters £2.95 or less like bhajias, samosas, spring rolls. Mains around £4.85 such as dosa, bhel puri, spicy pasta, pizza (can be vegan), stir–fry, special rice, cassava chips. Desserts £2.80–3.50 like gulfi, carrot halva. Vegan options and gluten free on request. Fully licensed with a bar. House wine £9.50 bottle, glass £2.80. Children welcome, high chair. Smoking at the bar only. No credit cards. Parking on the seafront as they're in a pedestrianised street.

Seasons of Lewes

Vegetarian Organic Cafe

199 High Street,
Lewes, East Sussex, BN7 2NS
Train Station: Lewes, five minutes walk
Open: Tue–Sat 9.30–17.00, Sun–Mon closed

Tel: 01273 473968

Vegetarian Organic cafe run by a mother and daughter team committed to vegetarianism and organic produce. Starters like soup with bread £2.90, salad bowl £2.90. Mains around £4.50. Cakes £1.50 (one usually vegan) and fruit crumbles too. Vegan ice cream available. Not licensed, but you can bring your own wine. Gluten free and wheat free diets catered for. No credit cards. No smoking.

Salad Bowl

Omnivorous cafe

21 High Street
Seaford, East Sussex
Open: Mon–Sat 9.30–15.00

Tel: 01323 890 605

Omnivorous café with veggie food and a veg hot pot for £2.15 which is very popular with local vegans. Also jacket potatoes.

Finbarrs Wholefoods

Wholefood shop

57 George St., Hastings
Open: Mon–Sat 9–17.30

Tel: 01424 443025

Trinity Wholefoods

Wholefood shop

3 Trinity St., Hastings

Tel: 01424 430473

Holland & Barrett

Health food shop

21 Queens Road,
Hastings, East Sussex TN34 1QY

Tel: 01424–427 253

Essex

The UK's answer to New Jersey, Essex is next to London and near to "Veggie Capital of Europe" Brighton. If we can survive famous Essex girl/man jokes we can survive anything!

Lively clubs, reasonably priced theatres, new cinemas, country walks, seaside towns, good shops, shopping malls, some decent eateries and like minded people – what more could you want?

by Karin Ridgers
Viva! Essex

For the latest on what's on in Essex see www.thisisessex.co.uk

Places in Essex

Hotels and Guest Houses

Vegetarian Restaurants

Omnivorous Restaurants

ESSEX England

Places in Essex

Shops

England
ESSEX

Vegetarian Catering Services

Beckneywood House

Vegetarian owned omnivorous B&B set in four acres of garden with a lake. There are two double ensuites and two twin ensuites at £50 per room per night, or £30 for sole occupancy.

Wake in the morning to a breakfast of cereal with soy yoghurt followed by veggie sausages, tomatoes, beans and toast. Soy milk available.

Beckneywood House has a quiet country setting where you can relax and unwind enjoying the fish, wildlife, ducks, moorhens and herons. The veggie and vegan owners particularly welcome other veggies and vegans. Their aim is to create a quiet retreat for people to escape their hectic lives.

Beckney Woods is within a few minutes walk from the house giving you the opportunity to explore the countryside. The small market town of Rochford is one mile away, and five miles further on Southend On Sea offers seaside fun for all the family. The old spa town of Hockley is one and a half miles in the opposite direction. Continue another couple of miles and you will be at Battlesbridge where you will find a variety of antiques all housed in historic barns. There are also some great riverside pubs and tearooms.

Visitors are welcome to stroll the grounds. There is a television lounge. Children of all ages are welcome. Pets welcome by arrangement. No smoking throughout.

*Lower Road
Hockley
Essex SS5 5LD
England*

Tel: 01702 201543

*www.beckneywood
house.co.uk*

*Train Station: Hockley or
Rochford, 1 1/2 miles*

Open: all year

*Directions: Six miles from
Southend Seaside/Pier.
One mile from Southend
Airport. Twelve miles
from Chelmsford on A130*

Parking: available

Café Pulse

Vegetarian world cuisine. They use locally grown produce with many organic ingredients and 95% of the food is made on the premises.

Salads £2.60–2.95 such as soup of the day and roll; paté (mint or Chinese brown lentil and mushroom) with pitta or rice cake plus Mediterranean chutney; hummous and curried fruit chutney with warm pitta or rice cakes.

Main meals (11am–4pm) £4.25–4.85 like chilli bean wrap with couscous; lentil and red pepper flan with garlic mash plus carrot, peanut and banana salad.

Pulse power salad £3.95 with fresh leaves, organic sprouting beans and seeds in balsamic dressing. Tabouleh salad £3.80 with bulgar wheat, fresh herbs, tomatoes, onions, green pepper in lemon and olive oil dressing.

Sandwiches £1.95–2.20 with salad or multi fillings, vegan friendly. Vegetarian hot dogs in a roll and salad £2.05. Toast 60p.

Teas 90p pot for one, £1.60 for two. Coffee, barleycup, hot chocolate £1.20. Organic carbonated drinks, mineral water (500ml) £1. Fresh fruit juice of the day £1.60. Fresh fruit smoothie (banana or strawberry) £2.95.

Desserts £1.60–1.75 include home made cakes.

The cafe can be hired in the evening.

Strong recycling initiative and they support local alternative therapists.

Vegetarian
Cafe

80 Leigh Road
Leigh-on-Sea
Essex
SS9 1BZ

Tel: 01702-719 222

www.clix.to/cafepulse

Open:
Mon–Sat 9.00–16.00

Child friendly
High chairs

No smoking

No credit cards

They can adjust items to cater for special diets

England ESSEX Restaurants

Tropical Emas

Chinesetern exotic authentic Singaporean, Malaysian, Indonesian, Chinese and vegetarian cuisine. Separate vegetarian and vegan menu.

10 appetizers £2–£5.20 like crispy "duck", spring rolls, crispy seaweed, veg wraps, deep fried bean curd.

32 vegetarian main dishes £3–£4.95 include Szechuan beancurd, dried tofu with green pepper and chilli black bean sauce, diced veg and cashew nuts in yellow bean sauce.

7 desserts £1.50–2.20 include banana fritters, crisply deep-fried noodles with syrup, toffee apple with sesame seeds.

Special lunches £4.90 Mon–Sat. Sunday buffet 12.30–3.30pm eat as much as you like for £12.80 (£8.80 under-7). Multi-course set meal £12.50 or £13.50 each for minimum of two people.

House wine £10.95 bottle, £2.60 glass. Beer £1.40 half, £2.60 pint. Coffee £1.20 with free refill.

Omnivorous Oriental Restaurant

6 Station Parade
Victoria Rd
Romford
Essex RM12JA

Tel: 01708–752 218

Open:
Mon 18.00–23.00,

Tue–Sat 12–14.30,
17.30–23.00
(Fri 23.30, Sat 24.00)

Sun and bank holiday
12.30–15.30,
17.30–22.30

High chairs for children

Fully licensed

Air conditioned

Smoke free area

Visa, MC, Amex

No service charge

Gluten–free, wheat–free and vegan diets catered

Vegetarian proprietor

Josephine's Tea Room

Vegetarian tea rooms

Arts & Crafts Centre, High Street
Dedham, Essex CO7 6AD
Open: every day 10.00–17.00
Closed Mondays Jan–March

Tel: 01206–322 677

Vegetarian tea rooms. Serve light lunches, £2.60–£6, but not much for vegans unless you call in advance. Tea 95p for a pot. Non smoking. No credit cards.

Leeora Vegetarian Food

Vegetarian take–away & delivery

Sunshine House, 63 London Road
Stanway
Colchester, Essex CO3 5PT
www.leeoravegetarianfood.co.uk
Business hours: Sun–Fri 12.00–14.00, 16.30–22.30,
Saturday 19.00–23.00

Telephone orders:
01206–514 953

Organic vegetarian/vegan take–away and delivery. Extensive menu includes soya specials, tofu dishes, dips, pates, desserts, pastries and barbecue dishes from around the world.
Healthy lunch delivered to your office, minimum order £10. Parties catered for.
National mail order of ready to eat meals (vegan and allergy care). New range of chilled or frozen vegetarian meals. You can order online through their website.
They also offer vegetarian cookery courses.

Vegan Essex!

Several years ago I woke up!

I found vegetarianism! A revelation! I had to share this new found obvious answer to the world's problems and to start this, form a veggie group in Essex. Despite being in the local press, my novice attempts at Viva! Essex were dashed. Well kind of. I carried on campaigning on my own.

However now in Essex we have a strong group known as Vegan Essex, Viva! Essex and Essex Animal Rights, and we are mainly vegan. We are networking with other veggie groups throughout Essex, such as Southend Veggies, Southend Animal Aid and St Francis Foundation. So we can maybe assume that veganism and vegetarianism are growing in our affluent county.

For more info please email veganessex@hotmail.com

Webber's Wine Bar & Bistro

Omnivorous restaurant

2 Western Road/ 11 High Street
Billericay, Essex CM12 9DZ

Tel: 01277-656 581
www.winecases.com

Varying menu and will be something suitable for vegetarians. Run by Gail and Brett Jones who are 'sympathetic' – Brett knows which wines are vegan.

Pizza Express

Omnivorous pizza restaurant

5 High Street
Brentwood, Essex CM14 4RG
Open: Mon–Sun 12.00–23.00

Tel: 01277-233 569

Pizza restaurant chain that can make vegan pizzas.

Cosmopolitan

Omnivorous restaurant

8-10 Broomsfield Road
Chelmsford, Essex CM1 1SN
Open: Mon–Sat 18.30–22.00

Tel: 01245-493 929

Omnivorous restaurant and patisserie with a vegetarian menu including vegan items. Starters such as avocado and mango salad £5.25. Main include Ragu di ceci £9.50, a rich sauce of chickpeas with tomato on pasta; Vegetali Delizia £10.25, sauté of potato, pepper and onion baked in Italian style. Organic produce used whenever possible.

Pizza Express

Omnivorous restaurant

219 Moulsham Street
Chelmsford, Essex CM2 OLR
Open: Mon–Sun 11.30–24.00

Tel: 01245-491 466

Pizza restaurant.

The New Street Brasserie

Omnivorous restaurant

Atlantic Hotel, New Street
Chelmsford, Essex CM1 1PP
Open: Mon–Sat 7.00–22.30, Sun 7.00–21.30

Tel: 01245-268 179

Starters include layered tian of Mediterranean vegetables, salsa verde, aged balsamic vinegar and cherry plum tomatoes. Mains include baked avocado filled with butternut squash purée on confit potatoes with lemon chili oil.

Waterfront Place

Italian bar and restaurant

Wharf Road
Chelmsford, Essex CM2 6LU
Open: Mon–Thu 11.00–22.00,
Fri–Sat 11.00–22.30, Sun 12.00–17.00

Tel: 01245–252 000
Fax: 01245–252 048
www.waterfront–place.co.uk
info@waterfront–place.co.uk

Italian bar and restaurant, expensive and classy, good atmosphere, with many vegan options. Starters such as bruschetta £5. Mains (which can also be starters) £10 include mild korma butternut squash with mushroom pilau & coriander pesto (parmesan free); stuffed Piedmont pepper with saffron and vine tomato risotto and red pesto.

Chef Canton

Chinese restaurant

2A Crouch Street
Colchester
Open: evenings every day and lunchtimes except Sunday

Tel: 01206–572 703

Chinese restaurant and take away service. Advisable to give advance vegan notice but not necessary, will also do vegan meals that don't appear on menu. Helpful staff. Approx price of 2 courses with no drink £13.

China Chef

Chinese restaurant

73 Crouch Street
Colchester
Open: from 17.30 every day

Tel: 01206–546 953

Chinese restaurant and take away service. They do a special set vegetarian dinner (min 2 persons) £10.20 per person which they say is vegan.

Food On The Hill

Omnivorous restaurant

28 East Hill
Colchester, Essex CO1 2QX
Open: Mon 18.00–late, Tue–Sat 12.00–late,
essential to book Fri & Sat

Tel: 01206–791 393
www.foodonthehill.com

Omnivorous restaurant which caters well for vegetarians and vegans. All food freshly prepared from well sourced, seasonal and wherever posssible organic ingredients on premises. Menu changes weekly. Starters from £3.75 and mains from £8. Large garden with outside seating area. Open policy on smoking. No credit cards.

England ESSEX Restaurants

Garden Café

Omnivorous cafe

74 High Street
Colchester, Essex CO1 1UE
Open: Mon–Sat 10.00–16.30, serving meals 12.00–15.00

Tel: 01206–500 169

Café at the back of the Minories art gallery boasts a fair selection of vegan lunches and cakes. 2 soups daily £3.90, vegan home made bread, and at least one of the main meals is vegan. Recommended by vegans and they are looking into introducing more vegan items, planning dairy free fruit smoothies/power drinks and oat milk. Soya cappuccinos available.

Pizza Express

Pizza restaurant

1 St Runwald's Street
Colchester
Open: Mon–Sun 11.30–24.00

Tel: 01206–760 680

Pizza restaurant.

Platypus Creek

Omnivorous restaurant

44 Lower Holt Street
Earls Cone, Colchester
Open: Wed–Sun 12.00–14.30, Wed–Sat 18.30–late

Tel: 01787–220 400

Situated on main road between Colchester and Halstead. Advance vegan notice required. Good selection of dishes to choose from– ask about the vegan chocolate mousse dessert. The Australian chef has been on a veggie/vegan cookery course. Approx price of two courses without drink £15.

The Lemon Tree

Omnivorous brasserie

48 St John's Street
Colchester
Open: open lunchtime and evenings

Tel: 01206–767 337

Brasserie in centre of town, built into old Roman City Wall. Advance vegan notice advisable but not necessary (more choice of meals if notice is given). Approx £15 for two courses without drink.

Keralam

South Indian restaurant

200 Main Road, Hawkwell
Hockley, Essex SS5 4EH
Open: every day 17.30–23.30 inc. bank holidays

Tel: 01702–207 188
www.keralam–essex.co.uk

'The first South Indian restaurant in Essex', famous for its cuisine from the south–west Indian state of Kerala. Recommended by vegans, lots of choice for veggies/vegans. Dosas from £3.25.

Suruchi

South Indian restaurant

506 High Road
Ilford, Essex IG1 1UE
Open: every day except Tuesday 12–15.00
and 18–24.00, last order 23.00

Tel: 020–8598 2020

Specialists in south Indian and Chinese vegetarian dishes in an Indian style. Many vegan items marked with 'v'. Value for money, good-sized portions, recommended by many vegans! Starters from £2.50 and mains £3.25–£4.25.

Pizza Express

Pizza restaurant

410–412 Cranbook Road
Gants Hill, Ilford
Open: Mon–Sun 12.00–23.00

Tel: 020–8554 3030

Pizza restaurant.

Pizza Express

Pizza restaurant

281–283 High Road
Loughton, Essex IG10 1AH
Open: Mon–Sun 11.00–23.30

Tel: 020–8508 3303

Pizza restaurant.

Churchills Café Bar

café–bar

Tylers Avenue
Central Southend
Open: Mon–Tue 11am–01.00am, Wed–Fri –02.00am,
Sat 9am–02.00am, Sun 12.00 noon –12.30 am

Tel: 01702–617 866

Trendy, clubby café–bar. Lovely food, reasonably priced. Dining from early evening, three courses £9.95. Our vegan researcher was well looked after on a hen night here.

Pizza Express

Pizza restaurant

9–11 London Road
Southend–on–Sea
Open: Mon–Sun 11.30–23.30

Tel: 01702–435 585

Singapore Sling

Oriental restaurant

12 Clifton Parade
Southend–on–Sea
www.locallife.co.uk/singaporesling
Open: Tue–Sun 12–15.00, 18.00–late

Tel: 01702–431 313

Friendly omnivorous restaurant with food from China, Japan, Thailand, Singapore and Malaysia. They have several vegetarian items on the menu and can cater for vegans with dishes such as green curry, Japanese udon noodles and Thai crispy tofu. Smoking permitted. Visa, MC.

Pizza Express

Pizza restaurant

131–133 St Mary's Lane
Upminster, Essex RM14 2SH
Open: Mon–Sun 12.00–23.00

Tel: 01708–224 111

Kia

Omnivorous restaurant

264 London Road
Westcliff–on–Sea
Open: Tue–Sat 18.00 till late,
Sun 12.30 – no set closing time

Tel: 01702–342 424
www.kia–worldcafe.co.uk

Omnivorous restaurant with some vegetarian and vegan options, particularly on the tapas menu. Starters such as melon, pear and hazelnut salad with elderflower dressing £4. Main courses include baked aubergine stuffed with onions, tomatoes, peppers and garlic served with tabouleh £8.50.

The Milton Restaurant

Omnivorous restaurant

61 Milton Road
Westcliff–on–Sea
Open: Tue–Sat 18.30–22.00

Tel: 01702–333 731

Omnivorous restaurant that can cater for vegetarians and vegans with advance notice with imaginative dishes such as puy lentils and chestnut soup, sweet potato and chervil rosti, ratatouille niçoise, and fennel, salsify and cauliflower casserole.

Holland & Barrett

Health food shop

42 Eastgate Centre, Eastgate
Basildon
Open: Mon–Sat 9.00–17.30

Tel: 01268–282 084

Nature's Table

Health food shop

Unit 8, The Walk, 128 High Street
Billericay
Open: Mon & Wed 9–17.30; Tue, Thu–Sat 9–17.00

Tel: 01277–655 444

Centre of Natural Health

Health food shop

20 New London Road
Chelmsford
Open: Mon–Sat 9.30–17.30

Tel: 01245–350 881

Holland & Barrett

Health food shop

4–5 Exchange Way
Chelmsford
Open: Mon–Sat 9.00–17.30

Tel: 01245–258 748

All Natural

Health food shop

27 Pier Avenue
Clacton-on-Sea
Open: Mon–Sat 8.45–17.00

Tel: 01255–435 629

Avalon Natural Health & Therapy Centre   Health food shop

6 St Johns Road
Great Clacton, Clacton-on-Sea
Open: Mon–Fri 9.00–17.00, closed Tue,
occasional Saturday mornings

Tel: 01255–436 059

Holland & Barrett

Health food shop

7 Pelhams Lane
Colchester
Open: Mon–Sat 9.00–17.30

Tel: 01206–546 009

Natural Foods

Health food shop

27 Sir Isaacs Walk
Colchester
Open: Mon-Sat 9.30-17.30

Tel: 01206-542 844

Natural Bodycare & Giftshop

Health food shop

55 High Street Wivenhoe
Colchester
Open: Mon-Fri 9.30-17.30, Sat 9.30-17.00

Tel: 01206-822 478

The Healthfood Centre

Health food shop

130 High Street
Epping
Open: Mon-Sat, closed Wed, 9.30-17.30

Tel: 01992-570 100

Holland & Barrett

Health food shop

1 Broad Walk
Harlow
Open: Mon-Sat 9.00-17.30

Tel: 01279-437 166

Sunrise Health Foods

Health food shop

31 Spa Road
Hockley
Open: Mon-Sat 9.00-18.00

Tel: 01702-207 017

The Vitamin Service

Health food shop

8 Madeira Avenue
Leigh-on-Sea
Open: Mon-Fri 9.00-16.00

Tel: 01702-470 923

GNC

Health food shop

16 Laurie Walk, Liberty Shopping Centre
Romford
Open: Mon-Sat 9.00-17.30

Tel: 01708-747 192

Shenfield Health Food Shop

Health food shop

27 Hutton Road
Shenfield
Open: Mon–Sat 9.00–17.30

Tel: 01277–260 739

Health Lines

Health food shop

32 Corbets Tey Road
Upminster
Open: Mon–Sat 9.00–17.30, Wed close 13.00

Tel: 01708–220 495

Abbey Health Foods

Health food shop

3 Sun Street
Waltham Abbey
Open: Mon–Sat 9.00–13.00, 14.00–17.00

Tel: 01992–650 014

T.M. Health Shop

Health food shop

348 London Road
Westcliff-on-Sea
Open: Mon–Sat 9.00–17.00

Tel: 01702–335 327

Minerva

Mail order chocolate

7A Eld Lane
Colchester, Essex CO1 1LS
www.MinervaChocolates.com
Amanda@MinervaChocolates.com
Business hours: Mon–Sat 10.00–17.30, closed
Sundays and Bank Holidays

Tel: 01206–560 338

Mail-order chocolate company, all chocolates vegetarian with wonderful vegan selection and Easter eggs. Gift boxes and gifts in boxes made from chocolate! Worldwide postal service.

Land & Liberty

Vegan books and permaculture

www.landandliberty.co.uk
http://pages.unisonfree.net/gburnett/happy/

Land & Liberty is a vegan, ethical initiative based in Essex. Earthright books, posters and T-shirts, forest gardening, permaculture design, consultancy and teaching. Books for young green vegans.

Leon's Vegetarian Catering

Gourmet vegetarian catering

132b London Road
Brentwood CM14 4NS
http://website.lineone.net/~leon.lewis/

Tel: 01277-218 661
leonsveg@aol.com

Vegetarian and vegan catering, buffets, cookery demonstrations, any event nationwide.

Nutbush Catering

Vegetarian outside caterers

Big or small events, parties and business lunches. For information and prices contact Viv Bird or Chris Coventry on 01702-524 460. Vebird@tinyworld.co.uk

Cavanagh's Catering Services

Gourmet vegetarian catering

Kathleen and David Smith
13 Rose Valley
Brentwood, Essex CM14 4HZ

Tel/Fax: 01277-227138
Mobile: 07930 432035
cavanaghs@lineone.net

Vegetarian and vegan catering for all events. Large outdoor functions to a small gourmet dinner at your home. Vegan proprietors.

Pimiento Vegetarian Cookery School

Contact Louise Bernard on 020-8502 1616
courses@pimiento.co.uk

Vegetarian cookery school based in Loughton in Essex. They run day long courses and demonstrations. One of the courses is specifically vegan, and where the course is vegetarian they can offer vegan alternatives. Vegetarian Society approved and owner holds the Cordon Vert Diploma.

Viva! Essex

Vegan activism

www.veganessex.org.uk
veganessex@hotmail.com

Tel: 07092 369280

Want a local campaigning group? We meet the first Tuesday of the month at the Brentwood School Sports Hall.

Gloucestershire

The Orange Tree

The only vegetarian restaurant for miles around with vegan, wheat-free and sugar-free options too. They even have vegan desserts. All the food is freshly prepared on the premises and a take-away service is available.

Starters £3-4 include watercress soup with organic wholemeal bread; yellow split pea dahl with warm chapatis and salad; spicy Thai sweetcorn and parsnip fritters with chutney, mixed leaves and alfalfa salads.

Main courses £7.95 include roasted butternut squash filled with moist saffron and pinenut cous cous and roasted peppers; red bean and chilli enchiladas topped with tomato and chilli sauce served with tortilla chips and salsa; cashewnut and sesame seed patties with spicy tikka masala sauce. All are served with salad or vegetables.

House wine £2 a glass or £9.95 a bottle. Beers £2.75. Coffee £1.35. Also soya smoothies and cappuccinos.

Open for private parties and outside catering.

Delightful courtyard garden.

317 High Street
Cheltenham
Gloucestershire
GL50 3HW

Tel: 01242-234 232
Fax: 01242 234 232

Open:
Sun & Mon 09.30-15.00

Tue-Thu 09.30-21.00

Fri & Sat 09.30-22.00

High chairs

Outside seating available in the summer.

Smoke-free area

Visa, MC, Switch

5% discount for members of The Vegetarian Society, Vegan Society, Viva! and people presenting this book.

Restaurants GLOUCESTERSHIRE England

Ruskin Mill Arts & Crafts Centre

Organic cafe

Old Bristol Road
Nailsworth
Gloucestershire GL6 0LA
Open: Tue–Sat 10–16.00;
Sun 15–18.00 summer and bank holidays,
14–17.00 winter.

Tel: 01453 837537

Organic café, vegetarian and fish. £3.80 for a meal, vegan and gluten free available. No smoking anywhere in the centre. No credit cards. Organic veg and craft shop open Tue–Sat 10–17.00. Gallery of contemporary local artists open every day 10–17.00 all year, and sometimes they have environmental exhibitions. Evening lectures, day classes and weekend workshops. The centre has artists, stained glass, felt, paper maker, jewellery etc, who can be visited by prior appointment through the above number.

Mother Nature

Vegetarian cafe

2 Bedford Street
Stroud
Gloucestershire GL5 1AY
Open: Mon–Sat 9–17.30, closed Sun

Tel: 01453 758 202

Vegetarian café which sometimes has vegan food. Fresh salads every day. Main meals from £4. Vegan ice cream available. Non smoking. Visa, MC.

Holland & Barrett

Health food shop

20 Regent Arcade
Cheltenham

Tel: 01242–528 749

24 Crickdale Street
Cirencester

Tel: 01285–641 068

3 St Michaels Buildings
Gloucester

Tel: 01452–311 281

Hampshire

Hamilton House B&B

Centrally located bed and breakfast, close to all the attractions of Portsmouth, the resort of Southsea, and the ferry terminals.

There are eleven rooms: two doubles and two twins at £22 per person per night, three double ensuites and two twin ensuites for £25 per person, and two family rooms for £25 per person.

The standard cooked breakfast is offered, but if you fancy anything different, just say what you would like and they will shop accordingly. Veggie sausages, vegan muesli, soya milk, vegan margarine and soya yoghurt are all available on request.

Dinner is not offered but there are restaurants just five minutes walk away and they all have vegetarian options.

It is five minutes drive to all parts of the city including shopping centres, museums, the historic ships complex and the Continental/Isle of Wight ferry ports.

Hamilton House has a booklet which guests can use that will get you 20–50% off entry tickets for the local attractions.

All rooms have a television, clock, hairdryer and tea and coffee making facilities. There is a television lounge.

**Omnivorous
Bed & Breakfast**

*95 Victoria Road North
Southsea
Portsmouth
Hampshire PO5 1PS
England*

*Tel and Fax:
023 9282 3502*

www.hamiltonhouse.co.uk

Email: sandra@hamilton house.co.uk

*Train station:
Portsmouth and Southsea, 1/2 mile then bus no. 17 stops outside the house, or get a taxi for £3.*

Open: all year

*Directions:
At junction 12 on M27 take M275 road into Portsmouth past the Continental Ferry port. At Charles Dickens roundabout take first exit and follow road round to right and then left. Follow Holbrook Road across three roundabouts (1/2 mile) into Victoria Road North. Hamilton House is second block on the right hand side.*

Parking: on street

Children are welcome and those sharing with two adults have a reduced rate.

No smoking throughout

The Gallery Café/Bar

Vegetarian café

Vegetarian café in relaxed arts centre setting, with Chinese, Greek, Indonesian, Italian, Mediterranean, Mexican, Thai and South Indian influences and cuisines. All main foods, salads and cakes are home made, they can cater for special diets such as gluten free and wheat free and there are always vegan options available.

Starters include range of soups and sandwiches at £2.65, various salads with cous cous, bean, potato and pasta, £1.75 for small, £3.45 for large.

Mains are usually 2 bakes and 2 quiches daily from £4.15 and usually 6 desserts with some vegan.

They have organic, vegan wines, vegan ice cream, mayonnaise, margarine and soya milk.

Sometimes open for supper evenings and special events depending on art centre programme.

Special functions can also be catered for.

Havant Arts Centre
East Street
Havant
Hampshire PO9 1BS

Tel: 02392–480 113
Fax: 02392–498 577

www.havantartsactive.org

Train: Havant

Open:
Mon–Sat 9.30–15.30,
Sun closed

Visa, Switch

10% discount to
Vegetarian Society and
Viva! members

Ashlee Lodge   Omnivorous bed & breakfast

36 Atherley Road   *Tel: 02380 222095*
Shirley
Southampton SO15 5DQ

Vegetarian friendly bed and breakfast. 1 single, 1 twin, 1 double, 1 family, £20-23 per person. Plenty of pubs, restaurants and nearby Chinese with vegetarian choices.

Koh I Noor   Omnivorous Indian restaurant

2 Portswood High Street, Portswood   *Tel: 02380 584339*
Southampton
Open: every day 18-24.00

Omnivorous Indian restaurant with a good vegetarian selection.

Country Kitchen   Vegetarian restaurant

59 Marmion Road   *Tel: 023-9281 1425*
Southsea, Hampshire PO5 2AX
Open: Mon-Fri 9.00-17.00, Sat 8.00-17.00

Vegetarian restaurant. Soup from £2.25 and bakes and mains at £3.95, such as vegan shepherd's pie or chilli bean and potato gratin. Cakes from 95p with gluten-free and vegan choices. No smoking. No credit cards.

Sweet Joe Pye   Wholefood shop

31 St Thomas Street   *Tel: 01590-672 931*
Lymington, Hampshire SO41 9NE
Open: Mon-Fri 9-17.30, Sat 9-13.00

Wholefood shop but no take-aways, at the top end of the High Street near Waitrose (where a lot of people park), away from the tourist strip.

The Bran Tub   Wholefood shop

20 Lavant Street   *Tel: 01730-267 043*
Petersfield,Hampshire GU32 3EW
Open: Mon-Sat 9-17.30 (Thu - 17.00, Sat - 16.00)

GM free veggie shop, with take-way pasties, cashewnut rolls etc delivered Wednesday from St Clements veggie restaurant (so might be sold out by Tuesday). They even have vegan ice-cream like choc ices and Cornettos.

GNC

Health food shop

48a Kingswell Path, Cascades
Portsmouth
Open: Mon–Sat 9–17.30

Tel: 023–9285 1552

Scoltocks Natural Foods

Health food shop

1 Market Place
Ringwood, Hampshire BH24 1AN
Open: Mon–Sat 9–17.30

Tel: 01425–473 787

Winchester Health Food Centre

Health food shop

Sheridan House, 41–42 Jewry Street
Winchester, Hampshire SO23 8RY
Open: Mon–Fri 9.15–17.00, Sat 9.15–17.45

Tel: 01962–851 113

Health food shop which sells a range of produce, GM–free where
possible, and some organic fruit and vegetables

Holland & Barrett

Health food shop

240 Commercial Road
Portsmouth, Hampshire PO1 1HG

Tel: 02392–825 416

27 Southampton Road
Ringwood
Hampshire BH24 1HB

Tel: 01425–483 950

18 East Street
Southampton
Hampshire SO14 3HG

Tel: 02380–211 859

33 High Street
Winchester
Hampshire SO23 9BL

Tel: 01962–843 194

17 Mayfair House
Hollins Walk
Basingstoke, Hampshire RH21 7LJ

Tel: 01256 346170

233 Fleet Road
Fleet, Hampshire GU13 8BN

Tel: 01252–625 671

Herefordshire

Places in Herefordshire

Hotels and Guest Houses

Restaurants

Shops

Bramlea Bed & Breakfast

Vegetarian
Bed and Breakfast

Small vegetarian B&B offering friendly personal service. There are three rooms; one single, one twin and one family all costing £20 per person per night.

Breakfast is fruit and soya yoghurt with a selection of cereals followed by a full cooked veggie breakfast. Special diets are catered for and they have soya milk, vegan margarine, vegan muesli and veggie sausages.

Dinner is not offered but Bramlea is a ten minute walk from the cente of Leominster where there are hotels, restaurants, pubs and cafes which offer vegetarian food. There is a selection of menus at the house and they can book a table for you. There are also a few health food shops where you can pick up picnic supplies.

Leominster has a medieval priory church and boasts many antique shops. There are many gardens, National Trust Properties, specialist nurseries and historic buildings in the area. Local artists display and sell their works. The cities of Hereford, Ludlow and Shrewsbury are not far away. Also nearby are the medieval villages of Woebley and Eardesland.

As it is a bungalow, the house is suitable for people with limited mobility (with a walking frame or stick), however it is not suitable for wheelchairs as the doorways are too narrow.

Children aged three and over are welcome. Pets welcome. Tea and coffee making facilities in the rooms. There is a TV lounge. Guests are asked not to smoke inside.

Barons Cross Road
Leominster
Herefordshire HR6 8RW
England

Tel and Fax:
01568 613406

Email:
lesbramlea@netlineuk.net

Train station: Leominster,
1 1/2 miles, they will
collect you.

Open:
1 March to 31 October

Directions:
Bramlea is one mile from
the centre of Leminster
situated on the A44
towards Wales. They are
directly opposite a
Safeway supermarket.

Parking:
three off street spaces

Bredwardine Lodge

Listed Victorian Gothic building built in 1857, formerly a school but now a family home and vegetarian bed and breakfast. There are two spacious rooms; one double and one family (with an oriental four poster bed) at £25 per person per night.

Breakfast is served in the library and is organic as far as possible. A typical breakfast comprises of juice, various fruits and cereal or muesli, followed by veggie sausages, tomatoes, mushrooms, toast and spreads. Rice milk, oat milk, almond milk and soya milk are all usually available as well as vegan margarine, vegan muesli and soya yoghurt. Vegan, gluten-free and sugar-free diets are catered for.

Dinner is not usually offered but can be if requested. The local pub serves home cooked meals with veggie options.

The house is set in a quiet garden amidst fields, hills and woodland. Alongside the house is a public footpath and Bredwardine is on the Wye Valley walk. On the hill above the village is Arthur's Stone, a prehistoric burial chamber, from which there are splendid views of the Black Mountains and the Golden Valley. Five minutes down the hill is the River Wye. Bredwardine Bridge is popular in summer with people sun bathing, swimming, paddling and canoeing.

Bredwardine Lodge is eight miles from Hay-on-Wye, the second hand book town which has a literary festival each May. The ancient cathedral city of Hereford is twelve miles away.

Children are welcome and they have toys and a cot. No TV but there is plenty to read. No smoking throughout.

Vegetarian
Bed & Breakfast

Bredwardine
Herefordshire HR3 6BZ
England

Tel: 01981 500113

Train station:
Hereford, 12 miles

Open: all year

Directions:
On the edge of the rural village of Bredwardine off the A4352 between Hereford and Hay-on-Wye.

Parking: available

Haie Barn

Vegetarian Bed and Breakfast

Vegetarian B&B in a barn conversion at the western end of the Golden Valley. There is one double ensuite room with a king sized bed which can also serve as a twin for £24 per person per night and two doubles for £19–£21 per person per night. Single occupancy of a room is £25–£30 per night.

Try their Big Barn breakfast consisting of mushrooms, tomatoes, baked beans, veggie sausages (six varieties to choose from) and potato wedges. If you'd like something different though, there is always a daily special which could be buckwheat pancakes with fruit compote. And there are always five other breakfasts to choose from. There is also fruit, cereal and toast. Ingredients are sourced locally wherever possible. They have vegan margarine and soya milk. Special diets are catered for. Let them know your needs when booking.

Dinner is £12 for two courses and £15 for three courses and could be carrot soup, then mushroom and chestnut cobbler with seasonal veg and for dessert, poached pears on a pastry bed. There are also restaurants around who cater for veggies.

There are many walks in the area including the Wye Valley walk and the Offas Dyke walk. You'll find solitude exploring the Brecon Beacons and Radnorshire Hills. Hay-on-Wye is nearby where days could be spent browsing in the many second hand book shops, or visit the the historic city of Hereford. Lovers of gardens, historic houses, country churches, cider, walking and other outdoor activities will all find something of interest in the area.

Guest lounge. Rooms have bath robes, a hair dryer, wash basin, TV, radio alarm, and tea and coffee making facilities.

The Bage
Dorstone
Herefordshire HR3 5SU
England

Tel: 01497 831729

www.golden-valley.co.uk /haiebarn

Email: goodfood@ haie-barn.co.uk

Train station: Hereford, 16 miles, then bus or taxi

Open: March-end October

Solely for adults.

No smoking throughout

Directions: On the B4348 you will pass the road sign for Dorstone, followed by a sharp left bend. Do not enter the village but continue on this road, passing St. Faith's church on your left, for 1 1/2 miles. Haie Barn is the first habitation on your left as you approach the hamlet of the Bage.

Parking: plenty of off road parking available.

Cafe @ All Saints

Bill Sewell's modern English veggie cafe is in an award winning refurbishment of a superb medieval church.

All food, even the bread, is freshly made on the premises. The menu changes regularly and includes a hot special for around £5.65, such as pasta with roast Mediterranean vegetables, basil and puy lentils in a balsamic vinaigrette. Generally speaking, if the main course is vegan, the soup contains dairy products, and vice-versa.

Soup £2.45, such as spiced tomato with olive oil roll or a slice of one of their breads.

Salad combination £2.95, such as mixed leaves; broccoli, carrots and mint with parsley, olive oil and lemon dressing; and wholegrain rice, puy lentils, herbs and fresh vegetables in a soy balsamic vinaigrette.

Sandwiches £2.95-3.65, such as roast mushroom and roast tofu, are made on their own breads baked each morning. Grilled 30p extra.

Cakes, tarts and puddings, 85p-£1.95 such as flapjacks, scones and brownies. None appear to be vegan.

Organic local apple juice, £1.25, freshly squeezed orange or pink grapefruit, £1.25, spring water or home made lemonade or elderflower cordial 95p.

Beer and cider £1.90-£2.50. Wine £2.35 glass, £8.75 bottle.

As well as the existing Place Below in London, Bill is opening a new restaurant in Cambridge soon after we go to press.

Vegetarian gourmet cafe

All Saints Church
High St
Hereford
HR4 9AA

01432 370 415

billgrub@aol.com

Mon-Sat
8.30-17.30,
closed Sundays

Near Hereford station

No smoking

Licensed

Children's portions and high chairs

Outside seating area

Switch, Visa, MC

The Old Post Office

Vegetarian bed & breakfast

Llanigon, Hay-on-Wye,
Powys HR3 5QA,
Wales

Tel: 01497 820008
www.oldpost-office.co.uk

Veggie bed & breakfast in an outstandingly beautiful area with the Brecon Beacons national park on the doorstep. Right on the Wales and Herefordshire border. Full details in the Wales section.

Oscars

Omnivorous restaurant

High Town
Hay-on-Wye, Herefordshire HR3 5AE
Open: Mon–Sun 10.30–17.00

Tel: 01497 821193

Omnivorous restaurant with typically 3 vegetarian main dishes daily, £6.50, and also always something vegan. They will try to cater for special diets. Non smoking. Visa, MC.

Nutters

Vegetarian restaurant

2 Capuchin Yard, Off Church Street
Hereford HR1 2LT
Open: Mon–Sat 9.00–18.00

Tel: 01432–277 447

Vegetarian restaurant with several vegan options, including at least 3 main dishes which start at £4.50. Large selection of home made cakes also including vegan choices. Wine £7.50. Non smoking, but outside area where smoking is permitted. No credit cards.

Café 47 at Harveststore

Wholefood cafe & health food shop

47 Eign Gate
Hereford HR4 0AB
Open: Mon–Sat 9.00–17.30,
also pavement café March–Oct

Tel: 01432 268209

Wholefood café and take-away in a health food shop, with 75% of the menu vegetarian. Always something vegan too, and they have soya milk. Sandwiches from £2.50, baked potato £3.75 to eat in, main courses such as curries £3.95. Vegan burgers, £2.50. The shop sells vegan ice-cream. Non smoking. Visa, MC. 5% discount to Vegetarian and Vegan Society members.

Salad Bowl

99% vegetarian take–away and shop

30 Union Street
Hereford HR1 2BT
Open: Mon–Sat 9.00–17.30

Tel: 01432–355 712

Take away and shop which does a lot of vegetarian dishes, though little for vegans.

Oat Cuisine

Vegetarian cafe & take–away

47 Broad Street
Ross on Wye, Herefordshire HR9 7DY
Open: Mon–Sat 08.30–17.00, Sun 11.00–16.00

Tel: 01989 566 271
www.oatcuisine.uk.com
trevor@oatcuisine.uk.com

38 seat vegetarian café & takeaway. Several vegan items on menu. Main courses, £2.70–£3.95. Desserts, £1.35, including vegan options. 5% discount for Vegetarian Society members. Non smoking. No credit cards. Wheelchair accces..

Hay Wholefoods

Wholefood shop

1 Lion Street
Hay on Wye
Open: Mon–Sat 9.30–17.30

Tel: 01497 820708

Wholefood shop with some take–away but you need to get there early, and they have vegan ice–cream.

Fodder

Wholefood shop

26–27 Church Street
Hereford
Open: Mon–Sat 9–17.30

Tel: 01432 358171

Veggie wholefood shop with take–away sandwiches, pasties and Tofutti vegan ice–cream.

Holland & Barrett

Health food shop

1–2 Commercial Street
Hereford

Tel: 01432–370 662

Hertfordshire

King William IV

Omnivorous pub with Olde Worlde restaurant and quiet alcoves around the pub for a business lunch or something more romantic. Big vegetarian menu that you can view on their website.

10 main dishes, a couple of them vegan, £7.95–8.95, such as chestnut and leek cottage pie; nutty and date curry with basmati wild rice served with garlic and coriander naan bread; spicy three bean chilli in a corn cup with saffron scented rice; grilled field mushroom filled with Thai risotto; Mediterranean vegetable moussaka.

Desserts £4.95–£6.00.

Weekday lunchtime panini baguettes from £4.25. Jacket potatoes £4.95.

Reserve evenings, and lunchtime if you want a good table.

Omnivorous country pub and restaurant

Heydon
Royston
Hertfordshire SG8
On the main road through Heydon.
Tel: 01763 838773
Fax: 01763 837179

www.kingwilliv.freeuk.com

kingwilliv@freeuk.com

Open pub hours lunchtime and evening, food till 22.00

Car park

Children ok in restaurant except Saturday night, though they can eat in the bar

Some smoking areas, restaurant is no smoking

10 tables outside

MC, Visa

Cook's Delight

Vegetarian fair trade shop

360 High Street
Berkhamsted,Hertfordshire HP4 1HU
Open: Tue–Sat 9.00–19.00

Tel: 01442–863 584
www.organiccooksdelight.co.uk

Vegetarian organic fair trade shop with treatment rooms upstairs offering accupuncture, reflexology and massages, amongst others. Very aware of corporate social responsibility and everything is bought ethically including organic hemp and cotton clothing. Extensive range of fruit and veg, vegetarian alcohol, and some takeaway food items such as chilli bean or curry pies. They even have vegan hemp ice cream!

Holland & Barrett

Health food shop

Unit 187c The Marlowes Centre
Hemel Hempstead

Tel: 01442–211 356

Holland & Barrett

Health food shop

25/27 Birchley Green
Hertford

Tel: 01992–504 751

Holland & Barrett

Health food shop

99 Hermitage Road
Hitchin

Tel: 01462–451 643

Holland & Barrett

Health food shop

61 St Peters Street
St Albans

Tel: 01727–845 333

Holland & Barrett

Health food shop

Unit 44 Queensway
Stevenage

Tel: 01438–727 749

Isle of Wight

Just below Southampton and Portsmouth, in the centre of the south coast of England, is the Isle of Wight, the perfect escape from the mainland.

PASSENGER AND CAR FERRIES

Wightlink: Portsmouth to Ryde/Fisbourne and Lymington to Yarmouth
National rate 0870 582 7744
Portsmouth 02392–827 744
www.wightlink.co.uk

Red Funnel: Southampton to Cowes
023–8033 4010
www.redfunnel.co.uk

Hovertravel: Southsea to Ryde (foot passengers only)
Southsea 02392– 811 000
Ryde 01983–811 000

Island Line: railway from Ryde to Shanklin
Ryde 01983–811000
Southsea 023–9281 1000

GENERAL INFORMATION ABOUT THE ISLAND

www.islandbreaks.co.uk
01983–813 818

Brambles

Vegan
Bed and Breakfast

A warm, friendly welcome awaits you at Isle of Wight's only vegan B&B. Brambles is set in a quiet location only five minutes walk to miles of sandy beaches. There are two double ensuites (which can become family rooms) for £22 per person per night and two twin ensuites (which can be occupied by a single person) for £23 per person per night (or £25 for a single person). Cheaper rates for weekly stays and for children under twelve.

Breakfast begins with fresh fruit juice, cereal with soya or rice milk, soy yoghurt and fresh or dried fruit, followed by French bread or toast, and warm scones or soda bread with a selection of preserves. A cooked breakfast is available for £3 and could be veggie sausages, marinated mushrooms, tomatoes and toast. Various teas, coffee and Barley Cup are available.

Dinner is available by request for £12 and could be Potato Wedges with scoralia dip, followed by Special Occasion Tofu with basmati rice and fresh green salad. For dessert, Chocolate Orgy Pudding. Bring your own wine. Open to non-residents for dinner too. They can also make you a packed lunch for £4.50 which includes sandwiches, fruit juice or flavoured soya milk, fruit and a flapjack. 50-100% of the food is organic.

Shanklin town centre is only five minutes from Brambles, with its many interesting shops and lively theatre. It is an ideal location for ramblers and cyclists who will enjoy the magnificent countryside.

Tea and coffee making facilities, televisions, clock radios and hairdryers in the rooms. Guest lounge with TV.

10 Clarence Road
Shanklin
Isle of Wight PO37 7BH
England

Tel: 01983 862507

www.freespace.virgin.net/brambles.vegan

Email: brambles.vegan@virgin.net

Train Station: Shanklin, five minutes walk

Open: all year, except Christmas period

Directions: for foot passengers travelling from Portsmouth via Wightlink or from Southsea via Hovertravel, the Islands railway runs from Ryde through to Shanklin

Parking: available on road

Well behaved children welcome

No smoking

No pets

10% discount given to members of the Vegetarian Society, Vegan Society, Viva!, PETA, Animal Aid and people presenting this book, for stays of one week or more.

Seaward Guest House

Omnivorous
Guest House

Omnivorous guest house on the Isle of Wight, two minutes' walk from the hovercraft terminal, railway station (for ferry), and bus station.

Seven rooms: one double, one twin and two family rooms at £15–£18 per person per night, one single at 18–20 per night and two double ensuites at £18–£22 per night.

A veggie breakfast could be hash browns, tomatoes, mushrooms, baked beans and toast. You'll need to ask in advance for vegan margarine and soya milk.

Dinner is not offered but there are local pubs and restaurants with vegetarian choices. There is a Holland & Barrett on the High Street for snacks and picnic goodies.

Nearby are the pier, ice rink, ten pin bowling alley, swimming pool, bowling green, fun fair and dotto train. Parallel to George Street is Union Street, the main shopping area, which has gift shops, pubs, cafes and restaurants, as well as banks and a post office. A car or bus ride away are amusement parks, steam railway, Osborne House and Carisbrook Castle.

There is a ground floor room which has wheelchair access.

Tea and coffee making facilites, washbasins and televisions are in all the rooms.

Public telephone in the hall for guests' use. Iron, ironing board and hairdryer available.

14/16 George Street
Ryde
Isle of Wight PO33 2EW
England

Tel and Fax:
01983 563168
Mobile: 0787–929 6979

Email:
seaward@fsbdial.co.uk

Train station: Ryde
Esplanade, 200 yards

Open: all year

Children are welcome and they have a cot

Smoking in rooms only

Secure cycle storage

Directions: George Street is opposite Ryde bus and railway station. Seaward is about 100 yards up George Street on the right hand side.

Parking: on street unrestricted except for 10–12.00 noon Mon–Fri. Several public carparks within easy walking distance.

Dimbola Restaurant   Vegetarian restaurant

Julia Margaret Cameron Trust   *Tel: 01983–756 814*
Terrace Lane   *Fax: 01983–755578*
Freshwater   *www.dimbola.co.uk*
Isle of Wight PO40 9QE
Open: Tue–Sun 10–17.00, also Mon in school holidays

Vegetarian restaurant and tea rooms. Light meals for about £5 like soups, veggie burgers with salad, chips, cakes, some vegan. No alcohol. No smoking. Visa, MC. Dimbola Lodge is the former home of one of the first Victorian lady photographers. The centre contains photographic galleries, a small camera museum, studio, dark room, and they run courses. Admission charge £3.50 adults, children free under 16. But you don't have to go in to use the restaurant.

Cowes Health Food   Health food shop

8 High St   *Tel: 01983–282 070*
Cowes   *Open: Mon–Sat 9–17.00*

Prime Foods   Food shop

62 High Street   *Tel: 01983–291 111*
Cowes   *primefood@aol.com*
Open: every day 11–18.00, sometimes later,
and almost round the clock in Cowes week

Godshill Organics   Health food shop

Yard Parlour, Newport Rd
Godshill, Isle of Wight

Ralph's Health Foods   Health food shop

64/65 St James St   *Tel: 01983–522353*
Newport, Isle of Wight   *or 528627*
Open: Mon–Fri 8.30–17.30 , Sat –17.00, closed Sun

Health food shop with lots of vegetarian pasties, plus both Swedish Glace and Tofutti vegan ice–cream.

Holland & Barrett   Health food shop

52 Upper St James St   *Tel: 01983–522 121*
Newport, Isle of Wight and   *and*
1 High Street   *Tel: 01983–565 257*
Ryde

Kent

Roydon Hall

Tudor Manor house with many original sixteenth century features. It is set in ten acres of woodlands and lawns with a magnificent view of the Weald of Kent. There is a large selection of rooms – singles, doubles, twins and families, all available with or without ensuite facilities. For a single room, prices range from £30–£50 per night, twins and doubles £40–£65 per room per night and triple/family rooms £55–£75 per room per night.

A continental breakfast is served. Vegan margarine and soy milk available. Dinner is offered from £8 and could be Baked Tomato with nut and millet stuffing, ginger squash sauce, confetti rice and green beans. They are open to non residents for dinner. Lunch is also available by arrangement. As much organic produce as possible is used.

Roydon Hall lies on the Greensand Way, a long distance footpath stretching from Hythe to Dorking and beyond. It is also within easy walking distance of the Weald Way and the North Downs Way. Half an hour's drive away, you'll find Leeds Castle, Bodiam Castle, Scotney Castle and Penshurst Place. The historic town of Royal Tunbridge Wells, the Medway towns, and the cathedral city of Canterbury are also within easy reach.

Roydon Hall caters for conferences and public events with accommodation for up to thirty people. It is also a centre for teaching Transcendental Meditation.

Tea and coffee making in the rooms and wasbasins in some.

Vegetarian
Guest House

Roydon Hall Road
East Peckham
Tonbridge
Kent TN12 5NH
England

Tel: 01622 812121

Fax: 01622 813959

Email: roydonhall@
btinternet.com

Train Station: Paddock Wood, five miles, then taxi

Open: all year, except Christmas, New Year and Easter

Directions: less than one hour's drive from central London off the M20. Phone for a brochure which contains detailed directions.

Parking: available

Children welcome and they have cots

No pets

No smoking throughout

The India Restaurant

Omnivorous Indian
Restaurant

Omnivorous Indian restaurant close to the ferry terminal with a dozen vegetarian and vegan dishes, but they can prepare any other traditional Indian dish with prior notice. Freshly cooked and grease free food is a speciality and they don't use any animal fat or butter ghee though vegans should watch for butter in the naan bread or parathas. They even have vegan dessert which is unusual for an Indian restaurant.

*1 Old High Street
Folkestone
Kent CT20 1RJ*

Tel: 01303-259 155

*Open:
Tue–Sun 12.00–14.00
& 18.00–22.30,
closed Mon*

Start with vegetable or tomato soup £2.50, samosa £2.50, onion pakora £2.25.

Main course vegetable biryani with pillau rice mixed with vegetables £5.25. Vegetable side dishes £2.15 like spinach, mushroom bhajia, okra, cauliflower, potatoes with peas, Bombay alu, plain or Tarka daal (lentils), chana masalla (chick peas). Green salad £1.50. Rices from £1.50.

If you're heading for France through the tunnel, get in the mood with French ratatouille provençale with tomatoes, courgettes, aubergines, garlic and basil for £4.95.

Various desserts £1.75–2.25 including lemon sorbet.

Tea or coffee £1. Irish (with whisky), French or Calypso coffee £2.95.

French and German spoken.

The Fig Café

Virtually vegan and organic café based in an art gallery, centrally and picturesquely located near the sea. All food and cakes are vegan apart from cow's milk for tea/coffee. Menu changes every two days.

Deluxe muesli breakfast with banana and soya yoghurt for £2.95. Several baguettes £3.25 with fillings such as avocado, tomato and onion. Main dishes such as mild vegetable coconut and apricot curry with rice £4.95. Snacks and light meals including watercress soup, and hot tortilla chips with salsa and avocado dip £3.95.

Vegan ice cream and homemade cakes, lemon, apricot and almond, and chocolate, £1.95.
Organic juices and smoothies. Wine is available with meals for a donation for the gallery in which the café is housed.

**Virtually Vegan
Organic Cafe**

*The Metropole Galleries
The Leas
Folkestone
Kent CT20 2LS*

Tel: 01303 211379

www.thefigjohnchip.com

*Open:
Tue–Sun 10.00–17.00,
phone to confirm*

Small children's menu

*No smoking
No credit cards*

*10% discount to members
of the Vegetarian or
Vegan Society and people
presenting this book
They can adapt for special
diets with advance notice*

Brockhill Country Park

Amazingly good value vegetarian café in a 54 acre park which includes a lake, children's play area and a beautiful valley. Great for picnicking, or eat in the café.

Mexican or Tandoori bean burgers £1.50 in a bun with salad. Avocado salad, garlic bread, Greek salad (can be with vegan cheese) £1.90, chips, even veggie sausages with chips and beans. Organic wholewheat pasta £1.40. Soups in Spring and Autumn 80p with a roll.

Swedish Glace and Tofutti ice-cream which they make cornets from. Tea 40p, coffee 60p, fruit juices.

**Vegetarian
Cafe**

*Sandling Road
nr Saltwood
nr Hythe
Kent CT21 4HL*

Tel: 07798 752555

*Open: Easter–Halloween
every dry day 11–17.00;
park open every day but
Xmas 9–19.00 or dusk*

*Directions:
Junction 11 off the M20
but poorly signposted,
aim for Saltwood not
Hythe or you'll miss it.*

Cornerstone Wholefood Restaurant   Omnivorous

25a High Street
Ashford, Kent
Open: Tue–Sat 10.00–17.30

Tel: 01233 642 874

Wholefood restaurant with many vegetarian dishes. Mains such as quiches, flans, pastas , £4.55 with baked potato and salad. Non smoking. Visa, MC.

Canterbury Environment Centre Café   Vegetarian café

The Canterbury Environment Centre
St Alphege Lane
Canterbury
Kent CT1 2EB
Open: Tue–Sat 10.00–16.00

Tel: 01227–457 009
cantenv@talk21.com

Vegetarian café based in the Canterbury environment centre which is set within a medieval church. Nothing over £2.70 with jacket potatoes starting at £1.80, but not much else for vegans. Non smoking. No credit cards.

Café des Amis   Omnivorous International Restaurant

93 St Dunstan Street
Canterbury
Open: Mon–Thu 12–22.00, Fri–Sat 12–22.30, Sun 12–21.30

Tel: 01227–464 390

Busy omnivorous restaurant with Mexican, French, Japanese and North African influences. Main courses range between £6.95–£12.95, they always have vegetarian options and can adapt items for vegans. Near Westgate Towers. Smoking section. Visa, MC.

Canterbury Wholefoods   Vegetarian Cafe & Wholefood Shop

1–2 Jewry Lane
Canterbury
www.canterbury–wholefoods.co.uk
info@canterbury–wholefoods.co.uk
Open: Shop Mon–Sat 9.00–18.00, Café 10–17.00

Tel: 01227–464 623

Wholefood co-op shop with a vegetarian café upstairs. Fresh bread baked daily, cruelty free toiletries, organic fruit and vegetables, lots of supplements and free delivery service in Kent if your order is worth £30 or more. Eat in the licensed café for no more than £5, which caters for vegans and special diets. Non smoking. Visa, MC.

Health House
Vegetarian cafe

116 High Street
Chatham
Kent ME4 4BY
Open: Mon–Sat till 9–16.00, closed Sun

Tel: 01634 409 291

Vegetarian café opposite Argos, with bakes, soups and salads. Sandwiches £1.50–1.70. Some vegan food, including the soup and some cakes.

Holland & Barrett Restaurant
Vegetarian cafe & shop

80 Sandgate Road
Folkestone
Kent CT20 2AA
Open: Mon–Sat 9.30–17.00 closed Sunday

Tel: 01303 243 646

Wholefood vegetarian café and take away in a Holland and Barrett shop. Selection of 6 salads 50p–£2.70, Bakes, baked potatoes etc. £1–£2.10. And for that sweet tooth they have fruit tarts, cheesecakes £1.25–£1.55. Non smoking. No credit cards.

Blackthorn Trust Café
Vegetarian cafe

Blackthorn Medical Centre
St Andrew's Road
Maidstone, Kent ME16 9AN
Open: Mon–Fri 10.00–15.00 (12.00–14.00 for lunch)

Tel: 01622–725 585
Fax: 01622–725 774
www.blackthorn.org.uk
(no menu)
info@blackthorn.org.uk

Vegetarian café based behind medical centre. Soup from £1.50, mains from £3.75 and desserts from £1.75. Can cater for vegans, coeliacs and other special diets on request. Non smoking. No credit cards.

El Loco
Omnivorous Mexican restaurant

Oxford Street
Whitstable
Open: Tue–Sat 19–22.30, last food orders 22.00

Tel: 01227–771914

Mexican restaurant with plenty of vegetarian food, mostly cheesey, on the site of the old veggie restaurant Beanies. Vegans can have a vegetarian burrito £7 with lots of vegetables like aubergines plus beans, all cooked with sunflower oil – just ask them to leave the cheese out. House wine from £7.50 a bottle. Smoking allowed but they'll seat non-smokers nearer the door. Visa, MC, Amex.

Holland & Barrett

Health food shop

87 High Street
Ashford
Kent TN24 8SQ

Tel: 01233 620392

41 High Street
Canterbury
Kent CT1 2RY

Tel: 01227–787 861

35 Biggin Street
Dover
Kent CT16 1BU

Tel: 01304–241 426

80 Sandgate Road
Folkstone
Kent CT20 2AA

Tel: 01303–243 646

8 St Georges Centre
Gravesend
Kent DA11 OTA

Tel: 01474–321 838

Unit 345, Dukes Walk, Chequers Centre
Maidstone
Kent ME15 9AS

Tel: 01622–765 277

10 The Centre
Margate
Kent CT9 1JG

Tel: 01843–228 131

219 High Street
Orpington
Kent BR6 OLZ

Tel: 01689–874 773

15 The High Street
Ramsgate
Kent CT11 9AB

Tel: 01843–852 568

Unit SU22 Blighs Walk
Sevenoaks
Kent TN13 7DB

Tel: 01732–465 061

23 Mount Pleasant Road
Tunbridge Wells
Kent TN1 1NT

Tel: 01892–533 077

Lancashire

Cameo Hotel

Omnivorous hotel

30 Hornby Road
Blackpool
Lancashire FY1 4QG
www.cameo-hotel.co.uk
janetandphil@cameo-hotel.co.uk
11 rooms, from £16 per person b&b,
£110 weekly b&b with evening meal

Tel: 01253 626144
Fax: 01253 296048
Open: all year

New vegetarian owned hotel, though not actually vegetarian but they'd love to be if they can get enough of us. Close to the Tower, seafront, piers, Winter Gardens and town centre. Smoking allowed in rooms. No credit cards.

Wildlife Hotel

vegan hotel

39 Woodfield Road
Blackpool
Lancashire FY1 6AX
Open: 12 room, all en suite,
£20 per person per night

Tel: 01253 346143

The only vegan hotel in Blackpool, animal rights folk especially welcome. Evening meal when available £6, vegan wine available. No smoking throughout. No credit cards. Dogs by arrangement. TV in rooms and in the lounge. Close to pleasure beach and those wonderful trams, between central and south piers. 10% discount for VSUK & Vegan Soc, Animal Aid, PETA and Viva members.

Lennard's Eating House

Omnivorous restaurant

8 Deansgate
Blackpool
Open: Mon–Sat 8.30–17.30

Tel: 01253–628 167

Omnivorous restaurant with a separate vegetarian menu featuring some vegan options. Mains from £4 such as nut and lentil roast and desserts from £1.45 with non dairy choice amongst the offerings. smoking section. No credit cards.

Surya Vegetarian Restaurant

Indian vegetarian

98 Derby Street
Bolton
Lancashire BL3 6HG
Open: Mon–Fri 11.30–14.30, 16.00–23.00,
Sat & Sun 12.00–23.00

Tel: 01204–380 679

Very vegan friendly Indian vegetarian restaurant with dishes from throughout the sub continent. Starters, £1.50–£4, with samosas and kachoris, and mains from £2–£6.99 with stir fried aubergines, dosas and spinach daal. All day buffet for £6.99. Plan to introduce menu with vegan items clearly indicated. Desserts, £2, including they tell us, vegan gulab jamun. Licenced with house wine from £4.89 for a bottle. Private function room and outside catering available. Separate smoking section. Visa, MC. Offer 20% discount to members of Vegetarian and Vegan Societies.

Patagonia Cafe

Omnivorous café

116 Bradshawgate
Bolton
Lancashire BL2 1AY
Open: Mon–Sat 9.00–17.00

Tel: 01204–528 533
Fax: 01204 528533

Omnivorous café that considers itself a cross over for mixed families with members from all camps. Half the menu is vegetarian, everything is under £5 and there is always something vegan. Non smoking. No credit cards.

Sokrates

Omnivorous Greek

80–84 Winter Hey Lane, Horwich
Bolton, Lancashire BL6 7NZ
Open: every day 18–22.30 last orders

Tel: 01204 668033

Omnivorous traditional Greek restaurant, with lots of vegetarian dishes. Around £8–16 for dinner. House wine £11, glass £1.90. Visa, MC, Amex, Diners. No smoking room. Children welcome. Reservations advised.

Red Triangle Cafe

Vegetarian restaurant

160 St James Street
Burnley
Lancashire BB11 1NR
Open: Tues–Sat 10.30–19.00,
Fri & Sat night 19.30–22.30 (only open for
bookings in evenings). closed Sun & Mon

Tel: 01282–832 319

Vegetarian café and restaurant that also has occasional music nights. Mains £3.25 during the day and £5.50 in evenings. Always something vegan including a few desserts. House wine £5.50 for a bottle, £1.30 glass. Non smoking. No credit cards.

The Jigsaw Pantry

Vegetarian restaurant

33 Moor Lane
Clitheroe
Lancashire BB7 1BE
Open: Tue & Thu–Fri 9.00–17.00, Wed 9.00–14.00,
Sat 9.00–16.00

Tel: 01200–443 916
Fax: 01254–398 843

Vegetarian wholefood and organic restaurant which involves local schools in education in diet and nutrition. Lite bites, 65p–£1.65, such as toasted fruit loaf, bagels and homemade soup. Sandwiches from £2.10 include hummus with carrot and coriander salad and toasted roasted vegetables sandwich for £2.50. Jacket potatoes from £2.50 with filling and side salad. Can cater for special diets – gluten-free, wheat-free and vegans. Non smoking. Will soon be able to accept credit cards.

Vegetarian Restaurant (Jim's Caff)

Vegetarian restaurant

19–21 New Market Street
Colne
Lancashire BB8 9BJ
Tel: 01282 868 828
Open: Open: Thu–Sun 19–23.00

Tel: 01282 868 828

Licensed vegetarian restaurant with world food influences. Specials such as Peruvian mountain potatoes and okonomiyaki (Japanese stuffed pancake), £6.45. Always something vegan but can offer more variety with advance notice including for dessert options. Smoking permitted. No credit cards.

The Whale Tail

Vegetarian cafe

78a Penny Street
Lancaster
Lancashire LA1 1XN
Open: Mon–Fri 9.00–16.00, Sat 9.00–17.00,
Sun 10.30–15.00

Tel: 01524 845 133

Vegetarian café which always has vegan options available. Soups at £2.10 and mains for £2.85–£4.75. Have vegan chocolate cake, £1.50. House wine £8 for a bottle, £2 glass. Non smoking inside but have a patio garden. No credit cards.

Waterslack Tearoom

Omnivorous tea room

Waterslack Garden Centre
Silverdale
Lancashire LA5 OUU

Tel: 01524–701 862

Tea room based in garden centre. Can cater for vegetarians with mains including quiches, jacket potatoes, £3.50.

Bear Cafe

Vegetarian café

29 Rochdale Road
Todmorden
Lancashire OL14 7LA
Open: Mon, Wed–Sat 9.30–17.00, Tue 9.30–15.30,
Fri & Sat 18.00–21.00

Tel: 01706–813 737

Vegetarian café above a wholefood shop. Café serves light meals and snacks with sandwiches from £1.75, Mexican, Greek and Italian ciabattas at £3, various wraps, plated salads, jacket potatoes and mini flans. Plenty for vegans with almost everything having a vegan alternative – such as a Ploughman's lunch with vegan cheese, £2.75. In their desserts they are famous for their vegan hot chocolate cake, £1.60, which can be served with non dairy cream or ice cream. Friday and Saturday nights they stay open as a tapas bar, average £15 for 2 people, BYO or buy from their choice of organic and vegetarian wines and beers from the shop below. Additionally, they have ongoing exhibitions in the café which change every 6 weeks. Child friendly with books, toys and baby changing facilities. Can cater for private functions. The shop stocks everything wholefoody and lots of cruelty free items. Separate smoking area. No credit cards.

Holland & Barrett

Health food shop

3 Cobden Court
Blackburn

Tel: 01254 693010

33 Corporation Street
Blackpool

Tel: 01253 299393

26 Newport Street
Bolton

Tel: 01204 385954

33 The Mall
Burnley

Tel: 01282–459 833

26 Penny Street
Lancaster

Tel: 01524–848 633

24 Euston Road
Morecombe

Tel: 01524–401 383

Lower Mall, 37 The Spindles Shopping Centre
Oldham

Tel: 0161–622 0180

Unit 1, 13 Friargate Walk, St Georges Centre
Preston

Tel: 01772–259 357

Unit 51 Market Wa, y, Rochdale Exchange
Rochdale

Tel: 01706–353 445

97/99 Princess Street
Stockport

Tel: 0161–480 2314

Leicestershire
Leicester

Leicester is a great place for vegetarians to live and visit, as it has a good range of veggie eateries, possibly due to the large populations of Hindus, Jains and students who live here.

Leicester city centre has a lot of character, with more small shops than chain stores, and lots of lovely old buildings, but it certainly isn't quaint. It is a small city, yet has good facilities, including a huge library, friendly pubs and possibly the largest outdoor market in Britain, where you can buy very cheap fruit and veg, textiles and clothes. There are several large parks on the edges of the city centre, plus a canal, which runs from North to South through the middle of the city.

There is a strong green movement in Leicester, and cycling paths are better than average, though air pollution can be a big problem in hot weather. The city also seems to have a strong spiritual feel.

by Ronny

Leicestershire Backpacker's Hostel

Omnivorous
Hostel

Small warm hostel catering for the 16–26 age group only. There are two rooms; one with three beds and one with two. Prices for B&B are £8 per person per night if you stay for two nights or more or £10 if staying for one night only. Your seventh night is free. There is also a summer house which can sleep five. Bedding is included in the price.

Breakfast is a large home-made roll with any filling and tea or coffee. Veggies and vegans are catered for. A full cooked breakfast is available for £2. Richard, the proprietor is almost veggie and bakes vegetarian white bread and vegan wholemeal bread as well as vegan cakes. Dinner is available for £4 and there is always a veggie or vegan option but it helps to let him know in advance if you are. Near the hostel are late opening shops, takeaways and a pub.

The hostel backs on to Watermead Park, a wetland area with lakes and ponds. It is a great place to watch wildlife, walk, jog, cycle or have a picnic. You can walk through the park and Riverside Way, past three pubs to visit the National Space Science Centre and Victorian Pumping station.

Half a mile from Birstall village is Charnwood forest, a great place for walking and cycling.

Leicester is only three miles away and there are several buses there every day.

Some form of photo ID is required to stay. Unlimited hot water. Check in after 5pm unless otherwise arranged. No self-catering.

157 Wanlip Lane
Birstall
Leicester
Leicestershire LE4 4GL
England

Tel: 0116 267 3107

Train Station: Leicester, 3 miles, then bus

No curfew, so can arrive late, but owner does not want people coming and going in the early hours during their stay in case they disturb other guests

Directions:
Birstall is 3 miles north of Leicester on the A6. In Birstall look for the Somerfield store at no.1 Wanlip Lane. From M1 and A46, go through Wanlip village to Birstall.

No parking, although there is a layby opposite where cars can be left at owners' risk

No smoking

Mirch Masala

Family oriented Indian vegetarian restaurant with Mexican, Italian and South Indian menus and several pizzas.

South Indian starters from £1.90–£3.25, such as kachoris – spiced crushed lentil balls covered in deep fried pastry, and pani puri – crispy puri filled with potatoes and chickpeas served with tamarind chutney and coriander mix.

Main dishes include favourites like masala dosa, £4.60; idli sambhar – flat rice and lentil flour cakes served with coconut chutney and sambhar (lentil soup); and mixed vegetable curry, £3.95.

6 Italian menu mains with Mirch Masala special spaghetti £4.50.

Large Mexican menu with various starters including nachos £3.45, and burritos, tacos, enchiladas, £3.75–£5.25 as mains.

They also have wraps for £3.75 with fillings ranging from herb and garlic to Mexican rice or chilli.

The snack menu includes jacket potatoes from £1.20, corn on the cob £1.40, vegetable burgers, chips and toasted sandwiches £1.99–£2.25.Pizzas for takeaway only £10.95–£16.65.

Weekday lunchtime specials, with a choice of one of three meals with a drink from £2.50.

Fully licensed plus a fresh juice bar with smoothies.

*Unit 19/20 Belgrave
Commercial Centre
Belgrave Road
Leicester
Leicestershire LE4 5AV*

Tel: 0116–261 0888

*Open:
Mon–Sun from 11am*

*Small children's menu
High chairs*

*Non smoking inside but
small outside seating area
where it is permitted.*

Visa, MC

England **LEICESTERSHIRE** Restaurants

Bobby's

Indian vegetarian restaurant

154 Belgrave Road
Leicester
Leicestershire LE4 5AT
Open: Tue–Sun 11–22.00 (Fri–Sat 22.30), closed Mon

Tel: 0116 266 0106

Indian vegetarian restaurant with some vegan curries, chapattis and snacks.

Chaat House

Indian vegetarian restaurant

108 Belgrave Road
Leicester
Open: Wed–Mon 12.00–20.30

Tel: 0116–2660 513

Indian vegetarian restaurant. There is no such thing as bad Indian food in Leicester which has curry houses everywhere. However there is such a thing as outstanding Indian food which you'll find here being munched by the local vegetarian Buddhists, Hindus, Sikhs and vegan Jains. Mains from £8. Non smoking. Visa, MC.

Good Earth Restaurant

Vegetarian restaurant

19 Free Lane
Leicester
good.earth–restaurant@virgin.net
Open: Mon–Fri 10–15.00, Sat 10–16.00

Tel: 0116–262 6260

Vegetarian buffet style restaurant which always has something vegan. Salads, £2.25–£2.95, and mains, £2.95–£3.95. Desserts, £1.75. Separate smoking section. No credit cards.

Pizza Pride

Vegetarian fast food

21 Melton Road
Leicester
Leicestershire
Open: Tue–Thu 11–15.00, 16.15–21.00, Fri 11–
15.00, 16.15–22.00, Sat 12–15.00, 16.15–22.00,
Sun 16.00–22.00

Tel: 0116–2669 522

Vegetarian pizza take–away and delivery which also does burgers, chips and jacket potatoes, from £1.20. Pizza bases are vegan and they can make them without cheese. Pizzas start at £3 for an 8 inch pizza, £1.50 when they run special offers. No credit cards.

Sayonara Thali Restaurant

Indian vegetarian restaurant

49 Belgrave Road
Leicester
Open: All week 12.00–21.30, Sat till 22.00

Tel: 0116–266 5888

Indian vegetarian restaurant and take away, choice of 50 starters from £2.25, all the usual mains from £7 and always vegan options. Separate smoking section. Visa, MC.

Sharmilee Restaurant

Indian vegetarian restaurant

71–73 Belgrave Road
Leicester LE4 6AS
Open: Tue–Fri 12–14.30, 18.00–21.00, Sat 12–
21.30, Sun 12–21.00

Tel: 01162 610503
Fax: 01162 681383

Indian vegetarian restaurant and take away. All the usual favourites. Can adapt items for vegans.

Sonal's Bhajiya House

Indian vegetarian restaurant

122 Narborough Road
Leicester LE3 0BT
Open: Wed–Mon 14.00–21.30, closed Tue

Tel: 0116–2470 441

Vegetarian Indian restaurant with vegan food too.

The Whole Truth

Vegetarian cafe

19 Belvoir Street
Leicester
Open: Tue–Sat 9.00–16.00, open for gourmet
evenings fortnightly, call to confirm.

Tel: 0116–254 2722
www.flavourlines.com/wt

Friendly alternative vegetarian and vegan café. Starters from £3, and mains, £4.50–£6, such as Mexican pancakes and chickpea and sweet potato casserole. Desserts, £1–£3, with vegan chocolate cake and organic apple strudels. Non smoking. No credit cards. Also do outside catering for functions for 15–150 people, for weddings, parties etc and plan to develop and extend the service.

Oriental Chinese
Chinese omnivorous restaurant

70 High Street
Leicester
Open: every day 12–15.00, 17.30–23.30

Tel: 0116–2532 448

Omnivorous Chinese restaurant with lots of vegetarian dishes such as stir–fried veg, crispy veg with chili and garlic, monk's veg, bean curd, £3–4 per dish. House wine £8 a bottle, £2 glass. Smoking and non-smoking sections. Visa, MC. Free home delivery take–away.

Currant Affairs
Vegetarian and vegan natural food

9A Loseby Lane
Leicester LE1 5DR
Open: Mon–Sat 9.00–17.30, closed Sunday

Tel: 0116–251 0887

Vegetarian and vegan natural food store with onsite bakery and an emphasis on using organic ingredients. Vegan takeaway snacks such as tomato and garlic sausage rolls, mexican pasties, 70p–95p. Have a range of vegan cakes including carrot and almond, 65p a slice.

Holland & Barrett
Health food shop

5–6 Humberston Mall
Haymarket Centre
Leicester LE1 3YB

Tel: 0116–251 6270

33 The Horsefair Street
Leicester LE1 3BP

Tel: 0116–262 1547

11 Manor Walk
Market Harborough
Leicestershire LE16 9BX

Tel: 01858–431 250

Lincolnshire

Maud Foster Windmill

Vegetarian cafe

Willoughby Road
Boston
Lincolnshire PE21 9EG
Open: Wed 10–17.00, Sat 11–17.00, Sun 13–17.00,
in addition in July & August Thu & Fri 11–17.00

Tel: 01205 352188

Vegetarian café serving light meals and snacks throughout the day and occasionally open evenings, phone to check. Meals from £2.50–£5, such as Chinese mushroom soup and vegetable fajitas. Always vegan choices available. Cakes from £1. Non smoking. Visa, MC. Offer 10% discount to members of the Vegetarian Society.

Jew's House

French/International restaurant

15 The Strait
Lincoln, Lincolnshire LN2 1JD
rolandbainbridge@yahoo.co.uk
Open: Mon–Sat 12–14.30 18.30–21.30;
Sun 12–16.00

Tel: 01522 524851

French and international omnivorous restaurant in the Jew's House, a twelfth century stone built house and one of the oldest buildings in Europe. Good selection of vegetarian dishes. Menu changes every two months. Evening starters £6.25 such as puy lentils, artichoke and chick peas with canals of guacamole and herb salad; main course £10.25 like baked avocado with vine cherry tomatoes and timbale of black rice. If a vegan books ahead or just turns up, the chef can provide something. Desserts £5.75, and the summe fruit champagne jelly is vegan. House wine £10.95 bottle, £2.95 glass. No smoking in the dining areas, but there's a separate lounge where you can smoke. MC, Visa, Diners, Amex. Children welcome but no high chair. Car park opposite. In the centre of Lincoln, close to the cathedral.

Holland & Barrett

Health food shop

47 Market Place *Boston PE21 6NF*	Tel: 01205 359712
61 Friargate, Freshney Place Shopping Centre *Grimsby DN31 1ED*	Tel: 01472–344 115
319 High Street *Lincoln LN5 7DW*	Tel: 01522–567 615
37 High Street *Scunthorpe DN15 6SB*	Tel: 01724–278 157
37 Lumley Road *Skegness PE25 3LL*	Tel: 01754–764 412

London

This chapter includes a selection of key places from our 384 page book *Vegetarian London*. (available from all central London bookshops, Planet Organic and Fresh & Wild supermarkets, and Country Life wholefood shop, any UK, US or Canada bookshop, and mail order from www.vegetarianguides.com)

We start with veggie-friendly **accommodation (page 238)** from camping to five star hotel. This is all you need before coming to London.

Next we list dozens of fabulous venues to eat out and shop in the **West End – Soho and Covent Garden (page 250),** the central area to the south of Oxford Street, where visitors normally spend the majority of time. Here there are a hundred cinemas and theatres, shopping galore, cafes and sightseeing. A two page munchie map enables you to locate the closest place in seconds. Some of the most popular and good value veggie eateries include the all-you-can-eat buffets for £6 at **Tai** in Greek Street and £4.99 at **Govinda's** off Soho Square. Don't miss the new falafel bar **Maoz** at 43 Old Compton Street, where you can fill up for only £3.

Then we cover the veggie treasures of the lesser known areas that estate agents have started calling **Noho (north of Oxford Street, page 262) – Marylebone/Fitzrovia,** from Oxford Street in the south to Madame Tussaud's and Regents Park in the north, and **Bloomsbury,** where you'll find the British Museum. These are ideal for tanking up before catching a train north at Euston or Kings Cross.

Finally we list a selection of terrific restaurants and stores outside the centre in the **Rest of London (page 271),** chosen from the 120 vegetarian restaurants and 150 shops covered in detail in *Vegetarian London*. These are either close to our accommodation recommendations, on main roads into London, or simply so good that they're worth a special journey.

London is truly the vegetarian capital of Europe. Have a great trip.

by Alex Bourke

London Accommodation

Guest Houses and Hotels

Hostels

Campsites

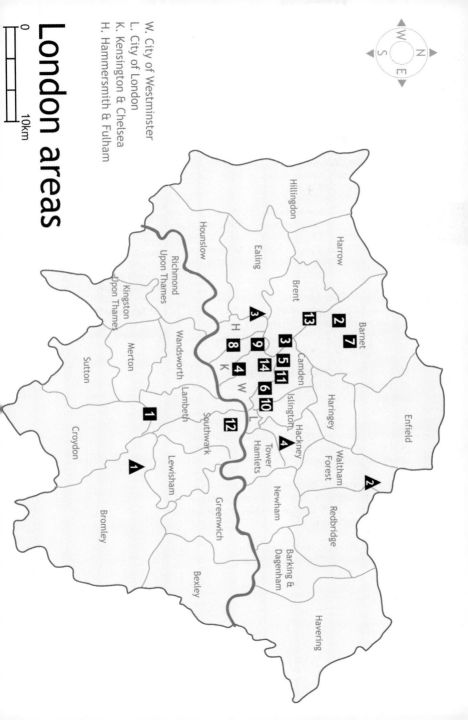

London areas

0 ——— 10km

W. City of Westminster
L. City of London
K. Kensington & Chelsea
H. Hammersmith & Fulham

Hampstead Village Guest House

Veggie friendly 1872 Victorian guest house in a peaceful setting close to the heath and tube. In the heart of lively Hampstead Village, a fun area with art cinema, restaurants with veggie food, coffee shops and pubs.

The large, very comfortable rooms are full of character with sitting area, writing desk, remote control TV, hairdryer, iron, fridge (brilliant for veggies), kettle, telephone, books and even a hot-waterbottle to cuddle.

En suite double £84, en suite single £66. Double £72, singles £48 and £54. Large studio with kitchen and shower £90 for 1, £120 for 2, £138 for 3, £150 for 4, £162 for 5. Parking £10 per day.

Optional breakfast £7 from 8.00 a.m., 9.00 at weekends until late, can be in the garden in summer and you can invite guests.

Booking requires credit card, pay on arrival in cash, sterling (travellers) cheques or credit card (5% surcharge).

No meals except breakfast, but there are veggie restaurants and a wholefood store in the area and veggie dishes in other nearby restaurants.

www.HampsteadGuesthouse.com
info@HampsteadGuesthouse.com

Veggie friendly hotel

2 Kemplay Road
Hampstead
London NW3 1SY

Tel:
020–7435 8679

Fax:
020–7794 0254

Tube:
Hampstead

5 rooms from
£48–66 single,

£72 upwards for double

No smoking anywhere

HAMPSTEAD VILLAGE GUESTHOUSE

2 Kemplay Road, Hampstead
London NW3 1SY

www.hampsteadguesthouse.com
tel: +44 (0)20 7435 8679 **Fax:** +44 (0)20 7794 0254
e-mail: info@hampsteadguesthouse.com

- Peaceful setting, close to Hampstead Heath, yet in the heart of lively Hampstead Village.

- Close to underground and bus. Centre of London in 10 minutes.

- Large rooms full of character, plus modern amenities: TV, kettle and direct-dial telephone.

- Breakfast in the garden, weather permitting.

- Accomodation from £48.

- No smoking.

"If you're looking for something a little different, make a beeline for Annemarie van der Meer's Hampstead home."

Chosen as one of the "Hotels of the Year". The Which? Hotel Guide 2000.

Temple Lodge

Temple Lodge is a quiet oasis in the middle of London. There are five single rooms at £30 per night or £195 per week and three twin rooms at £50 per room per night or £330 per week.

A hearty continental breakfast is served. Soya milk and vegan margarine are available on request.

You won't have to walk far for lunch or dinner as **The Gate** vegetarian restaurant is on the same premises. (closed Sunday)

Visitors are invited to join in with activities of the Christian Community and will have the opportunity of joining the Temple Lodge Club for a nominal fee. The house offers many facilities for the use of guests, such as a kitchen, a quiet and secluded garden and a large library.

The house is thought to be built on the foundations of a seventeenth century building. Attempts have been made to restore the house and garden to its former glory.

All major tourist attractions are reached easily by public transport. Pleasant walks along the River Thames are easily accessible. Historical houses, Kew Gardens, the Waterfowl sanctuary of the Wetlands Centre and three theatres are all within walking distance.

Children aged six and over only.

Washbasins in rooms.

No smoking throughout.

Vegetarian
Bed and Breakfast

51 Queen Caroline Street
Hammersmith
London W6 9QL
England

Tel: 020 87488388

Fax: 020 87488322

Tube Station:
Hammersmith, 5 minutes

Open: all year

Directions: By car, directly from the west along A4/M4 and from westerly directions along A3 and A40. The North/South Circular Roads give access from other directions.

Parking: metered parking available on the street.

The Lanesborough

Magnificent central luxury hotel, popular with veggie rock and movie stars and C.E.O.'s. 25 singles ensuite £265, executive single £320. 24 doubles and 3 twins £370, executive £450. 46 suites: junior £570, executive junior £705, small suite £780, medium £1060, large £1600, Royal suite £4500 with 3 bedrooms, dining room, kitchen, personal butler, chauffeur and Bentley. Rates include tax and service.

If a veggie/vegan breakfast is required you should give notice at the time of booking. Breakfast can be served in your room.

24 hour butler service for all rooms, includes (un)packing, assistance with co-ordination of social and business itineraries. Change of clothing pressed on arrival. In room services include CD and DVD players, e-mail, internet, MS-Office and printer, mobile phones for use throughout the hotel, private telephone line, dedicated fax machine, voicemail. Suites have mobiles which operate throughout Europe. Digital music library, on screen film library. Fitness studio, local health club membership, business center.

The in-house restaurant **The Conservatory** (also 5 private dining rooms) features a separate gourmet vegetarian menu, prepared under the supervision of celebrity chef and top food writer Paul Gayler. Choice of 12 hot and cold appetisers £9–15 such as spicy sweet potato fritters with sweet chili sauce; artichoke, French bean and mushroom salad with pumpkin seed dressing. 8 main dishes £17–19.50 such as Champagne risotto with artichoke fritters; pumpkin and ginger spring rolls, Asian stir fry. Extensive dessert menu £8–10.50 includes sorbets for vegans. House wine £6 glass, £22 bottle. Beer £4.90, coffee £4.90.

Hyde Park Corner
Knightsbridge
London SW1X 7TA

Tel:
020–7259 5599
Fax:
020–7259 5606

Tube:
Hyde Park Corner
5 minutes by taxi from
Victoria rail station

Very close to Hyde Park
and Buckingham Palace

www.lanesborough.com
info@lanesborough.com
www.stregis.com

Parking £4 per hour or
£30 overnight

Smoking allowed

Children welcome

Pets accepted

There is live music every
night and dancing on
Friday and Saturday
nights.

For reservations in USA
call toll free
1–800 999 1828,
fax 1–800 937 8278
or St Regis reservations
877–STREGIS
(877–787 3447)

Dora Rothner B&B

Vegetarian B&B in a friendly home twenty minutes by tube from central London.

There are three rooms: one single and two doubles costing £18 per person per night.

A light breakfast is served and includes fresh grapefruit, muesli, a selection of cereals, and toast with various jams. Soya milk, vegan margarine and vegan muesli are available.

Dinner is not offered but Rani Indian Vegetarian restaurant is just a few minutes away.

The B&B is close to shops, bus routes and the tube station. It is set in a well kept garden overlooking the park.

All rooms have televisions.

No children or pets.

No smoking throughout.

**Vegetarian
Bed and Breakfast**

*23 The Ridgeway
Finchley
London N3 2PG
England*

Tel: 020 83460246

Tube Station: Finchley Central (Northern Line), then an eight minute walk.

Open: all year

Directions: Close to Finchley Central tube, the North Circular Road and the M1.

Parking: available

Stephanie Rothner B&B

Friendly B&B with a well kept garden on a quiet residential road. There is one single room and one double room both costing £16 per person per night.

A light breakfast is served comprising of fresh grapefruit, fruit juice, cereals and toast with various preserves. Other types of fruit can be provided on request. Soya milk and vegan margarine are always available.

Dinner is not offered but Rani Indian Vegetarian Restaurant is not far away in Finchley, N3.

The house is very close to public transport and there are plenty of shops and restaurants serving veggie food nearby. From Woodside Park tube, it takes about twenty five minutes to be in central London.

Two friendly resident cats.

Short stay guests welcome.

Televisions in the rooms.

44 Grove Road
North Finchley
London N12 9DX
England

Tel: 020 8446 1604

Mobile: 07956 406446

Tube Station: Woodside Park (Northern Line), then a 15 minute walk.

Open: all year

Directions: Close to the M1 and off the A406 North Circular Road. Follow signs to Finchley.

Parking: on street

No children

No pets

No smoking

England LONDON Accommodation

Barrow House

Vegetarian bed & breakfast

45 Barrow Road
Streatham Common
London SW16 5PE

Tel: 020-8677 1925
Fax: 020-8677 1925
Open: all year round

Vegetarian and vegan bed and breakfast in south London, in a Victorian family house in a quiet location,.15 minutes by rail from Victoria Station and close to the A23. Three double/twin rooms, £60 double or £40 single. Non smoking. No pets. No credit cards. Two vegetarian restaurants and a wholefood store nearby.

Liz Heavenstone

Self catering b&b

192 Regents Park Road, Hampstead
London NW1 8XP
Tube: Chalk Farm
heavenstone@btinternet.com

Tel: 020-7722 7139
Fax: 020-7586 3004
Open: all year

Top floor apartment in a Regency terrace in Primrose Hill village, on the edge of Regent's Park. Two double/twin rooms, £50-60 per room per night, one with own bathroom, one with shower, which become a self contained apartment with living room when both rooms are taken. There's also a futon for an extra bed in one room. Good for self-catering as the double comes with a fridge and microwave with oven. Add £5 for self-service vegetarian or vegan organic breakfas. Children welcome. No pets. Discreet smokers tolerated. Prior telephone booking is essential, do not just turn up.

Quaker International Centre

Central vegetarian b&b

1-3 Byng Place, Bloomsbury
London WC1E 7JH
Tube: Euston, Warren Street

Tel: 020-7387 548
Open: all year except
Xmas to New Year

Accommodation set within this International Quaker Centre for Christians. Open to all, 16 singles at £36, four family rooms/dorms for 3-4 persons £20 per person, 7 twins and one double for £60. Breakfast included which is home made bread, cereal and fruit. Vegan margarine or soya milk can be available and there are two wholefood shops nearby anyway. They have basic cooking facilities, microwave plus fridge which is free. You are close to an Indian vegetarian restaurant opposite a wholefood shop in Marchmont Street, Planet Organic in Torrington Place, CTJ Chinese vegan restaurant in Euston Road, and Drummond Street with its veggie curry heaven. The centre is also available for hire for group or organisation meetings.

The Palace Hostel

Travellers hostel

48–49 Princes Square, Bayswater, London W2 4PX
Email: info-palacehotel@quista.net

Tel: 020-7221 5628
Fax: 020-7 221 5890
Price: £12

On the north side of Hyde Park. Open 24 hours.

Generator Hostel

Travellers hostel

Compton Place, off 37 Tavistock Place, WC1H 9SD
Email: info@the-generator.co.uk
Web: www.the-generator.co.uk

Tel: 020-7388 7666
Fax: 020-7388 7644
Price: £15

Huge tourist hostel with 800 beds at Russell Square in Bloomsbury. Fantastic location and great facilities. Open 24 hours.

St Christopher's Inn, Camden

Travellers hostel

48–50 Camden High Street, London 1NP
Tube: Camden Town
Email: bookings@st-christophers.co.uk
Web: www.st-christophers.co.uk

Tel: 020-7407 1856
Fax: 020-7403 7715
Price: £12–13

Near Camden Market, which is brilliant at weekends, 44 bed hostel in a cool, young area with lots of nightlife.

St Christopher's Inn, South Bank

Travellers hostel

121 Borough High Street, London SE1 1HR
Tube: London Bridge
Email: bookings@st-christophers.co.uk
Web: www.st-christophers.co.uk

Tel: 020-7407 1856
Fax: 020-7403 7715
Price: £12–13

Party atmosphere hostel with a bar, handy for the City.

North London Backpackers

Travellers hostel

1st Floor, Queens Parade, Queens Road, London W4
Tube: Hendon Central
Email: info@ukhostel.com

Tel: 020-8203 1319
Fax: 020-8203 9339

International Students House

Student hostel

229 Great Portland Street, London W1N 5HD
Tube: Great Portland Street
Open: All Year, Reservations phone 020-7631 8310

Tel: 020-7631 8300
Fax: 020-7631 8315

Long term accomodation for students, with dorms. £18 – £25 per night. Cooked veggie breakfast options available.

Crystal Palace Campsite

Crystal Palace Campsite
Crystal Palace Parade, London SE19
Tube: Crystal Palace BR

Tel: 020–8778 7155
Open all year round

This is a caravan park so electricity is available but no shop or cooking facilities. They do have laundry and washing facilities though. Rates vary according to the time of year. Average is £2.50 per tent, then £3.75 per adult in winter rising to £4.50 adult in summer. Car and tent is £3.50.

Lee Valley Park Campsite

Pickets Lock Centre, London N9
Tube: Tottenham Hale or Edmonton BR
Open: All Year Round except Xmas Day, Boxing Day & New Year

Tel: 020–8803 6900

Huge well equipped site set in 6 acres with sports centre and leisure complex with 12 screen cinema, swimming pool, golf course, kids' play area, 3 pubs and pizza restaurant. Acts as bus terminal for those going into town. There is a minimum charge for everyone £5.65 for adult or £2.35 for children 5–16, for individuals this goes up to £8.00 (i.e. one person and tent). Electricity is £2.40 per night. No charge for dogs or awnings. Another site is nearby at Sewardstone Road, Chingford, E4 7RA Tel 020–8529 5689, closed in winter.

Tent City Acton

Old Oak Common Lane, Acton, London W3
Tube: East Acton

Tel: (020) 87435708
Open: May –Oct 24 hours

Bunk beds in large dorm tents, or bring your own. Prices start at £5 per person. Showers, toilets, basic snack bar.

Tent City Hackney

Millfields Road, Hackney, London E5 OAR
Tube: No. 38 Bus route to Clapton Pond
Open: May– October

Tel: 020–8985 7656
Fax: 020–898 7656

3 large dormitories in tents with bunk beds. Separate and mixed dorms. Prices start around £5 per person, Under 5's free. Snack bar with salad, sandwiches and fruit open 8–12.00 then 19.00–22.00. Free cooking facilities, on site entertainment, free hot showers, laundry, valuables lock–up, no curfew. Canalside pubs nearby. Profits go to charity.

Other accommodation

If you're planning on foraging outside and just want a very cheap roof over your head, there are numerous private hostels and bargain bed and breakfasts near the West End in Paddington, W2, (north of Hyde Park), Victoria and Pimlico, King's Cross, South Kensington and Earl's Court, otherwise known as Kangaroo Valley being packed out with Australians and Kiwis on working holidays, from £10 per night depending on length of stay. Find them in the London Tourist Information Board, the accommodation section of free travellers' magazines in pavement dispensers around central London such as *TNT, Southern Cross* and *LAM*. If you're not already in London, our favourite guidebooks for budget places are Lonely Planet, Rough Guides or Let's Go London, England, Britain or Europe books. Or go to the fabulous site **www.hostels.com**. If you've just got off a coach or Gatwick airport train at Victoria station, there are some accommodation agencies that can sort out your first night's stay for a small commission.

Youth Hostels Association members can stay at one of London's seven youth hostels, including St Paul's (City), Earls Court, Oxford Street, Hampstead, Kensington, Rotherhithe, King's Cross/St Pancras, though watch out for higher prices (around £20) than elsewhere in the country and single sex dorms. Details at www.yha.org.uk. Reservations lonres@yha.org.uk, Tel: 020-7373 3400, Fax: 020 7373 3455.

If you're moving to London for at least six months, advertise free for a flatshare or sublet in LOOT, the free ads paper from newsagents, and let the landlords come to you. (www.loot.com) You can repeat the ad every two days. Getting an apartment in London is a full time job for a few days but it can be done if you're persistent. They are expensive, but if you're on a working holiday and pack it with friends, it works out cheaper than a hostel in the long run and much quieter. A single or double room in a houseshare will be £70-120 per week, a studio flat £100 per week and up. You'll need a month's deposit, a month's rent up front, and the contract will normally be a six months assured shorthold tenancy. So staying in a hostel for the first few weeks is definitely a lot less hassle while you find a job and you can get some mates there.

Places in the West End – Soho and Covent Garden

■ Vegetarian restaurants

● Wholefood & health food shops

Neal's Yard, Covent Garden, three veggie cafes

Soho - Covent Garden

Country Life Restaurant

3-4 Warwick Street, near Piccadilly
London W1
Open: buffet Sun–Fri 11.30–16.00 (last orders),
also Thur eve a la carte 18.00–22.30, closed Sat.

Tel: 020–7434 2922
Tube: Piccadilly Circus
exit 1

Herbivore heaven. All–you–can–eat lunch of mixed salads and hot dishes which you pay for by weight, maximum £5.95. Thursday night a la carte gourmet vegan. Gorgeous desserts. No alcohol or smoking. Wholefood shop upstairs. Resident vegan GP for private consultations.

Plant

Vegetarian fast food

47 Poland Street
London W1F 7VB
Open: Mon–Fri 11.00–19.00, closed Sat–Sun
www.plantfooddrink.com

Tel: 020–7734 7528
Tube: Oxford Circus,
Piccadilly Circus

New vegetarian take–away with a few seats, now with more vegan food. Soups, sandwiches and a salad bar. Smoothies, fresh juices, some organic juices, decaffeinated and specially blended coffee.

Beatroot

Vegetarian cafe & take–away

92 Berwick Street
Soho, London W1V 3PP
Open: Mon–Sat 9.00 –18.30

Tel: 020 7437 8591
Tube: Oxford Circus,
Tottenham Court Rd.

Our favourite central London café, with almost all desserts vegan, near the south end of Berwick St by the fruit and veg market. Point to whatever you fancy from 16 hot dishes and salads such as cottage pie, tofu stir–fry, Moroccan tagine. Small box £2.80, medium £3.80 or large £4.80. Lots of cakes, mostly vegan, £1–£2 including fabulous vegan chocolate dream cake with custard, tofu cheesecake, carrot cake, hemp flapjacks. Fresh juices, soya smoothies. No credit cards.

Mildreds

Vegetarian restaurant

45 Lexington Street
Soho, London W1
Open: Mon–Sat 12–23.00, Sun 12.30–17.30

Tel: 020–7494 1634
Tube: Piccadilly Circus,
Oxford Circus

Stylish vegetarian restaurant with hip young clientele to match, crowded and enthusiastic. The food is modern European with some Asian influences. Fully licensed. Cheques but no cards.

Crazy Salads

Omnivorous salad bar

128 Wardour Street
Soho, London W1
Open: Mon–Fri: 8.00–16.00

Tel: 020–7439 2462
Tube: Tottenham Court
Rd, Oxford Circus

Great salad bar, serve yourself and fill up a carton with a from selection of 40 hot and cold salads for £3.00.

Red Veg

Vegetarian burger bar

95 Dean Street,
Soho
London W1V 5RB
Open: Mon–Sat: til 22.00, closed Sun

Tel: 020–7437–3109
Tube: Tottenham Court
Road

London's first veggie burger and falafel bar with a few tables, just off Oxford Street near Tottenham Court Rd. The whole menu is GM free. Veggie burger £2.65, can be made spicy. Jamaican roll £2.65, Oriental noodles £2.95, falafel £2.95, noname nuggets £2.65. Medium fries 75p, large 95p, plantain chips £1.15, crispy zucchini £1.15, breaded mushrooms £1.15. Vietnamese style coffee, cappuccino, café latte, espresso, and tea all £1.00. Herbal teas £1.10. One of our contributors reports that many staff of nearby Waterstones bookstore stopped going to McDonalds and started to come here after reading *Fast Food Nation* by Eric Schlosser, which has to tell you something.

Woodlands Leicester Sq.

Vegetarian South Indian

37 Panton St (off Haymarket)
London SW1Y 4EA
Open: every day 12.00–23.00

Tel: 020–7839 7258
Tube: Piccadilly Circus,
Leicester Square

Vegetarian Indian restaurant off the south–west corner of Leicester Square. Lunchtime all you can eat buffet on weekdays for £5.99 alongside their regular menu.

Govinda's

Vegetarian Hare Krishna

9/10 Soho Street
Soho, London W1V 5DA
Open: Mon–Sat 12.00–20.00, closed Sun

Tel: 020–7437–4928
Tube: Tottenham Court Rd.

Indian restaurant and café, with some fast food, next door to the Hare Krishna temple, just off Oxford Street and near Tottenham Court Road. 7 dish all–you–can–eat buffet £4.99, after 7pm £3.99. No eggs. Non smoking. They go through phases of using vegetable ghee or butter ghee so vegans need to check.

Tai
Chinese vegan buffet restaurant

10 Greek Street
Soho
Open: Mon–Sat 12.30–21.30, Sun 3.00–21.00

Tel: 020–7287 3730
Tube: Tottenham Court Rd

All you can eat Chinese vegan buffet for only £6, incredibly popular with veggies and carnivores alike for its amazing value and delicious food. £3 for a take–away box. Rice, spring rolls, tofu, stir–fry veg, salad, soya meats, noodles. Unlimited Chinese tea £1. Cash only. Non–smoking. No alcohol but plenty of pubs nearby.

First Out
Gay/Lesbian vegetarian café and bar

52 St Giles High St
Covent Garden
Open: Mon–Sat 10.00–23.00, Sun 11–22.30

Tel: 020–7240 8042
Tube: Tottenham Court Rd.

Very popular gay and lesbian vegetarian café and basement bar, close to Tottenham Court Road tube and handy for fuelling up before hitting the nightclubs. Soups, salads, dips with pitta, veg chilli or curry, pies, bakes, or nachos. Generally good for vegans until you get to the many cakes. Glass of house white £2.95 to £3.95, £12–14.00 a bottle, beer £2.00 to £2.70. Smoking only in the bar downstairs. No credit cards. Friday night is 'Girl Friday' with men as guests.

Neal's Yard Salad Bar
Vegetarian wholefood café

2 Neal's Yard
Covent Garden
Open: Mon–Sat 10.00–20.00, Sun 10.00–19.00

Tel: 020–7836 3233
Tube: Covent Garden

Vegan owned café with a Brazilian, English, Italian, Lebanese and Oriental twist. Point to the food you want at the counter then chill out in the sun at an outside table. Main dishes small £5.50 (take–away £3.50), large £6.50 (£4.00). Lots of vegan desserts £2.00–£3.40 such as chocolate mousse or banana cinnamon cake. Drinks £2–£3 include mango juice, mixed berry, Brazilian fruit shake, wine and beer.

Neal's Yard Bakery
Vegetarian cafe and bakery

6 Neal's Yard
Covent Garden
Open: Mon–Sat 10.30–17.00, Sun closed

Tel: 020–7836 5199
Tube: Covent Garden

Café and organic wholemeal bakery with seating upstairs overlooking the courtyard. Soups, salads, hot dishes and desserts to eat in or take away, plus all kinds of bread. No credit cards. Bread from 6.30a.m.

Food For Thought

Vegetarian restaurant & take-away

31 Neal Street
Covent Garden
Open: Mon-Sat 12.00-20.30, Sun 12.00-17.00

Tel: 020-7836 9072/0239
Tube: Covent Garden

Extremely popular veggie take-away and café on fascinating Neal Street in a vaulted basement. They offer good value and the food is very fresh with a global menu. Crowded at peak times and you'll need to queue on the stairs at lunchtime. Scrummy vegan desserts such as apple and plum crumble. BYO, free corkage. No credit cards.

World Food Café

International veggie restaurant

First Floor, 14 Neal's Yard
Covent Garden
Open: Mon-Fri 11.30-16.30,
Sat 11.30-17.00, Sun closed

Tel: 020-7379-0298
Tube: Covent Garden

Upstairs international wholefood vegetarian restaurant, overlooking Neal's Yard. 90% vegan. There's an open plan kitchen in the centre so you can see all the food being prepared. Meals from every continent £5.95-£7.95. Minimum charge £5.00 at lunchtime and Saturdays.

Chi

Chinese vegan buffet restaurant

55 St Martin's Lane
Covent Garden
Open: every day 12.00-23.00, Sunday -22.00

Tel: 020-7836 3434
Tube: Leicester Square,
Charing Cross

All you can eat Chinese vegan buffet, like the busier Tai in Greek Street, one block back from Charing Cross Road in the heart of theatreland. Fill up on fried and boiled rice, noodles, stir-fry vegetables, tofu, mushrooms and several kinds of fake meat, with as many visits to the buffet as you like for just £5 before 5.30pm, £6 afterwards and all day Sunday. Take away £3.

Wagamama Lexington St.

Omnivorous Japanese restaurant

10A Lexington Street
Open: Mon-Sat 12.00-midnight, Sun 12.30-22.00

Tel: 020-7292 0990
Tube: Piccadilly Circus,
Oxford Circus

Omnivorous fast food Japanese noodle bar with over nine veggie and vegan dishes. Very busy, totally authentic, heaps of fun. Allow about £12-£15 for a belt-buster, less if your're only eating mains. Prices start at £1.25 for miso soup.

Maoz
Falafel cafe

43 Old Compton Street
Soho, W1
Open: 11am–02.00am, later at weekends

Tel: 020-7851 1586
Tube: Leicester Square
www.maozfalafel.nl

Fantastic new falafel bar like the ones in Amsterdam, at the west end of the gay zone, specialising in falafel in pitta, £2.50–£3.50. Self serve salad bar with large choice of salads and tahini which you pile on top of your falafel, all of which are vegan apart from the coleslaw and mayonnaise. Eat in or take–away. Non smoking. No credit cards.

Wagamama Haymarket
Omnivorous Japanese fast food

8 Norris Street
off the Haymarket, SW1Y
Open: Mon–Sat 12.00–23.00, Sun 12.30–22.30

Tel: 020-7321 2755
Tube: Leicester Square
www.wagamama.com

One of the newer branches of the omnivorous Japanese noodle chain and close by all the theatres.

Wagamama Leicester Sq.
Omnivorous Japanese fast food

14A Irving Street
West End, London WC1
Mon–Sat 12–23.00, –24.00 Fri–Sat, Sun 12.30–22.00

Tel: 020-7839 2323
Tube: Leicester Square,
Charing Cross

One of the many branches of this omnivorous fast food Japanese noodle bar with over nine veggie and vegan dishes. This one is just off Charing Cross Road, opposite the Garrick Theatre. Allow about £10 or more for a starter and main course with drink. Prices start at £1.25 for a small miso soup up to £6.50 for an enormous bowl of miso ramen (noodles).

Falafel Cafes Leicester Sq
24–hour omnivorous cafes

North E–est corner of Leicester Square
opposite the Hippodrome
Open: 24 hours

Tube: Leicester Square

When you've staggered out of a night club at 3am , there are a couple of busy all night cafes where you can get falafel, chips and coffee while you wait for the tube to open.

Gaby's

Mediterranean omnivorous cafe

30 Charing Cross Rd.
by Leicester Square
Open: Mon–Sat 11.00–24.00, Sun 11.00–21.00

Tel: 020–7836 4233
Tube: Leicester Sq.

Omnivorous Mediterranean café close to Leicester Square tube station on the Covent Garden side of Charing Cross Rd. Stacks of veggie and vegan eat-ins and take-aways for a fiver or less. Point to what you want in the deli style counter, such as stuffed aubergine or pepper £5.50, pasta with herb and tomato sauce £4, falafels £2.50. 20 salads £2-3. Chips £1.30. Alcohol, coffee, lemon and herb tea.

Carrie Awaze Designer Sandwiches

Omnivorous cafe

27 Endell Street
Covent Garden
Open: Mon–Fri 10–20.00,
Sat 12.00–19.00, Sun 12–17.00

Tel: 020–7836 0815
Tube: Covent Garden

Omnivorous Indian and international take-away with stacks for veggies and vegans. 6 vegan and 21 veggie sandwiches £1.95-2.95 take-away or £2.3-3.80 eat in, such as onion bhajia with hummous and salad. Filled jacket spud £5.95-6.25 such as with dhal and onion bhajia, or veg curry and cashews. Vegetarian thali or curry and rice £7.95. Beer, wine, teas, even soya milk.

Wagamama, Covent Garden

Japanese omnivorous

1 Tavistock Street
Covent Garden, WC2
Open: Mon–Sat 11.00–23.00

Tel: 020–7836 3330
Tube: Covent Garden

Omnivorous fast food Japanese noodle bar with over nine veggie and vegan dishes.

Country Life Shop

Wholefood shop

3–4 Warwick Street
near Piccadilly
Open: Mon–Thu 9–18.00, Fri till 15.30,
Sun 13.00–17.00, closed Sat

Tel: 020-7434 2922
Tube: Piccadilly Circus

Wholefood shop with vegan restaurant in the basement. Stock up for a picnic in the park with vegan yoghurt and ice-cream, wholemeal bread and rolls, biscuits and snacks. They sell *Vegetarian London*.

Fresh & Wild

Health food supermarket and cafe

75 Brewery Lane
Brewer Street
London W1R 3SL
Open: till late night and all weekend

Tel: 020-7434 3179
Tube: Piccadilly Circus

Huge organic wholefood supermarket on two floors in the middle of Brewer Street, with heaps of take-aways, a salad bar and juice bar with seating, organic fruit and vegetables, remedies and some books, including Veggie Guides. There's a great value self serve area right at the back upstairs where you can load up on grains, beans, nuts and dry fruit. This is where you'll also find Provamel soya desserts and at least six flavours of Swedish Glace vegan ice-cream. If you haven't tried this, just do it, we need say no more.

Lush

Cruelty-free bodycare

40 Carnaby Street
London W1

Tube: Oxford Circus

Unit 11, The Piazza
Covent Garden
London WC2E 8RA

Tube: Covent Garden

Now that a certain "against animal testing" high street chain no longer tells you or even their own staff whether their cosmetics are truly cruelty free, i.e. vegan, unless you get them to call Head Office which is pretty unlikely on a Saturday afternoon, many of our veggie and vegan friends have switched to shopping at Planet Organic, Fresh & Wild and Lush, where over 70% of the gorgeous soaps, shampoos etc are vegan and clearly labelled in the free catalogue. (though unfortunately not yet labelled on the shelves, but it's not really a big deal) The shop smells wonderful and you can have fun playing with the products. Carnaby Street itself is full of groovy hippy clothes shops and cute boutiques to get you dressed up and made up for an Austin Powers or Goth party.

Berwick Street Market

Fruit & veg market

South end of Berwick Street
Mon–Sat 9–18.00

Tube: Oxford Circus,
Tottenham Court Road,
Piccadilly

Oh gor bloimey, a real London fruit, vegetable and flowers street market. Rest your plates of, er, anyway, feet at Beatroot cafe then load up with £1 bowls of seasonal veg. Bargains to be had just before 6pm, as it's more than me street trader's licence's worf guv to sell after that time. One stall has nuts, spices and dried bananas and will give you a resealable bag to keep your bananas fresh.

Holland & Barrett

Health food shop

Unit 16, Embankment Shopping Centre,
Villiers St, WC2
(down the East side of Charing Cross Station)
Open: Mon–Sat 9–18.00, Sun closed

Tel: 020–7839 4988
Tube: Embankment,
Charing Cross

21 Shorts Gardens
Covent Garden
Open: Mon–Sun 10.00–19.00

Tel: 020–7379–0298
Tube: Covent Garden

123 Oxford Street
between Oxford Circus and Tottenham Court Rd
Open: Mon–Wed: 8.30–18.45, Thur–Fri: 8.30–19.45,
Sat 10:00–18.45, Sun 12:00–16.45

Tel: 020–7287 3624

Unit C12, downstairs in West One Shopping Centre
corner of Davis St. and Oxford St.
by Bond Street underground

Tel: 020–7493 7988
Tube: Bond Street

65 Charing Cross Rd
by Leicester Square
Open: Mon–Sat 10.00–20.00, Sun 11.00–18.00

Tel: 020–7287–3193
Tube: Leicester Sq.

Places in
Marylebone & Bloomsbury

■ Restaurants

● Wholefood & health food shops

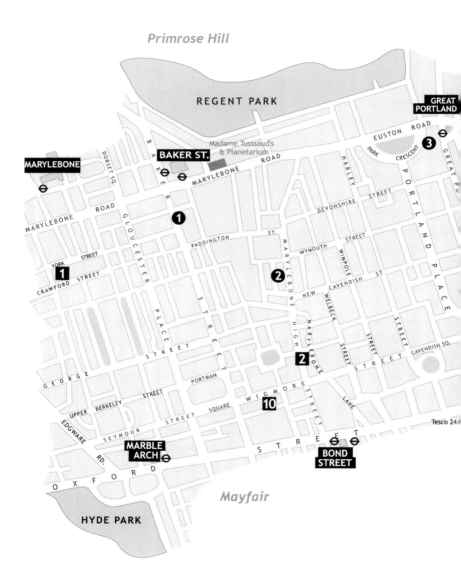

Primrose Hill

REGENT PARK

Madame Tusssaud's
& Planetarium

GREAT
PORTLAND

BAKER ST.

MARYLEBONE

EUSTON ROAD

3

MARYLEBONE ROAD

DORSET SQ.

BAKER STREET

PARK CRESCENT

PORTLAND PLACE

GREAT PO

MARYLEBONE ROAD

GLOUCESTER PLACE

PADDINGTON

DEVONSHIRE STREET

HARLEY STREET

1

ST.

WYMOUTH STREET

WIMPOLE STREET

PORTLAND PLACE

YORK STREET

1

CRAWFORD STREET

2

MARYLEBONE HIGH STREET

NEW CAVENDISH ST.

WELBECK STREET

STREET

STREET

STREET

CAVENDISH SQ.

STREET

2

CAVENDISH SQ.

GEORGE STREET

PORTMAN

LANE

Tesco 24/

UPPER BERKELEY STREET

SEYMOUR STREET

PORTMAN SQUARE

WIGMORE STREET

10

STREET

EDGWARE RD.

MARBLE ARCH

STREET

BOND STREET

OXFORD STREET

Mayfair

HYDE PARK

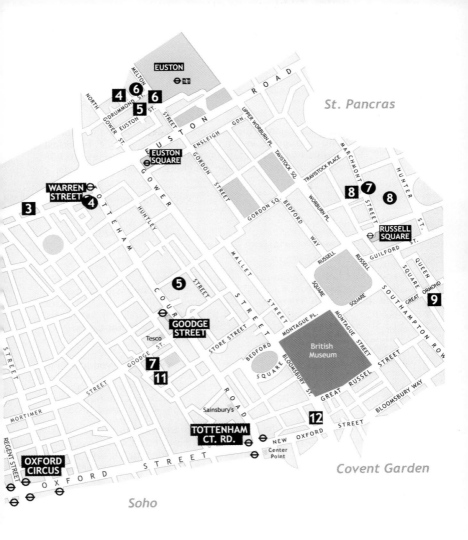

Marylebone - Bloomsbury

Raw Deal

Vegetarian café/restaurant

65 York Street, off Seymour Place
Marylebone, W1
Open: Mon-Fri 08.00-22.00, closed Sat-Sun

Tel: 020-7262-4841
Tube: Baker Street

All day week day cafe handy for Madame Tussauds, with a restaurant standard menu and great vegan cakes. Cooked veggie breakfast £3.50. Soup, filled jacket potatoes, salads. Main courses £6.00–£6.50. Licensed. Cheques, luncheon vouchers, but no credit cards.

Woodlands

Vegetarian Indian restaurant

77 Marylebone Lane, W1
(off Marylebone High St.)
Open: 7 days a week for lunch from 12.30 and
dinner 18.00-23.00.

Tel: 020-7486 3862
Tube: Bond St./Baker St.

Vegetarian Indian restaurant.   Nine varieties of dosa (vegetable stuffed pancake) from £3.95 to £5.50. Their specialty is uthappam or lentil pizza, with coconut, tomato, green chilli for £4.50, extra toppings 25p. 10 curries from £3.95 to £4.95 Thalis or set meals £12.50–£13.50. Licensed. They accept most major credit cards.

CTJ

Chinese vegan all-you-can-eat

339 Euston Road, NW1
Open every day 12.00-22.00

Tel: 020-7387-5450
Tube: Great Portland St,
Warren Street, Euston

Bargain restaurant close to Euston Station and Warren Street tubes. Eat as much as you like buffet for £5, take-out box £3. Choose from veg Thai curry, sweet and sour veg balls, lemon grass pot, spring rolls, crispy aubergine and black bean with mixed veg, seaweed spiced aubergine, tofu and all kinds of fake meats. Unlicensed but you can bring your own and pay a minimal charge for corkage.

Chutneys

Vegetarian South Indian restaurant

124 Drummond Street
Euston, NW1
Open every day, lunch buffet 12.00-14.25,
dinner through til 22.30

Tel: 020-7388-0604
Tube: Euston,
Euston Square

Apopular place for a quiet romantic dinner that won't stretch the wallet too much. Eat as much as you like buffet from 12 noon to 2.45pm every day for £5.45. Main courses include nine kinds of dosa £2.80–£4.85, 11 curries £2.50-3.40. Thalis start at £3.95.

Ravi Shankar

Vegetarian South Indian restaurant

133–135 Drummond Street
Euston, NW1
Open every day 12.00–22.45 (last orders 22.30)

Tel: 020–7388 6458
Tube: Euston,
Euston Square

One of three great value vegetarian South Indian restaurants in this street next to Euston station. Daily specials throughout the week, three course meal £6.95, two courses £5.70, or have a dosa or curry for £2 to £4. They have wine and lager. Most cards accepted.

Diwana Bhelpoori House

Vegetarian South Indian restaurant

121–123 Drummond Street
Euston, NW1
Open every day 12.00–23.30

Tel: 020–7387 5556
Tube: Euston, Euston
Square, Warren St

One of the larger Indian restaurants on Drummond Street. Eat as much as you like lunch buffet £4.80 and a full a la carte menu all day. Thalis £4 to £6. Lots of dosas and vegetable side dishes like bombay starting at £2.40. Several desserts, alas as in most Indian restaurants there is not much for vegans. Not licensed but you can bring your own with no corkage charge. Off licence nearby.

Crazy Salads

Omnivorous take-away

47 Goodge Street
London W1
Mon–Fri: 10–16.00

Tel: 020–7323 –9952
Tube: Goodge Street

One of a chain of take-aways with a buffet of 40 dishes offering amazing value for money. You cram as much as you can into a plastic box for £3.

Vegetarian Paradise

Indian restaurant & take-away

59 Marchmont Street
Bloomsbury, WC1
Mon–Sun: 12–15.00 and then 17.00–23.00

Tel: 020–7278 6881
Tube: Fussell Square

Indian vegetarian restaurant with real value for money here, with a lunch time buffet, all you can eat for £4.50 per adult. Mains from £2.40 for curries or £2.50 for a plain dosa.

Mary Ward

Vegetarian cafe

42 Queen Square
Bloomsbury
Mon–Thu: 9.30–20.50, Fri 9.30–20.30,
Sat 9.30–16.00, Sun closed

Tel: 020-7831 7711
Tube: Russell Sq.,
Holborn

Completely vegetarian cafe in an adult education centre by green Queens Square. Breakfast served until 11.30, usually toast, jam and Danish pastries. Lunch menu includes four vegan salads, £1.30 small or £2.50 large. Light meals £1.70-3.20, main dishes £3.50. Not licensed. No smoking. Cheques but no credit cards.

Wagamama, Wigmore St

Omnivorous Japanese

101A Wigmore St
near Marylebone High Street
Mon–Sat 12.00–23.00, Sun 12.00–22.00

Tel: 020 7409 0111
Tube:
Marble Arch, Bond St

Large omnivorous Japanese fast food noodle restaurant, this was the third to open in London, they now have ten.
See Bloomsbury, below, for menu.

Rasa Express

Veggie & fish Indian

5 Rathbone Street
Off Oxford Street near Tottenham Court Road
Open: 12–3pm buffet

Tel: 020-7637-0222
Tube: Tottenham Ct.Rd.

Unlike their fish restaurant in parallel Charlotte Street, here most of the menu is veggie snacks and take-aways. Typical snacks for £1.50 are Mysore potato balls fried in chickpea flour, or crispy spongy dumpling in a crunchy case made from urad beans and chillies. Take-aways £2-£2.50 like masala dosa or vegetable biriyani.

Wagamama, British Museum

Omnivorous Japanese

4A Streatham Street
close to British Museum
Mon–Sat 12–23.00, Sun 12–22.00

Tel: 020-7323 9223
Tube: Tottenham Court Rd
www.wagamama.com

Noodle restaurant with over nine veggie and vegan dishes, long trestle tables and very noisy. Not great for a first date, but superb if you're out on the town for a laff. Raw mixed juices £2.55. Mains include veg soup with wholemeal ramen noodles, stir-fried veg and tofu £6.25; yasai katsu curry with rice, mixed leaves and pickles £6. Side dishes, £1.25–£4.25 like five grilled veg dumpling, miso soup, skewers of chargrilled veg coated in yakitori sauce.

Holland & Barrett, Baker St

Health food shop

78 Baker St
Mon–Fri: 8.30–18.00, Sat: 9.00–17.30, Sun closed

Tel: 020–7935 3544
Tube: Baker St.

Part of the national chain, this is a medium sized shop with a wide range of supplements, plus some take–away foods.

GNC

Health food shop

104 Marylebone High Street,
Mon–Fri: 9.00–19.00,
Sat: 9.00– 18.00, Sun: 12.00–17.00

Tel: 020–7935 –3924
Tube: Baker Street

Mainly vitamins and supplements at this shop, not much food apart from soya milk and rice cakes.

Nutri Centre Ltd

Cruelty free cosmetics & food

7 Park Crescent, London W1
Mon–Fri: 9.00–18.30, Sat 10–16.00, Sun closed

Tel: 020–7436–5122
Tube: Regents Park

In the basement of a natural health centre, this shop sells mainly supplements and body care products, plus a few foods like pasta There is a huge books section with a separate telephone: 020–7323 2382. They have an impressive mail order books catalogue.

Health Food Centre

Health food shop and take–away

11 Warren Street
at the top of Tottenham Court Road
Mon–Fri 8.30–19.00, Sat 12.00–16.00

Tel: 020–7387 9289
Tube: Warren Street

Vegetarian health food shop and take–away tucked away down the side of Warren Street tube. Handy for Euston or Regents Park. A staggering range of veggie and vegan sandwiches, like (fake) chicken and salad, lentil burger and houmous, veggie BLT, all £2.60 for two which is stunning value for central London. Savouries like spicy Mexican slice, cartons of pasta and couscous salad. Hot take–away dishes include brown rice and curry, and pasta bake. Lots of cakes, some sugar free or suitable for vegans like date crumble. Juice bar. Extensive range of cruelty–free toiletries, herbal remedies and oils.

Planet Organic

Organic supermarket and cafe

22 Torrington Place
half way up Tottenham Court Road down the side of
Barclays Bank
Open: Mon–Fri 9–20.00, Sat 11–18.00, Sun 12–18.00

Tel: 020-7436-1929
Tube: Goodge St

Organic wholefood supermarket off Tottenham Court Rd, with a juice bar and deli-style café. Most dishes, snacks and cakes have ingredients displayed and if they're gluten, sugar free or vegan. Hot and cold dishes and salads, some of which are always vegan, for take-away or eat in at the handful of tables by the tills and outside. The shop sells everything for veggies including fifteen types of tofu and tempeh, every kind of pasta you ever had some you didn't (spelt, quinoa) as well as lots of macrobiotic products for home sushi. Huge section devoted to health and body care. A great place for presents like pretty candles, incense and aromatherapy oils. They even sell *Vegetarian London, Britain, France* and *Europe*.

Alara Wholeoods

Wholefood store

58 Marchmont Street
Bloomsbury
Open: Mon–Fri 9–18.00, Sat 10–18.00, Sun closed

Tel: 020-7837 1172
Tube: Russell Square

Vegetarian healthfood shop that is very popular with the locals. Large take-away section and one of the best places to grab lunch to go. Loads of vegan and organic produce including: fruit & veg, cosmetics, food supplements, wide variety of bread, and a small selection of veggie beers and organic juices.

Ambala Sweets

Indian sweet shop

opposite Diwana and Ravi Shankar
Drummond Street NW1

Tube: Euston

Indian sweets and savouries like samosas to take away. Load up here before catching a train north from Euston.

Holland & Barrett

36 Brunswick Shopping Ctr
Bloomsbury
Open: Mon–Sat 9.30–17.30, Sun closed

Tel: 020-7278 4640
Tube: Russell Square

Part of healthfood shop chain in UK, small branch with many veggie/vegan munchies like dried fruit, nuts and seeds.

Places in Rest of London

Vegetarian Restaurants

Wholefood and Health Food Shops

The Place Below

Bill Sewell's long-established cafe and take-away is located in the Norman Crypt of a Wren church, handy for St Paul's Cathedral.

This place provides a quiet retreat from the regular noisy circus that is Cheapside. The café has been refurbished by a young designer, to give it a sophisticated feel.

Sandwiches £5 eat-in, £3.50 take-away, grilled 50p extra, such as hummous, roast red onion and courgette. Soups, £2.90 eat-in, £2.30 take-away, for example carrot and tarragon, or lentil and lemon.

Hot dish of the day £7 eat-in, £5.50 take-away, such as Morrocan casserole with chickpeas, cinnamon and coriander, served with cous cous.

Salads and 'health bowls' £5.50–£7 (£1.50 less for take-away). Pitta pockets have just been introduced at the time of writing.

Cakes, crumbles and other puddings £2.80 eat-in or £2.20 take away. Only the fruit salad is vegan.

The menu changes daily. If the main course is vegan, the soup normally contains dairy and vice versa. A vegan salad and sandwich (such as satay pitta pockets) are normally available. Nuts are used in many dishes.

Two offers daily: £1.50 off hot dish of the day, i.e. £5.50, for eat in purchases 11.30–12.00; and coffee or tea only 50p (a real bargain in London) with any food purchase 07.30–11.30.

Bill is opening a new place, Michael House cafe, in Cambridge in early 2003.

Vegetarian cafe and take-away

St Mary Le Bow
Cheapside
London
EC2V 6AU

020 7329 0789

Tube: Bank or St Paul's

Mon–Fri
07.30–15.30

Closed Sat and Sun

www.theplacebelow.co.uk

Not licensed,
no corkage

Outside seating available
in churchyard

No smoking

Visa, MC, Amex

CTB

The City, Chinese vegan restaurant

88 Leather Lane, The City EC1
Open: Mon-Fri 12-22.00, Sat-Sun 17.30-22.00

Tel: 020-7242 6128
Tube: Moorgate

Oriental buffet restaurant in the heart of the city. All you can eat for £5 (all day) or take-away for £3.

RED of Knightsbridge

Knightsbridge Chinese vegan

8 Egerton Garden mews, Knightsbridge SW3
off Yeomans Row, past Harrods
Open: Mon-Fri 12.30-14.30, 18.30-23.00;
Sat 13.30-15.30, 18.30-23.00

Tel: 020-7584 7007
Tube: Knightsbridge,
South Kensington

Top class Chinese vegan restaurant in posh London, in a basement on a quiet street behind Brompton Rd. Fake flesh is a real speciality, an ideal stepping stone for the carnivore in your party. Huge menu. Starters £3-5.50, mains £5-7.50, desserts £3.50. Set menus £13.50-21.50. They now serve vegan organic wine. No smoking. No credit cards. 10% discount to people presenting this book.

Coopers

South Bank vegetarian cafe

17 Lower Marsh, Waterloo SE1
Open: Mon-Fri 08.30-17.30

Tel: 020-7261 9314
Tube: Waterloo

Family run deli with cafe round the back of Waterloo station. Savouries like potato and onion bhaji, veg rissoles, carrot and onion cutlet, chickpea roti, kibabs and cottage pies. Sandwiches, appetizers like olives, vine leaves and houmous, salads, soup, and 5 cakes of which at least one is vegan. Organic booze and health food shop produce. They plan to open a restaurant soon.

Aum

Kings Cross Oriental vegetarian & fish

52 Caledonian Road, Kings Cross N1
Open: Mon-Sat 12-15.00, 18-23.00, closed Sun

Tel: 020-7278 5298
Tube: Kings Cross,
Thameslink

Vegetarian and fish (only four dishes) restaurant with a global menu, near the new Almeida Theatre. Vegans well catered for with 13 clearly marked dishes. Starters £2.40-4.25 like Burmese crisply fried rolls. Main courses £5.25-6.95 such as Thai green curry with veggie ham, augergines, peppers and coconut milk; New Orleans stew with sweet potato, black-eyed peas, okra and sweetcorn. Lots of appetizers, side orders and desserts. Hot and cold drinks, non-alcoholic cocktails. Bring your own alcohol, corkage £1 per head. No credit cards.

Oshobasho

Highgate Wood vegetarian cafe

Highgate Wood, Muswell Hill Road, Highgate N10
Open: every day except Mon, 8.30 till dusk

Tel: 020-8444 1505
Tube: Highgate

Vegetarian cafe in the middle of ancient Highgate Wood, with a huge enclosed garden and seating outside for 200. In summer they have live instrumental jazz, classical and jazz singers. Global food. Winter porridge £3.75, gigantic grilled breakfast £5. Sandwiches, soup. Main rice or pasta dishes with salad £5.80 such as winter root veg stew, chickpea curry, ratatouille. Desserts like apple pie and carrot cake, at least one vegan. Mulled wine in winter. Children's portions.

Fiction

Crouch End vegetarian restaurant

60 Crouch End Hill, N8
Open: Wed–Sun 18.30–22.00,
Fri & Sat till 22.30 (last orders 21.30)

Tel: 020-8340 3403
Tube: Finsbury Park then bus W7,
or Archway and bus 41

British and international cuisine with fusions from Mediterranean, Asia and North Africa. Starters £3.95–4.45 like roasted spiced pumpkin soup, couscous. Five mains £9.25–10.45, three vegan, such as Vietnamese vegetables, roasted stuffed butternut squash. Desserts £4.35. Extensive wine list. Reservations on Fri and Sat recommended.

Peking Palace

Holloway Chinese vegetarian restaurant

669 Holloway Road, N19
Open: Mon–Sat 12–15.00, 18–23.00
Sun 18–23.00

Tel: 020-7281 8989
Tube: Archway, or
Holloway Rd then bus

Gorgeous new vegetarian restaurant in the centre of north London. All you can eat lunch buffet (not Sunday) £4.95. Huge a la carte menu. Appetizers £3–4.80 like grilled Peking dumpling, vegetarian satay, soya drum sticks. Soups £2.50. Mains around £5 like soya meat, tofu, curries, soya fish, soya king prawn, soya duck and chicken. Desserts include vegan ice-cream. No smoking. Bring your own wine.

Rani

Finchley Indian vegetarian restaurant

7 Long Lane, Finchley N3
Open: every day 18–22.00, also Sun 12.15–14.30

Tel: 020-8349 4386
Tube: Finchley Central

Home-style Gujarati cooking at the top of Long Lane, just off the North Circular Road. Vegan friendly as they don't use egg and only vegetable ghee. Starters £2.50-3.20. Mains £4-5, some with African influence. Great breads. House wine £1.80 glass, £9.70 bottle. Braille menu available.

Cafe 79

Primrose Hill vegetarian cafe

79 Regents Park Road, NW1
Open: Mon–Sat 8.30–18.30, Sun 9–118.30

Tel: 020–7586 8012
Tube: Chalk Farm

Cafe in a picturesque street on edge of Primrose Hill. Vegans will find most dishes contain dairy or eggs. All day cooked breakfast £3.45–5.75. Soup and organic roll £3.95, houmous and warm pitta £3.25, veggie burger and salad £4.25, baked potato £2.25 or £3.35 with filling. Sandwiches, baguettes and bagels from £2.10. Mains £5.45–5.75 such as burger and deep fried potatoes, pasta. Giant salads £5.95. Pot of tea £1.35, for two £1.95. (Soya) milkshakes £2.45.

Manna

Hampstead gourmet vegetarian restaurant

4 Erskine Road, Primrose Hill NW3
Open: every day18.30–23.00,
also Sat–Sun 12.30–15.00

Tel: 020–7722 8028
Tube: Chalk Farm

Classy international restaurant with lots of vegan food. Starters around £5.50 such as organic fritata, artichoke tempura. 3 salads or have a Manna Meze of any 3 starters or salads for £13.75. 7 mains, nearly all with vegan option, £8.95–11.95, like Indonesian coconut and cumin pancakes with tempeh and vegetables. Desserts £2.95–5.95, many vegan. Early evening 2 courses for £12.50 6.30–7.30pm.

The Gate 2

Primrose Hill gourmet vegetarian restaurant

72 Belsize Lane, Belsize Park NW3
Open: every day 18–23.00; also Wed–Sun 12–15.00

Tel: 020–7435 7733
Tube: Belsize Park

Sister to the long established Gate in Hammersmith. Starters £3.50–6.25 include soup, mushroom bruschetta, salad. Main courses around £11.25 such as vegan Mussaman curry. Side dishes £3.25–4.50. Desserts like chocolate mud cake £5.50, ice-creams and sorbets. Extensive wine list with veggie and vegan ones clearly labelled. Smoke free. Reservations recommended Fri and Sat night.

VitaOrganic

West Hampstead south–east Asian vegan

279c Finchley Road, West Hampstead NW3
Open: Mon–Sun 12 noon to 23.00

Tel: 020–7435 2188
Tube: Finchley Road,
BR Finchley Rd & Frognall

Oriental organic (and no MSG) restaurant with a self-serve buffet £5.90 before 6pm and then £6.90. Malaysian, Thai, Chinese and Japanese dishes. Also a la carte £2.50–£12. Sushi and noodle bar. Noodles from all parts of Asia. Soft drinks £1.50. Organic wine.

CTV

22 Golders Green Road, NW11
Open: every day 12.30–22.30

Tel: 020-8201 8001
Tube: Golders Green

Thai, Chinese and Japanese vegan buffet restaurant. Mouthwatering eat-as-much-as-you-like buffet for £5, or £6 after 6pm. Chow mein, crispy aubergine, spring rolls, Singapore noodles, Thai curry rice, sweet and sour won ton, black beans hot pot. Take out box £3. Bring your own alcohol for minimal corkage.

Rajens

West Hendon Indian vegetarian

195-197 The Broadway, West Hendon NW9
Open: every day 11.00–22.00

Tel: 020-8203 8522
Train: Hendon BR

Excellent value Indian vegetarian restaurant and take-away close to the mega-crossroads where the M1 meets the North Circular meets the Edgware Road. East as much as you like buffet thali £5 till 3pm, £6.50 evenings and all weekend. Also a la carte. Soft drinks only. Free car park at the back.

Veg

West Hendon Chinese vegan

244 The Broadway, Weset Hendon NW9
Open: Mon–Sat 12.30–22.30, Sun 17–22.00

Tel: 020-8203 6925
Tube: West Hendon

Close to the entrance to the start of the M1 and North Circular, Chinese vegan buffet restaurant where you can eat as much as you like for just £5. Scoff till you drop from boiled and stir-fried rice, spring rolls, tofu, stir-fry veg, soya meats and noodles. No alcohol but you can bring your own and pay 50p corkage.

Chai

Edgware Chinese vegan

236 Station Road, Edgware
Open: Mon–Fri 12–14.30 and 18–23.30,
Sat 12–15.30, 18.30–23.30; Sun 12–23.30

Tel: 020-8905 3033
Tube: Edgware
www.chai-veg.co.uk

Almost entirely vegan Chinese restaurant, Buddhist owned, with astonishing range of fake meats and lots of other dishes, ideal night out for both avid and reluctant veggies with 132 items on the menu. Appetizers £2.50-5.00, main courses £3.50-4.00. Set meals £11.50 or £13.95 per person. Corkage £2.50 per bottle. Visa, MC.

Cafe Pushkar

Brixton vegetarian restaurant

424 Coldharbour Lane, Brixton SW9
Open: every day 11–23.00

Tel: 020–7738 6161
Tube: Brixton

Cafe and restaurant near Brixton market. Soup, falafel, burgers from £2.50. Salads £2.50 or £2.40. Substantial mains £4–5 like sesame tofu with pineapple and mange tout, or Thai green curry. Vegan cakes from £1. Wine from £8.50 bottle, £2.50 glass.

Cicero's

Clapham Common vegetarian cafe

2 Rookery Road, Clapham Common SW4
Open: daily 10–18.00 summer, 10–16.00 winter

Tel: 020–7498 0770
Tube: Clapham Common

On the common. 50% vegan. All day breakfast £5. Starters £3.50 like sushi, soup, stuffed aubergine. Mains £5.50 such as grilled tofu with peanut sance and rice, aubergine moussaka. Sandwiches, veggieburgers, vegan desserts. Drinks 60p–£1.25. BYO. No smoking.

Sayur Mayur

Clapham Oriental vegetarian

87 Battersea Rise, SW11
Open: every day 17.30–23.00; Fri–Sun 13–15.00

Tel: 020–7350 0900
Train: Clapham Junction BR

New Oriental vegetarian restaurant and take–away with lots of fake meat and tofu dishes. No MSG.

Shahee Bhelpoori

Norbury Indian vegetarian restaurant

1547 London Road, SW16
opposite Norbury British Rail station
Open: every day 12–14.30, 18–23.00

Tel: 020–8679 6275
Train: Norbury BR

On the A23 to Brighton. Mains from £2.95, dosas from £4.10. 10 thalis £4.50–6.95. 14 desserts £1.85 include vegan ice–cream. Sunday all day and weekday lunch all you can eat buffet £3.95. Wine £6.50 bottle, £1.60 glass. 10% discount to VSUK and Vegan Society.

Wholemeal Cafe

Streatham vegetarian restaurant

1 Shrubbery Road, Streaham SW16
Open: every dat 12.–24.00. Closed bank holidays.

Tel: 020–8769 2423
Train: Streatham BR
Streatham Hill BR

Wholefood restaurant with world cuisine. Large vegan selection. Starters £2.0–2.90, mains £2.90–6.25 like Thai curry, hot bake of the day, homity pie. Desserts £2.25. Organic wines, beers, cilders, ales.

Mangoes
Wimbledon vegetarian restaurant

191–193 Hartfield Road, Wimbledon SW19   Tel: 020-8542 9912
Open: Mon–Fri 07-17.00, Sat 9–17.00, Sun 11–16.00   Tube: Wimbledon

New colourful vegetarian cafe and take–away with British, Mediterranean and Indian dishes and great vegan cakes. Lots of lunch sandwiches or have a platter of them. Baked potato or rice with many toppings, pasta, soup, home–made desserts.

Blah Blah Blah
Shepherds Bush vegetarian restaurant

78 Goldhawk Road, Shepherds Bush W12   Tel: 020-8746 1337
Open: Mon–Sat 12.30–14.30 & Mon–Sun 19–23.00   Tube: Shepherds Bush

Vegetarian restaurant on two floors. Starters £4.95–5.95. Main courses £9.50 such as Thai green curry with basmati rice and fruit salsa. One starter and main at least are always vegan, but of the desserts, £4.95, not one, they say there is no demand! Bring your own wine and pay £1.25 corkage per person. No credit cards.

The Gate
Hammersmith gourmet vegetarian

51 Queen Caroline St, hammersmith W6   Tel: 020-8748 6932
Open: Mon–Sat 12-15.00, 18-23.00, Sun closed   Tube: Hammersmith

Top class international vegetarian restaurant. 9 starters (7 vegan options) £1.95–8.50. 6 mains £9.50–10.50 such as Malaysian curry with basmati and wild rice, garnished with papaya salsa. 6 desserts (3 vegan) like damson and pear crumble with vegan ice–cream or sorbet. Wine £9.75 bottle, £2.95 glass. Smoking allowed in restaurant. Book at least 2 days ahead at the weekend.

Vegan Thai Buffet
Acton Chinese all–you–can–eat vegan

167 The Vale, Acton W3   Tel: 020-8740 0888
Open: Mon–Sat 12-22.00, Sun 17.30–22.00   Tube: Shepherds Bush

Vegan Oriental buffet restaurant west of Shepherds Bush where you can eat as much as you like for just £5, £3 take–away, from boiled and stir–fried rice, spring rolls, tofu, stir–fry veg, soya meats and noodles.

Revital Health Place

Victoria health food shop

3a The Colonnades, 123–151 Buckingham Palace Rd,
SW1 (behind Victoria train station)
Open: Mon–Fri 9–19.00, Sat 9–18.00, Sun closed

Tel: 020–7976 6615
Tube: Victoria

Between Victoria coach and train stations. Vegan desserts, pasties, pizza, cakes, macrobiotic foods, Nelsons products and books.

Planet Organic

Westbourne Grove wholefood supermarket

42 Westbourne Grove, W2
Open: Mon–Sat 9.30–20.00, Sun 12–18.00

Tel: 020–7221 7171
Tube: Bayswater

Picnic heaven. Load up here with 15 aisles of every kind of organic veggie food and heaps you never even knew existed, alcoholic and non-alcoholic drinks, exotic flowers. They sell Veggie Guides. Also meat, but it's hidden at the back of the store.

Greenlands

Greenwich health food shop

Unit 3a, Greenwich Craft Market, Greenwich, SE10
Open: Mon–Sun 9.30–18.30

Tel: 020–8293 9176
Tube: Greenwich

Take–away pies, pasties, sandwiches, salads, snacks, cakes and health drinks. Near National Maritime Museum and Cutty Sark.

Fresh & Wild

Wholefood supermarket

194 Old Street, The City EC1
Open: Mon–Fri 9.30–19.30,
Sat 11.30–17.30,Sun closed

Tel: 020–7250 1708
Tube: Old Street

49 Parkway, Camden Town NW1
Open: Mon–Fri 08–21.00,
Sat 9.30–21.00, Sun 11–20.00

Tel: 020–7428 7575
Tube: Camden Town

210 Westbourne Grove, Notting Hill W11
Open: Mon–Sat 03–20.00, Sun 10–18.00

Tel: 020–7229 1063
Tube: Notting Hill Gate
(7 minutes)

Stoke Newington Church Street, N16
Open: Mon–Fri 9–21.00, Sat 8.30–20.30, Sun 10–20.00

Tel: 020–7254 2332
Tube: Angel then 73 bus

305–311 Lavender Hill, SW11

Tel: 020–7585 1488
Tube: Clapham Common

House of Mistry

Hampstead health food shop

15-17 South End Road, Hampstead NW3
Open: Mon-Fri 9-19.00, Sat 9-18.00, Sun closed

Tel: 020-7794 0848
BR: Hampstead Heath

Health food shop by the Heath. Clinic attached for advice on healing. Cosmetics, body products, oils, toiletries.

Bumblebee Wholefood Co-op

N7 wholefood store

30, 32 and 33 Brecknock Rd, N7
(south end of Brecknock Rd, just off Camden Road)
Open: Mon-Sat 9-18.30, Thu till 19.30

Tel: 020-7607 1936
Tube: Kentish Town

Three shops with a massive selection of wholefoods, organic produce, macrobiotic foods and a bakery. Vegan and organic wines and beers. Take-away lunches 11.30-15.00, always 4+ vegan options.

Haelan Centre

Crouch End wholefood store

41 The Broadway, Crouch End N8
Open: Mon-Sat 9-18.00 (Fri -18.30), Sun 12-16.00

Tel: 020-8340 4258
Train: Crouch Hill,
Hornsey

Large independent shop with a complementary health clinic upstairs. A great place to buy presents or pamper yourself.

Bushwacker

Hammersmith wholefood store

132 King Street, Hammersmith W6
Open: Mon-Sat 9.30-18.00,
Tue 10-18.00, Thu 9.3.0-19.00, Sun closed

Tel: 020-8748 2061
Tube: Hammersmith

GM free wholefood shop. Organic fruit and veg too. Plenty for vegans.

The Grain Shop

Portobello Road bakery and take-away

269a Portobello Road, Notting Hill W11
Open: Mon-Sat 9.30-18.00, Sun closed

Tel: 020-7229 5571
Tube: Ladbroke Grove

Vegetarian deli, take-away, organic bakery and wholefood shop. Hot dishes, half vegan. Bakery caters well for special diets.

Natural's Way

Streatham health food shop

252 Streatham High Road, SW16
Open: Mon-Sat 9.30-18.30, Sun closed

Tel: 020-8769 0065

Manchester

Manchester is a large, hectic city, famous for its nightclub culture. There is a strong gay scene, and a massive population of students, so the city has had a cosmopolitan feel for a long time.

The shopping centre is mainly huge chain stores and offers little of interest, but the city really comes alive at night.

Vegetarians are quite well catered for in Manchester. There isn't so much in the way of good restaurants, but there are some excellent cafes and health food shops, including an entirely vegan super-market.

by Ronny

Eighth Day Café

Vegetarian cafe and wholefood shop

Vegetarian café and health food shop run by a workers co-op, with an international wholefood menu. Currently in temporary premises housed in a large portakabin in Sidney Street whilst the main site (107-111 Oxford Road) is rebuilt. They hope to move back early 2003 when they will increase to 100 seats.

Breakfast, served until 11.30, from £1.40 for beans on toast and £3.40 for a full (veggie) house. Salads £2 for small bowl, £3.40 for a large. Mains such as baked potatoes with various fillings from £2.50; pitta bread, small salad and vegan pate £3.10; specials from £3.25. Desserts are also usually vegan friendly such as chocolate cake £1.40. Special diets catered for and they always soya milk, vegan margarine and cheese.

All food is available for take-away.

Sidney Street
All Saints
Manchester M1 7DU

returning in 2003 to
107-111 Oxford Road

Tel:
0161-273 1850/4878
Fax: 0161-273 4878

www.eighth-day.co.uk
mail@eighth-day.co.uk

Open:
Mon-Fri 10.00-18.15,
Sat 10.00-16.30

Non smoking

Visa, MC

5% discount to Vegetarian Society members and 10% for students

v2go

Vegetarian cafe and take-away

Vegetarian food on the move.

Traditional veggie burger or spicy Mexican beanburger £2.80.

Falafel £3.50. Hummous and salad pitta £3.00. Mixed salads £1.90. Crunchy potato wedges £1.50. Fries £1.50.

Soup with a roll ££2.50.

Cakes or apple pie £1.70.

Mineral water £1.00. Freshly squeezed juices from £1.20. Fizzy drinks 75-95p.

At The Orient
in the Trafford Centre
Manchester

Tel: 0161-747 2700

www.v2go.co.uk
menu and job
opportunities on line

Open:
Mon-Fri 07.30-20.00
Sun 07.30-19.00

Earth Café

Central vegetarian café near the Arndale shopping complex, housed in the same building as the Manchester Buddhist centre, and run by Buddhists.

95% of the food is organic, everything is prepared on the premises and suitable for vegans. 50 seats with counter service.

Organic juice bar with juices from £1.50 and soya smoothies from £2.50.

Soups and sandwiches £2–£2.50, with fillings such as olive tapenades, vegetable pates or brazil nut and tofu.

There are at least 2 mains every day with 3–4 side dishes and a choice of 5 different accompanying salads – tabouleh, carrot and raisins, and bean sprouts and beatroot featuring amongst those available. Main dishes £2.50–£5.40, examples include Indonesian stew, cauliflower roulade, and sweet vegetable curry.

Cakes for dessert from £1.40, with regulars including chocolate and coffee and walnut.

16–20 Turner Street
Northern Quarter
Manchester
M41 1DZ

Tel: 0161–834 1996
Fax: 0161–839 4815

www.earthcafe.co.uk
fabulousfood@
earthcafe.co.uk

Train/Tube Train:
Manchester Piccadilly

Open:
Tue–Sat 10.00–17.00,
closed Sun–Mon

Can cater for special diets

High chairs

No smoking

No credit cards

England MANCHESTER Restaurants

Cafe Pop

Mostly vegetarian cafe

34-36 Oldham Street
Manchester M1 1JN
Open: Mon-Thur 09.30-17.30, Fri-Sat 09.30-
19.00, Sun 10.30-17.00

Tel: 0161-237 9688
www.cafepop.co.uk

Mostly vegetarian café (some meals have tuna) with cosmopolitan cuisine and a wide selection for vegans. Vegan breakfast, £3.90, selection of salads from £1 and mains at £4.20. Always have soya milk and vegan ice cream and are planning to introduce a vegan dessert menu. Separate smoking section. No credit cards. Offer 10% discount to Vegetarian and Vegan Society members.

Zumbar

Omnivorous cafe-bar

14 Oxford Road
Manchester, M1 5QA
Open: every day midday to midnight for food

Tel: 0161 236 8438

Omnivorous modern café-bar that attracts a lot of vegans, formerly called Amigo's, by the university opposite the BBC. Starters like nachos, garlic mushrooms, pitta with hummous, potato skins with chili filling. Mains £7.50 include enchiladas with rice and stir-fried vegetables; enchirito; Peking style sir-fry with cashews. Guacamole salad. Falafel £4.95 with salad and hummous dip. Vegan burger £2.40, you can have a jacket potato or rice with it.
Vegan cakes and ice-cream. Bottle of house wine £8.50-9.00, glass £1.80.

Eighth Day Café

Catering service

49 Old Birley Street
Hulme
Manchester
Greater Manchester M15 5RH

Tel: 0161-227 8848
Fax: 0161-273 4878

Sister of the main Eighth Day café, this place is a vegetarian and vegan catering service which offers national coverage for functions of any size and any special diet needs.

Misty's Vegetarian Café

Vegetarian & vegan café

Unit 3, Longsight Shopping Centre
531 Stockport Road
Longsight
Greater Manchester M12 4JH
mistys.vegetarian.café@ntlworld.com
Open: Mon–Sat 9.00–18.00, Sun 11.00–17.00

Tel: 0161 256 3355

Vegetarian café with food from around the world and predominantly vegan menu. Mains such as chickpea curry with rice, £3, and they specialise in vegan desserts, with typically 9 to choose from including strawberry vegan cheesecake and apricot and pistachio cake, £1–£1.50. Always have soya milk. Smoking permitted. No credit cards.

The Greenhouse

Vegetarian & vegan restaurant

331 Great Western Street
Rusholme
Greater Manchester M14 4AN
Open: Mon–Sun 12 noon to late, close afternoons
when no bookings.

Tel: 0161–224 0730
Fax: 0161–256 0943

The original vegetarian restaurant in Manchester since 1983 with 160 a la carte dishes, half of them vegan. Starters £1.95–£3.85. Mains £4.95–£9.85. A stunning 30 desserts, of which just under half are vegan. 10% discount for Vegetarian or Vegan Society members (except Sat after 17.00, Xmas, New Year and Valentine's). Non smoking. Visa, MC.

Punjab Sweet House

Indian omnivorous

177 Wilmslow Road
Rusholme
Greater Manchester M14
Open: Open every day 12–23.00, Fri–Sat till 24.00

Tel: 0161–225 2960

Indian omnivorous restaurant with about half the menu vegetarian. Many South Indian dishes, main meal from £4.50. Offer 10% student discount. Smoking section. Visa, MC.

Greens Restaurant

Ethnic vegetarian restaurant

43 Lapwing Lane
West Didsbury
Greater Manchester M20 2NT
Open: Mon–Sun 17.30–22.30, Tue–Fri 12–14.00,
Sun 12.30–15.30

Tel: 0161–434 4259
Fax: 0161–448 0120

Modern international and ethnic vegetarian restaurant. Salads from £4.75. Mains such as aubergine and potato mussamam curry with peanuts served with thai sticky rice, £9.75. Always vegan options available including in dessert options but vegan desserts change and are not always on menu so worth asking about. Bring your own booze, no corkage charge. Smoking permitted. Visa, MC.

Fuel Café Bar

Vegetarian café

448 Wilmslow Road
Withington
Greater Manchester M20 3BW
Open: Mon–Sat 9.00–24.00, Sun 9.30–23.30

Tel: 0161 2826040

Vegetarian café with internet access. Some vegan items on menu but vegetarian items can also be made vegan, such as a full breakfast at £4.50. Mains, £2.20–£5.90, include paninis, bruschettas and burritos. Desserts, £1.90. Licensed with house wine £2.30 for a glass, £8 for a bottle. Smoking permitted. Visa, MC.

Holland & Barrett

Health food shop

Unit 34, Lower Mall
Trafford Park
Manchester
Greater Manchester M17 2BL

Tel: 0161–747 2699

87 Deansgate
Manchester, M3 2BW

Tel: 0161–834 5923

Unit 122 Market Way
Upper Mall, Arndale Ct
Manchester

Tel: 0161–834 5975

607 Wilbraham Road
Chorlton Cum Hardy
Greater Manchester MX1 1AN

Tel: 0161–881 1539

Liverpool

Liverpool attracts a lot of tourists due to the worldwide success of the band the Beatles who put it firmly on the map in the 1960's. Today's fans can visit a museum, a shop and can even see the houses where the "fab four" grew up.

Liverpool boasts some splendid Victorian architecture including many unspoiled city centre pubs. Most of its docks are still in operation but Albert Dock has now been turned into a tourist attraction with lots of little shops and cafes and the impressive Tate modern art gallery. There are lots of museums to visit, including ones with certain historical themes, such as the Maritime Museum and the Museum of Liverpool Life.

Liverpool is a very compact city and it is easy to walk around the city centre. If you want all the usual high street shops, leave Central Station and walk straight up Church Street. The Beatles attractions and the Tourist Information Centre are also situated off this and the Docks are at the far end.

The most interesting area for vegetarians is Bold Street, which runs to the left of the station in the opposite direction. The small streets running parallel to and branching off Bold Street are full of pubs, clubs and cafes and are very lively in the evenings.

Liverpool is well served by railways and motorways and is a good base for exploring North Wales and the North West.

By Ronny

Places in Liverpool

Restaurants

1	**Green Fish Café** – Vegetarian café	158
2	**Green Fish Café** – Vegetarian café	158
3	**The Egg Café** – Vegetarian café	158
4	**Everyman Bistro** – Omnivorous restaurant	158
	The Pod – Omnivorous bar-restaurant	158

Shops

5	**News From Nowhere** – Bookshop	158
6	**Mattas International Foods** – Health food shop	158
7	**Holland & Barrett** – International food shop	158

MERSEYSIDE England

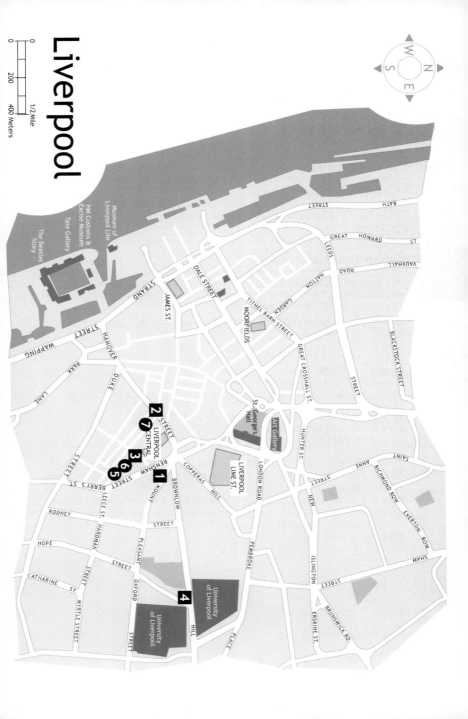

Green Fish Café

Vegetarian café

11 Upper Newington, Off Renshaw Street
Liverpool,Merseyside L1
Open: Mon–Sat 11–17.00

Tel: 0151–707 8592
www.greenfishcafe.co.uk
Train Liverpool Central

Cheap, modern–looking vegetarian café with at least two vegan meals per day. Smaller and more up–market in appearance than The Egg. Starters £1.50 upwards include soup and salads. Main courses £2.75–£3.50 include curry, mousakka, burritos and pasta. Desserts £1.20 upwards but no vegan cakes. Tea and coffee 70–80p. Sometimes have soya milk, but always have soya spread.

Turn left out of the central station, and it's opposite Black's Camping Shop on the ground floor of the Merseyside Youth Association building.

Green Fish Café

Vegetarian café

The Door, 65–67 Hanover Street
Liverpool,Merseyside L1 3BY
Open: Mon–Fri 10–17.00, closed weekend

Tel: 0151–702 0705
www.greenfishcafe.co.uk

New second branch, same menu as the other one. Directions: turn left out of the central station.

The Egg Café

Vegetarian café

Top Floor, Newington Buildings,Newington
Liverpool, Merseyside L1 4ED
Train/Tube Liverpool Central or
Lime Street (main railway Station)
Open: Mon–Sat 10–22.30, Sun 10–17.00

Tel: 0151 707 2755

Vegetarian café with majority of menu vegan. Mains, £2.90–£3.95. Always have vegan desserts – cakes and crumbles, £1.65. Smoking section. No credit cards.

Walk up Bold Street and turn right at the big Oxfam shop onto Newington (it is not signposted) and about half way along look out for a tall scruffy building on your right. Climb the stairs to the top (2nd) floor and you're there.

Everyman Bistro

Omnivorous restaurant

5-9 Hope Street
Liverpool, Merseyside L1 9BH
Open: Mon-Wed 12.00-24.00, Thu 12.00-01.00,
Fri & Sat 12.00-02.00. Closed Sun.

Tel: 0151-708 9545

Omnivorous restaurant with 45% menu vegetarian. Mains at £5.30 include aubergine and potato curry, spicy vegetable enchilladas and vegetable daal. Can cater for vegans and other special diets, but get there early as vegan options can run out. Licensed. House wine is £1.70 for a glass, £8.45 for a bottle. Separate non smoking section. Visa, MC.

The Pod

Omnivorous bar-restaurant

137-139 Allerton Road
Liverpool, Merseyside L18
Open: Mon-Sat 12-15.00 lunch, Sun 10.3-14.30
brunch menu, every day 18.00-21.30 tapas menu

Tel: 0151 724 2255
Fax: 0151 281 1391

Omnivorous bar-restaurant with a lot of vegetarian food. Lunch main meal £5 such as garlic focaccia with aubergine, salad, tomato and olive penne. They can make anything vegan and charge less. Soup £3. For a tapas evening meal you'll need about three dishes to make a meal at £3 each, such as potato agnioli, arancini (deep fried risotto balls), chick peas and sage, tortilla, stuffed chilli, patatas bravas (roasted new potatoes with chili, tomato and red pepper sauce), braised cabbage, vegetable tempura, olives, salads.

Smoking allowed in the whole restaurant as it's quite small. Visa, MC, Diners, Amex. Children over 14 welcome with parents, younger ones before 8pm when the drinking gets going. Reservations advised for evenings as they get quite busy though you can just turn up.

News From Nowhere

Bookshop

Bold Street (almost right at the top)
Liverpool, Merseyside L1

Train: Liverpool Central
Open: Mon-Sat 9-5.30

Radical bookshop run by a women's workers' co-op. Stocks a wide range of human and animal rights, gay and lesbian, environmental and personal development books, postcards and magazines. Good selection of vegetarian and vegan cookbooks. Very knowledgeable and helpful staff. Huge noticeboard by the door packed with events and contacts in Liverpool.

England **MERSEYSIDE** Restaurants – Shops

Mattas International Foods

International food shop

Bold Street
Liverpool

Train : Liverpool Central

Open: Mon–Sat 9–18.00, Sun 10–16.00

Cheap international food shop, selling some meat but also very well stocked with vegan products. Cheapest soya milk, tofu and take away vegan pasties and samosas in town. Delivery of vegan Turkish Delight every Thursday, ask at the counter! Walk up Bold street and it's on the left, near the top.

Holland & Barrett

Health food shop

17 Whitechapel
Liverpool, Merseyside L1 6DS

Tel: 0151–236 8911

3a Bold Stret
Liverpool, Merseyside L1 4DG

Tel: 0151–708 9343

6 Borough Pavement
Birkenhead,Merseyside L41 2XX

Tel: 0151 647 7327

28 Marina Walk
Ellesmere Port
South Wirral, Merseyside L65 0BS

Tel: 0151–355 9228

Unit 12 Station Arcade
Chapel Street
Southport, Merseyside PR8 1BH

Tel: 01704–530 734

Middlesex

Places in Middlesex

Restaurants

Shops

MIDDLESEX England

A1 Sweet

Vegetarian Indian cafe

106 The Broadway
Southall
Open: Tue–Fri 9.00–18.00, Sat: 9.00–19.00, Sun:
10.00–18.00, closed Mon

Tel: 020–8574 2821
Tube: Southall BR

Vegetarian Indian café with good honest food at no frills prices. 13 starters like Dhal Kachori £1.50–2.00. 15 main meals include Masala Dosa or Saag & Makki Roti £2.75–3.50, some of them vegan. 14 desserts £1.50–2.50, but none vegan. Soft drinks 50p with food.

Chai

Chinese vegan restaurant

353 High Road
Harrow Weald
Open: Mon–Fri 12.00–14.30 and 18.00–23.30;
Sat: 12.00–15.30 &18.30–23.30; Sun 12.00–23.30

Tel: 020–8863 8881
Tube: Harrow Weald BR

Chinese vegetarian restaurant, sister to the one in Edgware (north-west London). Run by committed Buddhists, they can guarantee that all the food is free from egg and animal products. Eat as much as you like buffet Mon–Sat lunch £3.80, Sun lunch £6.90, every evening £8.90. Also a la carte menu.

Chetna's

South Indian vegetarian restaurant

420 High Road
Wembley
Open: Mon closed, Tue–Fri 12–15.00 & 18–22.30;
Sat–Sun 13.00–22.30

Tel: 020–8903 5989
Tube: Wembley Park,
Wembley Central

Gujarati and South Indian vegetarian restaurant with take–away service specializing in Indian snacks, dosas, simple curries and pizzas. Starters such as bhelpoori, pani poori, from £2.40. Lots of dosas under £5. Large pizza £5.90–£6.70. Range of vegetarian desserts but nothing vegan. Wines and beers.Minimum charge of £5.50 per person. Credit cards ok. High chairs available.

Jashan

Indian vegetarian restaurant

1–2 Coronet Parade, Ealing Road
Wembley
Open: Mon–Fri 12–15.30, 18–23.00, Sat–Sun 12–23.00

Tel: 020–8900–9800

Indian vegetarian restaurant that aims to "promote healthy vegetarian food, that's rightly spiced and less oily". Extensive menu and low prices. Many cold drinks like fresh coconut water and fresh lime juice with soda water. Outside seating in the summer for around 25 people. This is an alcohol and smoke free zone.

Jhupdi

South Indian restaurant

235 Station Road
Harrow
Open: Sun–Thu 18.00–22.00, Fri–Sat 18.00–23.00;
also Tue–Sat 12.00–14.30

Tel: 020-8427-1335
Tube:
Harrow-on-the-Hill

South Indian vegetarian restaurant and take–away with a wonderfully extensive menu drawing on the culinary traditions of the Punjab and East Africa. Starters £2–£3. Main courses £6–£7 include thali, special thali, masala dosa, a stuffed tomato dish, vegetable spaghetti. 10 desserts but none vegan. Licensed and they do take–away.

Maru's Bhajia House

Indian café

230 Ealing Road
Alperton, Wembley
Open: Mon–Thu 12.30–20.30,
Fri–Sun 12.30–21.30,closed Monday in summer

Tel: 020 8903– 6771
Tube: Alperton,
Wembley Central

Ealing Road has a number of inexpensive Gujarati and south Indian restaurants. Maru's Kenyan Asian cuisine has been a firm favourite for over 20 years with bhajias of course, samosas, maize and assorted snacks. Asian film stars fill up here on pani puri, kachori and vada. £2.90 for a portion, £5.80 for a double portion. This is a café and gets very busy at lunchtimes and weekends.

Naklank Sweet Mart

Gujarati Indian restaurant

50b Ealing Road
Wembley
Open: Mon–Sat 10.00–19.00, Sun: 11.00–19.00

Tel: 020-8902 8008

Gujarati vegetarian Indian eat in or take–away. 39 different sweets and savouries, samosas, pakoras, 20 kinds of bhajia. Curries from £2.50 and mostly vegan. All traditionally made. Small seating area with two tables inside. Outside catering service.

Natraj

Indian take–away

341 Northolt Road
South Harrow
Open: Mon–Tue, Thu–Sat 10.00–19.30, closed Wed,
Sun 10–16.00

Tel: 020-8426 8903
Tube: South Harrow

Indian vegetarian take–away with plenty for vegans. Starters/snacks such as bhajias, sweets, samosas, etc. A regular take–away box of curry is £2.50, large £3.50. Box of rice £1.50 and £2.50. Or get a box of half curry, half rice for £2 or £3, ideal for lunch.

Sakonis

Vegetarian Indian & Chinese restaurant

5-8 Dominion Parade, Station Road
Harrow
Open: Mon-Sat 12.00-22.30

Tel: 020-8863-3399

Vegetarian Indian restaurant that also serves lots of Chinese dishes. Same menu as Wembley, below.

Shahanshah

North Indian veggie restaurant

60 North Road
Southall
Open: every day 10.00-20.00

Tel: 020-8574-1493
Tube: Ealing Broadway,
Southall BR

North Indian vegetarian restaurant, take-away and sweet centre with 50% of their ingredients organic. Starters £1-1.25 such as two samosas or pakora. Main meal £5. Vegans note, they use butter ghee. Outside seating . Alcohol and smoke-free. No cards.

Sakonis

Vegetarian Indian snack bar & take-away

119-121 Ealing Road
Wembley
Open: every day 11.00-22.30

Tel: 020-8903-9601
Tube: Wembley Central,
Wembley Park

Vegetarian Indian snack bar, take-away and delivery service with over 100 Gujarati, North Indian and Chinese dishes. Starters £1.40-£3.95. Main dishes £2.50-£6.50 such as masala dosa, biriyani, burger and chips, Szechuan spicy noodles, aubergine and chilli in hot black bean sauce. Lots of sweets, fruit shakes and fresh juices for £2.50.

Supreme Sweets

Indian take away

706 Kenton Road
Kenton, Harrow
Mon-Fri 10-19.00, Sat: 9.30-19.00, Sun 8.30-17.30

Tel: 020-8206 2212
Tube: Kingsbury

Indian vegetarian take-away. Sweets and savouries like bhajias £6 per kilo, samosas and pakoras from 40p. Also a range of frozen products like samosas, kachoris and spring rolls. 75% vegan, no eggs.

Woodlands

Indian restaurant

402a High Road Wembley
Open: Mon-Fri 12-15.00, 18-23.00;
Sat-Sun 12-23.00

Tel: 020-8902 9869
Tube: Wembley Central,
Wembley Stadium

Long established vegetarian Indian restaurant, one of three in London serving classic Indian dishes. This branch is decorated in vibrant colours with a bright and airy feel.

Bodywise Health Foods

Health food shop

249 Station Road
Harrow
Open: Mon–Sat 9.00–18.00, Sun closed

Tel: 020–8861–3336

Health food shop with in-house complementary therapy clinic with different practitioners visiting daily for reflexology, kineseology, homeopathy and Swedish massage.

Gaia Wholefoods

Wholefood shop

123 St Margarets Road
Twickenham
Open: Mon–Fri 9.30–19.00, Sat 17.00, Sun closed

Tel: 0181–892 2262

Wholefood shop selling fresh organic bread, fruit and vegetables, gluten free ranges. Also some vegan take-aways like pastries.

Food for Thought

Wholefood shop

154 High Street
Hounslow
Open: Mon–Sat: 9.00–17.30, Sun closed

Tel: 020–8572–0310

Wholefood shop near Heathrow airport with lots of organic food. Take-away sandwiches, pies, pasties, salads and burgers, some of which are vegan.

The Healthy Harvest Food Store

Wholefood shop

In Squires Garden Centre, 6 Cross Road
Twickenham
Mon–Sat 9.30–17.30, Sun from 10.00–17.00

Tel: 020–8943–0692

Get your gardening goodies and tank up on grub at this wholefood shop (not vegetarian) in a garden centre between Twickenham and Hampton Court. One variety of fresh veggie pastie available.

Holland & Barrett

Health food shop

Unit 21 Wembley Sq, High Road, Wembley

Tel 020–8902 6959

13 King Street, Twickenham

Tel: 020–8891 6696

22–24 College Road, Harrow

Tel 020–8427 4794

Norfolk

Whalebone House

Veggie B&B set in the small flint village of Cley, situated on the unspoilt north Norfolk coast. One double ensuite room at £27.50 per person per night and one twin with private bathroom at £25 per person. Minimum of two nights stay.

Breakfast is always a special occasion and is taken at a big round table in their cafe. Start with organic juices, cereals and fruit, then move on to the cooked main course which could be a crostini of roasted field mushroom with marinated and roasted smoked tofu or coriander and red chilli gram flour pancakes with roast tomato filling, amongst other dishes. If you still have room, finish with organic bread or toast with home made preserves and freshly brewed tea or coffee. Soya milk, vegan margarine, veggie sausages, vegan muesli and soy yoghurt are all available. Gluten-free and many other diets are catered for. Just tell them when you book. Produce is local, organic and seasonal.

Lunch and dinner are available in their cafe, 'thecafe at Whalebone House', North Norfolk's only veggie restaurant. The proprietors see thecafe and the guest rooms as an extension of their home so expect a friendly hands on approach.

Cley is a perfect base for walkers, birdwatchers, photographers, painters, writers and anyone wanting to spend some time in beautiful surroundings. Cley Marshes Nature Reserve is one mile away. Bring walking boots, binoculars and warm clothes and leave mobile phones behind! Whalebone House offers meditation and awareness retreats in Winter and Spring.

Rooms have tea and coffee making facilities, hot water bottles, CD player, television, hairdryer, torch and binoculars.

High Street
Cley next the Sea
Norfolk NR25 7RN
England

Tel: 01263 740336

www.whalebonehouse.co.uk

Email: whalebone.house@virgin.net

Train Station: Sheringham, 8 miles, then bus or taxi

Open:
February–November

Directions: On the A149 in the heart of the village, 4 miles from the nearest small town of Holt.

Parking: plenty of safe parking on the street

No smoking throughout

Greenbanks Hotel

Omnivorous
Hotel & Restaurant

Hotel and restaurant with vegetarian proprietors in the heart of the Norfolk countryside. There are nine luxury ensuite rooms consisting of doubles and twins for £68 per room per night and family rooms for £90 per room per night.

Begin your day with cereal and juice followed by a cooked breakfast of herbed potato pancakes, beans, spiced tomatoes, home made veggie sausages and muffins or nut scones. Soya milk, soya yoghurt and vegan margarine are available. Have breakfast in your room if you desire.

A three course dinner is offered in their licensed restaurant for £18. It could be miniature vegetable spring rolls followed by ginger roasted root vegetables with stuffed peppers and for dessert, apple cake and coconut custard. 50% organic. Open to non-residents. Special diets catered for.

Greenbanks is set in eight acres of meadows and has a bog garden, wild flower walk and lakes. They also have a heated indoor hydrotherapy pool.

The coast and beaches are nearby as well as Peddars Way walk and Thetford Forest where you can walk or cycle.

Not far away is the thriving city of Norwich with its huge churches, interesting castle and museums. It has the best night life in the region behind Cambridge.

Tea and coffee making facilities and televisions are in the rooms.

Swaffham Road
Wendling
Norfolk NR19 2AB
England

Tel and Fax:
01362 687742

www.greenbankshotel.
co.uk

Email:
greenbanks@skynow.net

Train station: Norwich,
20 miles, then bus

Open: all year

Directions: Midway between Swaffham and East Dereham on A47, turn off at sign saying Wendling/Longham.

Parking: 20 spaces

Children are welcome and they have facilities such as high chairs.

Pets by arrangement

Disabled access

No smoking throughout

England NORFOLK Restaurants – Accommodation

thecafe@
Whalebone House

Dinner at thecafe is a set menu which changes daily. If you have any dislikes or preferences or you follow a special diet, let them know in advance and they will do their best to accommodate you. It is £16 for two courses, £19.50 for three courses and £21.50 for four courses.

Dinner could be saffron and butterbean cous cous with a watercress and pink grapefruit salad to begin, then coconut and cumin pancakes with spiced aubergine and cabbage and coriander-lime oil, followed by a green salad and for dessert, hot buttered Moroccan dates with an orange-flower rice pudding. Aperitif, mineral water and coffee included.

Licensed. Vegan organic wines are available from £2.90 a glass or £9.50 a bottle. Booking is essential. No credit cards. No smoking.

Vegetarian
Cafe/Restaurant

Whalebone House
High Street
Cley next the Sea
Norfolk NR25 7RN
England

Tel: 01263 740336

www.thecafe.org.uk

Email: whalebone.house@ virgin.net

Train Station: Sheringham, 8 miles, then bus or taxi

Opening hours Jun–Oct:
Tue–Fri:12.00–15.00,
19.30 onwards
Sat:12.00–17.00,
19.30 onwards
Sun:12.00–17.00
Mon: closed

Opening hours for rest of year (except Dec and Jan):
Fri: 19.30 onwards
Sat: 12.00–15.00,
19.30 onwards
Sun: 12.00–15.00
Mon–Thurs: closed

Dec and Jan: closed

The Greenhouse

The Greenhouse is both a café and an environmental centre which offers cheap food and a relaxed atmosphere, so mobile phones should be turned off at the door!

Soup of the day with bread, £2.50.

Salads £1.50 side dish, £2.50 plate.

Ploughmans salad with the option of vegan cheese £4.

A selection of sandwiches is also available.

There are a range of cakes, including vegan and gluten-free options.

Hot and cold cordials, 60p. Organic teas, mug 60p, large pot, £2. Organic, fair-trade coffees from 60p-£2. Soya milk and soya cappuccinos.

Wines, beer and cider are available with meals, for around £2 a glass or £4-8 for a bottle of wine.

A strong emphasis is placed on ethics, so fair-traded and organic ingredients are used where possible.

Vegetarian Restaurant

42–46 Bethel St
Norwich
Norfolk NR2 1NR

Tel: 01603 631007

Open:
Tues–Sat 10.00–17.00,
closed Sun and Mon

Licensed

High chairs

No smoking

Credit cards accepted,
but not Switch

Red Lion

Vegetarian Bed and Breakfast

Bailey Street,
Castle Acre,
Norfolk, PE32 2AG
www.oldredlion.here2stay.org.uk

Tel: 01760 755557
Train Station: Downham
Market, 12 miles

Two doubles (one ensuite), two twins, one dorm room and one family room £15–£25 per person per night. Evening meal by arrangement. Can use the kitchen to cook own meals if desired.
Dogs and children by arrangement. No smoking.

The Tree House

Vegetarian restaurant & take-away

14–16 Dove Street
Norwich
Norfolk NR2 4DE
Open: Mon–Wed 10–17.00, Thu–Sat 10–21.00

Tel: 01603–763 258

Vegetarian wholefood café-restaurant with mostly organic and vegan food. Starters from £2.75 such as lentil and miso soup and mains start at £4.90 and change daily. Normally all desserts are vegan with tofu cheesecake, £2.40, and they always have vegan ice cream. Non smoking. No credit cards. Offer 10% discount to students.

Les Amandines

Vegetarian restaurant & shop

Norfolk House Yard
St Nicholas Street
Diss
Norfolk IP22 4LB
Open: Wed–Thu 10–15.00, Fri–Sat 10–16.00,
ring to confirm

Tel: 01379 640449

Vegetarian and vegan café-restaurant established 12 years, in the centre of the town, a stone's throw from the old church and market place. Breakfasts, teas, cakes and lunches.
The adjacent shop called Natural Food Store sells organic bread, scones, pasties, cakes, savouries, deli stuff like wrapped vine leaves, and vegan cheeses. Shop open Mon–Fri 9–5.30, Tue till 5pm, Sat 9–5. Shop number 01379–651 832.

Restaurants – Accommodation **NORFOLK** England

Holland & Barrett

Health food shop

9/10 Victoria Arcade
Great Yarmouth
Norfolk

Tel: 01493–855 316

15 Norfolk Street
Kings Lynn
Norfolk

Tel: 01553–765 969

19/21 White Lion Street
Norwich

Tel: 01603–762 955

Northamptonshire

Daily Bread Co-op

The Old Laundry
Bedford Road
Northampton NN4 7AD
Open: Mon-Fri 8.30-17.30, Sat -17.00,
closed Sun

Tel: 01604 621531
www.dailybread.co.uk
northampton@dailybread.co.uk

Vegetarian wholefood shop, not a bakery as you might think, and they sell vegan ice-cream. On the town side of the Bedford Rd roundabout, near the Council offices. The best place in Northampton we know of for veggie food, though they told us there's a café in Kettering Road that has a few veggie things.

Holland & Barrett

Health food shop

8 Mercer Row
Northampton NN1 2QL

Tel: 01604-639 603

43 Queens Square
Corby
Northamptonshire NN17 1PD

Tel: 01536-408 914

34 High Street
Kettering
Northamptonshire NN16 8SU

Tel: 01536-417 209

33 Long Causeway
Peterborough
Northamptonshire PE1 1YJ

Tel: 01733-311 268

Northumberland

The Byre

19th century stone-built farm byre which has been converted into a modern unique house offering vegetarian bed and breakfast. There are two rooms; one double ensuite and one double with private bathroom £18-£20 per person per night from October to March and £20-£22 per person per night from April to September. £24 on public holidays.

Breakfast could be fresh fruit salad and cereal or porridge followed by veggie sausages, rashers, baked beans, tomatoes and mushrooms.

A two course dinner is offered for £10 and could be spaghetti bolognaise, Chinese stir fry, Malaysian coconut milk curry, Indonesian Mee Goreng, ratatouille or naan bread with chickpea cholay, followed by fruit crumble, pancake strudel, fruit compote or banana split for dessert. Meals are served with red, white or non-alcoholic wines and tea or filter coffee. As much local fresh produce as possible is used and they cater for special diets.

Harbottle is a small village in the Northumberland National Park. The park offers glimpses of ancient landscapes and wilderness found nowhere else in England.

The ancient ruins of Harbottle castle overlook the Reivers Way along the Coquet Valley. Harbottle is at the foothills of the Cheviots making it a perfect base for walking, cycling and birdwatching and it is just fifteen minutes from the village of Rothbury. Northumberland has a magnif-icent coastline with wide sandy beaches, quaint villages and dramatic castles.

Tea and coffee making facilities, television and video in the sitting room.

*Harbottle
near Rothbury
Northumberland
NE65 7DG
England*

Tel: 01669 650476

www.the-byre.co.uk

Email: rosemary@the-byre.co.uk

Train station: Morpeth, then taxi or bus or they can collect

Open: all year

Directions: A1 north past Newcastle, A697 to Coldstream, B6344 to Rothbury, go west for 4 1/2 miles, turn right at signpost marked Sharperton/Harbottle/ Alwinton

Parking: available off road

Children welcome by arrangement

No smoking throughout.

Disabled access, category three

Brookside House

Vegetarian Bed and Breakfast

Town Foot,
Haltwhistle,
Northumberland, NE49 OER

Tel and Fax:
01434 322481
Open: all year

Two rooms; one twin ensuite and one family with private bathroom £23–£25 per person per night. Evening meals by arrangement. No smoking.

The Town House

Vegetarian restaurant & coffee house

15 Narrowgate
Alnwick
Northumberland NE6 1JH

Tel: 01665 606336
www.townhouse.alnwick.org.uk
townhouse@alnwick.org.uk

Vegetarian restaurant and coffee house owned by two vegans. Light lunches from £2.20 to £5.95. Evening meal starters £1.50–4.45, mains £6.95–7.50, desserts around £4.

Organic wines and beers, house wine £2.25 glass, £9.45 bottle. Non smoking. Gluten free and allergies no problem. High chairs. Credit cards ok. Conference room facilities, private room for events.

The Chantry Tea Room

Omnivorous restaurant

9 Chantry Place
Morpeth
Northumberland NE61 1PJ

Tel: 01670–514 414
Open:
Mon–Sat 9.00–16.45

Omnivorous restaurant. Several vegetarian choices on menu, jacket potatoes, sandwiches, various pies and hot dishes, from £2.85. Can cater for vegans with advance notice. Non smoking. No credit cards.

Bay Horse Inn

Omnivorous pub

West Woodburn
Near Hexham
Northumberland NE48 2RX
cowens@bayhorseinn.fsnet.co.uk

Tel: 01434–270 218
Open:
Mon–Sun 8.00–23.00

Omnivorous pub which caters well for vegetarians and also vegans, with everything clearly marked on the menu. Vegan breakfast from £4, soup from £1.95. At least 3 vegan mains, £3.45–£5.50, with vegetable chilli, mixed nut loaf and stir fried vegetables in blackbean sauce amongst the offerings. Restaurant is non smoking. Visa, MC.

Holland & Barrett

Health food shop

31–33 Fore Street
Hexham
Northumberland

Tel: 01434–609 067

SCRUMPTIOUS FOOD FROM

Suma is one of the UK's leading independent distributors and manufacturers of vegetarian foods and ethical products.

We have been trading and evolving for over 25 years. And as one of the largest workers co~operatives in the UK **Suma** provides a high quality service to customers and a rewarding working environment for its workers, within a sustainable, ethical business structure.

We aim to create a healthier, more balanced & greener lifestyle for the future by working with the environment ~ not against it.

We have deep ethical & social concerns and endeavour to respond and educate in a conscientious way on issues such as GMO's and the benefits of natural and organic foods.

The **Suma** brand encompasses the highest quality vegan, vegetarian, fairly traded and organic foods all of which are approved by the Vegetarian Society. So look out for our products in your local Health Food Shop. You will find a huge range, from organic beans, nuts and grains through to delicious pasta sauces, and that all time essential ~ recycled toilet paper!

For more information about **Suma** please contact us on 0845 458 2290.

Nottingham

Nottingham relies on the legend of Robin Hood to pull in tourists from all over the world.

The city centre itself could at first sight be considered quite ugly, sprawling and clogged with traffic, but there is plenty of outstanding scenery a bus or train ride away. What remains of Sherwood Forest is situated north of the city, close to Mansfield. Within the city is Woolaton Park, a beautiful place for a stroll with lakes, woodlands and resident deer.

Nottingham has some unique attractions for veggies, including an entirely vegetarian burger bar, and an entirely vegan social club run by ethical green campaigners! There are some good, well-stocked health food shops, along with plenty of veggie-friendly cafes and pubs.

by Ronny

Anson's Place

Veggie B&B in a large Victorian house situated in Gedling Village, three and a half miles north east of Nottingham city. There are two rooms, one double and one twin costing £35 per room per night. If you are alone, the room will cost you £30. One of the rooms overlooks the garden and can be made into a family room.

Breakfast is comprised of fruit juice, a selection of cereals or muesli with fresh fruit salad or grapefruit, followed by baked beans, tomatoes and mushrooms on toast with tea or coffee. Soya milk, vegan margarine and vegan muesli available. Food is organic when possible. It's best to give notice if you are vegan.

No evening meal is offered, but there are a few veggie restaurants in the city.

Sherwood Forest (an S.S.S.I) is thirty minutes drive away.

The Peak District is forty minutes away and historic Newark is twenty five minutes away.

Visit Nottingham Castle, The River Trent, Greens Windmill and The Lace Market. There are also many museums, shops, nightclubs and theatres in town, as well as a National Ice Arena, water sports and Tennis Centre.

Tea and coffee making facilities and televisions in the rooms. Guests are welcome to use the garden.

21 Waverley Avenue
Gedling
Nottinghamshire
England NG4 3HH

Tel: 0115 9618090

Email: ansonsplace21@ hotmail.com

Train Station: Midland Nottingham, 3 1/2 miles, then bus or taxi

Open: all year

Directions: 3 1/2 miles north east of Nottingham off the A612 Nottingham to Southwell Road

Parking: available

High chairs for the little ones

No pets

No smoking

10% discount for stays of three nights or more

Alley Café

Vegetarian and vegan organic cafe

Friendly vegetarian and vegan organic café in the centre of Nottingham opposite the main library, located in a courtyard near the market square.

Starters, £2–£2.95, include organic potato wedges with spicy salsa relish; chickpea and courgette fritters with a mint soya yoghurt dip; and crunchy Oriental tofu orbs.

Large selection of sandwiches, with a choice of 5 different breads (foccacia, Italian, baguette, granary and rye) all of which are £2.75 and come with names, a few of which follow with introductions: Ethel is a vegan cream cheese, avocado and pineapple sandwich; Mildred – smoked tofu, vegan pesto with artichoke hearts; and Winston – roasted vegetables and hummus.

Specials are usually vegan and change daily. Regular mains such as loaded herb crepes with creamy garlic mushroom filling (vegan), £4.25; tandoori tofu kebab, £3.95 and choice of 2 burgers at £4.25 – a tempeh burger and a hemp burger.

Desserts typically like tofu cheesecake which changes flavours, carrot cake and Belgian chocolate biscuit cake (all vegan), from £1.50 a slice.

They try to cater for special diets and there is usually a wheat-free special on the board.

There is a DJ Thu–Fri evenings with a mellow funk sound.

They try to have environmentally sound initiatives using eco products and recycling waste wherever possible.

1 A Cannon Court
Long Row
Nottingham
NG1 6JE

Tel: 0115–955 1013

www.alleycafe.co.uk
alleycafe@hotmail.com

Open: Mon–Sat 11.00–23.00

Fully licensed and all wines are organic and vegetarian or vegan

Smoking permitted

Visa, MC

England **NOTTINGHAMSHIRE** Restaurants

V1 Vegetarian Fast Food

Vegetarian fast food, where you'll usually get your food in just 2 or 3 minutes and no more than 6.

Oven-baked veggieburgers are a speciality, choose from spicy, chilli, nut, benay, tikka, VLT, ranch with fries and a drink £3.90-4.20, or burger only £2.20. Or have the organic version with organic mushroom burger, organic tortilla chips and organic drink for £4.90, burger only £2.90. Vegan cheese add 20p, double burger +£1. Jungle box for kids with sausages or nuggets or mini VLT with fries & drink £2.20.

Extras 95p-£1.70 fries, hash browns, onion rings, sausages & dip, spicy wedges & dip, garlic mushrooms, beany chips. Nuggets & dip £2.20, nachos £2.50, spicy bag & dip £2.75. Bhaji, samosa & wedges combo bag & dip £2.75.

Chilli or ratatouille with rice or chips £3.20.

Breakfast served until 11am, sausage, rasher & beans in a bun with hash browns & drink £2.75. Hot sausage sandwich £1.75. Toasted teacake 75p. Toast & jam 60p.

Dozens of freshly made sandwiches & wraps on white, granary or tomato bread from £1.60.

Soft drinks 80p-£1.20, fresh OJ £1.2-1.50, hot drinks including cappuccino 75p-85p. Also fruit smoothies, iced tea, mineral water, soya and organic drinks. Special offers include soup & sandwich £2.50, 25% student discount off-peak weekdays and all day Sunday. 3-6pm doughnut or tea cake & hot drink £1.

Vegetarian and vegan burgers and cafe

7 Hounds Gate
Nottingham
NG1 7AA

Tel: 0115-941 5121

Open:
Mon-Sat 08.00-18.00,
Sun 12-16.00

Full menu and details of external catering on their superb website:
www.v-1.co.uk
mail@v-1.co.uk

Kids parties for 10 or more with balloons, birthday cake and a present for the birthday child, £3.70 per child. Entertainment - face painting, balloon modelling, games & prizes - from £50.

No eggs used

10% discount for members of The Vegetarian and Vegan Society, Viva!

Croft Hotel

Omnivorous Hotel

6–8 North Road,
West Bridgford,
Nottinghamshire, NG2 7NH
Train Station: Nottingham, 1 mile

Tel: 0115 9812744
Open: all year

Fourteen rooms £20–£25 per person per night.
Children and pets welcome. Smoking allowed in some rooms.

Heart and Art

Vegetarian cafe & art gallery

121 Mansfield Road
Nottingham NG1 3FQ
Open: Tue 10.00–15.00, Wed–Thu 9.00–16.00, Fri–
Sat 10.00–18.00, Sun 10.00–15.00

Tel: 0115–950 6022

Vegetarian café and art gallery. Homemade meals, £3; salads,
sandwiches and cakes, £1. Eat in, take away and catering service.

Squeek

Gourmet vegetarian restaurant

23–25 Heathcote Street
Hockley
Nottingham NG1 3AG

Tel: 0115–941 0710
Open:
Mon–Sat 18.00–22.00

Vegetarian gourmet restaurant where everything on the menu can be
made vegan. Starters from £3.95, mains from £ £8.95. Prix fixe 3
course, £13.50. Desserts, £3.95 including vegan ice cream. House
wine, £8.95. Separate smoking section. Visa, MC.

The Vegetarian Pot

Indian vegetarian restaurant

375 Alfreton Road
Radford
Nottingham NG7 5LT
Open: Mon–Sat 11–14.00, 17–21.00, closed Sun

Tel: 0115–970 3333
www.vegetarianpot.com

Friendly vegetarian North Indian restaurant and takeaway with a
predominantly vegan menu. Non–vegan items are clearly indicated
with a star. Main meals, £2.85–£4, such as channa (chickpeas), aloo
bhangan (potatoes and aubergine) and saag (spinach and mustard
leaves flavoured with freshly ground ginger and garlic). Set meals
include choice of 2 thalis which comprise vegetable dishes, daal, pilau
rice and chapattis or pooris. Desserts happily include vegan friendly
yellow rice (rice cooked with sugar and raisins), £1. Non smoking. No
credit cards. Offer outside catering.

Sumac Centre

Vegan cafe & campaigns centre

245 Gladstone Street
Forest Fields
Nottingham NG7 3HX
Open: Fri–Sun 10–18.00,
phone for further openings

Tel: 0845–458 9595
www.veggies.org.uk/sumac
sumac@veggies.org.uk

Campaigning resource centre for animals, humans and the environment. Pure vegan café with meals, snacks, cakes and fresh local produce. Eat from £1.50 – £3.50. Vegan social club/bar from around October 2002. They can host gatherings, meetings. Wed–Sun internet access, library. Home of Veggies Catering Campaign, volunteers always needed.

Screaming Carrot

Vegetarian bakery & wholefood shop

42 Foxhall Road
Forest Fields
Nottingham   NG7 6LJ
www.screamingcarrot.co.uk
screamingcarrot@hotmail.com
Open: Mon–Fri 7.00–18.00, Sat 10.00–16.00

Tel: 0115–910 3013

Vegetarian bakery, natural food shop, wholesale and consultancy, on the way to the veggies' Sumac centre, that does vegetarian and vegan savoury foods, take away items and cakes. Operate an organic veg box scheme and have friendly and helpful staff.

Broadway Café

Omnivorous cafe in cinema

Broad Street
Nottingham

Tel: 0115–952 1551

Omnivorous café within the Broadway cinema, serving drinks, snacks and meals. Vegetarian and vegan dishes identified on the menu. Often have veggie and vegan staff.

Lincolnshire Poacher

Real ale pub with food

161–163 Mansfield Road
Nottingham
Open: Mon–Sat 11.00–23.00, Sun 11–22.30

Tel: 0115–941 1584

This real ale pub usually has 5 veggie dishes, and they are happy to cater for vegans.

The Angel

Omnivorous pub

7 Stoney Street
Hockley
Nottingham

Tel: 0115-950 2303

Busy pub with regular music events and a large selection of vegetarian and vegan meals, including veggie breakfast.

Muchachas

Omnivorous Mexican restaurant

140 Alfreton Road
Nottingham
Open: Mon-Sat 12.00-14.00, 18.00-23.00,
Sun 18.00-22.00

Tel: 0115-948 3001

Co-operative run Mexican restaurant, training people with learning difficulties. 8-9 veggie dishes, served with rice or potatoes – many can easily be made vegan.

Q in the corner (at Ziggis)

Omnivorous cafe

3 Victoria Street, Nottingham
Open: Mon-Sat 9.30-16.00

Tel: 0115-950 6956

Omnivorous café at rear of boutique, with good selection of homemade vegetarian and vegan dishes.

Royal Thai

Omnivorous Thai restaurant

189 Mansfield Road
Nottingham

Omnivorous Thai restaurant. 12 main courses on vegetarian menu, 7 suitable for vegans, from £1.95-£6; set meals £14/£17.

Durham Ox

Omnivorous inn

Newark Road
Wellow NG22 0EA
Open: Mon-Sun 11.30-21.30

Tel: 01623 861026

17th century coaching inn with vegetarian menu lunch and evening, £4.95 for main of which there are usually 11. With advance notice will cater for vegans. Non smoking dining areas. Visa, MC. Also a resident ghost apparently.

Natural Food Company

Wholefood shop

37a Mansfield Road
Nottingham

Tel: 0115 955 9914
Open: Mon–Sat

Vegan–friendly, all–vegetarian wholefood shop. Cakes and savouries. Natural remedies.

Roots Natural Foods

Wholefood shop

526 Mansfield Road, Sherwood
Nottingham NG5
www.geocities.com/rootsnaturalfood

Tel: 0115 960 9014
Open: Mon–Sat

Natural foods, organic fruit and veg, take–away foods, free range eggs, cleaning and health products and Veggies burgers and sosages.

Holland & Barrett

Health food shop

95c Victoria Centre
Nottingham NG1 3QE

Tel: 0115–958 0753

14 Broadwalk, Broadmarsh Centre
Nottingham NG1 7LE
Tel: 0115–979 9409

Shops **NOTTINGHAMSHIRE** England

VEGGIES

CATERING CAMPAIGN

245 Gladstone Street, Nottingham NG7 6HX
0845 458 9595 email: info@veggies.org.uk
www.veggies.org.uk

Providing catering services, using no animal ingredients whatsoever, and giving practical suppport, to the animal rights movement.

Resources for local groups and individuals, campaigning for human and animal rights, on environmental issues, and for peace, co-operation and social justice worldwide.

CATERERS TO THE ANIMAL RIGHTS MOVEMENT

Oxfordshire

Cotswold House

Omnivorous Bed and Breakfast

363 Banbury Road, Oxford, OX2 7PL
www.house363.freeserve.co.uk
Email: d.r.walker@talk21.com
Train Station: Oxford, 2 1/2 miles

Tel and Fax:
01865 310558
Open: all year

Two single ensuites £50–£55, two double ensuites and one twin ensuite £75 and two family rooms £75–£95 per room per night. Vegans catered for by prior request. Children six and over only. No pets. No smoking throughout.

Gables Guest House

Omnivorous Guest House

6 Cumnor Hill, Oxford, OX2 9HA
www.oxfordcity.co.uk/accom/gables
Email: stay@gables-oxford.co.uk
Train Station: Oxford, 1 mile
Open: all year, except Christmas and New Year

Tel: 01865 862153
Fax: 01865 864054

Two singles £30–£35 per night, two doubles and two twins £50–£55 per room per night, all with ensuite bathrooms. Children welcome. No pets. No smoking throughout.

Highfield West B&B

Vegetarian owned Bed & Breakfast

188 Cumnor Hill, Oxford OX2 9PJ
highfieldwest@email.msn.com
Open: all year except Christmas and New Year

Tel: 01865 863007

Vegetarian owned bed and breakfast that would like to go entirely veggie. Two and a half miles from the centre of Oxford in Cumnor village on the west side of Oxford. One family £82 if full; 1 double and 1 twin £52; 2 singles £29; all ensuite except singles which share a bathroom. No smoking. No credit cards.

Oxford Youth Hostel

Omnivorous Hostel

2a Botley Road, Oxford, OX2 OAB
Train Station: Oxford, just behind the hostel

Tel: 01865 727275
Open: all year
oxford@yha.org.uk

Twin rooms £41 per room per night, or £18.50 (£13.75 under 18's) per person per night in a four bed or six bed dorm. All rooms are ensuite. Dorms are segregated by sex unless filled with a group of friends. Lockers and hanging space.

Vegans and those on special diets can be catered for with adavanced notice. Evening meals available, but they also have a self catering kitchen. Internet access. 24 hour access. Disabled access. Smoking allowed in some areas.

Alpha Bar
Mainly vegetarian take-away

89 The Covered Market
Oxford OX1
Open: Mon–Sat 10.00–16.00, closed Sun

Tel: 01865 250499
info@alphabar.co.uk

Mostly vegetarian take-away in the covered market. Sandwiches £2.30–2.60 according to the type of bread. All kinds of mostly vegan spreads, falafels, tofu, tempeh. Salads £2.70–3.70. Sometimes soups. Organic drinks, vegan cakes £1 such as banana and apple muffin, apricot flapjacks.

Café MOMA
Omnivorous cafe

Museum of Modern Art, 30 Pembroke Street
Oxford OX1 1BP
Open: Tue–Sat 11–17.30, also Thur 11–20.00. Sun
12–17.30, closed Mon

Tel: 01865 722 733
Fax: 01865 722 573
www.moma.org.uk

Basement café in the Museum of Modern Art, next door to the back entrance to Marks & Spencer, which has a largely vegetarian menu. There are veggie main meals, as well as salads, soup, baked potatoes and cakes. Some food is vegan. Relaxed atmosphere. No smoking. The refurbished café and gallery are closed for renovations until 10th November 2002, when they will be reopening with a new name. Free admission to exhibitions of modern art and lots of events.

The Magic Café
vegetarian café

110 Magdalen Road
Oxford OX4 1RQ
Open: Mon–Sat 10.00–16.00

Tel: 01865–794 604

Spacious vegetarian café featuring cheerful décor and art exhibitions. Always vegan options available and you can have lunch for under £5. Non smoking. No credit cards. Great New Age bookshop next door.

England OXFORDSHIRE Restaurants

Chutneys Indian Brasserie

Indian omnivorous restaurant

36 St Michaels Street
Oxford OX1 2EB
Open: Every day 12–23.00

Tel: 01865–724 241

South Indian restaurant near Gloucester Green coach station with lots of vegetarian and vegan dishes. Licenced.

The Crooked Billet

Omnivorous restaurant

Newlands Lane
Stoke Row, Oxfordshire
Open: Mon–Sat 12–14.30, 19–22.00;
Sun 12–22.00

Tel: 01491 681 048
Fax: 01491 682 231
www.thecrookedbillet.co.uk

Omnivorous up–market restaurant, close to Reading, with a separate vegetarian menu, can always do something vegan. Starters £5.95–8.00, mains £9.50–12.00, desserts £5–6.80 though none vegan. Lunch menu £11.95 for two courses or £14.95 for three, a la carte evening anything up to £35 or more a head with wine. House wine £12.75 bottle, £4–5 a glass. Smoking throughout. Visa, MC. Well behaved children welcome but no reductions apart from a Sunday menu. Car park. You should book for evenings.
In the heart of the Chilterns, a great walking and mountain biking area, close to the start of many footpaths. Long hours at weekends if you want lunch at 4pm on a Sunday.

Uhuru Wholefoods

Wholefood shop

48 Cowley Road
Oxford OX4 1HZ
Open: Mon–Fri 10–18.00, Sat 9.30–17.30

Tel: 01865–248 249

Independent wholefood shop east of the city centre. Well stocked with a range of ethical products and very pro–vegan. Take–away counter with pasties etc, some of which are vegan.

GNC

Health food shop

17 Westgate Centre
Oxford
Open: Every day 9–17.30 (18.00 Sat), Sun 11–17.00

Tel: 01865 249219

Holland & Barrett

Health food shop

6 Golden Cross Arcade
Cornmarket Street
Oxford OX1

Tel: 01865 792102

6 Suffolk House, Banbury Road
Summertown
Oxford OX2

Tel: 01865 552523

100 London Road
Headington
Oxford OX3

Tel: 01865 764578

6 Castle Centre
Banbury, Oxfordshire

Tel: 01295 277909

47 Market Place
Wantage, Oxfordshire OX12 8AW

Tel: 01235 768965

Nature's Harvest

Health food shop

6 Castle Centre
Banbury,
Oxfordshire OX16 8LR
Open: Mon–Sat 9–17.00

Tel: 01295 253208

Health foods, alternative remedies, essential oils, but no take-away.
Chiller and freezer with tofu and non-dairy ice-cream.

England OXFORDSHIRE Shops

Shropshire

Bottom End Cottage

Vegetarian owned self catering cottage, tucked away on the edge of a wood, against the buttresses of the old Railway Station. The cottage has wonderful views of the Bridge and Gorge. It is centrally heated and sleeps four people, with one double room and one twin room, or six people if using the double sofa bed. Prices range from £175–£425 for seven days hire of the cottage. Short breaks and weekends usually available. Offers may apply.

The cottage has a custom made kitchen with a fridge, 'Rayburn' gas fired range style cooker and a dual microwave/oven. Everything you should require is provided. Across the yard, there is a laundry room with a washing machine, tumble dryer and sink. The lounge room has an open log fire, a television, video and radio/cd player. The two bedrooms and the bathroom are upstairs. Only hand towels are provided, so don't forget to bring your own bath towels. Bed linen is provided free of charge. If you stay for more than a week, their housekeeper will change the beds and clean the cottage. The cottage garden is a quiet santuary, should you wish to have a lazy day. There is a small artist's studio opposite the garden, which can be made available for your sole use on request. The owner runs introductory two day art courses from this studio, which you may like to enrol in.

The cottage is set in a conservation area, and The Gorge is a World Heritage Site. There are many beautiful walks around. Relive the area's pioneering past by visiting one of the museums. The local shops and a bus stop are within easy walking distance. There is plenty of night time entertainment, including a jazz bar, a wine bar, and many pubs and restaurants, including a veggie bistro.

*8 Ladywood
Ironbridge
Shropshire TF8 7JR
England*

Tel: 01952 883770

Fax: 01952 884647

www.theironbridge.co.uk

info@theironbridge.co.uk

Train Station: Telford, 4 miles, then bus or taxi

Open: all year

Directions: on the Jackfield side of Ironbridge, drive onto the bridge as if you were going to cross it. You will see an unmarked lane on your left. Continue down this lane bearing right at the hairpin bend. Proceed under the Ironbridge until you see Bottom End Cottage in front of you.

Parking: one space

Cot available by prior arrangement

No pets

No smoking

5% discount to members of the Vegetarian Society, Vegan Society, Viva!, PETA and people presenting this book

Mynd House

Omnivorous
Hotel

Ludlow Road
Little Stretton
Church Stretton
Shropshire SY6 6RB

Tel: 01694 722218
Fax: 01694 720163

www.myndhouse.co.uk
info@myndhouse.co.uk

Station: Church Stretton 1
mile, taxi available

Omnivorous hotel in a 1902 house in "Little Switzerland" in the quiet hamlet of Little Stretton, close to Church Stretton and Cardingmill Valley. The village has pubs and a thatched church.

All rooms en suite, prices per person. One single £40-50. 3 doubles £30-60, one with sitting room, a 4-poster bed and double bath spa. Two twins £35-45. One family room for £100. No single supplement except in deluxe rooms.

Open: mid Feb to mid Nov plus Xmas and New Year for group bookings

Cereals and cooked veggie breakfast. They have vegan margarine, soya milk and yoghurt.

Children welcome, cot available but no high chairs

Evening meal £17.50 resident, £20 non resident by prior booking. They specialise in Western and Malaysian Chinese (Nonya) cuisine to add a touch of spice to your holiday. 8 starters, 6 vegan, include vegetable dim sum, garlic mushrooms on toast, spring rolls, creamy mushrooms, soup. 8 mains, 3 vegan such as vegetable curry as spicy as you choose; mushrooms sauteed with red onions and leeks in ale encased in puff pastry topped with mustard seeds; Louisisana vegetable roast; vegetable chow mein.

Pets welcome, one double room has direct access to the car park without passing through the main part of the hotel.

Open to non-residents for dinner by prior reservation only

The hotel has a bar. The lounge has a cosy log fire for winter evenings.

Rooms have remote control TV, tea and coffee making, adjustable central heating.

Directions: 2 hours from Birmingham, Manchester, Liverpool or Bristol. Main line train services connect Shrewsbury with Hereford stopping off at Church Stretton.
On B4379 off A49 between Shrewsbury and Ludlow, 1 mile south of Church Stretton.

Nearby attractions include Long Mynd National Trust, walking the Shropshire hills, Shrewsbury with its abbey and tudor buildings, Ludlow's 900 year old castle, 13th century Stokesay castle (English Heritage), Ironbridge world heritage site, gliding club, hillside golf.

Smoking only in the bar

Acorn wholefood restaurant and coffee shop in Church Stretton

Olivers Vegetarian Bistro

Vegetarian
Restaurant

Vegetarian bistro with at least 50% of the menu vegan including desserts.

All day veggie breakfast.

Starters £3.95 like roasted pepper with white beans, pesto optional; fennel and four onion tartlet.

Main courses £8.95 such as chickpea and lentil dhansak; cashew nut, celeriac and caramelised onion tart; Moroccan spiced stew with couscous. Mains all served with mixed leaf salad and Oliver's own savoury Cajun style potatoes.

Desserts £3.95 such as rhubarb, pear and apricot crumble; toffee and banana sundae. Swedish Glace vegan ice-cream available.

Weekend daytime menu is more snacky, for example veggieburgers £3.90 with salad, Mexican burger £4.40 with chili and salsa, pasta Italiano £5.90.

Toasted baguettes with any three fillings from 20 for £4.40, extra fillings 40p, with a side salad. Also filled baked potatoes from £3.30.

Fully licensed with lots of beers. Bottle of house wine £7.95, glass £2.20.

Pot of all kinds of tea 95p per person. Cappucinos, lattes etc and can be with soya milk.

33 High Street
Ironbridge
Shropshire TF8 7JR

Tel: 01952-433 086

www.
olivers@theironbridge.co.
uk

Open:
Tue-Thu 19-21.30,
Fri-Sat 19-22.00,
Sat 12-15.00,
Sun 11-17.00.
Closed Mon.

Licensed

Credit cards ok

Can do kids portions

Non smoking unless you
go outside

Lost Leet Mill B&B

Omnivorous Bed and Breakfast

Hopton Heath,
Craven Arms SY7 0QB

Tel: 01547 530384
lostleetmill@clara.co.uk

Omnivorous B&B with full veggie cooked breakfast, in beautiful Clun valley. One double and one twin, both en suite, £18–25 per person. Local pubs and restaurants have vegetarian food. 10% discount to VSUK and Vegan Society. Well behaved dogs welcome. No smoking.

Goodlife Wholefood Restaurant

Vegetarian

Barracks Passage
Wyle Cop
Shrewsbury SY1 1XA
Open: Mon–Fri 9.30–15.30 Sat 9.30–16.30, closed Sun

Tel: 01743 –350455

Vegetarian wholefood restaurant and coffee shop in one of historic Shrewsbury`s passageways. Everything made fresh on site daily with local produce. Soup £1.90. Several kinds of nutloaf £2.15 for a big slice. Savoury potatoes £2.15, jackets £1.55, plus 60p per filling. Salad bar from £1.60 for two generous portions. Desserts including vegan crumble from £1.80, scones and flapjacks. Pots of many kinds of tea £1, coffee cup 90p, mug £1. Wine and beer £1.50 glass.

Acorn Wholefood Café

Omnivorous café

26 Sandford Avenue
Church Stretton SY6 6BW
Open: Mon & Thu–Sat 9.30–18.00 (17.00 winter),
Sun and bank holidays 10.00–18.00. Wed on school
hols only. Closed Tue.

Tel: 01694 722 495

Omnivorous wholefood café, with always a main veggie dish £4.75 with jacket potato or rice, and a nut roast with salad £3.60. Jacket potato £2.90 with one filling. Vegan cakes £1.20–1.75, desserts like vegan crumble £2–3, cakes including wheat, dairy or sugar free. 30 kinds of teas, hot spiced apple. Bring your own alcohol, 99p corkage.

Holland & Barrett

Health food shop

4 Butchers Row, Shrewsbury

Tel: 01743–272 016

3 The Square, Shrewsbury

Tel: 01743–357 611

Unit 34 Sherwood St.,Telford Shopping Ctre
Telford

Tel: 01952–291 356

Glastonbury

Vegan Läyne Kuirk-Schwarz-Waad has a degree in chemistry, has worked as a buyer and advisor in the remedies and toiletries section of one of London's biggest organic food stores, and has a private practice as a natural health practitioner. She believes that as well as eating good food, it's important to regularly get away from the city, and loves to go on retreats both in Britain and abroad. Here she tells us about her favourite place to go and recharge, with no animal ingredients!

Glastonbury is another world. Another world where everybody seems a little bit kinder and more sensitive. Vegetarian, vegan, organic, earth-friendly, cruelty-free, fairly traded are terms that are not merely acknowledged as being in existence (but only really relevant somewhere else), here people genuinely support, embrace and LIVE these and other ethical life-choices!

Glastonbury is magical. And not just because of Arthurian legends or claims of the first Christian church or culdee (similar to wattle and daub hut) being built on the site where the Abbey now stands or belief in the Holy Grail resting within the Chalice Well. Glastonbury's particular magic is much, much older and it continues to draw modern and ancient pilgrims of all belief-systems and none.

Interestingly enough, most people immediately associate Glastonbury with Michael Eavis' legendary 'Glastonbury Festival', which in fact takes place in a field 6 miles away!

The Isle of Avalon has so much to offer, it is hard to know where to begin!

ACCOMMODATION

Glastonbury Tourist Information
Tel: 01458 832 954
Email: glastonbury.tic@ukonline.co.uk
You really will find that you are spoilt for choice!

My own particular favourite is The Barn, a beautiful organic, vegetarian and vegan bed & breakfast with amazing views and an even lovelier host, Adrian Goolden.

Everywhere, but everywhere, serves vegetarian and vegan food! Some places serve exclusively vegetarian and vegan food, and I've listed lots of them in this chapter.

Pretty much all food stores sell vegetarian and vegan goodies, and organic is normal not freakishly trendy in Glastonbury! There is a good health food store on the High Street ... tofu galore.

THINGS YOU MUST SEE: The Tor, The Red Spring, The White Spring, Chalice Well and Gardens, Glastonbury Abbey, The Tithe Barn...

Have a wonderful time...you won't want to leave!

That's all folks!

Läyne Kuirk–Schwarz–Waad
BSc.(Hons), MRSS, MCOM, Dips.(III)ACHM, Dips.(II) Dietary Therapy, Dips.(NutriScience) ESNS Fr.
Based in London, Läyne Kuirk-Schwarz-Waad can be contacted for a variety of treatments on 07985-120 101 or schwarzwaadkuirk@btopenworld.com

Places in Somerset

Hotels and Guest Houses

Restaurants

Shops

Lavender House

Vegetarian owned omnivorous B&B in Bath. There are five rooms; one single with private bathroom at £45 per night, three double ensuites and one twin ensuite at £70–£90 per room per night.

Imaginative veggie and vegan breakfasts like three seed bread with vegan pesto, vine tomatoes, avocado and fried potoatoes, or field mushrooms stuffed with cous cous, veg and herbs. Standard cooked veggie breakfasts with veg sausages are also on the menu. Vegan margarine, soya milk, home made vegan muesli and soya yoghurt are all available. A light supper to a three course dinner for £15.20 is available during the week by request. Main course could be pasta with vegan pesto, pinenuts and olives served with salad leaves from their greenhouse. Organic home grown produce used when possible. There is a veggie restaurant, cafe and pub in town and several other restaurants cater for vegetarians.

Everyone comes to Bath to see the Roman Baths, but there are many other attractions including Royal Crescent, the Jane Austen Centre, Assembly Rooms and the Costume Museum, Beckfords Tower, the Postal Museum, the American Museum and the Sally Lunn Oldest House and Museum (1482). There's also the Victoria Park Botanical Gardens and the Prior Park Landscape Gardens. Bath has many beautiful walks in its vicinity like the Bath Skyline walk and the Kennett and Avon Canal walk. There is much to explore in the area around Bath, like Cheddar Gorge.

Guest lounge with TV. Rooms have TV's and tea and coffee making facilities.

Omnivorous
Guest House

17 Bloomfield Park
Bath
Somerset BA2 2BY
England

Tel: 01225 314500

Fax: 01225 448564

www.lavenderhouse-bath.com

Email:
lavenderhouse@btinternet.com

Train Station: Bath Spa, 1.8km then bus, taxi or collection is posible.

Open: all year

Children over eight only or non walking babies.

No pets

No smoking throughout

Directions: From A36 ring road, take A367 Wells Road, then fork right into Bloomfield Road and take second right turn into Bloomfield Park.

Parking: available on and off road

Marlborough House

Vegetarian
Guest House

1 Marlborough Lane
Bath
Somerset BA1 2NQ
England

Tel: 01225 318175
Fax: 01225 466127

www.marlborough-house.net
mars@manque.dircon.co.uk

Train: Bath Spa, 3/4 mile, then bus or taxi.

Open: all year

Cots and high chairs

Pets welcome

Directions: From M4, take the Bath exit #18 (A46 to Bath), through the green hills surrounding Bath. Get in correct lane to exit towards Bath again. The roundabout will lead you to the A4. Keep straight on this road through Bath as if you were heading to Bristol. You will drive around Queen Square (a small green) which will join up with the Upper Bristol Road (the A4 again). You will pass a string of B&B's, then just after some pedestrian lights, with a Vauxhall Dealer on your left, will be Marlborough Lane. Turn right there and then immediately into their driveway.

Parking: sometimes available, three spaces

No smoking throughout

Impressive stone Victorian house with spacious and elegantly furnished rooms close to the city centre of Bath. There are seven rooms, comprising of double ensuites at £65– £85 per room per night, twin ensuites and family rooms at £65–£95 per room per night. Children are £10 per night. A single person in any room is £45– £75 per night.

Breakfast could begin with cereal and soya yoghurt, followed by vegan pancakes or veggie sausages, breakfast potatoes and sauteed mushrooms. Soya milk, vegan muesli and vegan margarine are available. Dinner is available for £15 and could be a French Country Dinner of Roasted Artichoke Pate and French Bread to start, then a Roasted Pepper Salad, followed by a main course of Marseilles Spinach Stew finished with a dessert of Chocolate Tarte and Swedish Glace ice cream. All food is organic. Vegans, diabetics and the allergy sensitive are happily catered for. If you fancy going out for dinner, Bath has a veggie restaurant and a veggie pub.

Marlborough House is situated close to Queen Square, the heart of Bath, and at the edge of Royal Victoria Park. All the sites are within walking distance, like the Roman Baths, Assembly Rooms, Museum of Costume, the Jane Austen Centre and the Royal Crescent Circus. Bath is a perfect base for exploring other nearby historical sites all within 45 minutes of Marlborough House, such as Stonehenge, Wells, Glastonbury, Lacock, Castle Comber, Cheddar and Longleat. There are also many beautiful walks nearby.

Rooms have telephones, TV's, tea and coffee making facilities, homebaked cookies and complementary sherry.

Poplar Herb Farm

Veggie B&B situated rurally on the Somerset Levels, an area of outstanding natural beauty renowned for its abundant wildlife. There are three rooms; one double ensuite at £20 per person per night, one twin and one family room at £18 per person per night.

Breakfast begins with juice, fruit, soy yoghurt and cereal followed by a cooked feast of veggie sausages, mushrooms and tomatoes with home made bread and spreads, washed down with tea or coffee. Soya milk, vegan muesli and vegan margarine are available.

Dinner is offered by request for £9.50 and could be carrot and coriander soup, followed by nut fritters, home grown salad and herbed potatoes, finished with a dessert of apricot fool. There are excellent veggie restaurants in nearby Glastonbury and several local inns serve veggie food.

Poplar Herb Farm is a 2 1/2 acre nursery and organic smallholding. Enjoy the serenity of the herb gardens and nursery or meet the rescued animals.

The farm is an excellent base for a walking or cycling holiday in the unspoilt Somerset countryside. Seven miles away is historic Glastonbury, with its famous Tor and Abbey Ruins. There are fascinating caves in Cheddar and Wookey Hole, twelve miles away, and numerous coastal resorts and attractive villages to explore.

Meditation room which guests can use. Astrological consultations or personal tuition in astrology or meditation can be arranged. Tea and coffee making in rooms.

Burtle
nr Bridgwater
Somerset TA7 8NB
England

Tel: 01278 723170

Email:
richardfish@lineone.net

Train Station: Bridgwater
or Highbridge, 9 miles,
then taxi from Bridgwater.

Open: all year

Children are welcome and
they have a cot and high
chair.

Well behaved pets are
welcome by prior
arrangement.

Directions: Take the A39
from Glastonbury. After
approximately 7 miles
turn right (left if you are
coming from Bridgwater)
at the sign for Edington
and Burtle into Holy Well
Road. Upon arriving at
Burtle, turn right at the
junction by the Church.
Poplar Herb Farm is the
first property on your left.

Parking: available

No smoking throughout

The Ramala Centre

Beautifully converted old stable block nestled at the foot of Chalice hill in the heart of Avalon. The Ramala Centre functions primarily as a day centre for spiritual retreat but it also accommodates up to five residential guests. There are three rooms; one double and one twin at £25 per person per night and one twin ensuite at £30 per person per night.

Breakfast is a selection of cereals and fruit with rice cakes and oat biscuits or it could be a full cooked English breakfast. Vegan margarine and soy milk are available.

The High Street is five minutes walk from the Ramala Centre and has four excellent wholefood restaurants and cafes, a wholefood store and many interesting 'new age' shops. The Centre is in a very quiet position and is ideally situated for visiting all the various sites of The Tor, Chalice Well and the Abbey.

The Ramala Centre embraces the work of many Spiritual Teachers and tries to be universal rather than denominational. The Centre has its own spiritual routines which include an early morning and a midday meditation every day and a Sai Baba meeting every Thursday evening. Both guests and visitors are free to use all the facilites of the centre which include a video library on spiritual topics and a reading/meditation room. You can choose to be alone and to walk around the sacred sites of Glastonbury in peace and solitude or mingle with the other guests and the custodians of the Ramala Centre.

Tea and coffee making facilities in the kitchen. There is a television in the ensuite room. Guest lounge.

The Old Stables
Dod Lane
Glastonbury
Somerset BA6 8BZ
England

Tel: 01458 832459

Fax: 01458 833678

www.ramalacentre.com

Email:
ramalaceasynet.co.uk

Train Station: Castle Cary, 15 miles.

Open: all year

Children are welcome

Directions: Junction 23 off M5. On arrival in Glastonbury town centre, turn right at the top of the high street. Dod Lane is the second road on the left.

Parking: available

10% discount to members of the Vegetarian Society, Vegan Society and people presenting this book.

No smoking throughout

The Barn

Vegetarian bed & breakfast

84b Bovetown
Glastonbury BA6 8JG

Tel: 01458 832991
Open all year.

Organic vegetarian bed and breakfast, vegans welcome. Two twins and one single, all en suite, £24 per person. Quiet and secluded with wonderful views. Non-wheat cereals and muesli, local stewed fruit, toast, croissants, local and home-made jams, local apple juice. On the Tor side of the town. No smoking. No credit cards.

Rosemullion–The Fisherking Centre

Vegan detox centre

54 Roman Way
Glastonbury, BA6 8AD
Train Station: Castle Cary, 40 minutes drive, collection possible
Open: all year, except Easter and Christmas

Tel: 01458 831182
www.ploughshares.co.uk

One double, one twin and one single room available. £750 per week per person for cleansing programme, includes all therapies, supplements, organic fruit and vegetables, and a meal at the end of the week. There is a beautiful garden and a guest lounge to relax in, a sauna and a meditation/treatment room. A maximum of three people are there at a time, so you will receive very individual treatment. They also run training courses in vegan cuisine. No smoking throughout.

Between The Oaks

Vegetarian bed & breakfast

45 Benedict Street
Glastonbury BA6 9NB
Open from Easter 2003

Tel: 07866 692693
philip@plus44.com

New veggie b&b in the town centre in a 16th century stone cottage with a ley line through the garden. One double/twin room for £16 single, £25 double. Help yourself to a basic breakfast of cereal, coffee, teas, soya milk available. Smoking in garden only. One well behaved dog by appointment. TV in living room.

Tordown

Vegetarian guest house

5 Ashwell Lane
Glastonbury BA6 8BG
www.tordown.com

Tel: 01458 832287
Fax: 01458 831100
info@tordown.com

Vegetarian guest house on the southern slopes of Glastonbury Tor, a haven of tranquility. 7 rooms: 2 singles £20.50-22.50 (one has a toilet), twin £41 for 2, double or twin ensuite £47, family ensuite with kitchen £51 for 2 or £80 for 4. 75% for double room for one person. No smoking. Visa, MC. Pets by apppointmnent. Healing. Spa pool.

Cafe Galatea

Vegetarian and vegan café which is also an internet café and art gallery. They have a varied and extensive menu and source locally and organically as much as possible. Soup, £2.75, salads from £4.

Mains start at £4.75 for lunch and £7.50 in evenings and include pizza (with option of vegan cheese), pasta bakes and aviyal, a South Indian dish of stir-fried vegetables with spices.

In the evenings they do a mezze plate with assorted popular dishes and have an a la carte menu.

A good range of speciality coffees, soya lattes and barleycinos. They can cater for special diets. Live music in evenings and weekends, when it's best to book.

5a High Street
Glastonbury
Somerset BA6 9DP

Tel: 01458-834 284

www.cafegalatea.co.uk

Open: Mon 11-16.00;
closed Tue;
Wed-Thu, Sun 11-21.00;
Fri 11-22.00,
;
Sat 10.30-22.00

Licensed

Non smoking

Visa, MC

Disabled access

Shambhala

Not a health farm, more a cross between an ashram and a B&B, offering rest, healing or spiritual regeneration. 6 very beautifully decorated rooms, one en suite. Health and healing break, from £128, includes vegetarian buffet breakfast, light soup and salad lunch, use of meditation sanctuary, jacuzzi and a heart opening and consultation session. Individual treatments £38-60 such as Indian head massage, Reiki, Bowen, personal empowerment, aromatherapy, reflexology, metamorphic technique, detox massage, colonic hydrotherapy. Sauna £6. 3 day de-tox break (includes all therapies) £288, that extra day may make all the difference to the depth to which you can unwind and really let go into a new harmony, confidence, well being and peace. 15 page brochure can be emailed to you.

Coursing Batch
Glastonbury
Somerset BA6 8BH

Tel: 01458 831797
Fax: 01458 834751

www.shambhala.co.uk
findyourself@
shambhala.co.uk

Train: Castle Cary then taxi

50% deposit
4% credit card charge

Directions: from Glastonbury, A361 towards Frome, one mile, at the crest of the hill take slip road on left Ashwell Lane.

The Assembly Rooms Café

Vegan organic cafe

The High Street
Glastonbury
Telephone in advance to check opening times
www.assemblyrooms.org.uk

Tel: 01458 834677

Cooperatively run, this is a cosy organic, vegan café with very friendly staff and wholesome, home-cooked food at very reasonable prices.

Rainbow's End Café

Vegetarian cafe

17a High Street
Glastonbury
Open 6 days, morning till early evening

Tel: 01458 833896

Look for a board on the High Street, just before you reach the George & Pilgrim Pub. Walk down the little alleyway and there it is. You will find some very nice hot dishes, fresh salads and cakes with some seating outside. Predominantly vegetarian with plenty for vegans.

Spiral Gate Café

Vegetarian organic cafe

24 High Street, Glastonbury
Open 7 days. Closes about 8.00pm most evenings
and earlier on Sundays.

Tel: 01458 834633

Layne really loves the food here. Everything is organic, from the fresh juices to the very substantial main courses. The Red Dragon Pie sells out quickly and for a very good reason – pounce on it! The prices are reasonable with a main course for £5 and most of the dishes are vegan. There is seating upstairs and art on the walls. No smoking. Booking recommended for busy times.

White Spring Café

Wholefood café

Well House Lane, Glastonbury
Telephone to check opening hours, but they are
usually open 7 days, 11.00am till early evening.
www.sacredsites.co.uk/sites/whitespring/info.html

Tel: 01458 830406

This is a very unusual place. Descend the steps into what is essentially a cave with a stream (The White Spring) running through the middle of the floor and you'll discover a wonderful little wholefood café with very friendly staff, other-worldly atmosphere and a nice selection of snacks and mains. Soups, salads, chips, hot bagel sandwiches. Majority of dishes are vegetarian, but plenty for vegans. Cheap food and very filling. You can collect White Spring water free from a pipe outside. Very welcome after a trip up the Tor!

The George and Pilgrim   Omnivorous pub/hotel/restaurant

7 High Street   *Tel: 01458 831146*
Glastonbury

This building was constructed in the late 15th century as accommodation for wealthy pilgrims. It continues to be one of the more highly priced of places to stay and is also a pub which serves food 7 days from 12.00 noon till 9.00pm, some of which is vegetarian and vegan. This is a beautiful building with a sense of history and well worth a visit.

The Rifleman's Rest   Omnivorous pub

Chilkwell Street   *Tel: 01458 831023*
across the road from 'Ariel's Cottage'
Glastonbury

This is a lovely, warm and very friendly pub with very hard-working staff and a good mixture of people, including lots of musicians. They also serve extremely nice food, some of which is vegetarian and vegan. Dogs are very welcome and there is huge beer-garden. Highly recommended!

The Who'd A Thought It Inn   Omni hotel/pub/restaurant

17 Northload Street   *Tel: 01458 834460*
Glastonbury

This gorgeous place is a hotel, restaurant, pub and occasional music venue, with a lovely atmosphere, great staff and an entire menu just for vegetarians and vegans. They even knew which of their wines and beers were veggie. There is also a separate area for non-smokers and seating outside. I'll be back!

Demuths

Vegetarian restaurant

2 North Parade Passage, Off Abbey Green
Bath
Open: Every day 10.00–22.00 (Fri–Sat till 23.00,
Sat from 09.00), closed every day 17.30–18.00

Tel: 01225–446 059
Fax: 01225–314 308

Vegetarian dishes from all around the world, half of them vegan and clearly marked, including the desserts. Menus change every 3 months. 12 entrées £2.75–4.95 such as soup, hummus, guacamole, roasted squash and pumpkin, nachos. Fabulous main courses £5.95–6.95 day, £10.50–11.50 evening. Vegans, who get a lousy deal in the dessert department in some vegetarian restaurants, will think they've landed in heaven. House wine £10.25 a bottle or £2.25 a glass.

Metropolitan Café

Vegetarian cafe

15 New Bond Street
Bath
Open: Mon–Fri 9.30–17.00, Sat 9–17.00, Sun 11–16.00

Tel: 01225 482 680

Vegetarian café in the shopping area near the Abbey, above Bloomsbury crafts shop and opposite The Gap clothing store. Take-away style food like wraps, sandwiches, bruschetta. Average £3.75 for a sandwich. Some vegan food. Smoothies and milkshakes (can be soya) around £2.35. Cup of tea £1.30. Children's menu, one high chair. No smoking. Visa, MC.

The Porter

Vegetarian pub

15 George Street
Bath
Open: Mon–Sat 11.00–23.00, Sun 11.00–22.30

Tel: 01225 424104
www.theporter.co.uk
info@moles.co.uk

Vegetarian pub. Everything is under £5 and includes traditional pub food and a varied menu, half of it vegan, with cashew nut curries, ratatouille, Trinidadian casseroles and homemade soups. All the alcohol is vegetarian. Small glass of white wine £2–£2.25, large £2.80–£3.20, bottles 11–£12.80. Small glass of red wine £2–£2.15, large £2.80–£3.05, bottles £11–£12. Beer £2.20–£2.50 for a bottle. Smoking permitted. Visa, MC.

Riverside Café

Vegetarian cafe

Riverside Walk,17 Argyle Street
Bath
Open: Every day 9.30-17.30

Tel: 01225-480 532

Vegetarian with traditional café food. 1 veggie and 1 vegan salad £1.95-3.50. 10 vegetarian main courses £4.25, though only jacket potatoes for vegans. Lots of cakes £1.60, none vegan.. Wine £9 bottle, £2.25 galss. Tea 85p, coffee £1. No soya milk. Children's portions but no high chairs. No smoking.

Tilley's Bistro

Omnivorous restaurant

3 North Parade Passage
Bath
Open: Mon-Sat 12.00-14.30, 18.30-23.00

Tel: 01225-484 200
www.tilleysbistro.co.uk

Restaurant specialising in French and English cuisine with plenty of vegetarian choice. Lunch set menu, £7.50 for 2 courses, £9.50 for 3. At dinner there is a separate a la carte vegetarian menu, £4.50-£8.50. Can cater and adapt dishes for vegans and special diets. Separate smoking section. Visa, MC.

The Good Earth

Vegetarian restaurant

4 Priory Road
Wells
Open: Mon-Sat 09.00-17.00 closed Sunday

Tel: 01749-678 600

Licensed vegetarian restaurant and take away in wholefood store. Salads from £2.50 and main meals from £3.75 such as ratatouille and jacket potatoes. Non smoking. Visa, MC.

The Wholefood Store

Wholefood shop

29 The High Street
Glastonbury

Tel: 01458 831004

In Harmony With Nature

Hemp shop

1a The Market Place
Glastonbury

Tel: 01458 835769

Organic hemp everything and very cheap Nagchampa incense.

Stone Age

Crystal shop

2–4 High Street
Glastonbury

Tel: 01458 835514

Beautiful, beautiful crystal shop.

The Speaking Tree

Spiritual bookshop

5 High Street
Glastonbury
Open 7 days, 9.00–18.00

Fantastic range of books on all matters spiritual, herbalism to witch–craft, massage to permaculture. Other alternative/ spiritual shops include Growing Needs in Magdalene Street and Gothic Image.

Country Harvest

Health food shop

8 The Courtyard, St James Street
Taunton

Tel: 01823 252 843

Evergreen

Health food shop & wholesaler

61 Station Road
Taunton

Tel: 01823 322 414

County Stores

Health food shop & take–away

52 North Street
Taunton
Open: Mon–Sat 8.30–17.30, closed Sun

Tel: 01823 272235

Food shop with a health food section. Also an omnivorous restaurant and deli take–away open the same times.

Holland & Barrett

Health food shop

42 Stall Street
Bath

Tel: 01225 330812

Unit 20, Angel Place Centre
Bridgwater

Tel: 01278–452 567

6 Station Road
Clevedon

Tel: 01275–342 049

5 Old Market Centre, Paul Street
Taunton

Tel: 01823–274 347

22 High Street
Wells

Tel: 01749–677 665

19 Meadow Street
Weston Super Mare

Tel: 01934–620 020

13 Glovers Walk
Yeovil

Tel: 01935–421 785

Staffordshire

The Arch

Omnivorous Chinese restaurant

Units 1– 3 The Mall, Brunswick St
Newcastle, Staffordshire

Tel: *01782 630849*

Omnivorous Chinese restaurant with a reasonable selection of vegetarian food, especially popular at weekends.

Passion of India

Omnivorous Indian restaurant

Snow Hill,Howard Place
Shelton

Tel: *01782 266360*

Omnivorous Indian restaurant between Hanley and Stoke in a student and ethnic area, near the College of Further Education. The English owners were constantly asked for Indian dishes so they went to Delhi and recruited a chef. The food is authentically Indian unlike every-where else in Stoke with is Bangladeshi or Pakistani, hence more expensive.

Al Shafiq's Balti Centre

Omnivorous Indian restaurant

58 Church St
Stoke on Trent

Tel: *01782 410080*

Reasonable choice for veggies for about a fiver. Jug of cold table water brought to you on arrival and you can bring your own drinks.

Bauhinia

Omnivorous Chinese restaurant

Parklands,A34
Stoke on Trent

Tel: *01782 719709*

Omnivorous Chinese restaurant outside town with its own car park. Popular at lunchtimes for business lunches. Our reader said the MSG there gives him a headache but there's a reasonable selection for veggies/vegans. Piano player in the evening.

Cranberry's Eating House

Omnivorous restaurant

Hanley
Stoke on Trent

Tel: 01782–204499

Omnivorous restaurant, the only place in Hanley to serve soya milk with tea. They will even rustle up a vegan pudding though it's not on the menu, and it won't be just fresh fruit.

Dylans

Omnivorous restaurant

99 Broad St, Hanley
Stoke on Trent
Open: Thu–Sat evening if prebooked, can open other times for parties.

Tel: 01782 286 009

Vegetarian restaurant, under new management, now serving some fish and shellfish. Menu changes weekly and everything can be made suitable for vegans. 3 course meal £10, for example roast tomatoes stuffed with falafel and mint Yofu; followed by curried mango and courgette with coconut and avocado plus rice; then vegan chocolate cake or apple crumble with Swedish Glace ice-cream or Provamel cream. House wine from £4.95 bottle, glass £1.60, get there soon before they put it up! Smoking discouraged. No credit cards. Call to book, though you may be able to just turn up. But they only open if they've got booking by 5pm.

Fortune Rendez-vous

Omnivorous Cantonese retaurant

19-21 Broad St
Hanley, Stoke on Trent

Tel: 01782 271179

Omnivorous Cantonese restaurant with reasonable veggie choice. The mock duck is very ducky. Very bright inside.

Lazees

Omnivorous Indian restaurant

The Cultural Quarter, 56 Piccadilly
Hanley, Stoke on Trent

Tel: 01782 261717

Stoke is blessed with lots of omnivorous Indian restaurants but this is one of the best, almost opposite the Regent Theatre. A screen downstairs shows Bollywood movie extracts.

Naseeb

Omnivorous restaurant

131 Etruria Raod
Hanley, Stoke on Trent

Tel: 01782 212240

Omnivorous restaurant a few minutes walk from the centre of town with its own carpark. Buffet nights Monday and Thursday with a good selection for veggies, and a dial a curry service.

Ria

Thai omnivorous restaurant

65 Piccadilly
Hanley, Stoke on Trent

Tel: 01782 264411

Omnivorous Thai restaurant in the Cultural Quarter, with many veggie dishes most of which are or can be vegan. Service can be slow and restaurant is dark and can be a bit smoky.

Robertos

Italian omnivorous restaurant

25 Pall Mall
Hanley, Stoke on Trent

Tel: 01782 287410

One of many omnivorous Italian pasta and pizza places in Stoke, but this is our favourite, in the "Cultural Quarter." The vegetariana comes with olives and capers and dishes can be made up vegan as long as they remember to leave the cheese off. Around the corner is another Italian called Portofino.

Breckles Wholefoods

Wholefood store

14 Stanley Street
Leek

Tel: 01538 387660

Health Matters

Health food shop

21/23 The Strand
Longton

Tel: 01782 319333

Wholefoods, vitamins, herbal and homeopathic stuff. Handy for the Gladstone Pottery Museum and various factory shops such as Doulton and Portmeirion.

Boots Health and Herbal Stores

Wholefood shop

39–41 Merrial St
Newcastle, Staffordshire

Tel: 01782 617463

Wholefood shop with with fresh and frozen veggie and vegan food.

Health Rack

Health food shop

17 Castle Walk
Newcastle, Staffordshire

Tel: 01782 662045

A B Wholefoods

Wholefood shop

75 Broad Street
Hanley, Stoke on Trent

Tel: 01782 219363

Wholefood store just outside the centre of town, near Dylans, with West Indian and Chinese foods, woks, frozen patties, some vegetables.

Armstrongs Health and Herbal Store

22 Town Road
Hanley, Stoke on Trent

Tel: 01782 215417

Holland & Barrett

Health food shop

8 Underhill Walk Shopping Centre
Burton on Trent

Tel: 01283–740 078

41 Market Street
Lichfield

Tel: 01543–256 782

29 High Street
Newcastle Under Lyme

Tel: 01782–713 059

1 Goalgate Street
Stafford

Tel: 01785–252 758

8 Upper Market Square
Hanley, Stoke On Trent

Tel: 01782–266 126

Suffolk

Church Cottage

Vegetarian Guest House

Saxtead, Woodbridge, Suffolk, IP13 9QR
Train Station: Darsham or Campse Ashe/Wickam
Market, 1/2 hour's drive, but collection is possible
Open: all year, except Christmas, New Year and
Easter weekend

Tel: 01728 724067

Eight rooms, £25 per person per night. A three course organic dinner is only £10. Special diets catered for. Children and pets welcome. Smoking allowed, with respect to other guests.

Western House

Vegetarian Bed and Breakfast

High Street, Cavendish, Suffolk, CO10 8AR
Train Station: Sudbury, seven miles
Open: all year

Tel: 01787 280550

One single, one double and two twins at £17–£18 per person per night. Vegan catered for with notice. Children aged two onwards welcome. No pets. No smoking throughout. Small wholefood shop on the premises.

Diva Vegetarian Café

Vegetarian cafe & New Age shop

in The Genesis Therapy Centre
40–44 Upper Orwell Street
Ipswich
Open: Mon–Fri 10.00-18.00, Saturday till 20.00

Tel: 01473 226385
www.forewarn.com

Vegetarian and vegan meals and snacks to eat in the café or take away. Also The 7th Chakra New Age Gift Shop open Mon–Sat 10.00-18.00 for crystals, clothing, candles, CDs, gifts. The Therapy Centre offers hynotherapy, Reiki healing and tuition, massage and readings.

Kwan Thai

Thai omnivorous restaurant

14 St Nicholas Street
Ipswich
Open: Mon–Fri 12.00-14.00, 18.00-23.00, Sat
12.00-14.00, 18.00-23.30

Tel: 01473-253 106

Thai restaurant with several vegetarian dishes. Vegetarian set menus are from £16.00 per person for 2 people and include sweet and sour, panang, stir fried mushroom and sweetcorn, phad thai and steamed rice. Separate vegetarian mains, £2.75–£6, such as phad puk nam mun hoy – fried mixed vegetables in soya sauce; and gairng keow wahn – bean curd, mushroom and bamboo shoots cooked with coconut milk and fresh Thai herbs. Smoking section. Visa, MC.

The Linden Tree

7 Out Norgate
Bury St Edmunds
Open: Mon–Sat 12.00–14.00, 18.00–21.30,
Sun 12.00–15.00, 18.00–21.30

Tel: 01284 754600

Omnivorous restaurant which has at least 5 vegetarian mains daily and 1 vegetarian special, £6.99, and also always something vegan and indicated on the menu. House wine, £8.95 for a bottle, £1.75 for a glass. Separate smoking section. Visa, MC.

Holland & Barrett

Health food shop

6 Brentgrovel Street
Bury St Edmonds

Tel: 01284–706 677

91 Hamilton Road
Felixstowe

Tel: 01394–671 796

7 The Butter Market
Ipswich

Tel: 01473–219 153

27 Westgate Street
Ipswich

Tel: 01473–233 477

17 The Britton Centre
Lowestoft

Tel: 01502–500 832

8/10 Market Place
Stowmarket

Tel: 01449–676 046

Surrey

The Claridge House Vegetarian Guest House & Retreat Centre

Claridge House

Veggie Guest House & Retreat Centre

Dormans Road
Dormansland
Lingfield
Surrey RH7 6QH

Tel: 01342 832150

Fax: 01342 836730

www.claridgehouse.freese
rve.co.uk

Email: welcome@claridge
house.freeserve.co.uk

Train Station: Lingfield,
1 mile, then bus or taxi,
or they can pick up with
prior notice.

Open: all year

Directions:
From M25: leave at
Junction 6 (A22) following
signs to East Grinstead.
At Blindley Heath turn left
to Lingfield on B2029.
From M23: leave at
Junction 10 (following
signs to East Grinstead.
At the second roundabout
turn left to Lingfield
(B2028).
From Lingfield: about 1/2
mile out of Lingfield. past
the racecourse on your
right, you will go under a
bridge. About 1/4 mile
after the bridge, fork right
along Dormans Road.
Claridge House is situated
on the left just before the
30mph sign.

Parking: available

No children or pets.

No smoking throughout

Quaker centre standing in two acres of beautiful gardens in the small Surrey village of Dormansland. There are twelve rooms; three singles at £50 per night and nine twins at £40-£50 per person per night. Prices are for full board which includes all meals. £10 reduction if only B&B is required. A mid week break (Mon-Fri) with full board is £140.

A light breakfast is served and includes a selection of cereals, muesli, soya yoghurt and fresh bread. Gluten free and vegan muesli is available, as well as soya milk and vegan margarine. Dinner is a main course with vegetables followed by a dessert. What is served depends on the dietary needs of guests. Let them know when booking if you are vegan or on a special diet.

Courses are run at weekends on a variety of subjects. The house is open to anyone who is seeking healing, rest or renewal as the emphasis is on spirituality, not on religion. This unique centre offers a sanctuary away from the stresses of every day life or it could act as a bridge between hospital and home.

The house is well situated for exploring the surrounding areas of Surrey, Sussex and Kent. There are more than a dozen National Trust and private properties and gardens open to the public within easy reach. There are also miles of attractive walks in the immediate vicinity.

Two guest lounges and a Quiet Room. Rooms have washbasins and tea and coffee making facilites. Good disabled access as there are four ground floor rooms, two of which were purpose built to suit those with disabilities. No TV.

Tekels Park
Vegetarian Guest House & Study Centre

Tekels Avenue,
Camberley, Surrey, GU15 2LF
www.accommodation.uk.com/surrey/tekels-park
Train Station: Camberley, one mile

Tel: 01276 23159
Fax: 01276 27014
Open: all year,
except Christmas

Theosophical Society owned guest house with twenty two rooms comprised of singles, twins and doubles, from £30 per person per night. Evening meal with advanced notice, from £8 for one course. Children by arrangement. No pets. Disabled access. No smoking.

Blubeckers
Omnivorous restaurant

Gomshall Mill
Gomshall, Surrey GU5 9LB
gomshall.blubeckers@btopenworld.com
Open: every day 12-14.30,
17.30-22.00 (Fri-Sat -22.30)

Tel: 01483 203060
www.blubeckers.co.uk

Omnivorous restaurant with at least half a dozen vegetarian main dishes from £10, some of which can be made vegan. Only sorbets for vegan desserts. Smoking section. House wine £11 bottle, from £2 for a glass. High chairs for children, ballonn and crayons! Some outside seating. Credit cards ok. Big white building on the A25, between Guildford and Dorking.

Riverside Vegetaria
Vegetarian restaurant

64 High Street
Kingston-upon-Thames
Open: Every day 12-23.00

Tel: 020-8546 7992
Train/Tube Kingston BR

Superb riverside vegetarian restaurant by the Thames. In warm weather you can eat under the sky. 70% vegan including some awesome desserts. Starters £3.95-£4.30. Main dishes £5.50-£6.70 include masala dosa, tofu marinated in teriyaki sauce, mushroom and lentil bake; all served with veg, salad and/or rice. Organic and vegan wines. Discounts for Vegetarian and Vegan Society members. Booking advised a couple of days ahead for weekends and outside.

Wagamama Kingston
Japanese omnivorous restaurant

16-18 High Street Kingston
Kingston-upon-Thames
Open: Mon-Sat 11.00-23.00, Sun 12.30-22.30

Tel: 020-8546 1117
www.wagamama.com
Train: Kingston BR

Omnivorous fast food Japanese noodle bar with at least nine veggie and vegan dishes.

Richmond Harvest

International wholefood restaurant

5 The Square
Richmond
Open: Mon-Sun 11.30-23.00

Tel: 020-8940 1138
Train: Richmond BR

International wholefood vegetarian restaurant using 80% organic ingredients with a small amount of outside seating. Many vegan dishes. Starters and salads from £3.25. Main courses £5.95 such as Chinese casserole with ginger and tamari sauce, or butterbean curry with brown rice. At lunchtimes jacket spuds with some of the main dishes as fillings for £4.50. Five desserts and the hot fruit crumble is vegan at £3.25. Vegetarian and vegan wine £2.50 a glass or £10.95 a bottle. Beer £2.95. 10% service charge applies after 5pm. Credit cards are accepted.

Tide Tables

Vegetarian café

2 The Archways, Richmond Bridge
Richmond
Open: daylight hours, phone ahead in winter as
they close if weather is bad

Tel: 020-8948-8285

Vegetarian café under the arch of a bridge near the town centre, with beautiful views of the Thames, a riverside terrace and outside seating in summer. Open for breakfast, lunch and tea. Vegan soup, spinach pastie with salad, stuffed focaccia, vegan shepherdess pie with salad, falafel, from £2.20 to £5.90. Handmade organic cakes. Hot and cold drinks and free corkage. Child and dog friendly.

Veggie One

Vegetarian Chinese

322 Limpsfield Road
Sanderstead, South Croydon
Open: Tues-Sun 18-23.00, closed Mon

Tel: 020-8651-1233
Train: Sanderstead

Vegetarian Chinese restaurant and take-away, GM free and completely organic. All their dishes are vegan except the egg fried rice. Evening meal £10-15 per person. Starters like crispy aromatic "duck", tempura vegetables £1.80-£6.00. Mains £2.00-£5.50 include aubergine and bean casserole, vegan pork, vegan fish, abalone mushrooms with sesame. 8 desserts £2.00-3.50 such as toffee apple, toffee banana, mango pancake. They want to promote health, so though licensed they don't sell alcohol and it's smoke free. But you can bring your own drinks. Non alcoholic wine £5.50 or £6 per bottle, non-alcoholic beer £1.50 or £2, soft drinks and soya milk. Cheques or cash, no credit cards.

Santok Maa's

Indian vegetarian restaurant

848 London Road
Thornton Heath
Open: Thu-Tue 12-22.00. Closed Wed.

Tel: 020-8665-0626
Train: Thornton Heath,
Norbury

North and South Indian vegetarian restaurant and take-away, with some Chinese dishes that use Indian spices like stir-fries. Nearly 100 veggie and vegan dishes. Starters average £2.95, main courses £3.95, rice £1.75. Desserts from £1.50 but no vegan ones. Bring your own wine, £1 per person corkage. Special offer on Monday, all food half price excluding dessert and take-away.Visa, MC, Amex.

Food for Thought

Wholefood shop

38 Market Place
Kingston, Surrey KT1 1JQ
Open: Mon-Sat 9-17.30, Sun closed

Tel: 020-8546-7806

Wholefood shop with plenty of staples like dried fruit, nuts, seeds, pulses etc. plus supplements, aromatherapy, skin-care ranges, and homeopathic remedies.

Oliver's Wholefood Store

Wholefood store

5 Station Approach
Kew Gardens, Richmond
Open: Open Mon-Sat 9-19.00, Sun 10-19.00

Tel: 020-8948 3990
TrainTube: Kew Gardens

Wholefood shop next to the tube station, handy for picking up something to nibble while you visit Kew Gardens. Veggie and vegan take-away snacks include sandwiches, pastries, salads, seaweed rice and wraps. They sell vegan wines as well as organic fruit and veg. Nutritionist and beauty therapist, regular lectures in-store.

Holland & Barrett

Health food shop

19 Grace Reynolds Walk
Camberley

Tel: 01276-64043

1098-99 The Mall, Whitgift Centre
Croydon
Open Thursday till 20.00 and
Sunday 11-17.00.

Tel: 020-8681 5174

Holland & Barret

Health food shop

185 High Street
Dorking

Tel: 01306–889 654

Unit 44, Ashley Centre
Epsom
Open: Mon–Sat 9–17.30, Sun 10–16.00

Tel: 01372–728520

Unit 3, Friary Centre
Guildford

Tel: 01483–537 207

12–13 Apple Market
Kingston
Open: Mon–Fri 9–17.30,
Sat 9–18.00, Sun 11–16.30

Tel: 020–8541–1378

68 High Street
Reigate

Tel: 01737–248 260

50a George St
Richmond
Open: Mon–Sat 9–17.30, Sun 11.30–16.30

Tel: 020–8940 1007

213 High Street
Sutton
Open: Mon–Sat 9–17.30, Sun 11–16.00

Tel:020–8642– 5435

13 King Street
Twickenham

Tel: 020–8891 6696

27 Wolsey Walk
Woking

Tel: 01483–772 978

Tyne & Wear

For what's on in the north-east, try
www.tyne-online.com with its unique Geordie Search facility.

Bob Trollop's Pub

Vegetarian pub

100% Vegetarian PUB with a terrific British veggie food menu and good value.

All day breakfast with sausages, burger, tomato, mushrooms, baked beans and hash browns. Mixed grill similar plus garlic mushrooms, onion rings, jacket wedges.

Starters like garlic bread, samosas, garlic mushrooms with tomato and garlic dip, mushroom pate with toast, pakoras, taco triangles. Dips and dippers with salad garnish like deep fried coated veg with peanut satay sauce, deep fried jacket wedges with garlic mayonnaise, vegetable nuggets with tomato and garlic dip.

Main courses: Tagliatelle Nicoise with salad and jacket potato, bean hot pot, lentil veggie chilli, mushroom Stroganoff, country vegetable casserole; all served with either hash browns, wholegrain rice, deep fried jacket wedges, or in a Giant Yorkshire pudding. Also veg curry, naan bread, jacket spuds with coleslaw, baked beans, ratatouille, chilli, bean hot pot, vegetable casserole or mushroom Stroganoff.

Hot butties made with wholemeal hoagie, baguette, or tortilla wrap, containin veggie sausages, spicy beanburger, quarter or halfpounder. Spice it up with chilli, beans, ratatouille, salsa, crispy onion rings, peanut butter or mushrooms. Extra veg and spuds available. Sandwiches can also be made with the same range of breads. .

Lots of desserts like blackcurrant and apple crumble, chocolate fudge cake, treacle sponge, banana splits, chocolate or blueberry muffin. They do coffee and teas.

32–40 Sandhill
Quayside
Newcastle
Tyne & Wear NE1 3JF
Tel: 0191 261 1037

www.wessextaverns.co.uk

Pub open:
Mon–Sat 11–23.00,
Sun 10–22.30

Full menu:
Mon–Sat 11–19.00
Sun 10–19.00

Children until 7pm

Happy hours 4–7pm with cut price wine, draught beers, lager and cider.

There's a list behind the bar of which dishes are vegan and a magic vegan button on the till to inform the chefs not to put butter in your sandwich etc.

Wine £8.50 bottle, glass from £1.75

Smoking allowed, no non smoking area

Visa, MC, Switch and they do cashback if you spend over £5

Directions: right by Tybe Bridge and opposite the Guildhall

The Last Days of Raj

Indian omnivorous restaurant

168 Kells Lane
Low Fell
Gateshead
Open: Mon–Sat 12.00–14.30, Mon–Sun 18.00–
24.00. Closed Sun lunch.

Tel: 0191 4826494

Indian restaurant with some vegetarian dishes and more that can be adapted.

Heartbreak Soup

Omnivorous Tex–Mex

77 Quayside
Newcastle
Open: Mon–Sat 12.00–14.00, 18.00–late

Tel: 0191–222 1701

Lively international Tex–Mex restaurant with big selection of veggie alternatives. Not much for vegans except a starter which is apparently big enough to serve as a main – a Japanese plate for £4.95. Visa, MC.

Out Of This World

Organic supermarket

Gosforth Shopping Centre
High Street
Gosforth NE3 1JZ
Open: Mon–Sat 9–18.00, late night Fri till 19.00

Tel: 0191 213 0421

Big ethical organic supermarket, with lots of veggie food. They do sandwiches Mon–Fri and pasties, though Wed–Fri are the best days for those when they have deliveries.

Holland & Barrett

Health food shop

5 Cameron Walk
Metro Centre
Gateshead

Tel: 0191–460 2546

Unit 12, Hill Street Centre
Middlesborough TS1 1SU

Tel: 01642–220 179

11 Bigg Market
Newcastle NE1 1UN

Tel: 0191–232 7540

21 Blandford Street
Sunderland

Tel: 0191–565 6249

27 Albany Mail
Washington

Tel: 0191–417 8451

Warwickshire

Parkfield

Omnivorous B&B in a Victorian house with a vegetarian proprietor. There are nine rooms; one single at £25 per night, one single ensuite at £35 per night, four double ensuites and two twin ensuites at £22.50–£24 per person per night and one family ensuite at £19 per person per night.

For breakfast start with cereal followed by pancakes and stewed fruit, or have a full cooked vegetarian English breakfast of veggie sausages, beans, tomatoes and mushrooms with toast and preserves. Vegan margarine and soya milk are available.

Parkfield is only one hundred metres from the Greenway cycle path which connects with the Heart of England way.

The town centre, where there are Shakespeare Birthplace Trust houses and three Royal Shakespeare theatres, is only a ten minute walk away.

Nearby there is a teddy bear museum, river rides and many small restaurants and shops.

Stratford is also an excellent base for visiting the Cotswold Hills, Warwick Castle, Blenheim Palace, Coventry, Oxford, Birmingham and the National Exhibition Centre.

Don't be surprised if you come back as many of their customers do.

Tea and coffee making facilities, radio alarms and televisions are in the rooms.

**Omnivorous
Bed and Breakfast**

*3 Broad Walk
Stratford upon Avon
Warwickshire CV37 6HS
England*

*Tel and Fax:
01789 293313*

www.parkfieldbandb.co.uk

*Email:
parkfield@btinternet.com*

Train Station: Stratford upon Avon, 1/2 mile, then taxi

Open: all year

*Directions:
Take the B439 towards Bidford on Avon from Stratford town centre.
Turn left into Broad Walk immediately before first roundabout*

Parking: planty available

Children over five are welcome

No smoking throughout

Rhubarb

Vegetarian cafe

50 Warwick Street
Leamington Spa, Warwickshire CV32 5JS
Open: Mon–Sat 9.30–18.00

Tel: 01926 425005

Vegetarian café. Three specials each day, around £6.50 such, as Mexican wrap.
They also have bagels, sandwiches, soup, nachos, cakes. Some of the food is vegan or can be adapted. Smoking allowed everywhere. No credit cards. There's a shop attached that sells artefacts from all over the world.

Summersault

Vegetarian restaurant

27 High Street
Rugby, Warwickshire CV21 3BW
Open: Mon–Sat 9.00–16.30, shop till 17.30, closed
Sunday,

Tel: 01788 543 223

75 seat vegetarian lunch restaurant. Entrees from £2.10, range of vegan and vegetarian salads from 90p per portion. Vegan and veggie mains from £4.55, menu changes daily. Desserts £1.40–2.25 all wholemeal, including vegan. Organic vegetarian wine £2.35 a glass, £12.95 bottle. Pot of tea for one £1.40, coffee £1.30. No smoking. Children's portions, high chairs.

Hussains

Indian omnivorous restaurant

6a Chapel Street
Stratford–upon–Avon
www.hussainsindiancuisine.co.uk
Open: daily 17–24.00, also Thu–Sun 12.30–14.30

Tel: 01789 267506

North and South Indian omnivorous restaurant. £6.99 for a three course lunch, dinner around £15 per head, individual dishes from £6.45. House wine £7.75 bottle, £2 glass. Smoking and non–smoking sections. Children welcome. Parking outside. Visa, MC, Amex.

Thai Kingdom

Thai omnivorous restaurant

11 Warwick Road
Stratford-upon-Avon
Open: Mon-Sat 12-14.00, 18-22.45, closed Sun

Tel: 01789 261103

Omnivours Thai restaurant. The bargain here is the £3.99 special lunch, popular with students and tourists, with vegetarian options such as veg or sweet and sour tofu with rice.
Vegetarian set menu £15.95 with choice of starter, 5 mains with rice, dessert and coffee. Everything cooked to order so they can make it vegan, nut free or whatever. A la carte starter £3.95, main dishes £5.95. Smoking and non smoking areas. House wine £10 bottle, £2.45 glass. Well behaved children welcome but no special facilities. Visa, MC, Amex, Diners. They have held private parties for Thai royalty. Booking advised for evenings as they sometimes do corporate meals.

The Vintner

Omnivorous bar and restaurant

5 Sheep Street
Stratford-upon-Avon
Open: every day, 10-22.00 for food,
till 23.00 for drinks

Tel: 01789 297259
www.v_vintner.co.uk

Omnivorous wine bar, café and restaurant, with several vegetarian dishes, recommended by veggies who've stayed at Parkfield. Breakfast, all day brunch and evening menus. The brunch menu includes vegetable tortillas £5.50 available till 7pm in the restaurant for pre-theatre diners, or later in the wine bar. Main courses include mushroom and potato pave with wine and veg £7.95, or polenta cake with aubergine and pepper. They use vegetable stock gravy and will prepare dishes for vegans according to what they have that day and what you like. Children's menu, they have high chairs. Smoking and non-smoking areas. Parking round the back. Visa, MC, Diners, Amex.

The Red Lion Inn

Omnivorous restaurant

Station Road, Claverdon
Warwick CV35 8PE
Open: Mon-Fri 12.00-15.00, 18.00-23.00,
Sat & Sun 12.00-21.30

Tel: 01926 842291

Omnivorous restaurant which typically has 3 vegetarian main dishes on menu, from £7.95, and they are happy to adapt things for vegans. Non smoking in dining area. Visa, MC.

Holland & Barrett

Health food shop

55 Warwick Street
Leamington Spa

Tel: 01926–421 775

2 Market Place
Nuneaton

Tel: 02476–352 649

36a High Street
Rugby

Tel: 01788–570 280

31 Bridge Street
Stratford Upon Avon

Tel: 01789–269 893

20 High Street
Warwick

Tel: 01926–409 305

West Midlands

Wolverhampton

Wolverhampton is not an obvious destination for tourists, but it is a cheap place to visit. It has a great health food shop, and some impressive Balti restaurants, so getting veggie food here isn't a problem.

by Ronny

Jyoti Vegetarian Restaurant

Indian vegetarian restaurant

569 Stratford Rd
Birmingham
Open: Tue–Fri 18.00–21.15, Fri 12.00–14.00, Sat
13.00–21.15, Sun 13.30–20.30

Tel: 0121–766 7199

Vegan friendly Indian vegetarian restaurant. Mains, £5.75–£6, with half of all items on menu suitable for vegans. Average £12 a head with a starter, main and dessert. Non smoking. Visa, MC.

The Warehouse Cafe

Vegetarian restaurant

54 Allison Street
Digbeth
Birmingham B5 5TH
Open: Mon–Sat 12.00–14.30.
Also some evenings on special occasions

Tel: 0121–633 0261

Vegetarian restaurant based in Friends of Earth building. 60% vegan, including salads, ice cream and burgers. Varied menu with a mixture of Indian, Mediterranean, Mexican, organic, Spanish, Thai, wholefood. Mains from £1.95–£3.75. Always have soya milk. Non Smoking. No credit cards. Discounts for FoE members.

Cathay

Oriental omnivorous restaurant

86 Holyway Head
Birmingham City Centre
B1 1NB

Tel: 0121–666 7788
www.cathayrestaurant.co.uk

Omnivorous Oriental restaurant which boasts not only a separate vegetarian menu (most of which is also vegan) but separate vegetarian chefs and kitchen, and can seat 110. Average main is £8 and includes several mock meat dishes such as sweet and sour chicken or crispy aromatic duck, and black bean aubergine. Several desserts including a vegan 'bunny bun' – steamed Chinese bun in the shape of a small rabbit with a sweet lotus filling, £3. Fully licensed. Non smoking in dining area. Visa, MC. Offer 10% discount to members of the Vegetarian and Vegan Societies.

London Sweet Centre

Indian vegetarian take–away

104 Soho Road
Handsworth
Birmingham B21 9DP

Tel: 0121–554 1696

Vegetarian sweet centre. Some savoury items with samosas and pakoras (with vegetable ghee), and lots of sweets.

Milan Sweet Centre

Indian vegetarian take–away

238 Soho Road
Handsworth
Birmingham B21 9LR
Open: Mon–Sun 10.00–19.45

Related to the Stoney Lane branch (below).

Milan Sweet Centre

Indian vegetarian take–away

191 Stoney Lane
Sparkhill
Birmingham B12 8BB
Open: Mon–Sun 9.00–20.00

Tel: 0121 551 5239

Indian vegetarian takeaway with some vegan friendly items including in the sweets.

Pritam Sweet Centre

291 Rookery Road
Handsworth
Birmingham
Open: Mon–Sun 9.30–19.30

Tel: 0121–449 1617

Indian vegetarian take away, with several savoury items and sweets.

Rogans Vegetarian Restaurant

Vegetarian restaurant

12 College Road
Handsworth Wood
Birmingham B20 2HX
Open: Mon–Sat 12.00–14.00, 17.30–21.00

Tel: 0121 551–5626
Fax: 0121 5540444

Highly recommended vegetarian restaurant with half of menu vegan and dishes suitable indicated as such. Lunch mains, £1.50–£4.25, with Italian herb burger, chilli beans with rice and falafels. Evening mains, £4.95–£5.75, include typically Caribbean pepper pot served with rice and Mediterranean butter beans with pitta bread. Vegan dessert offerings such as chocolate and orange gateaux, various crumbles and carrot cake, from £1.60. Non smoking. No credit cards.

Sangam

Indian vegetarian take–away

334 Soho Road
Handsworth
Birmingham
Open: Mon–Sat 11–20.00, Sun 12–18.00

Tel: 0121–523 9905

Indian vegetarian eat–in and take–away. £1.60 per bowl of curry or rice.

Browns

Omnivorous bar

Earl Street
Coventry,
West Midlands CV1 5RU
Open: Mon–Thu 9–23.00, Fri–Sat 9–01.00,
Sun 12–18.00, food always available

Tel: 024 7622 1100
www.browns–cafebar.co.uk

Omnivorous bar with a lot of veggie food. £5 for a meal. At least half of the 15 dishes are veggie and maybe 4 of those vegan. Choice of 5 or 6 veg and 3 kinds of potato. Desserts £2.50. Soya milk available. Bottle of house wine £9.85, glass £2.65. Non smoking section. Visa, MC. No under 18's. Roof terrace. Sometimes weekend DJ's. In the centre next to the Cathedral, art gallery and the university.

The Restaurant at Ryton Organic Gardens

Omnivorous

Woolsten Lane
Ryton–on–Dunsmore
Coventry
West Midlands CV8 3LG
Open: Mon–Sun 9.00–17.00

Tel: 024 76307142

Omnivorous restaurant based in gardens, with some outside seating area. Average of 5 vegetarian mains daily, £7.50, and happy to adapt things for vegans. Non smoking inside. Visa, MC.

Rosemary's Health Food Shop

Health food shop

3 Mander Square, Mander Centre
Wolverhampton
Open: Mon–Sat 9–17.30, Sun 10.30–16.30

Health food shop, not entirely vegetarian, but they do have pasties, sandwiches and cakes for us, and vegan ice–cream. 20% off if you buy two identical products.

Holland & Barrett

1–3 Corporation Square
Birmingham

Tel: 0121–236 7869

54–55 The Pallasades
Birmingham B2 4XH

Tel: 0121–633 0104

33 Alchester Road South
Kings Heath, Birmingham
West Midlands B14 7JQ

Tel: 0121–444 7000

6 City Arcade
Coventry CV1 3HW

Tel: 02476–222 752

Unit 30, West Orchards
Coventry CV1 1QX

Tel: 02476–230 107

12 Churchill Precinct
Dudley DY1 1PG

Tel: 01384–230 610

84 High Street
Solihull B91 3TA

Tel: 0121–709 2153

Sainsbury's Centre
Sutton Coldfield B72 1XX

Tel: 0121–321 2439

34–36 Park Street Arcade
Walsal WS1 1NJ

Tel: 01922–611 348

13 Queens Arcade, Mander Centre
Wolverhampton WV1 3NL

Tel: 01902–420 937

West Sussex

St Martin's Organic Tearooms

Almost vegetarian tea room

98% organic wholefood tearoom selling English food in the attractive Chichester town centre, close to the cross. All veggie and mainly vegan, apart from a salmon dish.

There are several types of vegan soup, around £4, including broccoli, mushroom, or tomato.

Salads around £5 include green salad or rice salad.

Potato cakes and sandwiches are also available.

Drinks include freshly squeezed orange or apple juice, vegan smoothies, coffee, caffeine-free coffee alternatives and hot chocolate.

House wine £2.80 glass, £11 bottle. Beer £2.70 a glass. Coffee 2.00.

Soya milk isn't offered, but they have organic oat milk and offer 'oataccino'. Also vegan organic margarine. Ingredients list available for everything.

All savoury dishes, soups and cakes are made on the premises and a list of their ingredients is available at the counter, making this a highly recommended place for people with allergies or special diets. The food is all low in fat.

3 St Martins St
Chichester
West Sussex

Tel: 01243 786715

www.organictearooms
.co.uk

Open:
Mon–Sat 9.00–18.00
closed Sunday.

Licensed

No cards

Cash or cheque only

No smoking

Earthwise Vegetarian Café

Vegetarian and vegan cafe

Commercial House, 19 Station Road
Bognor Regis
Open: Mon–Sat 9.30–17.30

Tel: 01243–828 246

Vegetarian and vegan café. Salads from £2 for small, £4 for large. Mains, £2–£6, with chillis, curries and nut roasts, and a changing daily specials board. Jacket potatoes with filling, £3.50. Vegan cakes, £1.50, and vegan ice cream, 60p a scoop. Smoking section. No credit cards.

Café Paradiso

Vegetarian cafe

9 Priory Lanes, Northgate
Chichester
Open: Mon–Sat 9.00–17.00 closed Sunday

Tel: 01243–532 967
Fax: 01243–532 967

Vegetarian café. Salads from £2.75, mains, £3.95–£4.95, such as falafel. Cater for vegans and coeliacs. Licenced. Non smoking. No credit cards.

Country Life

Omnivorous restaurant

The Old Candle Factory, 1 Terrant Square
Terrant Street
Arundel
Open: Mon–Wed, Fri–Sat 10.30–17.00;
Sun 11–17.00; closed Tue

Tel: 01903 883 456

Omnivorous restaurant with around half the menu vegetarian, such as Mexican bean hot pot, nut roast £4.95–5.50. Vegan fruit cake £1.65. House wine £2.25 a glass. Smoking allowed everywhere. No credit cards. Can do half portions for children, one high chair.

Holland & Barrett

Health food shop

17 London Road
Bognor Regis

Tel: *01243 830354*

19 North Street
Chichester

Tel: *01243–778 898*

Unit 6, County Mall,
Crawley

Tel: *01293–565 913*

Swan Walk, West Street
Horsham

Tel: *01403–274 353*

Wiltshire

Bradford Old Windmill

Bed and breakfast in a converted windmill hidden away amongst the trees with a vegetarian proprietor. There are three rooms, all double ensuites from £69–£109 per room per night. All have their own unique features such as the Damsel room with its queen sized water bed and whirlpool bath, the round bed in the round Great Spur room and the Fantail room with its spectacular views.

Of their seven breakfast choices, six are vegetarian such as devilled mushrooms on wholemeal muffins. Soya milk and vegan margarine are available. 95% organic.

Dinner is offered for £20 per person on most nights and will be a veggie adaption of a recipe collected from Mexican, Thai, Nepalese, Gambian or Jamaican cuisine. 80% organic. Nearby Bath (eight miles away) also offers restaurants serving plenty of veggie food.

Bradford on Avon is an unspoilt town with many charms, like secret courtyards and overflowing gardens viewed from narrow alleyways between weavers' cottages and clothiers mansions.

Nearby attractions include the Kennet and Avon canal, the cities of Bath, Glastonbury and Wells, Cotswold villages, the stone circles of Avebury and Stonehenge, Wookey Hole caves and the Forest of Dean.

Curl up on the sofa in the circular lounge and enjoy a log fire on cold winter nights.

Televisions and tea and coffee making facilities are in the rooms.

Omnivorous
Bed and Breakfast

4 Masons Lane
Bradford on Avon
Wiltshire BA15 1QN
England

Tel: 01225 866842

Fax: 01225 866648

*www.distinctlydifferent.
co.uk*

Train station: Bradford on Avon, 1/4 mile, then taxi.

Open: March–December

Directions: On A363 from north find mini round-about by Castle pub. Take Masons lane down hill towards town centre. Turn left after fifty metres into private unsigned drive immediately before first road side house.

Parking: available

Children over ten years are welcome

No smoking throughout

Berli's

Vegan restaurant overlooking Salisbury market square and situated above a shop called Julian Graves.

Soup of the day served with a wedge of wholemeal bread from £2.25. Deep fried potato wedges £3.50. Bean chilli with rice £3.60. Jacket potatoes £3.60 come with a salad garnish and choice of homemade toppings – chilli, hummus or sour 'cream' and chives.

Lunch mains courses £4.95–£6.25, include ratatouille, marinated tofu tortilla wrap, stir-fried vegetables and a Mediterranean platter – mixed salad with marinated aubergine and red pepper, hummous, kalamata olives, cous cous and a warm pitta bread.

Dinner menu mains, £7.60–£7.95, such as Thai green curry served with Oriental salad and rice; chestnut and mushroom goulash with green olives, served with a selection of vegetables; and black bean burrito served with salad and potatoes.

Desserts vary and are displayed on a dessert board. Homemade vegan cheesecake served in the evenings, with fresh mango, pecans and maple syrup, is a speciality, and they also do fresh fruit salads, homemade sorbets and apple crumbles. Cakes include fudge chocolate, carrot, orange drizzle and sugar free apricot flapjacks.

Special diets catered for. All chocolate products in cakes and desserts are organic and fair trade.

House wine, £9 for a bottle, £1.85 for a glass.

14 Ox Row
Market Square
Salisbury
Wiltshire SP1 1EU

Tel: 01722–328 923

veggie_debbie@
hotmail.com

Open:
Tue–Sat 10.30–15.00,
Fri–Sat 18.30–22.00,
call to confirm

Licensed

Non smoking

Visa, MC

Function room upstairs

England **WILTSHIRE** Restaurants

The National Trust Circle Restaurant Vegetarian

High St
Avebury SN8 1RF
Open: April–Oct every day 10–18.00; Oct–Mar
weekends only 10–16.00; Closed Xmas Day

Tel: 01672–539 514
Fax: 01672–539 683

Vegetarian and vegan restaurant in a 19th century stable block built of the same sarsen stone as the adjacent megalithic stone circle. Menu changes every ten days, with main courses £5–£5.95 including salad. Soup £2.95 is always vegan. Fruit wine, beer, usual hot beverages, soya milkshakes. One highchair. Wheelchair access.

Applebys Vegetarian café

5 Old Hughenden Yard
Marlborough SN8 1LT
Open: Mon–Sat 8.30–17.00, 10–17.00 Sunday

Tel: 01672–515200
Fax: 01672–515200

New vegetarian café which used to be called Stones. Hot lunch £5.95, cold lunch with salad £4.75, sandwiches £3.45–4.25, salads £3.50. You can have an alcoholic drink but only with a meal. Good range of organic and vegetarian wines, beers and ciders. House wine from £2.20 glass. Teas £1.35 pot. Soya milk not available, they'll keep yours in the fridge for you. Children's portions, 4 high chairs.

Holland & Barrett Health food shop

9 & 10 The Brittox
Devizes SM10 1AJ

Tel: 01380–722 025

59 Silver Street
Salisbury

Tel: 01722–324 064

1a, 17 Brunel Shopping Centre
Swindon

Tel: 01793–521 235

Unit 15, The Shires
Trowbridge

Tel: 01225–776 056

Unit 1, Market Place
Warminster

Tel: 01985–847 965

Salisbury Health Foods Wholefood shop

15 Queen Street
Salisbury
Open: Mon–Sat 9–17.30

Tel: 01722–335965
Fax: 01722–412519

Wholefood shop with lots of take-away food and vegan ice-cream.

Worcestershire

Lady Foley's Tea Room

Vegetarian restaurant

Great Malvern Railway Station
Imperial Rd, off Avenue Rd
Malvern
Open: Mon–Sat 9–18.00, Sun 3–18.00

Tel: 01684–893033
Fax: 01684–560923
margaretbaddeley@yahoo.com

Vegetarian restaurant on the platform of the railway station. Soup £1.70 is usually vegan. Salad £1.20. Main courses like ginger stir–fry veg or red bean chilli with rice, jacket potatoes. Various desserts but none vegan.

St Annes Well Cafe

Vegetarian cafe

Victoria Walk, St Annes Road
Malvern
Open: Mon–Sun 10–17.00 Easter–September,
Winter hours vary

Tel: 01684–560 285

Vegetarian café with mostly vegan menu. Cooked meals between midday and 3pm. Mains such as chillis, aubergine and mango curry £4.50–£6.70. Always some vegan desserts, 85p–£1.30. Most of seating outdoors. Non smoking. No credit cards.

King Charles II Restaurant

Omnivorous restaurant

King Charles House
29 New Street
Worcester
Open: Mon–Sat 12.00–14.00, 18.30–21.30

Tel: 01905 22449

Omnivorous restaurant that has several vegetarian dishes on the menu and can adapt things for vegans if asked. Typically mains are £9.95 such as pasta and vegetables. No smoking in dining area. Bar upstairs. Visa, MC.

Holland & Barrett

Health food shop

22 Mealcheapen Street
Worcester

Tel: 01905–28153

Yorkshire

Prospect Cottage, Ingleton, North Yorkshire
Vegetarian bed and breakfast in a cosy stone built home

Places in Yorkshire

Hotels and Guest Houses

Shops

Restaurants

England YORKSHIRE

Acorn Guest House

Omnivorous guest house with vegetarian owners. There are nine rooms all with ensuite bathrooms; two singles at £26, two doubles and three twin rooms at £19 per person per night and two family rooms at £50–£60 for the room. One of the rooms is a loft with doors and a balcony overlooking the garden.

A selection of cereals and a cooked breakfast is offered. Soya milk, vegan margarine, veggie sausages and veggie bacon are available.

There are many museums, cinemas, sports arenas and an ice rink. Shop until you drop at the Princess Quay centre on the river which is built almost entirely of glass. Check out the markets on Sunday.

There is plenty of night life including lots of old worldly pubs, restaurants and clubs.

The town is pedestrianised and flat so is very easy for wheelchair users to get around.

Acorn Guest House has disabled access. There are three ground floor rooms and one has access to a wheel-in shower room.

Televisions and tea and coffee making facilities are in the rooms.

Omnivorous
Guest House

719 Beverley High Road
Hull
East Yorkshire HU6 7JN
England

Tel: 01482 853248

Fax: 01482 853148

Train station:
Hull, 2 1/4 miles

Open: all year

Children welcome

Animals welcome

Smoking in some rooms

Directions:
2 1/4 miles north of Hull
city centre on the A1079
Beverley to York Road..

Parking: ten spaces

Disabled access

Archway Cottage

Two early Victorian cottages linked together make this large family home and B&B. Situated in the heart of Ilkley, it enjoys outstanding moorland views.

There are four rooms; one double ensuite at £20 per person per night, one twin at £17.50 per person per night, one family room at £35–£48 per night and a family ensuite at £40–£50 per night.

For breakfast choose from a selection of fruit juices and cereals with fresh fruit salad followed by tomatoes, mushrooms or beans on toast. With prior notice they can provide vegan sausages, soya milk and soya yoghurt. Tea, coffee, fruit and herbal teas are all available.

Dinner is not offered but Ilkley has a variety of restaurants most with veggie options.

Ilkley also has a nightclub and two bars with late night licences. There is a wide variety of shops and a museum. It is also an ideal walking base with the famous Ilkley Moor and Cow and Calf Rocks. The Dales Way walk starts here which goes all the way to Windermere.

The nearby villages of Otley, Grassington and Malham are lovely and well worth a look.

Packed lunches are available. Tea and coffee making facilities, washbasins and televisions are in the rooms.

Omnivorous
Bed & Breakfast

24 Skipton Road
Ilkley
West Yorkshire LS29 9EP
England

Tel and Fax:
01943 603399

Email:
thegreens@archcottage.fs
net.co.uk

Train Station:
Ilkley, 1/4 mile

Open:
all year, except
Christmas

Children are welcome and
they have a high chair.

They will accept one well
behaved dog.

Directions:
Situated on the A65, two
minutes from the town
centre.

Parking: 2 spaces

Cornmill Lodge

Small family run vegetarian guest house within fifteen minutes walk of York Minster. There are five rooms; two double ensuites, one twin ensuite, one single (with private facilities) and one family all priced at £20–£30 per person per night.

Breakfast is organic wherever possible and comprises of fruit juice, fruit salad and organic or gluten–free cereal. You are then spoilt for choice with a selection of mushrooms with sesame seeds on toast, banana with sunflower seeds on toast, grilled or scrambled almond and sesame seed tofu, vegetarian sausages or a vegan burger. Any of these can be accompanied by mushrooms, tomatoes, baked beans, and wholemeal toast with preserves. Organic tea and coffee, fruit and herb teas, soya and rice milk, vegan margarine, vegan muesli and soy yoghurt available.

Dinner is not offered but there are two veggie restaurants nearby.

Born in Yorkshire the owner, Jen, knows a lot about the county and is always willing to advise guests about the many attractions of the city and surrounding area.

For those who enjoy walking, Cornmill Lodge is only half an hour's drive to the Yorkshire Moors, Dales and the coastline. Or you could spend a day in the medieval city of York with its excellent shopping and restuarants.

Leave your soap at home as toiletries are free from animal ingredients and are not tested on animals.

Tea and coffee making facilities in the rooms.

120 Haxby Road
York
Yorkshire YO31 8JP
England

Tel and Fax:
01904 620566

www.cornmillyork.co.uk

Email:
cornmillyork@aol.com

Train Station: York, 2 kms then get bus no.1 towards Wiggington.

Open: all year

Children of all ages are welcome and those under fourteen are half price. They have cots and high chairs.

Directions: From outer ring road, A1237, follow signs to York District Hospital. Take a sharp left turn at traffic lights after hospital. Cornmill Lodge is on the right, just before the pedestrian crossing.

Parking: off street

No smoking throughout

10% discount to members of the Vegetarian Society, Vegan Society, Viva!, PETA, and people presenting this book.

Falcon Guest House

Vegetarian B&B set in a quiet part of Whitby, a town with an 'old world' feeling. Falcon Guest House has eight rooms; two singles at £20 per night, two doubles and two twins at £18 per person per night and two family rooms at either £50–£60 for the room per night or £18 per person per night for three adults.

You won't go hungry at this B&B where breakfast is more than ample! Choose from vegan organic muesli, organic cornflakes or weetabix along with bananas, dates, nuts and wheatgerm. Then follow up with a cooked brekkie of veggie sausages, organic baked beans, fried mushrooms and tomatoes and organic wholegrain bread and toast with organic marmalade. Tea and herbal teas are available as well as fairtrade coffee. Vegan margarine and soya milk are available.

No evening meals are provided, but there is a nearby wholefood restaurant which does daytime and evening meals for both veggies and vegans.

The town has several museums, including the Whitby museum, the Captain Cook museum and the Dracula museum.

If you're more of an outdoors type or just craving some fresh air Whitby is set in between a two mile beach and North Yorkshire Moors National Park.

There are tea making facilities in the rooms and there is a TV lounge.

**Vegetarian
Bed & Breakfast**

*29 Falcon Terrace
Whitby
North Yorkshire
YO21 1EH
England*

Tel: 01947 603507

*Train Station:
Whitby, 7 minutes walk*

Open: all year

Children welcome

No animals please

*Directions:
From train station, go along Windsor Terrace, skirting opposite side of train station from dockend side. Windsor Terrace soon winds up a short hill (North Road). Falcon Terrace is topmost street off North Road on the right.*

Parking: available on the street

No smoking throughout

England YORKSHIRE Accommodation

The Flower In Hand

Vegetarian owned omnivorous guesthouse in Scarborough's Old Town. The house is perched in the lee of the Castle Headland and looks down into the Harbour and across the bay, with views to Flamborough Head. There are five rooms, three doubles, two twins and one family, all with ensuite bathrooms and all costing £19.50 per person per night. Children stay for half price.

Wake in the morning to cereal and juice, followed by a sizzling veggie Yorkshire breakfast consisting of veg sausages, fresh tomatoes, mushrooms, beans and fried bread. Vegan muesli, vegan margarine and soya milk are available.

The Flower is a couple of minutes from the beach and seafront attractions, yet it is above and away from the hustle and bustle. The eleventh century castle is close by and the town centre with its many shops and busy nightlife is less than ten minutes walk away. There are lots of restaurants and pubs, as well as a variety of clubs to dance the night away.

Scarborough is a great place for a holiday whether you just want to relax and do nothing, or walk the cliffs and moors all day. There are lots of attractions for the kids too, such as the Kinderland play park and Atlantis Waterworld. The proprietor has lived in Scarborough all his life, so can advise you on everything there is to do in the area.

Rooms have TV's and tea and coffee making facilities.

Omnivorous Guest House

Burr Bank
Scarborough
North Yorkshire
YO11 1PN
England

Tel: 01723 371471

Email: bazflower@aol.com

Train Station:
Scarborough Central,
15 minutes walk or £3
taxi ride.

Open: all year

Children of all ages
welcome

Pets welcome by
arrangement

Directions: Follow signs
for South Bay. Head north
towards the castle. One
hundred yards after traffic
lights by lifeboat house,
turn right between
Princess Cafe and
Newcastle Packet Pub. Go
up hill and Flower in Hand
is straight ahead.

Parking: usually available

Smoking in rooms only

10% discount to members
of the Vegetarian Society,
Vegan Society and people
presenting this book.

Moorlands
of Hutton-le-Hole

Award winning Georgian guesthouse and self catering cottage within the North York Moors National Park. It is ideally placed for exploring Yorkshire's natural beauty, historical sites and the coast. There are three double ensuites and two twin ensuites at £32.50 per person per night.

Breakfast could be muesli or cereal with fresh fruit followed by fried potatoes, tomatoes, mushrooms, baked beans and veg kedgeree with home made bread and preserves. Soya milk, vegan muesli and vegan margarine are available. Local, organic and home made ingredients are used when possible. Dinner is offered by prior arrangement for £18 and could be Broccoli soup to begin, followed by Thai Green Curry, finished with Fruit Salad. Barry, the chef, has been vegetarian for fifteen years and serves excellent veggie and vegan meals. There are also a number of pubs within seven miles all offering veggie dishes.

Explore the ruined abbeys of Rieveaulx and Bylands. Ryedale Folk Museum is worth a visit. It is half an hour to dramatic coastline, sea bird colonies and the historic towns of Whitby and Scarborough. It's twenty minutes to Castle Howard and thirty five minutes to York. You can play croquet in the peaceful streamside garden surrounding the house, or play tennis at the court fifty yards away. If it's too cold for sitting outdoors, find a deep armchair by the fire and relax with a book and a glass of wine.

Self catering cottage sleeping six available. Rooms have TV's and tea and coffee making facilites. One has a four poster bed. Ground floor rooms so some disabled access.

Hutton-le-Hole
North Yorkshire
YO62 6UA
England

Tel: 01751 417548

Fax: 01751 417760

www.moorlandshouse.com

Email: veg@moorlandshouse.com

Train Station: Malton, 20 miles or York, 30 miles, then taxi.

Open: all year

No children

Pets in the cottage only

No smoking throughout

Directions: Hutton-le-Hole is within the North Yorkshire Moors National Park, a few miles north of the market town of Kirkbymoorside and about 25 miles north of York. From the A170 between Thirsk and Scarborough, the turning to Hutton-le-Hole heads north about one mile east of Kirkbymoorside, and is also signposted "Ryedale Folk Museum". As you enter the village, ignore the local residents turn off to the left. Moorlands House is on the left hand side.

Parking: off road

Myrtle Grove

Veggie B&B set in the busy thriving town of Hebden Bridge. There is one spacious double ensuite room with views over the garden, the town and across the valley to Heptonstall. It costs £25–£30 per person per night.

Begin your day with home grown organic fruit with soy yoghurt and cereal followed by a full cooked breakfast. Soy milk, vegan margarine and vegan muesli are available. The veggie proprietor uses organic produce where possible, bakes her own bread and makes preserves. She is happy to cater for special dietary requirements if given notice.

Walk from the B&B down to the canal and town centre to do some shopping, or eat dinner at one of the many restaurants providing veggie food. The town of Hebden Bridge promotes the arts and has theatrical performances, poetry readings, story telling and live music. There is an arts festival every June. There are alternative therapy and healing clinics as well as an Alternative Energy Centre, canal boats, a marina and a cinema providing a varied selection of films.

For walkers, Hardcastle Craggs are nearby and there are footpaths beginning at the house. You could take easy and relaxing strolls along the canal or do more challenging walks into the hills and onto the moors.

The room has tea and coffee making facilites, a television and radio. Dogs are welcome by arrangement.

Vegetarian Bed and Breakfast

Old Lees Road
Hebden Bridge
West Yorkshire HX7 8HL
England

Tel: 01422 846078

Email: myrtlegrove@ btinternet.com

Train Station: Hebden Bridge, 1km, then bus or taxi or collection is possible.

Open: all year

Directions:
At Hebden Bridge (A646) take A6033 to Howarth after the first set of traffic lights. Myrtle Grove is 200 metres on the right. (A B&B sign hangs from the railings).

Parking: available on the street

No smoking throughout

North Cliff

North Cliff Bed and Breakfast is a beautiful Victorian Villa still retaining many of its original features. There are two double rooms and one twin room all costing £22 per person per night and all with ensuite bathrooms.

Start your day with cereal followed by a full cooked English veggie breakfast consisting of veggie sausages, tomatoes, mushrooms and beans with potato fritters and toast. Vegan margarine, soya milk and soya yoghurt are all available.

An evening meal is available if you have pre-booked and asked for dinner. It costs from £6 for a main meal and £3 for dessert. Veggie and vegan meals aren't a problem. Packed lunches are also available, or there is a health food shop in Whitby where you can pick up supplies.

Robin Hood's Bay is a picturesque old fishing village with narrow cobbled streets and alleyways. It is situated on the Heritage Coast of the English North York Moors. There are plenty of pretty beaches and rock pools to explore as well as tennis courts, a bowling green, a croquet lawn and loads of walks including the coast to coast walk. There are pubs and restaurants for the evening.

A short ride away are the busier resorts of Scarborough and Whitby and the North York Moors National Park. Slightly further away is the city of York, Castle Howard and Flamingoland theme park.

Tea and coffee making facilities and televisions are in the rooms. The rear rooms have views over the bay.

Omnivorous
Bed and Breakfast

Mount Pleasant North
Robin Hood's Bay
near Whitby
North Yorkshire YO22 4RE
England

Tel: 01947 880481

www.north-cliff.co.uk

Email:
lmnorthcliff@aol.com

Train station:
Whitby, 6 miles, then bus

Open: all year

Children welcome
Cot and high chair

Small dogs welcome by
arrangement

Smoking in some areas

Directions: easy to find

Parking: off street parking
available

£2 off per night to people
presenting this book, if
staying more than one
night.

Prospect Cottage

Vegetarian B&B in a cosy stone built home, situated within the village of Ingleton. There are a double and a single room both costing £16.50–£18 per person per night.

Begin your day with a hearty breakfast in the dining room, which overlooks the valley of the River Greta. Start with fruit juice, fresh fruit and cereal or muesli followed by baked beans and mushrooms on potato waffles, wholemeal toast and fresh coffee. Veggie sausages, soya milk and vegan margarine are always available.

Local cafes and pubs have good veggie options and there is a superb Indian restaurant in the neighbouring village, High Bentham. Picnic supplies can be picked up from Ingleton's two bakeries or the health food shop in High Bentham. There is also an organic shop 'Growing with Grace' four miles away.

The village of Ingleton lies at the foot of Ingleborough (one of the famous Three Peaks) surrounded by fells, caves, crags and wooded glens. The unique limestone scenery includes the 4 mile Waterfalls Walk, the country's largest tourist cavern White Scar Caves, and Gaping Gill, the largest pot hole in the British Isles.

Ingleton is a centre for the Yorkshire Dales National Park and is on the doorstep of the Southern Lake District. Lancaster, Kendal and Skipton are 17 miles away with castles, museums, art galleries, cinemas, theatres and shopping.

There is no TV lounge, but on a summer evening it's much nicer to sit in the garden drinking tea and watching the sunset! There are tea and coffee making facilities in the rooms.

Vegetarian Bed & Breakfast

Bank End
Ingleton
via Carnforth
North Yorkshire LA6 3HE
England

Tel: 015242 41328

Train Station:
Bentham 3 miles
or Ribblehead 5 miles.
From Bentham get a bus
or collection from either
station is possible by
arrangement.

Open: all year

Directions:
From the A65 main trunk
road, turn into Main
Street, Ingleton. Prospect
Cottage is about 300
yards up on the left.

Parking: available on the
street

Secure bicycle storage

Children welcome

Dogs by prior
arrangement

No smoking throughout

5% discount off a one
night stay or 10%
discount if staying for two
nights or more to
members of the
Vegetarian Society, Vegan
Society, Viva!, PETA,
Animal Aid and people
presenting this book.

See picture at the start of
this chapter

Shepherd's Purse

Guest house with veggie owner, only two minutes from the beach. There are five double ensuite rooms costing £42–£52 per room per night, and one twin, one family and two doubles with shared bathroom at £37 per room per night.

Breakfast is served in the cafe next door and costs from £2.50–£4.95. A full veggie breakfast includes veggie sausages, veggie bacon, tomatoes, mushrooms, baked beans, toast and preserves. Soya milk and vegan margarine available. The cafe also has a good selection of veggie food for dinner.

There are some good museums around, including Captain Cook's Museum and the museum at Whitby Abbey. Whitby is the home port of the Bark Edeavor, an exact replica of Captain Cook's ship. North York Moors Steam Railway is close by and will take you on a picturesque journey. The town has many old pubs with live music and folk clubs.

Children welcome and they have cots and high chairs. No pets.

Tea and coffee making facilities and televisions in the rooms.

Smoking allowed in some areas.

95 Church Street
Whitby
North Yorkshire
YO22 4BH
England

Tel: 01947 820228

www.shepherds-purse.co.uk

Email: rosie@shepherds-purse.co.uk

Train: Whitby, taxi or five minutes walk

Open: all year

Directions: in the Old Market Square in the historic part of town

Parking: no, but there is a nearby public carpark

England YORKSHIRE Accommodation

Ranworth

Vegetarian guest house

Church Road, Ravenscar,
Scarborough,
North Yorkshire YO13 0LZ
Train Station: Scarborough, ten miles

Tel: 01723 870366
Open: all year

Two doubles, one double ensuite and one twin £20 per person per night. Evening meal available for £8. Children and pets welcome. No smoking throughout. Wonderful views. 10% discount given to members of the Vegetarian Society and Viva!

Vegetarian B&B

Vegetarian bed & breakfast

21 Park Grove,
York, YO31 8LG
Train Station: York, two miles

Tel: 01904 644790
Open: all year

One single, one double ensuite and one family ensuite, £22 per person per night. Children welcome. No pets.
No smoking throughout.

Dairy Guest House

Omnivorous GH owned by veggies

3 Scarcroft Road,
York, YO23 1ND
www.dairyguesthouse.freeserve.co.uk
Email: filcis@globalnet.co.uk
Train Station: ten minutes walk

Tel: 01904 639367
Open: all year

Single rooms £32, single ensuites £42, doubles and twins £22.50 per person, and double, twin and family ensuites £27.50 per person per night. Disabled access. Children and quiet dogs welcome. No smoking throughout.

Wild Ginger

Vegetarian
Cafe Bistro

Vegetarian and vegan award winning wholefood restaurant where everything on the menu is either vegan or has a vegan alternative, and much of it is organic.

Breakfast until 12 noon, £4.95, vegetarian rashers and sausages, mushrooms, beans, tomato and toast.

Homemade soup with roll, £2.75. Salads from £2.95 for a small, £3.95 for a Greek salad. Daytime menu includes several burgers £4.95 and hot and cold sandwiches £1.95–£2.95, including avocado with dairy free mayonnaise and spicy red bean and salad. Jacket potatoes from £4.50 with filling and salad.

Evening menu mains £4.95–£7.50 such as vegetarian roast haggis served with potato wedges, swede and carrot, seasonal vegetables and Wild Ginger gravy; pancakes with special filling of the day; and a pasta dish.

Large choice of tempting desserts start from 80p for a scoop of speciality dairy-free ice cream (vanilla, strawberry, chocolate and raspberry), ice cream sodas from £1.75 and hot chocolate cake with a rich chocolate sauce and ice cream, £3.95.

Can cater for special diets – gluten-free, wheat-free, raw, diabetic and will try to cater for anyone.

Fully licensed with all organic alcohol. House wine £7.50 for a bottle, £1.75 a glass. Lots of fruit winese.

They also hold special gourmet evenings and have a mailing list for information.

5 Station Parade
(behind the Greenhouse)
Harrogate
North Yorkshire HG1 1UF

Tel: 01423–566 122
Fax: 01423–505 439

www.wild–ginger.co.uk

Train: Harrogate

Open:
Mon–Thu 10.00–15.45,
Fri & Sat 10.00–20.45
(last orders)

Non smoking

Visa, MC

5% discount for Vegan Society members

England **YORKSHIRE** Restaurants

The Blake Head

Vegetarian world food café at the back of a bookshop which caters for vegans and has wheat-free options. It was recently described as 'Vegetarian Heaven' by a local newspaper.

Breakfasts, snacks and main meals are all available and there is even a children's menu.

Typical breakfasts, £3-6 include beans on toast; potato and parsnip rosti with sauteed mushrooms; or hot apricot muesli.

Lunches, £2.75-£6 include soup with bread; jacket potatoes with mixed salad; or spicy bean burger with ciabatta roll and salad.

Main courses include mushroom timbale with cranberry and onion gravy; sun dried tomato and olive puff parcels with a white wine sauce; and arame ginger filo parcels with toasted sesame seeds.

Children can tuck into burgers, salads, beans on toast or jacket potatoes, £2-4.

There is a good range of cakes and biscuits, 95p-£2.40. Their chocolate fudge slice; banana, apricot and nut loaf; and orange and syrup biscuits are all vegan.

A wide range of drinks is available, including teas and herbal teas, £1.25; coffees from £1.20; hot chocolate; barleycup, £1.50, soft drinks; juices and mineral water, from £1.25. Wines, £2.95 per glass, £10.95 per bottle. Beers are also available.

Organic and fresh local produce is used where possible and all food is prepared on the premises.

104 Micklegate
York
North Yorkshire YO1 1JX

Tel: 01904 623 767

www.
blakeheadvegetariancafe.
co.uk
Train: York

Open:
Mon-Sat 9.30-17.00,
Sun 10.00-17.00

Children are very welcome and high chairs are available.

No smoking except in the outside courtyard.

5% discount for Viva! members.

El Piano

Vegetarian tapas bar in the heart of York. Other than the nightclubs, it is the latest opening premises in the city.

Organic where possible, the menu is a mix of Hispanic and internationally influenced dishes and is typically presented in platter format.

Homemade soup £3.25, with bread or Spanish crisps. Any single portion of salad or savoury bread with olives or pate £2.95. All the salads with a savoury item from the deli for £5.95.

Breakfast, £4.50, is always served.

Tapas style choices are all at £12.95 and include 'Grab and Dab' where you can select at least 4 of the following: falafels and fire sauce, pakoras and mint sauce, fried mushrooms and garlic mayo, samosas and chutney, fried pineapple and Thai sauce, and aubergine slices and cumin sauce; a giant salad plate; and a mixed plate with 2/3 hot foods and 1/3 salads.

All special diets catered for – gluten-free, wheat-free, raw, macrobiotic, vegan, diabetic, candida and sugar free.

Desserts £2.45–£3.50, with several vegan choices – various flapjacks, chocolate brownies, chocolate and marshmallow pie, crema Catalana, carrot cake and oranges in tequila syrup; all of which can be served with non-dairy toppings.

There are musical instruments for customer use and live music on Fridays and Saturdays.

Vegetarian tapas bar

15/17 Grape Lane
York
North Yorkshire Y01 7HU

Tel: 01904–610 676
Fax: 01904–643 049

www.elpiano.co.uk

Train: York

Open:

Mon–Sat 10.00–00.30

Bring your own alcohol, no charges.

Wheelchair and pushchair access.

High chairs for children

3 function rooms upstairs for public use

Smoking permitted

Visa, MC

Hitchcock's

Superb vegetarian all-you-can-eat buffet restaurant that attracts lots of meat eaters and is worth stopping in Hull for. Anyone who misses Heather's in London will love this place. One price £12 (£10 concessions) for three courses and coffee, with one sitting starting from 8.15pm.

Being in a quiet area of the Old Town, they only open when enough people book, usually 10 or 15 are sufficient, either as a single group or several separate bookings.

The menu is chosen by the first person to book and is based around a particular country, such as Italian, Chinse, Mexican, Thai, Cajun, Indian, Afro-Caribbean, Russian. But they could do Nepalese, Patagonian, Israeli, Tibetan, German and even English. Or a mixture. Almost all food is vegan, for example the Cajun menu starts with salsa red bean, dips with crudites and toasted bread. The awesome main course buffet includes okra gumbo, red beans and rice, banana bread, Jamaican curry, fried plantain bananas and sweet potatoes, lemon spinach, sweetcorn, hot salsa, salads, chillies.

Several desserts such as pecan pie, crumble and (vegan) ice cream.

House wines from £1 glass, £5 bottle. Beer £2 pint. Spirits from £1. Or bring your own wine and pay £1 per bottle corkage.

Caters for coeliacs, nut-free and other diets on request.

This is one of the best vegetarian restaurants ever, anywhere.

1–2 Bishop Lane
Hull
East Yorkshire HU1 1PA
(on corner of Bishopsgate and High Street)

Tel: 01482–320 233
Fax: 01482–320 907

Open:
Tue–Sat 20.00–24.00,
Sun–Mon closed

Children welcome, prices to suit as they like haggling.

Licensed

Outside catering

£2 discount for members of the Vegetarian or Vegan Society

Hansa's

Award winning Indian restaurant. Starters £2.75–3.25 include deep-fried cassava wedges with tamarind sauce, banana bhajiya, or have a platter of mixed bhajiyas for two for £6.95. House specialities include mung bean dhosa £4.75, idli with daal £4.50. Mains from £3.50 such as whole Kenyan aubergine stuffed with spicy masala £6.25, curries and daals. Thali and dessert £8.95. Banquet for six £10.95 each. One of the few Indian restaurants where vegans have a choice of three desserts such as sweet vermicelli cooked in vegetable ghee with sultanas, almonds and cardamon, £2.95. All you can eat Sunday buffet £6.95, children £3.95.

Organic, vegetarian and vegan wine from £2.50 glass, £8.95 bottle. Beer £2.50 bottle. Coffee £1.50. Soya milk available.

Gujarati Vegetarian Restaurant

72–74 North Street
Leeds, West Yorkshire

Tel: 0113-2444 408

www.hansas.co.uk
(complete menu)

Open: Mon–Thur 17.30–22.30, Fri & Sat 17.30–23.00, Sun 12–14.00

High chairs for children

Visa, MC.
10% service charge

10% discount for Animal Aid, PETA, Vegetarian or Vegan Society, Viva!

Gift vouchers available.
Cookery demonstrations.

Roots and Fruits

Friendly vegetarian restaurant. All day breakfast which can be made vegan, £4.95, and starters from £2.50 include nachos, samosas and New York potatoes (wedges). Sandwiches £3.75 such as wild mushroom pate or hummus. Jacket potatoes £3.75 with various fillings.

Mains £4.50–£6.25 such as burgers and chilli burritos. There is a specials board, from £5.25, which varies and typically includes pasta salad or curry.

Desserts, £2.95, and although nothing for vegans they hope to introduce some vegan-friendly items soon. They always have soya milk.

Private parties for up to 30 people.

Vegetarian Restaurant

10 Grant Arcade
Leeds
West Yorkshire LS1 6PG

Tel: 0113-242 8313

Open:
Mon–Fri 11.00–18.50
(last orders),
Sat 10.00–19.00

Licenced

Separate smoking section

Visa, MC

10% discount to Vegetarian Society members

Hansa's Gujarati Vegetarian Restaurant

44 Great Horton Road
Bradford, West Yorkshire
Open: Mon-Thu 18-20.30, Fri-Sat 18-23.30, Sun 12-22.00

Tel: 01274-730 433
www.hansas.co.uk

Same menu as Hansa's Leeds, see previous page.

South Square Vegetarian Cafe   Vegetarian cafe

South Square, Thornton Road, Thornton
Bradford
Open: Tue-Sat 10.30-16.30, Sun 12-16.00. Mon closed

Tel: 01274-834 928

Vegetarian cafe. Mix of fast food, Indian, Mediterranean and Mexican dishes, with a wholefood approach.

Courtyard by Marriott   Omnivorous restaurant

The Pastures, Tong Lane
Bradford BD4 ORP

Tel: 0113 2854646

3-star hotel and restaurant 5 miles from both Bradford and Leeds city centres. Some vegetarian food in the restaurant such as pasta, and they say the can cater for vegans if you call ahead. Three course a la carte dinner £20, main meal £10-15. The hotel is £95 single occupancy Mon-Thur, falling at weekends to £70 double, £50 single, but watch out for weddings.

Bean There   Vegetarian cafe

10 Wellington Road
Bridlington, East Yorkshire
Open: Tue-Sat 11-15.00; Sat 18-20.30 last orders

Tel: 01262-679 800
www.beentherecafe.co.uk
sixwheelwrights@aol.com

Vegetarian café opposite the Cenotaph. Lunchtime soup and roll £2.50, main meals up to £3.95. Evening meal £6.95 including veggies such as carib stew or rice and vegetable bake with crunchy nutty topping. Desserts such as vegan fruit crumble £1.80 lunch, £3.50 evening, with Swedish Glace ice-cream. Bring your own alcohol.

Eating Whole

Vegetarian restaurant

25 Copley Road
Doncaster
South Yorkshire DN1 2TE
Open: Mon–Sat 09.00–16.00,
also Thu–Sat 19.30–22.30. Closed Sun.

Tel: 01302 738 730

Vegetarian restaurant with vegan food. Soups from £1.90 and mains such as spicy lentil rissole with chilli sauce at £4. Always a vegan dessert, fruit salad or treacle tart, £1.80. Smoking section. No credit cards. Vegetarian and Vegan Society members receive a 10% discount.

Swinstey Tea Gardens

Vegetarian cafe

Fewston House
Fewston
Harrogate
North Yorkshire HG3 1SU
Open: Sat & Sun 10.30–17.00 and Bank Holidays

Tel: 01943 880637
Fax: 01943 880637

Vegetarian café with French, Mediterranean, Balkan and wholefood cuisine. Main meals such as Moroccan cous cous, £5.50. Always something vegan, including amongst the cakes, like apple cake or mixed fruit and silken tofu, £1.80. Also always have soya milk. Non smoking. No credit cards.

Laughing Gravy

Vegetarian restaurant

The Birchcliffe Centre
Birchcliffe Road
Hebden Bridge
West Yorkshire HX7 8DG
Open: Thu–Sun from 19.30

Tel: 01422 844425
www.laughinggravy.co.uk

Vegetarian restaurant which you'll need to book for. They do a mezze menu, like a buffet that comes to your table, for £14.75, with loads for vegans. They change the menu every week based on what's in season. Ashley the chef has worked in many kinds of restaurants so the cuisine is taken from all over the world. Licensed for alcohol. Just outside Hebden Bridge, a four minute walk from the train station. No smoking. Visa, MC. Child friendly, two high chairs and they can get more. Will open for parties of 10+ other nights. During the day it's a residential centre running courses and they do the catering, and they do outside events too.

The Blue Rooms

Vegetarian restaurant

9 Byram Arcade
Huddersfield, West Yorkshire
Open: Mon–Fri 10.00–17.00, Sat 9.00–17.00

Tel: *01484 512 373*

Vegetarian restaurant. Mains, £3.90, and there are always vegan friendly dishes. Non smoking. No credit cards.

The Zoo Café

Vegetarian cafe

80B Newland Avenue
Hull, East Yorkshire
Open: Mon–Sat 10.00–18.00 closed Sunday

Tel: *01482–494 352*

Vegetarian café. Veggie burgers always available. Choices from soup, salads, burritos, casseroles. Desserts such as brownies, flapjack, treacle tart etc. Very dairy oriented and not always vegan options available, though they say they try to offer them and cater for gluten free diets too. Smoking. No credit cards.

Strawberry Fields Bistro

Omnivorous bistro

159 Woodhouse Lane
Leeds
West Yorkshire
Open: Lunch Mon–Fri 12–14.10,
dinner Mon–Sat 18–21.30, closed Sun

Tel: *0113 243 1515*

Omnivorous bistro in Leeds where they make everything themselves and cater well for veggies and vegans with Mediterranean and Mexican dishes. Starters £1.50–£3.50 include vegan garlic bread or hummous. Main dishes £4.99–6.00 such as pizzas (can be without cheese), wild mushroom enchillada. Wine £7.99 bottle, £1.95 glass. Very much a bar in the evening with spirits doubles for £1.20.

Cheerful Chili

Vegetarian restaurant

Yorkgate Farm, East Chevin Road
Otley
West Yorkshire
Open: Tue, Wed, Fri, Sat 18.30–late, last orders 21.30

Tel: *01943 466567*

Vegetarian evening restaurant that gets heavily booked. Call to reserve and they'll call you back. Bring your own alcohol. During the daytime it's called the Ramblers Cafe with non-vegetarian food.
Location: on the right-hand side of East Chevin Road, which comes south out of Otley and eventually, after changing its name to Otley Old Road, joins the A658 airport road a mile or so N.E. of the airport.

The Curlew Cafe

Omnivorous restaurant

11–13 Crossgate
Otley, West Yorkshire LS21 1AG
Open: Tue–Thu 17.00–21.00, Fri & Sat 17.00–22.00

Tel: 01943–464 351

Omnivirous restaurant that has some vegetarian options on black-board. Mains, £11. Licenced. Visa, MC.

Airy Fairy

Vegetarian coffee shop

239 London Road
Sheffield, South Yorkshire
Open: Mon, Wed–Sat 11–18.00, Tue 14.30–19.30

Tel: 0114–249 2090
www.airyfairy.org
anwen@airyfairy.org

Vegetarian fair trade gift and coffee shop. Coffee from 80p, lots of fruit and herb teas, vegan hot chocolate and cappucinos. Homemade soup. Cakes 60p–£1.10, such as fruit cakes and vegan blueberry crumble. Handmade and local crafts with pagan influences, and fair trade items from around the world. Also some cruelty free products.

Nirman Indian Tandoori

Indian omnivorous restaurant

189–193 Glossop Road
Sheffield

Tel: 0114–272 4054
Open: every day 18.00–24.00

Bombay South Indian omnivorous restaurant with many veggie dishes.

Olive Garden

Vegetarian cafe and take–away

117 Norfolk Street
Sheffield

Tel: 0114–272 8886
Open: every day 18–24.00

Vegetarian cafe over a health food shop.

Blue Moon Cafe

Vegetarian cafe

2 St James Street
Sheffield

Tel: 0114–276 3443
Open: Mon–Sat 8.00–20.00

Big vegetarian self service restaurant by the Anglican cathedral. Soup £2.50, mains £4.90 with salad, desserts from £1.40 for a range of vegan cakes. Organic wines and beers. Non smoking. Visa, MC.

Kick Ass Angel

Juice bar

232–234 London Road
Sheffield, West Yorkshire

Tel: 0114–258 4503
Open: Tue–Sat 11.00–18.00

Herbs Restaurant

Vegetarian restaurant

10 High Street
Skipton
North Yorkshire BD23 1JZ
Open: Mon & Wed–Sat 9.30–17.00
closed Sun & Tues

Tel: 01756 790 619

Vegetarian wholefood restaurant and take away in natural food centre. Starters from £2 and mains, £2.55–£5.20, which change daily. Desserts from £1.50. Most special diets catered for including vegan. Non smoking. Visa, MC.

The Old Oak Tree

English omnivorous restaurant

South Kilvington
Thirsk
North Yorkshire
Open: 11.45–14.00, 18.45–21.00 (last orders).
Closed Mon though the bar is open in the evening

Tel: 01845–523 276

English omnivorous restaurant with a vegetarian menu that changes, some vegan but best to ring first. Licensed. Smoking area. No credit cards, just cash or cheque. Children's menu, one high chair.

Magpie Café

Omnivorous restaurant

14 Pier Road
Whitby
North Yorkshire
Open: Mon–Sun 11.30–21.00

Tel: 01947–602 058

Omnivorous restaurant which has several hot and cold vegetarian dishes which they are happy to adapt for vegans. Mains at £5.95 which include a dried fruit and nut salad. Will try to cater for other special diets, some gluten-free items menu. Non smoking. Visa, MC.

The Rubicon

Vegetarian restaurant

5 Little Stonegate
York
North Yorkshire
Open: Mon–Sun 11.30–22.00

Tel: 01904 676 076
www.rubiconrestaurant.co.uk

Vegetarian restaurant. Lunch main dishes, £2.50–£6.50; dinner mains, £7–£9. Always something vegan available. Desserts such as rhubarb crumble, £4.50. Licenced and most of their alcohol is vegan. Non smoking. Visa, MC. 10% discount to Vegetarian Society members.

The Green House

Wholefood shop

5 Station Parade
Harrogate
North Yorkshire
Open: Mon–Sat 9–17.45

Tel: 01423 502 580

100% vegetarian, mainly organic, wholefood shop at the front of Wild Ginger award-winning vegan restaurant. Chiller and freezer cabinet so great for vegan cheeses, tofu, five flavours Swedish Glace. Also vegan wines, beers, cider and perry.

Trade for Change

Fair Trade shop

20 New Market Street
Leeds
West Yorkshire
Open: Mon–Fri 10–17.00, Sat 9.30–17.30

Tel: 0113 242 5356
www.tradeforchange.co.uk
info@tradeforchange.co.uk

Fair trade shop selling veggie foods, snacks, cards, gifts, home furnishings, clothes made from organic cotton.

The Beehive

Fair Trade shop

67 Potter Newton Lane
Chapel Allerton
Leeds
West Yorkshire
Open: Tue–Fri 10.30–16.30, Sat 10–17.00

Tel: 0113–262 2975

The other fair trade shop, out of town, like Trade for Change only smaller, with a good selection of crafts, gifts, some wholefoods and a mini-café (one table and four chairs), on the Roundhay Park.

First Season

Wholefood shop

1 St. Annes Lane
Whitby
North Yorkshire
Open: Mon–Sat 9.30–17.00

Tel: 01947 601608

Vegetarian wholefood shop with supplements, a few pasties and vegan ice-cream.

Holland & Barrett

Unit 1, 58 Kirkgate Bradford	Tel: 01274 723289
19 Cheapside Barnsley	Tel: 01262–676 006
Unit 1, 47/49 Kings Street Bridlington	Tel: 01422–365 794
1a James Street Harrogate	Tel: 01423–503 469
95 New Street Huddersfield	Tel: 01484–548 963
9 Jameson Street Hull	Tel: 01482–326 597
21 Whitefriargate Hull	Tel: 01482–225 829
11 Crossgates Centre, Arndale Leeds	Tel: 0113–264 8326
21 Bond Street Mall, Bond Street Centre Leeds	Tel: 0113–246 7011
37 The Merrion Centre Leeds	Tel: 0113–234 2828
Brunswick Pavillion, Westborough Scarborough	Tel: 01723–501 369
10 Barkers Pool Sheffield	Tel: 0114–275 5438
30 Market Place Thirsk	Tel: 01845–526 868
11 All Saints Walk, The Riding Centre Wakefield	Tel: 01924–367 195
28–30 Coney Street York	Tel: 01904–627 257

Spiral

Leeds West Yorkshire	Tel: 0113 248 4044

Catering service, cooking workshops, short courses, for animal and gluten free diets. All vegan.

Isle of Man

The Isle of Man is so different, with history going right back to the Vikings, and scenic, with beautiful coastal walks. Being in the Gulf Stream the weather is mild. There is lots of sea wildlife like seals and basking sharks.

Fly there from many places including Manchester, Liverpool and London, or get the ferry or Seacat from Liverpool, Heysham in Lancashire, Belfast or Dublin.

There's one vegetarian restaurant on the island, which is only open during the day. In the evenings and on Sundays you'll find plenty of pizza places, Italian and Indian restaurants, and we've heard that the owners of the French restaurant L'Experience in Summerhill, Douglas, have a veggie in the family so they can knock something up for us.

Fernleigh Hotel

Omnivorous hotel

Marine Parade
Peel
Isle of Man IM5 1PB
See accommodation at www.isleofman.com
4 en suite rooms £22 per person. 8 standard rooms
£18, no supplement for single occupancy.
Open: All year except around Christmas

Tel: 01624 842435
Fax: 01624 842435
ferneleigh@manx.net

Omnivorous hotel on the sunny West side of the island, 13 miles from Douglas, that is happy to do vegetarian or vegan bed and breakfast. They make their own own Glamorgan and chick pea vegetarian sausages, vegan lentil and carrotburgers, oat cakes, a different breakfast every day. Soya milk and soya cream available and they will get soya margarine if you ask beforehand.

Green's

Vegetarian restaurant

Steam Railway Station
Douglas
Isle of Man
Open: Mon–Sat 9.00–17.00
Web: nigelkermode@excite.com

Tel: 01624–629 129

Vegetarian restaurant at the railway station in Douglas. Substantial bowl of vegan soup £2.95. Main £4.95–5.95 such as Red Dragon pie, homity pie, pasta bake, wholemeal pizza, moussaka. Baked potatoes with fillings and 5 to 7 salads. Desserts like fruit crumble or sticky toffee pudding (not vegan). House wine £7.95 bottle, glass £1.50. Smoking section. Children welcome, 3 high chairs and a baby table. Parking outside. No cards, cash or cheque only.

Julian Graves Health Store

Health food shop

62 Duke Street
Douglas
Isle of Man
Open: Mon–Sat 8.30–17.30,
closed Sunday and sometimes for delivery

Tel: 01624–616 933

Health food shop with savoury take–aways, baguettes.

Castletown Health Store

Health food shop

21 Malew Street
Castletown
Isle of Man
Open: Mon–Fri 9.00–17.30, Sat 9.00–17.00

Tel: 01624–825 812
www.health–store.co.uk
mail@health–store.co.uk

Holland & Barrett

Holland & Barrett

Unit 2, 26–30 Strand Street
Douglas
Isle of Man IM1 2EG

Tel: 01624–676 527

Isle of Man Health Food Centre

Health food shop

90 Bucks Road
Douglas
Isle of Man IM1 3AG
Open: Thu 10.30–13.00, Sat 9.00–17.30,
Mon–Tue, Wed & Fri 9.00–13.15, 14.15–17.30

Tel: 01624–675 647
www.iomhealthfoods.com

Channel Islands
Guernsey & Jersey

The Green Olive

Omnivorous restaurant with about half the menu vegetarian and some of it vegan. (the rest is seafood and chicken)

Lunch starters include marinated mixed olives £2.25, hummus and dips with toasted bread sticks £3.95, soup of the day £2.95.

Four salads in small or large, £3.25–5.50.

Ciabatta sandwiches with side salad from £4.95.

Loaded potato bake with your choice of filling served with side salad £4.95-5.25.

Lunch main course aubergine boat £7.45, stuffed with asparagus, cherry tomatoes and courgettes, baked with red onion chutney and finished with filo pastry sails. Pasta with cherry tomatoes, olives, chilli and garlic £7.45. Char grilled vegetable and wild mushroom pesto £6.95, with basil grilled vegetables tossed with pine nuts and pasta. Plus specials on the blackboard.

Evening menu offers the lunch starters and four veggie mains, such as the aubergine boat for £9.95, char grilled vegetable and wild mushroom pesto £7.95; butternut and sun blushed tomato filo samosa £9.95, set on a bed of apricot and tarragon risotto with mango salsa. Plus specials.

Desserts £3.20 include vegan summer fruits pudding.

House wine £2 glass, £6.95 bottle. Over 20 more wines from around the world, or champagne £28.95. Beer £2.10. Coffee £1, cappucino £1.50.

1 Anley Street
St Helier
Jersey JE2 3QE

Tel: 01534-728 198
Fax: 01534-728 198

Open:
Tue–Fri 12–15.30;
Tue–Sat 18–21.30 last orders

10% service charge on groups of 7+.

Smoke-free area.

Visa, MC

Laska

Albert House, South Esplanade
St Peter Port, Guernsey GY1 1AJ
Open: Mon–Sat, food served 12–14.30,
18.30–21.30 (Sat from 17.30), closed Sun

Tel: 01481–727 444

Cocktail bar, previously called Four Seasons Restaurant, with food, several tapas and light meals and always a vegetarian special for £8.50–12.50. House wine £11.95 bottle, £2.60 glass. Non smoking tables available. Credit cards ok. Children ok.

Lido's Wine Bar

Omnivorous brasserie

4 – 6 Market Street, St Helier, Jersey JE2 4WY
Restaurant Mon–Sat 12–16.00, Mon–Thu 18–21.00;
bar every day 10–23.00 with pastries & afternoon teas.

Tel: 01534 722358

Up–market wine bar and brasserie which can do lunches later than most Jersey places. They always have a couple of veggie dishes, but with notification they'll cook anything as everything is made fresh. Starters £4–£6. £6.95–£9.00 for a main course such as pasta,
It's in a pedestrian precinct so you can sit out in the sun in the heart of town. There are lots of business folk for weekday lunches, quieter at night. It's next to the Victorian food market, open Mon–Sat dawn till 17.30, 14.00 Thursday.

Roberto's

Onivorous restaurant

1 Trinity Square
St Peter Port, Guernsey GY1 1LP
Open: Tue–Sun 12–13.30, 18–22.00, closed Mon

Tel: 01481–730 419
roberto@ciprom.co.uk

Omnivorous restaurant with some vegetarian dishes like pancakes or pasta for £6.95.

Hansa Wholefoods

Wholefood shop

20 Fountain St
St Peter Port, Guernsey
Open: Mon–Sat 9–17.30

Tel: 01481–723 412

Hansa Wholefoods

Wholefood shop

South Side
St Sampsons, Guernsey
Open: Mon–Sat 9–17.30

Tel: 01481–249 135

Leaders Health Foods

Wholefood shop

The Arcade, Bath St / Halkett St
St Helier, Jersey JE2 4WJ
Open: Mon–Sat 9–17.00

Tel: 01534–871588

Picnic and self-catering heaven, a veggie health food shop with organic foods, dried fruit, nuts, soya milk, vegan ice-cream. No take-away or vegetables.

Scotland

the Greenhouse

Edinburgh

14 Hartington gardens, Edinburgh EH10 4DL

Winner of The Vegetarian Society's Best Guesthouse Award 2001

Situated in heart of beautiful and historic Edinburgh providing quality vegan and vegetarian bed and breakfast accommodation. We offer a very extensive menu in a smoke free environment. The vegetable shampoo and the homemade vegetable soaps are free of any animal testing. Even the pillows and duvets are animal free. Refreshments in all rooms and en-suite facilities available.

Tina Fox, The Vegetarian Society's Chief Executive commented "If you ever needed an excuse to sample the delights of Edinburgh this is it, good food, great establishment and brilliant location, what more can anyone ask?"

Contact Hugh Wilson and Suzanne Allen on:

E-mail : greenhouse_edin@hotmail.com

Telephone : 0131 622 7634 Website : www.greenhouse-edinburgh.com

Scotland

A holiday in Britain is not complete without visiting Scotland. The Highlands are breathtaking, the people are incredibly friendly, and the cities are throbbing with life and culture.

Top of the list of places to visit is Edinburgh, the capital. From the ancient castle, museums and galleries to the many pubs and night clubs, you will never be without something to see or do. Then of course there is the famous Edinburgh Festival every summer. And you will not go hungry in this city! Edinburgh is excellent for vegetarians and vegans. The number of vegetarian restaurants just keeps on growing and it now rivals London as being the best city in Britain for vegetarian eating. Even if you are at an omnivorous restaurant, in Edinburgh they are used to catering for veggies and most know how to knock up a great meat-free meal.

If you want to wake up to a full vegetarian Scottish breakfast, stay at one of the veggie guesthouses in Edinburgh, such as the central Greenhouse where you will be in vegan heaven. The friendly proprietors Hugh and Suzanne will be more than willing to help you with tourist information on Edinburgh. They will even give you a free city map with veggie places highlighted!

Don't leave Scotland before you check out Glasgow, the country's second largest city. It is lively and cosmopolitan and just as cultural as Edinburgh. Glasgow is particularly known for its architecture due to Charles Mackintosh (1868-1928), the famous Glasgow born architect and designer, who is renowned world wide for his innovative style which helped shape European Art Nouveau. His influence can still be seen around the city. Although not quite the vegetarian paradise that Edinburgh is, there are still several veggie friendly restaurants. You will be spoilt mercilessly at the vegan West 13th and vegetarian 13th Note pub-restaurants. These places are the business!

Don't just stay in the city when visiting Edinburgh and Glasgow. Hire a car and go exploring! Around both cities there is much to see, such as coastal hills, parks, woodlands, historic towns and heritage sites.

If you want to go further afield into Braveheart country, you will find people more aware of vegetarianism than you might expect. Towns in the Highlands like Fort William and Aviemore are popular ski resorts and although sadly lacking vegetarian restaurants, you can still get decent veggie and vegan food. You can't go wrong in an Italian or Indian restaurant and you will find both in these towns. Inverness (north of Fort William and Aviemore) does however have a wonderful vegetarian restaurant called Herbivore, where you can try vegetarian haggis! If you are not staying in Inverness, the food is well worth the drive.

All over Scotland there are many vegetarian guesthouses, some in small towns but many in the remote and beautiful countryside. Imagine waking in the morning to the smell of vegetarian bacon and scrambled tofu, hearing the sound of birds chirping and knowing that all you have to do that day is enjoy yourself! And the Scottish people will do their utmost to ensure that you do.

For general tourist information on Scotland go to
www.visitscotland.com

Our Scotland chapter is in three parts. First Accommodation outside Edinburgh, then restaurants outside the capital, finally a giant section on Edinburgh itself, one of our Top Ten Veggie Destinations.

Places in Scotland

Hotels and Guest Houses

Shops

Places in Scotland

Restaurants

429

Scotland

0   50   100 km

Corry Lodge B&B

**Vegetarian
Bed & Breakfast**

Vegetarian B&B set in one and a half acres of garden surrounded by woodlands. The self-contained log cabin overlooks the loch and hills. It comprises of a kitchenette, lounge/dining room, bathroom, one twin room and one double room, both costing £20 per person per night.

Although self contained, it is not self catering as there is no cooker. However the vegetarian owner Liz, who cooks with seasonal organic ingredients, will bring breakfast over to you.

For breakfast start with fruit juice, cereal or muesli with soya yoghurt and stewed fruit, and then move on to the naughty stuff with veggie bacon, veggie sausages, tomatoes, mushrooms, waffles and bread or toast with homemade preserves and tea or coffee. Soya margarine and milk are always available.

Dinner is offered by arrangement for £10 and could be soup, followed by a curry, nut roast, casserole, hot pot, stuffed vine leaves or a pasta dish. Liz makes her own eggless pasta.

Nearby are nature walks, the beach and sailing. The picturesque port town is a walk away and has a museum, theatre, pubs with live music and numerous restaurants serving vegetarian food.

Animals and children are welcome. The cabin has high chairs and a toy box, with swings and a play area in the garden. Be careful not to trip over one of the many hens that run free there!

The cabin has all amenities including an iron and hairdryer. Televisions are in the bedrooms and lounge. A recent guest called it utopia.

*Garve Road
Lochbroom
Ullapool
Wester Ross IV26 2TB
Scotland*

Tel: 01854 612681

*Email:
lized.corry@btopenworld.com*

*Train station:
Inverness, 30 miles*

Open: all year

*Directions:
Corry Lodge is 58 miles northwest of Inverness on the A35, two miles from the village of Ullapool.*

Parking: available

Smoking is allowed on the porch only.

10% discount to members of the Vegetarian Society, Vegan Society and people presenting this book.

Cruachan

Vegetarian
Bed and Breakfast

Vegetarian B&B in Minard, a village on the banks of Loch Fyne. Spend some time just relaxing in this friendly home, in between taking some of the many local walks available, or going on day trips. There are three rooms; one single at £18.50, one double at £20 and one double ensuite at £22.50 per person per night.

Breakfast is a delicious feast. Begin with fruit juice, cereals and fresh fruit, followed by your choice of several dishes, including The Cruachan – veggie sausages, scrambled tofu, tomato, mushrooms, beans and potatoes; The Benedict – tofu in a rich sauce served on a muffin and garnished with herbs; or The Sunshine – French toast with summer fruits. Many items are organic. Soya milk, soya yoghurt, vegan margarine, vegan muesli and herbal tea are all available.

Dinner is offered for £12.50 and could be a Tofu and Roast Vegetable Plait or Moroccan Casserole. Special diets catered for with advance notice. Pintos Vegetarian Restaurant is nearby.

Cruachan is close to many places of interest, including Kilmartin Glen with its Standing Stones, Dunadd Iron Age Fortress and the Herb Garden at Lochgair. There's also the restored Highland village of Auchindrain and the Museum of Ancient Culture. At Cruachan, the grounds rise up to the forest and depending on the time of year, deer can be seen coming down the hill to feed.

Cooking breaks are offered at set times of the year. Tea and coffee making facilities in the rooms.

Inverae Farm Road
Minard
Argyll PA32 8YF
Scotland

Tel: 01546 886378

Email:
iswcruach@talk21.com

Train Station: Glasgow, 20 miles, then bus

Open: all year

Directions: follow the A83 through Inveraray going towards Campbeltown, come into Minard, turn first right up farm track after 40 mph sign. Cruachan is the third house on the right.

Parking: available

10% discount to members of the Vegetarian Society and the Vegan Society

No children or pets

No smoking throughout

5% discount to people presenting this book

Cuildorag House

Vegetarian
Bed and Breakfast

Veggie Bed and Breakfast with three rooms amidst some of Britian's most magnificent landscapes. The double and family room are £17.50 per person per night and the double ensuite is £21 per person per night. Children are half price or free if they're under three years old.

Breakfast is cereal or porridge followed by veggie sausages, potato scones, baked beans, mushrooms and tomatoes. Vegan margarine and soya milk are always available and soya yoghurt is sometimes available. A three course dinner is offered by arrangement for £12. Organic produce is mainly used. There are veggie options at restaurants in nearby Fort William.

Fort William is a popular tourist centre and is close to the ski fields of Ben Nevis (Britian's highest mountain) and Glencoe. Skiing, snowboarding, hiking, climbing and bike riding are the activities to do in the area and you'll find plenty of shops where you can buy or hire the equipment you'll need. There are walks for all levels, from strolls along Glen Nevis through the gorge to Steall Meadows, to the strenuous hike up Ben Nevis. Or you could embark on an eighty mile bike ride along the Great Glen Cycle route which links Fort William and Inverness.

The Isles of Skye or Mull make nice day trips.

There's a television in the lounge and both the double rooms. Rooms have tea and coffee making facilities.

Onich
nr Fort William
Highlands PH3 6SD
Scotland

Tel: 01855 821529

www.cuildoraghouse.com

Email: enquiries@
cuildoraghouse.com

Train Station: Fort William,
10 miles, then a bus.

Open: all year

Directions: Take A82
Glasgow Road. It's about
10 miles north of Fort
William.

Parking: available

There is a cot and high
chair for the youngster in
the family and the
proprietor may even
babysit for you.

Smoking in the garden
only

5% discount on stays of
two nights or more to
members of the
Vegetarian Society, Viva!
and people presenting
this book.

East Lochhead

Omnivorous
Bed & Breakfast & S-C

One hundred year old Scottish Farmhouse with views to the south east over the Barr Loch and Renfrewshire hills. It is set within twenty five acres of farmland and guests are encouraged to enjoy the two acres of beautiful garden.

There are three rooms; one double, one twin and one family, all with nice views, ensuite bathrooms and all costing £60–£70 per room per night. There are also five self catering cottages which can accommodate from one to six people.

The co-proprietor Janet is an enthusiastic and qualified cook and being almost vegetarian she specialises in veggie food. There is a large breakfast menu, which includes Scottish pancakes with maple syrup. Vegan muesli, veggie sausages, vegan margarine, soya milk and soya yoghurt are available.

They provide delicious evening meals for B&B guests and to those self-catering, if they wish. The vegetables are home grown.

Lochwinnoch is ony twenty five minutes drive from Glasgow. There is much to do in Lochwinnoch including watersports, golf, walking and cycling. There is a cycle track opposite the house. The Ayrshire coast is only twenty minutes away.

East Lochhead has received many awards including winning the Scottish Tourist Boards Thistle Award for customer care in 2001. They have also received two gold awards for Green Business Tourism.

Tea and coffee making facilities and TV's are in the rooms. There is a TV lounge.

Largs Road
Lochwinnoch
Renfrewshire PA12 4DX
(Glasgow outskirts)
Scotland

Tel and Fax:
01505 842610

www.eastlochhead.co.uk

Email:
eastlochhead@aol.com

Train station:
Lochwinnoch,
then phone for collection

Open: all year

Directions:
From Glasgow take M8, exit junction 28A to Irvine (A737). Road divides at Kilbarchan. Stay on right. At road head roundabout turn right on A760. Travel two miles. Look for East Lochhead on the left.

Parking: plenty of parking

Animals and children are welcome and there are cots and high chairs.

No smoking throughout

5% discount to people presenting this book

Glengarry House

Omnivorous B&B and self-catering chalet

Omnivorous bed and breakfast with vegetarian proprietor. Situated within the boundary of the Loch Lomond National Park, Scotland's first such park. Glengarry is surrounded by fantastic mountain scenery and is the ideal base for touring the Southern Highlands by car and for exploring the great outdoors. Uninterrupted views of Ben Lui to the north and the Crianlarich hills to the south.

All rooms have been recently upgraded and have private or en suite facilities. One double with shower, one twin ensuite (with great views of Ben Lui) and one family room, all £22 per person per night.

Full veggie cooked breafkast with sausages, bacon, tomatoes, mushrooms, potato scone. Vegan margarine, muesli, dairy free milk and yoghurt available.

Vegetarian or vegan evening meal £12–18, for example parsnip and fennel soup or roast vegetables and garlic bread, vegi crumble with chickpea patties, baked apples or individual toffee puddings.

The area is a hillwalkers' paradise with 20 Munroes within a ten mile radius.

In the grounds there is a self-catering chalet for 2 to 6 people. When walking the West Highland Way, stay for a week and avoid carrying big bags, no packing and unpacking each day, dry kit for the next day (not that it will rain!), the reassurance of vehicle back up at any time (coming back from the pub), all your food is provided, daily internet weather forecasts, £300 per person all inclusive.

Tyndrum,
Perthshire, FK20 8RY

Tel: 01838 400224

Train: Tyndrum Upper & Tyndrum Lower 1/2 mile then taxi

www.glengarryhouse. co.uk

glengarry@altavista.net

Open all year

Children over 10
No facilities for babies

No pets

Vegetarian proprietor

No disabled facilities

No smoking throughout.

Open for dinner to non-residents with prior arrangement

Directions: 1/4 mile south of Tyndrum Village, just off the A82 on the right heading north

10% discount to people presenting this book

Isle of Barra Hotel

Omnivorous hotel on the Isle of Barra, a perfect place to get away from it all. The hotel has forty rooms; seven doubles and thirty three twins for £39 per person per night for bed and breakfast or £57 per person per night for dinner bed and breakfast. Most rooms have views of the Atlantic Ocean.

Breakfast is served in the dining room overlooking the ocean and begins with a buffet of fruit juice, fruit, cereals and porridge followed by tomatoes, mushrooms and beans on toast. Soya milk and veggie sausages are available, though they sometimes need notice to get the sausages, so let them know you want them when you book.

A four course meal and coffee is £22.95 to non residents or £18 to residents. There is always one veggie dish on the menu and vegans can be catered for. Dinner could be breaded mushrooms to start, then soup, followed by vegetable risotto and for dessert a fruit crumble.

The beach is close by aswell as mountains which offer great walking and wildlife. There is a golf course with beautiful views, seals at Seal Bay, a wildflower and bird heritage centre and a thatched house museum. Expect to see lots of lovely sunsets and breathe pollution free air during your stay. The plane lands on Cocklestrand Beach every day except Sunday.

There are televisions and tea and coffee making facilities in the rooms.

Omnivorous
Hotel

Tangasdale Beach
Isle of Barra
Western Isles HS9 5XW
Scotland

Tel: 01871 810383

www.isleofbarra.com/
iob.html

Email: barrahotel@aol.com

Train station: none. A post bus meets the plane and drops at the hotel, or get a taxi.

Open: Easter–October

Directions:
The hotel is two miles from the ferry port and six miles from the airport.

Parking: available

Children are welcome and they have cots and high chairs.

Pets welcome

Smoking is allowed in the rooms, the bar and reception.

There is some disabled access.

10% discount to people presenting this book.

Inverdeen House B&B

Omnivorous
Bed & Breakfast

Omnivorous B&B in a 'B' listed Georgian townhouse. Built in 1820, it is one of the original buildings in the beautiful highland village of Ballater.

There are three guest rooms; two double ensuites, (one with a king sized bed) priced from £20–25 per person per night and a twin ensuite for the same price. A single person supplement of £3 per night is charged. All rooms have been newly renovated and furnished.

You are invited to choose as much as you want for breakfast and then to fill in a request slip. Veggie breakfasts are a specialty as the owner is vegetarian. Mention when you book or when you arrive if you are vegan or have any other dietary requirements. On offer is fresh fruit salad, prunes, cereals, porridge and a cooked breakfast of veggie sausages, mushrooms, tomatoes, baked beans, hash browns and fresh bread. Soya milk, vegan margarine and soya yoghurt is available. There is no evening meal offered.

Ballater is set amid pine forests and breathtaking mountains. It is a great base to pursue outdoor activities. Choose from hillwalking, climbing, mountain bike riding, golf, gliding, skiing or snowboarding. The Lecht and Glenshee ski centres are nearby. Of course you could just enjoy the fresh air and take gentle walks, check out the castles and do some whisky tasting.

Children are welcomed at discounted rates and they have high chairs for toddlers. Children under 2 stay for free. Televisions are in the rooms and the lounge has satellite TV. They have a secure cycle store and drying facilities. They are working towards the Green Tourism Awards.

Bridge Square
Ballater
Royal Deeside AB35 5QJ
Scotland

Tel: *01339 755759*

www.inverdeen.com

Email: *info@inverdeen*

Train station: Aberdeen, 42 miles away, then get a bus. They are two minutes walk from Ballater bus station.

They sometimes pick up from Aberdeen airport and train station for the cost of the petrol.

Open: all year

Directions:
From Aberdeen: when you reach the Bridge junction at the Aberdeen side of Ballater, with the village on your right and the bridge over the River Dee on your left, the house is directly opposite.
From Braemar: Drive on the main Braemar Road through the village, past the Kirk Green. When the road turns left for Aberdeen, the house is on your right.

Parking: one space

10% discount to people presenting this book if you are staying for three nights or more and you mention it when you phone them to book.

No smoking throughout.

437

Neptune Light House

Vegetarian
Bed & Breakfast

22–24 Tolbooth St
Forres
Morayshire IV36 OPH
Scotland

Tel and Fax:
01309 674387

Email:
neptunelitehouse@onetel.
net.uk

Vegetarian B&B set in an eco-friendly area with a strong organic movement. Neptune House has three guest rooms; one double, one double ensuite and one twin all at £18–£22 per person per night.

Breakfast is made from organic, local and seasonal ingredients and the menu is flexible. You can have anything from porridge or cereal to a continental breakfast or a cooked breakfast which can include mushrooms, tomatoes, potato rosti, scrambled tofu and toast with preserves. They make their own bread and biscuits. Juice, coffee and organic and herbal teas are available. Soya milk is always available but if you want vegan margarine it's safer to let them know in advance.

Train station: Forres,
15 minutes walk

Open: all year

Children are welcome

Smoking in the garden
only

There is a tourist information office up the road from Neptune House which will be able to help you with your plans for your stay. A main attraction in the area is Findhorn Foundation, a spritual community who do many ecological and sustainable projects.

Directions:
Leave the A96 Aberdeen
Inverness Road out the
first roundabout for
Forres. Follow the road to
the High Street. Turn
into Tolbooth St.
Neptune House is 200
yeard down on the right.
Look for the blue door.

Apart from a must visit to Findhorn you could do a tour of the whisky distilleries, go swimming at the nearby beaches, take in the beautiful wildlife on nature walks or visit some of the historical sites like Brody Castle.

Parking: free parking
around the back of the
house

There are washbasins and tea and coffee making facilities in the rooms and there is a TV lounge.

They run Italian vegetarian cookery classes, currently in the afternoons as we go to press but weekends are planned.

Old Sawmill Cottage

Cosy traditional cottage with wood burning stoves, set in a woodland garden on the banks of the River Girvan. One double ensuite room at £15-20 per person per night.

Breakfast is mostly organic and comprises of fruit juice, fresh and dried fruit with soya yoghurt, then porridge or cereal followed by bread, rolls or toast with preserves, as well as coffee, tea, herbal and fruit tea. Vegan muesli, vegan margarine and soya milk are all available. Breakfast is served in the conservatory but can be served in the bedroom if requested.

Dinner is not offered, but there are restaurants catering for veggies and vegans nearby.

There is an abundance of wildlife in the surrounding area including red squirrels, otters, woodpeckers, owls and kingfishers. Resident animals include one dog, two cats, three geese and three goats, so guest's pets are only accepted under special circumstances.

Old Sawmill Cottage is nine miles from sandy beaches and secret coves where you can swim or go on boat trips. Nearby are golf courses, theatres, castles, craft shops and Rabbie Burns National Heritage Park. There are many great walks and bike rides. Bikes are available to hire.

Make sure you have a go at wood turning in their workshop!

There are tea and coffee making facilities in the room and there is a lounge with a television.

Vegetarian Bed & Breakfast

Kilkerran
Maybole
Ayrshire KA19 7PZ
Scotland

Tel: 01655 740451

Email:
kilkerran@breathemail.net

Train station:
Maybole, 5 miles

Open:
March–October (inclusive)

No smoking throughout

Directions:
Turn left off A77 at Maybole onto B7023. Go through Crosshill turning right at the War Memorial towards Dailly. One and a half miles out of Crosshill, cross bridge over River Girval. Old Sawmill Cottage is on the left, fifty yards past the bridge.

Parking: available

Quiraing Lodge

Large Victorian house, set in an acre of garden overlooking Staffin Bay.

Quiraing Lodge not only offers B&B, but also has workshops and events throughout the year in photography, arts and crafts and mind and body.

There are seven rooms; one single, one double, three twin and two family rooms all £22 per person per night and all with hand basins.

Breakfast is cereal and a full cooked breakfast. They will gladly make vegan meals when requested, including homemade vegan bread. All the food is locally produced and/or organic if possible.

Evening meals cost £10 but are by arrangement only. There are four local options for dinner and all have good vegetarian dishes.

There are two sandy beaches nearby to Quiraing Lodge. There is excellent walking and wildlife and beautiful views to the Quiraing and the Outer Hebrides.

The house has a large living room and an extensive library featuring photgraphy, art, travel and local books. Both rooms have open fires.

There are no televisions. Some rooms have tea and coffee making facilities.

*Staffin
Isle of Skye IV51 9JS
Scotland*

Tel: 01470 562330

www.quiraing-lodge.co.uk

Email: sam@quiraing-lodge.co.uk

*Train station:
Kyle of Lochalsh, 50 miles away. From there get a bus to Portree. Then catch a local bus or they can collect from Portree by arrangement.*

Open: all year

Children are welcomed and they have a cot and high chair.

Pets are accepted by arrangement.

No smoking throughout

*Directions:
Quiraing Lodge is 16 miles north of Portree. Go through main village of Staffin. Turn right after 800 metres at signs for Quiraing Lodge and Staffin slipway. It is the large house at the bottom of the hill.*

Parking: available

The Rossan

Omnivorous
Bed & Breakfast

Early Victorian house, built in 1869 standing in a huge garden between the Screel Hills and the sea. The house overlooks Auchencairn Bay and Hestan Island. There are three family rooms all at £15 per person per night or £25 for dinner, bed and breakfast. All the beds have patchwork quilts made by the proprietor, Elizabeth who has been vegetarian for 49 years.

For breakfast there is fruit juice, fresh fruit, vegan organic muesli or cereal followed by a cooked breakfast of veggie sausages, tomatoes, mushrooms with homemade organic wholemeal bread and homemade marmalade. Vegan margarine and soya milk are available if you let her know when you book. As well as catering for veggies and vegans, she also caters for medical diets (especially coeliacs).

Dinner could be vegetable soup with home made bread followed by stuffed peppers or aubergines, baked potato with vegan cheese and at least two types of vegetables or salad. For dessert there is vegan or homemade ice cream.

There is an endless list of things to see and do in the area including birdwatching, bike riding, walking, swimming at the nearby sandy beaches, playing golf at one of the numerous courses, sailing on Loch Ken and visiting art galleries, museums, castles and ruined Abbeys. Galloway Forest Park, Threave Gardens and the Threave Wildfowl Reserve are all within easy reach.

Hairdryers and tea and coffee making facilities are in the rooms. TV in the dining room. Secure bicycle storage shed. Packed lunch is available for £5.

*Auchencairn
Castle Douglas
Kirkcudbrightshire
DG7 1QR
Scotland*

Tel: 01556 640269

Fax: 01556 640278

www.the-rossan.co.uk

*Email:
bardsley@rossan.freeserve.co.uk*

Train station: Dumfries, 20 miles, then get a bus or taxi

Open: all year

Children are welcome, cot and high chair

Well behaved dogs can come for free

No smoking throughout

Directions: Take the A711 from Dumfries, or coming from Stranraer take the A75, turn right at Castle Douglas, then right onto B736 then A711. From Glasgow go to Castle Douglas then take the B736.

Parking: plenty of off road spaces

10% discount off dinner, bed and breakfast to members of the Vegetarian Society and the Vegan Society.

Rhu Mhor Guest House

Traditional guest house set in an acre of wild tree-shrouded garden with resident roe deer, overlooking Loch Linnhe and the hills of Loch Eil. Owned for the last thirty years by the same veggie kilt-wearing proprietor!

There are seven guest rooms; one double, one twin and one family at £16–£19 per person per night, as well as two double and two twin ensuites at £20–24 per person per night. A single person supplement is charged. Weekly rates are also available.

For breakfast there is juice and oatmeal porridge, muesli or cornflakes. You then have the choice of either a continental breakfast or a full cooked breakfast which includes veggie sausages. Soya milk is available. Inform him when booking or upon arrival if you are veggie or vegan or have any other dietary needs.

Dinner is not provided, but there are a couple of Indian restaurants in Fort William where you can get a decent veggie curry.

Rhu Mhor is set amidst some of the most beautiful scenery in Britain and is just around the corner from Ben Nevis, Scotland's highest mountain.

Rhu Mhor is ideal for a quiet holiday taking in the beautiful scenery while on leisurely walks; or for a more active holiday involving long distance walking, ascending to the summits of some of Scotland's highest mountains, rock climbing, canoeing or cycling the quiet back roads and forest paths.

There are washbasins in the rooms as well as tea and coffee making facilities. There is a TV lounge and a separate sitting room.

Omnivorous
Guest House

Alma Road
Fort William
Inverness-Shire PH33 6BP
Scotland

Tel: 01397 702213

www.rhumhor.co.uk

email: ian@rhumhor.co.uk

Train station:
Fort William, 10 minutes walk

Open: Easter–October

Children welcome and there is a cot.

Animals welcome

Separate room for smoking

Directions:
From town centre go north on A82. Turn right into Victoria Road after the hospital, then left into Alma Road.

Parking: available

Sonnhalde

Victorian villa with an open outlook across the Spey Valley to the Cairngorm mountains. There are seven rooms; two double ensuites and one twin ensuite at £21 per person per night, two twins at £18 per person per night and two family rooms at £18–£21 per person per night.

Start the day with a hearty breakfast of fruit, muesli or porridge, wholemeal bread with various spreads and buckwheat crepes with tomatoes and mushrooms. Vegan muesli, margarine and veggie sausages are all available, as well as soya milk and soya yoghurt.

Dinner at £10 could be home made soup, then tomato, spinach and pine nut pie with fresh veggies and salad followed by plum and banana crumble. There are also a good selection of shops and restaurants in town catering for vegetarians.

Kingussie is an excellent centre for touring the Central Highlands. It's within easy reach of the popular tourist town Aviemore and the Cairngorm ski slopes. The Cairngorm area is in the process of becoming a National Park. There are loads of outdoor activities, such as hill walking and mountaineering, natural history tours and of course skiing and snowboarding. There is a Folk Museum, Wildlife Park and a Whisky Trail nearby. Inverness is 40 minutes drive away and Loch Ness one hour.

Tea and coffee making and washbasins in the rooms. Televisions in rooms by request. There is a lounge with a TV, the only room which smoking is allowed in.

East Terrace
Kingussie
Highlands PH21 1JS
Scotland

Tel and Fax:
01540 661266

*www.highlandguest
house.co.uk*

Email:
*bernard.jones_l.m.p.a@
virgin.net*

*Train Station: Kingussie,
approx 1/2 mile, then
owners can collect.*

Open: all year

*Children are welcome and
they have a cot and a high
chair.*

Pets by arrangement.

*Directions: Directly off A9,
take the second exit for
Kingussie (travelling
north). Turn left into
town, then right at traffic
lights, then first right.
It's the third house on the
left.*

Parking: available

Three Castle Terrace

Vegetarian B&B in a bungalow overlooking the sea. There are three rooms, one double ensuite at £20 per person per night, one twin at £18, and one single costing £18–20.

Wake in the mornings to fresh melon and strawberries with cereal and a full cooked English vegetarian breakfast. This comprises of veggie grills and burgers, grilled tomatoes and mushrooms as well as toast and jam. Vegan margarine, soya milk and vegan muesli are always available.

Penny, the veggie proprietor doesn't offer dinner but says there is plenty of veggie food and some vegan food available at the restaurants in Ullapool.

From Three Castle Terrace it is five minutes walk to the ferry terminal where you can jump on a ferry to visit nearby islands, such as Handa Bird Island.

There is unlimited hill walking, a golf course, an indoor pool and lots of pubs all in and around the town. The subtropical Inverewe Gardens are to the south of Ullapool.

There are no tea and coffee making facilities in the rooms, but you only have to ask and Penny will make you a cup.

Televisions are in the bedrooms and the lounge room.

Vegetarian
Bed & Breakfast

3 Castle Terrace
Ullapool
Wester Ross IV26 2XD
Scotland

Tel: 01854 612409

Train station:
Inverness, 30 miles, then a bus.

Open:
by arrangement, usually April–October.

Directions:
Coming from the south arrive at the pier head in Ullapool, turn right, go up hill for about 500 metres to a t–junction, turn left. It's the fourth house on the left.

Parking: available

Animals are accepted by arrangement

Smoking is allowed in the garden only

10% discount to people presenting this book, if staying more than one night.

Wheatears

Wheatears is off the beaten track in a tranquil location on the Scottish Borders Coastline. It is close to the National Nature Reserve at St Abbs Head with its sea bird colonies and the sandy beach at Coldingham Bay, yet less than an hour from Edinburgh. Renovated from stone farm cottages built in 1830, with over 2,000 native trees planted in their two acre wildlife garden. One double ensuite and one twin ensuite room for £25 per person or £35 for single occupancy. There's also the self-catering detached Curlew Cottage with a double bed in one room, and double and single in the other, £220–£390 per week, but you'll need to book ahead.

A comprehensive range of vegan dishes is provided, homemade using local, home grown, GM free and organic produce where possible. Dairy products can be requested and special diets by arrangement. Breakfast offers cereal, muesli, porridge, fruit salad, yoghurt, followed by a traditional Scottish breakfast with homemade sausages and scrambled tofu. Or try the International dish of the day, for example Haritha pancakes or noodle soup. Three course dinner (also available for self-caterers) is £15 and changes every day with selections from India, Asia and Africa, for example pate or felafel followed by Thai curry, then crumble or cheesecake.

The area around Wheatears is famous for bird watching and ideal for walking and cycling. There are golf courses, country houses, museums, small harbours and geological sites like Siccar Point. Guests can relax and browse in the library with natural history and travel books or select a wildlife video to watch in your room. A wood burning stove and classical CDs complete the cosy atmosphere.

Lumsdaine
Coldingham
Borders TD14 5UA
Scotland

Tel and Fax:
018907 71375

Email: susan_richard@ lineone.net

Train Station:
Historic Berwick–upon–Tweed, 12 miles, then taxi, or collection can be arranged

Open: March–end October

Directions: Take A1 from Berwick–upon–Tweed North, then take A1107 to Eyemouth. Keep on A1107 and pass through Coldingham (3 miles from Eyemouth). Wheatears is 3 miles from Coldingham, signed off the A1107.

Parking: available

Pets by arrangement

No smoking throughout

Drying room

Tea and coffee making facilities and televisions in rooms

Vegan proprietors

Children over five are welcome, younger if supervised (they have a pond)

Booking required

445

Woodwick House

Omnivorous
Hotel

Evie
Mainland
Orkney KW17 2PQ
Scotland

Tel: 01856 751330

www.orknet.co.uk/
woodwick

Email: woodwickhouse@
appleonline.net

Train Station: None

Open: all year

Children welcome and
they have cots and high
chairs

Dogs are welcome for a
fee of £7 for the duration
of the stay if they come
into the house

Smoking is allowed in one
of the sitting rooms

Directions: Evie is on the
east coast of the largest
island, Mainland. Fly to
Kirkwall Airport or catch
the ferry from Scrabster
to Stromness.

Parking: available

Small veggie friendly hotel in the tiny village of Evie. There are two doubles and one twin for £28 per person per night and two double ensuites and two twin ensuites for £33–£39 per person per night.

Breakfast begins with cereal or organic muesli and is followed by veggie sausages, tomatoes, mushrooms, baked beans and toast. Soya milk, vegan margarine and vegan muesli are available. They can cater for special dietary needs. A three course dinner is offered for £22 and could be soup or garlic mushrooms followed by spicy lentil puffs with spinach and roast veggies and for dessert, apple pie or treacle tart.

Woodwick House is set in a very special peaceful place which tends to attract those who care for the environment. Orkney has few trees and so has always had a lack of wood. Due to this, it is full of ancient historical sites which have survived because all the buildings were made from stone. The most impressive ancient monuments are all on Mainland like the Village of Skara Brae, the tomb of Maes Howe and the Ring of Brodgar. The best preserved example of a fortified stone tower in Orkney is only one and a half miles down a track from the village of Evie.

Wildlife is abundant and many people come to birdwatch. There are beautiful walks and sandy beaches nearby.

Televisions and washbasins in the rooms. TV lounge.

Avingormack Guest House

Guest house & retreat centre

Boat of Garten
Inverness-shire PH24 3BT
www.scotland2000.com/avingormack
www.motivationretreats.co.uk
Email: avin.gormack@ukgateway.net

Tel: 01479-831 614
Fax: 01479-831 344

Virtually vegetarian bed and breakfast, personal development and retreat centre in the heart of the beautiful Scottish Highlands. 2 doubles, 1 twin, 1 triple/family £21-23 per personincluding cooked veggie breakfast. Three course evening meal £15 is always vegetarian or vegan (unless a group of meat eaters is staying, they have two cookers and prepare separately). Bring your own wine. Children welcome. No pets. No smoking except in garden. Courses include hypnotherapy training, stop smoking, stress management, phobias.

Covenanter Hotel

Omnivorous Hotel

The Square, Falkland, Fife, KY15 7BU
www.covenanterhotel.com
Email: g.menzies@btinternet.com

Tel: 01337 857224
Train: Mark Inch, 4 miles
Open: all year

Five double ensuite rooms at £25 per person per night, or £39 for single occupancy. A two course meal in their restaurant is £15, or have three courses for £20. Vegans and those with special dietary requirements are catered for with advanced notice. Children welcome. No pets. Smoking in the cocktail bar only. 10% discount on food to people presenting this book.

Fearn House

Omnivorous b&b

High Street, Dornoch, Sutherland, IV25 3SH
Tel and Fax: 01862 810249

Train Station: Tain, eight miles
Open: March–October

Omnivorous bed and breakfast owned by vegetarians, Three rooms; one double and two double ensuites at £21 per person per night. No children. Dogs welcome. No smoking throughout.

Findhaven

Vegetarian bed & breakfast

16 Market Street, Forres, Moray IV36 1EF
Tel: 01309 674566
www.scotland-info.co.uk/findhaven
Open: all year, except Christmas

Train Station: Forres,
five minutes walk

One single/twin room and one double from £14–£16 per person per night. 10–15% discount on stays of four nights or more. Children of any ages welcome. No pets. No smoking throughout.

Glen Mhor Hotel

Omnivorous hotel

9–12 Ness Bank, Inverness,
Inverness-Shire, IV2 4SG
www.glen-mhor.com
Email: glenmhor@ukonline.co.uk
Open: all year, except New Year

Tel: 01463 234308
Train: Inverness,
ten minutes walk

Forty five ensuite rooms with prices for standard rooms ranging from £29.50 to £44 per person per night, up to £60 per person per night for an executive honeymoon suite. An evening meal is available and they are open to non residents too. Vegans catered for with advanced notice. Children welcome and they have facilities for them. Pets also welcome. Smoking allowed in rooms and some areas.

Grey Gables

Vegetarian Bed and Breakfast

Springwood Road, Isherwood, Peebles,
Borders, EH45 9HB
Tel: 01721 721252
Open: Easter–September

Train:
Edinburgh, 25 miles

One twin and one double room at £16.50 per person per night. 10% discount to members of the Vegetarian Society, Vegan Society, Viva! and people presenting this book. Evening meal available. No pets and no smoking.

Lazy Duck Hostel

Self Catering Hostel

Badanfhuarain, Nethy Bridge,
Inverness–Shire, PH25 3ED
Tel and Fax: 01479 821642
www.lazyduck.co.uk
Email: lazy.duck@virgin.net

Train Station: Aviemore,
then £10 taxi ride, or
bus
Open: all year

The Lazy Duck is one of Scotland's smallest hostels sleeping only eight people in an open plan sleeping gallery It's £8.50 per night per person. Private use by arrangement. Well equipped kitchen. Home baked bread available. Advance groceries delivery service. Village shop one mile. Linen provided, but bring own towels. Safe cycle storage. Washing machine and dryer. No smoking.

Sleeperzzz

Self Catering Hostel

Rogart Station
Sutherland IV28 3XA
www.sleeperzzz.com
kate@sleeperzzz.com

Tel: 01408 641343
Open: all year

It`s a hostel in a train carriage, with 8 rooms each with 2 bunks for £9 per person. 10% off for rail users and cyclists. Wonderful place for train lovers or a"brief encounter." Local attractions are hill walking or cycling in the lovely Scottish countryside, and sampling malt whiskies in the hotel 100m away which does vegetarian food though not vegan. However there's a kitchen in the hostel and an everything shop 100m away which even sells organic muesli. Directions: get off the train at Rogart or A9 north from Inverness then A839 towards Lairg and Rogart. See website for full details and pictures.

Pinto's Restaurant

New vegetarian and vegan restaurant with a fresh modern approach to international dishes and a Scottish flair. Plenty for vegans, with half of all dishes being suitable and clearly marked. Organic where possible.

Starters, £2.50–£3.50, such as polenta served with tapenade, or corn chowder, layered Mediterranean gateau, soup, green bean and sun dried tomato spring rolls.

Mains, £8.75, served with salads, potatoes and fresh vegetables, include Morrocan casserole with couscous, Greek pasta casserole, vegetarian haggis with clapshot stacks and whisky sauce, corn pancakes with sweet potato and ginger sauce, mushroom and salsify tartlet, and Southern Indian pasties.

Two course dinner £11.25, three courses £13.50.

Desserts, £2.50–£3.50, such as soya ice cream sundaes, gooseberry tartlet with vanilla sauce, Polynesian mud torte.

Wine £9.50–16.50 for a bottle. Beer £2.25. Coffee £1.

Can cater for gluten and wheat-free diets and they have organic and vegetarian wines.

The restaurant also serves as a venue for cookery courses and themed evenings such as a Chinese banquet.

1 Argyll Street
Lochgilphead
Argyll PA31 8L2

Tel: 01546-602 547

lswcruach@talk21.com

Open:
Tue–Sat 12.00–14.30,
19.00–22.00

Booking advisable

Non smoking

Visa, MC.

5% discount to people presenting this guidebook

The Booth Café

Vegetarian cafe and restaurant

Vegetarian and vegan café by day and restaurant in the evening, based in a wildlife sanctuary in a stunning location.

Food is by donation – pay what you can, and all the proceeds go to help upkeep of the sanctuary.

Wholefood and organic as much as possible, they have snacks and light eats during the day such as soup, filled pitta breads, broccoli and cauliflower bake and pizzas (with vegan option).

Evening meals include summer vegetable and cashew nut loaf, mushroom stroganoff and provencal vegetable plait.

For dessert there is a vegan chocolate cake with hot chocolate sauce and apple and strawberry crumble.

The menu changes as they like to experiment. They can always cater for special diets.

They run various children's projects, raising awareness and educating children on animal and environmental issues and hold storytelling and musical evenings.

Bring your own bottle.

Hillswick Wildlife Sanctuary
Hillswick
Shetland ZE2 9RW

Tel: 01806–503 348

Fax: 01806–503 747

thebooth@freeuk.com

Open: May–Sept, Mon–Sun 11.00–late, hoping to open all year from 2003

Non smoking

No credit cards

BYO

Directions:
Drive from Lerwick on A971 North as far as you can go until you get to Hillswick then turn left down onto Seafront.

Herbivore

Vegetarian
Restaurant

The only vegetarian restaurant in the Highlands. For lunch, try soup of the day with bread £2.50, falafels with pitta bread £4, or a Powerplate of raw veg, seaweed, nuts, seeds and fruit £4. Dessert could be chocolate and orange torte £4.

For dinner, try grilled asparagus with maple and lime roasted sweet potato wedges at £4, followed by haggis with veg and shallot gravy £8. Desserts such as caramel and apple pie £3.50. Vegan margarine, vegan ice cream, soya milk and organic vegan wine available.

Fair Trade tea and coffee. Organic vegan beer £2.75. House wine £2.30 per glass. Most dishes are are vegan or can be.

38 Eastgate
Inverness
Inverness-Shire IV2 3NA

Tel: 01463 231075

www.herbivore-inverness.co.uk

Open: Mon–Sat: 12–14.30 and 17.30–21.30, Sun: closed

High chairs for children.
Fully licensed
Most cards accepted
No smoking
Vegan proprietor

5% discount to Vegetarian Society and Vegan Society

Seagreen Restaurant and Bookshop

Omnivorous restaurant

Seafood restaurant which caters for vegetarians and vegans. About half the menu is veggie or vegan. Fantastic views to Skye. Garden and terrace. In the same building as a complementary therapy centre with residential courses.

Starters £3.25 such as hummous or soup of the day. Salads from £1.35 such as mixed organic leaves, or carrot and toasted sesame seeds with beetroot. Main courses £4–5 include red onion and pepper polenta tatin, potato rosti with roasted vegetables, aduki bean burger.

Desserts include vegan poppyseed and apricot tart, apple and plum crumble. Wine £2.45 glass, £8.65 bottle. Beer £1.65. Coffee, £1.50. Soya milk available.

Plockton Road
Kyle of Lochalsh
Western Isles IV40 8DA

Tel: 01599 534 388

Open: Mon–Sat 10–17.00

www.seagreenkyle.f9.co.uk

High chairs
Children's portions

Raw diets catered for

VISA, MC, Solo, JLB, Switch

5% discount to Vegetarian Society members and those presenting this guidebook

West 13th

Vegan pub

Vegan pub with a large imaginative menu, opened by the people who used to run the superb 13th Note pub. If they maintain their legendary quality, folk will be coming from as far afield as London to dine and sup here.

Starters from £1 include garlic bread, kalamata olives and home made soup.

Mains £4.50–£5 such as pan fried marinated courgettes, garlic mushrooms and creamy red pesto on ciabatta served with salad; vegetable stir fry with whole-wheat noodles topped with seitan in capital sauce; canneloni stuffed with baby spinach and creamy mushrooms with tomato sauce; filo parcels stuffed with smoked tofu and creamed leeks served with cider cooked carrots and salad.

Desserts from £2 like lemon and poppy seed cake or tofu cheesecake with various toppings including blueberry and chocolate.

House wine £9.50 for a bottle, £2.40 for a glass.

Breakfast served all day Sundays.

Live music at least twice a wee. Happy hour is 17.00–20.00 week nights.

They're currently working on opening a larger city centre place in Autumn 2002, which will be a totally vegan café–bar, and all the alcohol will be vegan too.

12–14 Kelvinhaugh Street
Glasgow
G3 8NU

Tel: 0141–576 5018

www.help13.co.uk

Open: Mon–Sat 12–21.00,
Sun 12.30–21.00

Smoking permitted

Visa, MC

10% discount to Vegan
Society members

453

Grassroots Cafe

Vegetarian restaurant

Vegetarian and vegan organic wholefood restaurant. Most dishes are either vegan or can be made vegan.

Full breakfast, £4.75. Starters, £2.50–£4.95, include soups, tempura and greek dips. Sandwiches, £4.50, with choice of breads and fillings – eg hummous and avocado.

Salads from £2.95. Mains, £4.20–£6.75, such as burgers, thai green curry, vegetable chilli and a pasta of the week.

Special diets catered for. Soya milkshakes and smoothies.

Fully licensed. BYO. Smoking allowed except in smoke-free area. Visa, MC.

97 St Georges Rd
Charing Cross
Glasgow G31 2RD

Tel: 0141–333 0534

www.grassrootsorganic
.com

Train/Tube Train:
St George Cross

Open: Mon–Sun 10.00–22.00

The 13th Note

Vegetarian cafe/bar

Vegetarian and vegan restaurant and bar.

Starters, £2–£3. Mains, such as filo wraps, £3–£5.

All desserts, from £3, are vegan including tofu cheesecake.

50–60 King Street
Glasgow G1

Tel: 0141 553 1638
Fax: 0141 552 5797

www.the13thnote.co.uk

Open:
Mon–Sun 12.00–24.00,
food served until 22.00

Smoking permitted

Visa, MC

10% discount to members
of the Vegan Society

Café na lusan

Vegetarian restaurant

9 Craigard Road
Oban, Argyll PA34 5NP
Open: Mon–Tue 10–17.00; Wed 10–17.00 winter,
10–21.00 summer; Thu–Sat 10–21.00; Sun summer
12–9, Sun closed winter.

Tel: 01631 567268

Very relaxed vegetarian restaurant. Practically everything is or can be vegan. Lunch around £4, dinner £7. Desserts include vegan coffee or chocolate coconut cake. Glass of organic vegan wine £2, bottle £10. Phone for bookings. Entering Oban along George Street take a left opposite the Pancake Place.

The Smiddy

Omnivorous restaurant

Smithy Lane
Lochgilphead, Argyll PA31 8TA
Open: Mon–Sat 10.00–17.00 (last orders 16.00)

Tel: 01546–603 606

Omnivorous place that caters well for vegetarians. Have mains such as vegetarian flans, baked potatoes, potato nests with ratatouille, nut roast, £5.80. Non smoking. No credit cards.

Opus Salad Bar

Omnivorous cafe

95 Queensbury Street
Dumfries, Dumfries & Galloway DG1 1BH
Open: Mon–Sat 9.30–16.30

Tel: 01387 255752

Omnivorous place with a few vegetarian dishes, £3, and various salads, but vegans will have to call in advance. Separate smoking section. No credit cards under £10.

The Green Tea House

Vegetarian tea rooms

The Old Bank, Chapel Street
Moniaive, Dumfries & Galloway DG3 4EJ
Open: Tue-Sun 11-16.00 (17.00 summer), closed Mon.
Talent evenings with local singers, bring your own wine.

Tel: 01848 200 131
www.moniaive.com

Vegetarian tea room that uses local organic products, 12 miles south-west of Dumfries. Homemade vegan soups and rolls £2. Vegetable pie with lemongrass served with salad £5. Vegan date and apple slice, gluten free chocolate brownies. Coffee and tea £1, served with vegan shortbread. Specialise in people with dietary sensitivities. Theme nights twice a month, folk evenings with local singers, £15 a head with a choice of four starters, mains and desserts and a complementary drink when you arrive; bring your own wine. No smoking. Pets welcome. Children welcome, they have high chairs. No credit cards. Parking. Large garden, you can sit outside. The artist James Patterson Museum, one of "the Glasgow Boys", is in Moniaive, lots of local arts and crafts in the village. Annual comic festival around the first weekend in September.

Abbey Cottage Coffee and Crafts

Omnivorous cafe

26 Main Street
New Abbey,Dumfries & Galloway DG2 8BY
Open: open for lunch and afternoon tea

Tel: 01387-850 377

Omnivorous café with lots for vegetarians. All vegetable based soups, and therefore suitable for vegans and other items can be adapted for vegans if asked. Little over £5.

Balti & Dosa House

Omnivorous Indian restaurant

11 Hyndland Street, off Dumbarton Road
Glasgow G11 5QE
Open: Mon-Thu 17.00-23.00, Fri-Sat 17-24.00,
Sun 17-23.00

Tel: 0141 334 0084

Omnivorous Indian Punjabi restaurant. Lots of vegetarian food, 29 dishes on the new menu. Approx £9-10 for dinner. All the popular Indian dishes, vegan no problem, they prepare dishes separately. Desserts, but as in many Indian restaurants none are vegan. Licensed for alcohol. No smoking area for 30 people, smoking area for 48. MC, Visa, Amex, Diners.

The Bay Tree

Omnvorous Middle Eastern restaurant

403 Great Western Road, Kelvinbridge
Glasgow G4 9HY
Open: Mon–Sat 9.30–22.00, Sun 9.30–21.00

Tel: 0141–334 5898

Middle Eastern cuisine. Separate vegetarian and vegan menu with an average main for £6.50. Separate smoking section. No credit cards.

Fast Food Bar

Omnivorous take–away

66 Woodlands Rd, Charing Cross
Glasgow G3 6HA
Open: Mon–Wed 8.00–18.00, Thu–Sat 8.00–03.00

Tel: 0141–332 5495

Fast food take away bar with 80% of menu vegetarian. Several burgers, pakoras and pizzas all of which have vegan options or can be made vegan. No credit cards.

Marmaris Restaurant

Turkish omnivorous restaurant

141 Elderslie Street
Glasgow G3 6JA
Open: Every day 17.00–23.00 or later

Tel: 0141–221 7144

Omnivorous Turkish restaurant with cold vegetarian mezze. Reckon on £6.50–7.50 for a meal. House wine £10 carafe, £5 half carafe.

Otago

Omnivorous restaurant

Otago Street, Off Great Western Road,
Kelvinbridge, Glasgow
Open: Mon–Sun 10.00–22.00

Tel: 0141–337 2282

Omnivorous restaurant with half of menu vegetarian. Starters, £4–£5, mains, £9–£12, such as asparagus risotto and mediterranean roast vegetables, and desserts from £3.95. Will always try and cater for special diets including vegans. Fully licensed. House wine, £10.95 for a bottle, £2.60 for a glass. Separate smoking section. Visa, MC.

Tempus Bar–Café

Omnivorous cafe in arts centre

Centre for Contemporary Arts, 350 Sauchiehall St
Glasgow G2 3JD
Open: Mon–Sat 11.00–23.00

Tel: 0141–332 7959

Omnivorous café based in centre for contemporary arts. Some vegetarian options though slim pickings for vegans. Chefs are happy to adapt dishes if asked in advance. Smoking section. Visa, MC.

Dunnet Head Restaurant

Omnivorous restaurant

Dunnet Head, Brough
Caithness, Highlands KW14 8YE
Open: Mon & Tue, Thu–Sun 12.00–15.00,
18.00–21.00. Closed Wed

Tel: 01847–851 774
www.dunnethead.co.uk

Omnivorous restaurant with separate vegetarian menu. 9 mains, £3.45–£6.50, which can be adapted for vegans. Not licensed, BYO. Non smoking. Visa, MC.

Cawdor Castle

Omnivorous restaurant

Nairn,Inverness
Inverness-Shire IV12 5RD
Open: 1st May–13th October, 10.15–17.00

Tel: 01667 404615

Omnivorous restaurant. Set within Cawdor castle, figuring famously in Shakespeare's Macbeth, and one of the Highlands' most romantic castles. Some vegetarian options on menu.

An Tuireann Arts Centre and Café

Omnivorous cafe

Sruan Road, Potree
Isle of Skye, Inverness-shire IV51 9EG
Open: Mon–Sat 12.00–15.00

Tel: 01478–613 306

Café based in arts centre with gallery opening times from 10.00–17.00. Cater well for vegetarians and also always have something for vegans including daily soups. Mains around £5. Visa, MC.

Achins Coffee Shop

Omnivorous cafe

Inverkirkaig, Lochinver
Sutherland IV27 4LS
Open: every day 10.00–17.00 Easter–October

Tel: 01571 844 262
Fax: 01571 844 262

Small coffee shop with some vegetarian options such as nut roast with salad, £3.75. Non smoking. Visa, MC.

Holland & Barrett

Health food shop

49 Netherkirkgate, Aberdeen	*Tel: 01224 648810*
61 High Street, Dumbarton	*Tel: 01389–730 754*
Unit 31, Kingsgate Shopping Centre Dunfermline	*Tel: 01383–624 915*
Unit 20, Wellgate Centre, Dundee	*Tel: 01382–205 726*
Unit 13, The Olympia, East Kilbride	*Tel: 01355–232 627*
45 High Street, Falkirk	*Tel: 01324–633 397*
Unit 3 Douglas Bridge, Galashiels	*Tel: 01896–754 256*
94 Sauchiehall Street, Glasgow G2	*Tel: 0141–331 118*
9 Queen Street, Glasgow G1	*Tel: 0141–221 3425*
34 Eastgate, Inverness	*Tel: 01463–234 267*
132 High Street, Kircaldy	*Tel: 01592–205 349*
34 Brandon Parade South, Motherwell	*Tel: 01698–230 929*
Thistle Centre, Stirling	*Tel: 01786–465 350*

Nature's Larder

Wholefood shop

60 Holburn Street, Aberdeen

Grampian Health Foods

Health food shop

Crown Street, Aberdeen

Edinburgh

by Ronny

Edinburgh is one of the most attractive and inviting cities in Britain, with stunning limestone buildings overlooked by an imposing castle, and lots of history and culture.

The city centre is full of lively pubs, cafes and shops, and it is almost as good as Brighton and London for vegetarian food. Walking around requires a degree of fitness, as Edinburgh is very hilly, which adds to its atmosphere and rugged good looks. There are several excellent free museums in the city, along with a thriving arts scene. The botanical gardens are also not to be missed.

The annual Edinburgh Fringe Festival draws thousands of people, so if you are planning to visit during August, book your accommodation as far in advance as possible.

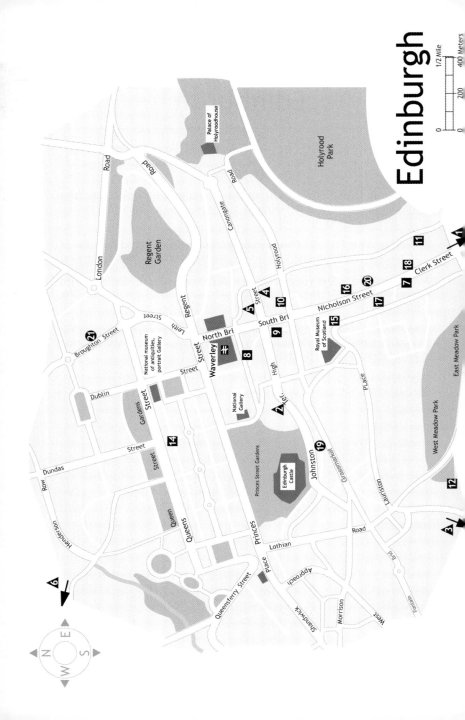

Edinburgh

0   200   400 Meters

0   1/2 Mile

Places in Edinburgh

Accommodation in Edinburgh

Restaurants in Edinburgh

Shops in Edinburgh

The Greenhouse

Vegetarian
Guest House

A warm welcome awaits you at this friendly veggie guest house. Situated in the heart of Edinburgh, it's only twenty minutes walk to the city centre. There are six rooms, comprised of doubles and twins. One can be converted to a family room. Four have ensuite bathrooms and two have private bathrooms. Stay for £35 per person per night from May–September (inclusive) and £27.50 the rest of the year.

The breakfast menu is extensive and mouth watering. Half of it's vegan and even more can be made vegan by request. Hugh and Suzanne are committed to providing good service and great veggie food. The full Scottish breakfast includes rashers, organic tempeh and home made veggie sausages (choose from mushroom, kidney bean and coriander, chickpea and black olive, walnut and rosemary, or herbed polenta); served with mushrooms, tomatoes, baked beans, hash browns, scrambled tofu and toast. Yum! Vegan kedgeree is on the menu too, or opt for one of the lighter choices like bagels with vegan cream cheese, scrambled tofu with mushrooms on toast, pancakes with maple syrup, Greenhouse tomato bruschetta, or Greenhouse mushrooms on sour dough bread. Soya milk, vegan margarine, vegan muesli and soya yoghurt are available. Organic and GM free ingredients used whenever possible.

No evening meal, but it's hardly necessary in the veg paradise that is Edinburgh! Hugh and Suzanne will give you a map of Edinburgh with veggie places highlighted.

TV's and tea and coffee making facilities in the rooms. Vegans who like their cuppa white don't miss out, as soya milk can be kept in a cooler in your room.

14 Hartington Gardens
Bruntsfield
Edinburgh EH10 4LD
Scotland

Tel: 0131 6227634

www.greenhouse-edinburgh.com

Email: greenhouse_edin@hotmail.com

Train Station: Waverley, 35 minutes walk or get bus or taxi

Open: all year

Directions: From the M8, go to Newbridge round-about and take the A8. Then take A702 (Lothian Road). This becomes Earlgrey Street, then Home Street, then Leven Street, then Bruntsfield Place. Turn right down Viewforth Street, then left into Hartington Gardens.

Parking: available

Vegan bedding.
Soaps are home made and vegan.

Children are welcome and those under twelve stay for £20. Cot available.

No pets

No smoking throughout

Discounts available depending on length of stay

Cameron Toll Guest House

Omnivorous guest house

299 Dalkeith Road, Edinburgh, EH16 5JX
Train Station: Waverley, then ten minute taxi ride
Open: all year

Tel: 0131 6672950
www.edinbed.com
camerontoll@msn.com

Three single ensuites at £25–£40 per night, three double ensuites and two twin ensuites at £21–£35 per person per night, and three family rooms at £40–£100 for the room per night, depending on number of people. Two course evening meal available for £9. Special diets catered for with advanced notice. House is fur and feather free for allergy sufferers. C hildren welcome. No pets. Smoking allowed in some rooms.

Six Marys Place

Omnivorous guest house

6 Marys Place, Raeburn Place
Stockbridge,
Edinburgh EH4 1JH

Tel: 0131 332 8965
www.sixmarysplace.co.uk

2 single & 3 double £28–£30 pp low season, £35-40 high, 2 twin en suite £30–£35 low season, £40 high
Restored Georgian townhouse, a short walk from the Royal Botanical Gardens. Tea/coffee and tv in room if requested, also tv lounge. Offers veggie breakfasts. Also has a family room that sleeps 5 for £120–140 depending on season, with double bed, double sofa bed and a single. 5% discount for Vegetarian Society members.

No. 1

Vegetarian guest house

1 Gayfield Place,
Edinburgh, EH7 4AB
Open: all year

Tel: 0131 5574752
Train Station: Waverley,
5–10 minutes walk

One twin, one single and one double £25 per person per night, and one double ensuite £30 per person per night. Children welcome but no pets. No smoking.

465

Castle Rock Hostel

Omnivorous hostel

15 Johnston Terrace,
Edinburgh EH1 2PW
Open: all year

Tel: 0131 2259666
TrainStation: Waverley,
ten minutes walk

Located next to the castle, this hostel has 225 beds. Dorms have 8–16 beds and cost £11 per night. Single sex dorms. No private rooms. Veggie continental breakfast is £1.60. Free tea and coffee. If you're vegan, you'll need to bring your own soya milk and margarine. There is a kitchen for self catering. 24 hour access. No lockers, but you can leave valuables at reception.

Royal Mile Backpackers

Omnivorous hostel

105 High Street,
Edinburgh, EH1 1SG
Open: all year

Tel: 0131 5576120
Train Station: Waverley,
ten minutes walk

38 beds costing £11 per night in a dorm of eight to ten people. Single sex dorms. No private rooms. Veggie continental breakfast is £1.60. Free tea and coffee. If you're vegan, you'll beed to bring your own soya milk and margarine. There is a kitchen for self catering. 24 hour access. No lockers, but there's a safe in reception. Smoking areas. No children.

High Street Hostel

Omnivorous hostel

8 Blackfriars Street,
Edinburgh, EH1 1NE
Open: all year

Tel: 0131 5573984
Train Station: Waverley,
five minutes walk

140 beds costing £11 per night in a dorm of six to sixteen people. A veggie continental breakfast is £1.60. Free tea and coffee. If you're vegan, you'll beed to bring your own soyaa milk and margarine. There is a kitchen for self catering. 24 hour access. Single sex dorms. No private rooms. No lockers, but there's a safe in reception. Smoking areas. No children.

The Baked Potato Shop

Not just your usual spud! Very friendly small vegetarian and vegan take away located just off the Royal Mile, in the heart of Edinburgh, and a favourite of local students.

Good value, generous portions with potatoes starting from £2.45 with fillings including pasta salad, curried rice peppers, mexican, spinach or avocado salad and cous cous. They do a superb vegan coleslaw. Hot fillings such as vegetarian haggis, chilli, vegetable curry or baked beans.

Varied selection of filled rolls, £1.25, and filled pittas from £2.25. Tasty sos rolls too.

They have vegan mayonnaise, margarine and soya milk, some gluten-free, wheat-free and raw foods and also make their own vegan cakes (carrot, chocolate, cranberry and apple) which start from 55p.

Lots of fliers for various holistic things and happenings and also leaflets on animal issues.

It can get very busy at lunchtime so be prepared to queue.

56 Cockburn Street
Royal Mile
Edinburgh EH1 1PB

Tel: 0131–225 7572

charlesveggie@aol.com

Train/Tube Train:
Waverley Station

Open: Mon–Sun 9.00–21.00 Extended hours during festival.

No smoking

No credit cards

10% discount to members of Animal Aid, PETA, Viva!, Vegetarian and Vegan Society and also to people presenting this book!

Bann UK

Vegetarian restaurant

Situated off the Royal Mile, a combination of modern décor with candlelight makes this gourmet eatery popular with tourists and locals.

Extensive world menu with snacks and starters from £3–5 and full meals around £10. Examples of food include: Lebanese flatbread stuffed with roasted Mediterranean vegetables; soup with bread; Mock duck and chutney in pitta; hummous and baba ganoush dips with wraps. Plenty for vegans. Desserts, £3.90.

Good range of drinks including a gorgeous foamy soya hot chocolate, though the fruit juices are a bit pricy. Licenced for alcohol.

*5 Hunter Square
(Royal Mile)
Edinburgh EH1 1QW*

*Tel: 0131–226 1112
Fax: 0131–226 1112*

www.urbann.co.uk

Licensed

Open: Mon–Thu 11.00–24.00, Sat & Sun 11.00–01.00, phone to confirm.

Visa, MC

Future Foods

Vegan cafe/takeaway

New ultra–modern vegan sandwich, juice, coffee and snack bar with computer controlled audio-visual system and broadband internet access. Starters, £1.30–£1.50, include soup of the day such as tomato and basil or lentil and coriander, and large choice of salads, £1.20–£1.50 which vary every day.

Sandwiches, 99p–£2.20, pre-packaged and to order (with wide choice of bread, rolls, tortilla etc) include spicy avocado salad and vegan BLT. Heated snacks and ready meals – burgers, pasties, chilli with rice also available. Desserts, 40p–£1.50, with soya yoghurts, cakes and strawberry vegan cheese cake.

Coffee £1.10–£1.30.

*2 Warrender Park Road
Marchmont
Edinburgh EH9 1JQ
Tel: 0131–662 8080*

www.futurefoods.biz/www.future–foods.co.uk

Open: Mon–Tue & Fri 8.00–16.00, Wed & Sat 8.00–14.00, Thu 8.00–18.00

Smoking permitted.

10% discount to members of Animal Aid, PETA, Viva!, Vegetarian and Vegan Societies and also to people presenting this book!

Black Bo's

Black Bo's been acclaimed for its vegetarian cordon vert dishes with the chef dedicated to providing imaginative and fllavoursome meals with a strong emphasis on fruit.

You won't find a menu like this anywhere else. The foods sounds bizarre, but somehow the combination of flavours really works. Modern, fashionable interior.

Almost half the menu is vegan and starters at around £5 include chickpea chilli with coriander and avocado, with lemon sorbet and blue bols.

Main courses at around £10 include mushrooms with back olive roulade; fried potato balls with fig and rum sauce; and aubergine with melon and chilli.

Our reviewers visited twice and found the service very variable.

Sorbet appears to be the only vegan dessert. All wines have been guaranteed vegetarian by their supplier.

House wine £10.50 per bottle. Selection of other wines available.

Vegetarian restaurant

57–61 Blackfriars Street
Edinburgh EH1 3RT

Tel: 0131–557 6136
www.blackbos.com

Open: Mon–Sun dinner
18.00– 22.30, also Fri–Sat
lunch 12–14.00

Open lunchtimes
throughout the week
during the festival.

Henderson's Bistro Bar

Vegetarian cafe-bar

Vegan friendly vegetarian wine bar with cosy atmosphere adjoining the Salad Table. Soup from £1.95, choice of pates £2.20, and bruschetta of wholemeal/Italian style bread from £2.50 or marinated wild mushroom bruschetta from £3.25. Mains include Thai curry with rice, £4.95; burgers, £3.95; and Moroccan stew – aubergine, butternut squash, tofu, apricot and spices served with rice, £4.50.

Bottled beers and ciders from £2.20, fresh juices and soft drinks 70p–£2.40, coffees from £1.20, pot of tea £1.10. House wine (vegan) £2.60 (175ml glass), £3.60 (260ml), £10 bottle, plus numerous other wines, many biodynamic, organic or vegan. Non-alcoholic wines £6.75 bottle.

25 Thistle Street
Edinburgh EH2 1DR

Tel: 0131–225 2605
Fax: 0131–225 3542

mail@
hendersonsofedinburgh.
co.uk
Train: Waverly Edinburgh

Open:
Mon–Wed 12.00–15.00,
Thu–Sat 12.00–21.00,
Sun 12.00–19.00
Extended hours during
festival.

Smoking permitted

Visa, MC

Henderson's Salad Table

Vegetarian fast food restaurant

Long established vegetarian café situated in the centre, celebrating 40 year anniversary in 2002.

Large selection of salads from £1.30. Pastries and savouries from £1.95. Up to 8 different hot dishes which change daily and start from £3.95 for lunch or £4.50 for dinner. Sweets such as fresh or dried fruit salad £2.40, or apple or cherry pie £2.20.

They aim to provide at least one hot vegan dish and try to be aware of and cater for special diets. Use seasonal, local and organic produce whenever possible.

Fruit juices, fruit and herb teas 85p–£1.10. House wine £2.60 for a glass. Bottled beers from £2.40.

94 Hanover Street
Edinburgh EH2 1DR

Tel: 0131–225 2131
Fax: 0131–225 3542

mail@
hendersonsofedinburgh.
co.uk
Train: Waverly Edinburgh

Open: Mon–Sat 8.00–
22.30, Sun 12.00–20.00

Separate smoking section

Visa, MC

Small health food shop
upstairs with take-away
food including fruit pies,
plus coffee bar.

Legume

New vegetarian restaurant with Scottish and French influences and a varied menu that has plenty of choice for vegans. On the lunch menu, 1 course is £7.95, 2 courses £9.95, 3 for £13.95. Dinner is £9.95, 13.95 or £17.95.

Typically you might begin with pea and mint soup, marinated avocado and cucumber tapenade; main dishes inlcude stir fry bean sprouts with lemon and garlic cous cous and caramelised chicory, and French pancake with Mediterranean vegetables and red pepper sauce. Desserts include paw paw with black-currant sorbet and lemon syrup, and sauteed apple and pear.

Special diets catered for with notice.

Vegetarian Restaurant

11 South College Street Edinburgh EH8 9AA

Tel: 0131 667 1597

www. legumerestaurant.com LegumeEdinburgh@ aol.com

Open: Mon–Sat 11–14.00, 17.30–22.00

Fully licensed. Non smoking.

Visa, MC

10% discount to members of the Vegetarian Society

Susie's Wholefood Diner

Vegetarian/vegan café were you can fill up for around a fiver and you'll be spoilt for choice with at least 7 (3 or 4 vegan) hot dishes, including Morrocan stew, sweet and sour tofu stir-fry, vegan cashewnut flan. Salads every day.

Relaxed menu rules allow you to combine several hot and cold dishes together and the portions are generous. Order a small plate for £4.50 or large £5.50 and make up your own feast.

Vegan desserts include banana and date and walnut cake or apricot slices.

Susie's is licensed and offers many house wines and beers.

Vegetarian cafe

51 –53 West Nicolson St opposite the pear tree Edinburgh EH8 9DB

Tel: 0131 667 8729

susies@ednet.co.uk

Licensed

Open: Mon –Sat 12.00– 22.00 (Mon 21.00), closed Sun except during festival. Extended hrs during festival.

Ann Purna

Indian vegetarian restaurant

45 St Patrick's Square
Edinburgh EH8 9ET
Open: Mon–Fri 12–14.00, 17.30–23.00; Sun 17.00–22.00

Tel: 0131–662–1807

Vegetarian Indian Gujarati restaurant

The Engine Shed Cafe

Vegetarian cafe

19 St Leonards Lane
Edinburgh EH8 9SD
Open: Mon–Thu 10.30–15.30, Fri 10.30–14.30

Tel: 0131–662 0040
engineshed@aol.com

Vegetarian café run by charitable organisation Garvald Community Enterprises which works with people with learning difficulties. Always vegan options available and a wheat-free choice in main dishes. Soup, £1.25, and mains, £2.75–£4.50, typically include chillis and casseroles. Salads, 90p for a portion, £2.50 for a plate of 3 salads, and £3.50 for a substantial plate which you can fill with a helping of all the salads on offer. Hot desserts are occasionally vegan and there is always a fresh fruit salad. Counter service. Non smoking. No credit cards.

Suruchi

Indian vegetarian restaurant

14A Nicholson St
Edinburgh EH8 9DB
Open: Mon–Sat 12–14.00, Sun 13–15.00

Tel: 0131 556 6583
Fax: 0131 622 7227

Indian vegetarian restaurant. 10% discount to Vegan Society members.

Kalpna

Indian vegetarian restaurant

2–3 St Patrick Square
Edinburgh EH8 9EZ
Open: Mon–Sat 12–14.30, Mon–Sun 17.30–23.00

Tel: 0131–667 9890

Indian vegetarian with plenty of choice for vegans. Mains, £4–£7.30. Non smoking. Visa, MC. Offer 5% discount for Vegetarian and Vegan Society members.

Filmhouse Cafe-Bar

Omnivorous cafe in cinema

88 Lothian Road, Edinburgh EH3 9BZ
Open: Mon–Thu & Sun 10.00–23.30,
Fri & Sat 10.00–00.30

Tel: 0131 229 5932

Always have vegan options available– vegan curries, baked potatoes and always a vegan daily special too. Exciting place because they also screen movie films.

The Elephant House

Omnivorous cafe

21 George IV Bridge, Edinburgh EH1 1EN
Open: 08.00–23.00, Sat 09.00–23.00,
Sun 9.30–23.00

Tel: 0131 220 5355

Popular with students, it has some veggie food though little in mains for vegans, but they do do vegan cakes such as carrot cake, chocolate cake and some biscuity things, all around £2.25. Good location.

Helios Fountain

Personal growth bookshop

7 Grassmarket
Edinburgh EH1 2HY
Open: Mon–Sat 10.00–18.00, Sun 12.00–16.00

Tel: 0131–229 7884
Fax: 0131–622 7173

Former coffee shop which has now become a personal growth bookshop with a range of crafts and eco-friendly kids stuff.

Jordan Valley Wholefoods

World food shop

8 Nicolson Street
Edinburgh EH8 9DJ
Open: Mon–Fri 9.30–17.30, Sat 10–18.00, closed Sun

Tel: 0131 556 6928

Jordan Valley make their own range of vegetarian and vegan pates, pies, dips and pastries.

Real Foods

Wholefood shop

37 Broughton Street
Edinburgh EH1 3JU
Open: Mon–Fri 9.00–19.00 (Thu 20.30),
Sat 9.00–17.30, Sun 10.00–18.00

Tel: 0131 557 1911

Edinburgh's largest retailer of wholefood and health products. Many of their products are organic. As well as snack foods they sell organic breads, also vegan wines and foods that are clearly labeled. There is a smaller branch at 8 Brougham Place EH3 9JH, open Mon–Sat 9.00–18.30, Sun 10–17.00. Tel. 0131 228 1201

Piemaker

Omnivorous pie shop

38 South Bridge
Edinburgh EH1 1LL
Open: Mon 10–19.00, Tue–Thu 10.00–midnight,
Fri & Sat 10.00–02.00(am!), Sun 11.00–19.00

Tel: 0131 556 8566

Several vegetarian pies and about 4 vegan sweet pies including apple, apple and raspberry, maple and pecan nut pie. Average of 5 savoury pies such as yummy chilli bean, all clearly marked if vegan, and very good value at £1–£1.29. Not far from Princes Mile and near the studenty area of Southside. They have a sister branch on Home St.

Hanover Health Foods

Health food shop

40 Hanover Street, Edinburgh EH2 2DR
Open: Mon & Tue 9.30–17.30, Wed 10–17.30,
Thu 9.30–19.00, Fri & Sat 9.30–17.30

Tel: 0131 225 4291

Wales

Heartspring Vegan Bed & Breakfast and Retreat Centre

Wales

Wales is a different country: The landscape sparkles with extra vitality when you venture west of Offa's Dyke.

History did not begin in 1066 here. Read the ancient stories collected in **The Mabinogion** and gain the satisfaction of locating the precise scenes. Listen to the language spoken by King Arthur and Myrddin (Merlin). The latter lived on a vegan diet of "roots, grasses, wild fruit and berries, or nuts and acorns." Even the patron saint, Dewi (David), was recorded to have eaten a vegan diet and drank water. And Welsh water is so pure... try "crystal clear Cerist."

The tradition continues, including amongst those labelled "hippies" for seeking refuge in Welsh valleys from English materialism. The self-sufficiency impetus, especially in West Wales where John Seymour lived and wrote his books, is strong and although Seymour killed his own animals, many of his followers chose to be at least vegetarian. Stay in the independent hostel at Brithdir Mawr, near Trefdraeth (that's the Newport in Pembrokeshire) to sample the simple life of a sustainable community.

Industrial erections known as windmills and which attract tempting government grants now threaten to desecrate the solitude of Mid Wales. Yet there need be no conflict of "green interest." The kitchens at the **Centre for Alternative Technology**, near Machynlleth, are powered by the much more environmentally-friendly and dependable source of renewable energy known as wood. The Vegan Society sponsored the first bio-fuel machine here in the early 1980s to demonstrate how subsidised and environmentally damaging sheep farming could be replaced with the return of the natural climax vegetation of oak woodland, surviving today in pockets such as at Dinas Emrys (National Trust) and Ynyshir (Royal Society for the Protection of Birds). The Foot and Mouth crisis of 2001, when the closure of footpaths devastated the tourist industry, emphasises the need to make this change. Dinas Mawddwy's Meirion Mill (on the site of King Arthur's last battle, at Camlan) now grows willow for renewable energy, while the Greenwood Centre, near Caernarfon, demonstrates the potential of switching from sheep to native broadleaved trees (not to be confused with the alien conifers planted by the Forestry Commission).

Anecdotal evidence suggests that there are more vegans per head of population in Wales than in England. They have their own little magazine, *Y Figan Cymreig*, while there's no trouble in buying vegan ice creams in little coastal resorts such as Aberaeron. Wholefood shops are everywhere and major centres – that's places like Aberystwyth and Haverfordwest – have several. Shop in confidence at Vegonia in Porthmadog, where all the stock is vegan. Spot the vegan restaurant as you tour the medieval walls of Conwy. Wales still has its share of flesh-eaters but vegetable samosas can be found in the most surprising of places.

Laurence Main is a director of the Vegan Society and was its Assistant Secretary in the early 1980s. The author of 50 walking guidebooks, he spends much of his life camping and recording dreams on sacred peaks. A Druid, he researches and gives talks on Earth Mysteries (including leys) and King Arthur. His guidebooks include the popular *Walk Snowdonia and North Wales*, published by Bartholomew (cartography by David Perrott), *The Spirit Paths of Wales* (Cicerone Press) and *A Meirionnydd Coast Walk* (Gwasg Carreg Gwaig). Laurence contributes walks in Wales to *Country Walking* and *Trail* magazines and writes weekly walks in *The Western Mail*. Guided walks are sometimes available (telephone Laurence on 01650 531354 or write to him at 9 Mawddwy Cottages, Minllyn, Dinas Mawddwy, Machynlleth, SY20 9LW – grid ref. SH859142).

Places in Wales

Hotels and Guest Houses

Ardwyn – Llanelli, Carmarthenshire – Veggie B&B	481
Chapel Guest House – Near Newport, Gwent – Omni Guest House	482
Fraser Cottage – Wrexham, Denbighshire – Veggie B&B	483
Graianfryn – Caernarfon, Gwynedd – Veggie Guest House	484
Green Haven – Haverfordwest, Pembrokeshire – Veggie B&B	485
Gwalia Farm – Machynlleth, Powys – Veggie B&B	486
Heartspring – Carmarthen, Carmarthenshire – Vegan Retreat Centre	487
Hendre Vegetarian B&B – Nantglyn, Denbighshire – Veggie B&B	488
The Old Post Office – Llanigon, Powys – Veggie Guest House	489
Plas Dolmelynllyn – Dolgellau, Gwynedd – Omnivorous Hotel	490
Plas Madoc – Llandudno, Conwy – Veggie Guest House & s/c	491
Trericket Mill – Builth Wells, Powys – Veggie Guest House	492
Ty'r Ysgol – Pwllheli, Gwynedd – Veggie Guest House	493
The West Usk Lighthouse – Wentloog, Gwent – Omnivorous B&B	494
Cefn Gribyn – Isle of Anglesey – Veggie B&B	495
Tremeifion – Talsarnau, Gwynedd – Vegetarian Hotel	495
The Old Rectory Hotel – Maentwrog, Gwynedd – Vegetarian Hotel	495
Caerleon House Hotel – Newport, Gwent – Omnivorous guest house	495
The Old Post Office – Pembrokeshire – Guest house & restaurant	496

Restaurants

Tomlins – Penarth, South Glamorgan – Vegetarian Restaurant	497
Hunky Dory – Newport, Gwent – Vegetarian coffe shop	498
The Wall Place – Conwy, Gwynedd – Vegetarian cafe	498
The Harvest Moon – Isle of Anglesey – Vegan cafe & healing centre	498
Waverley – Carmarthen, Pembrokeshire – Vegan and veggie restaurant	498
Beehive Café – Newport, Pembrokeshire – Omnivorous cafe	499
Great Oak Cafe – Llanidloes, Powys – Vegetarian cafe	499
Centre for Alternative Technology Restaurant – Machynlleth, Powys	499
Quarry Café – Machynlleth, Powys – Vegetarian cafe	500
Crumbs – Cardiff, South Glamorgan – Vegetarian cafe	500
The Chapter Arts Centre Cafe – Cardiff – Omnivorous cafe	500
Cafe Naz – Cardiff Bay, South Glamorgan – Omnivorous Indian	501
Govindas – Swansea – Vegetarian Indian restaurant	501

Places in Wales

Shops

Wales

Ardwyn

Vegetarian Bed & Breakfast

Vegetarian B&B with views of the Black Mountain. There are one double and one twin room. Both have ensuite bathrooms and cost £20 per person per night. The rooms have mountain views.

Breakfast could be mushrooms, tomatoes, beans, hash browns and toast. Dietary requirements can easily be catered for by the vegetarian proprietor, Paula. Vegan margarine, vegan muesli and soya milk are available.

Dinner is offered for £10 and could be avocado with hazelnut dressing followed by spinach, mung bean and lime casserole and for dessert, baked cinnamon oranges with Grand Marnier.

There are many attractions in the area, such as the Gower Peninsular, West Brecon Beacons, National Botanic Garden of Wales, Aberglasney Historic House and Gardens, Llyn Llech Owain Country Park, Gelli Aur Country Park, Carreg Cennen Castle, Pemberton Chocolate Farm and the Dylan Thomas Centre to name a few!

If you're there at the right time, don't miss the Swansea Bay Summer Festival.

Televisions and tea and coffee making facilities in the rooms. Satellite TV in the main lounge.

192 Gate Road
Penygroes
Llanelli
Carmarthenshire
SA14 7RW
Wales

Tel: 01269 832739

www.ardwyn-veg.co.uk

Email:
enquiries@ardwyn-veg.co.uk

Train station:
Ammanford, 5 miles or Carmarthen, 11 miles. Can get a bus or taxi from Ammanford centre.

Open: all year except 24–26 December

Directions:
From the end of the M4, take the A48 towards Carmarthen. After four miles, at the end of the Crosshands roundabout take the A476. After 1 1/2 miles turn right on to the B4297. Ardwyn is 400m on the right.

Children are welcome

No smoking throughout

Parking: private parking available

Chapel Guest House

Chapel Guest House lies in the pretty village of St Brides, between Newport and Cardiff. There are four rooms, all with ensuite bathrooms; one single at £25–£30, one double, one twin and one family all priced at £22–£23 per person per night.

Breakfast is fruit and muesli or cereal followed by a full cooked English breakfast. Vegan sausages, soya milk, vegan margarine and vegan muesli are all on offer.

Dinner is not available, but there are two restaurants in the village and there is a veggie cafe in Newport.

Chapel House, formerly Rehoboth Baptist Chapel built in 1828, fell into disrepair and in 1982 was converted into the 3 star accommodation it is now. It is only half a mile from the 'special scientific interest' site of the Severn Estuary which can be accessed across footpaths. Tredegar House Stately Home with its boating lake, park and gardens is two miles away. There is a golf course a mile away.

The village is ideally placed for touring South Wales and the Wye valley. It is only four miles from Newport with its premier indoor Go-Kart track and eight miles from Cardiff which has one of the finest Civic Centres in Europe and a great night life.

Children are welcome and those under twelve are half price. There is a high chair. Pets are accepted by arrangement.

There are televisions and tea and coffee making facilites in the rooms. TV lounge. There is a ground floor room so disabled access is possible.

Omnivorous Guest House

Church Road
St Brides Wentloog
Near Newport
Gwent NP10 8SN
Wales

Tel : 01633 681018

Fax: 01633 681431

www.smoothhound.co.uk/ hotels/chapel1.html

Email: chapelguesthouse@hotmail.com

Train station: Newport, 4 miles, then bus or taxi

Open: all year

Directions: Leave M4 at junction 28. Take A48 towards Newport. At roundabout take third exit, signposted, 'B4239 St Brides'. Follow B4239 for approximately three miles to village centre, turn right into Church Road, then first left into Church House Inn car park. Chapel Guest House is on the left.

Children welcome High chair

No smoking throughout

Parking: available

Fraser Cottage

Pure vegetarian B&B in Bangor-on-Dee, a small rural village situated in the Welsh Borderlands.

There are three guest rooms; two double ensuites and one twin ensuite costing £20–£25 per person per night.

Breakfast is vegan and is cooked with a wide selection of fresh organic ingredients. Vegan proprietors Helen and Winny offer a choice of hot and cold food but don't have a menu as they like to surprise you!

Fraser Cottage is within short walking distance to the pub and the church, both of which have picturesque views over the River Dee and its medieval bridge.

Nearby attractions in Chester include an historic walled city, guided tours, boat trips, museums and a cathedral. In LLangollen attractions include steam railways, a canal and Horseshoe Pass. There are also the National Trust Properties Erdigg Hall and Chirk Castle nearby.

But if that doesn't excite you, Bangor-on-Dee is perfectly situated to enjoy the countryside of Cheshire, Shropshire, the North Wales cost and Snowdonia. Also within easy reach are the major cities of Liverpool and Manchester.

The house has an informal atmosphere, is centrally heated and carpet free. The rooms have televisions, videos, clock radios and tea and coffee making facilities. Dogs are welcome. Children under three stay for free and those between three and twelve get a 20% discount. There are high chairs.

Vegetarian
Bed & Breakfast

High Street
Bangor-on-Dee
Wrexham
Denbighshire LL13 OAU
Wales

Tel and Fax:
01978 781068

www.frasercottage.com

Email:
helen@frasercottage.com

Train station:
Wrexham, 5 miles, then bus, or if necessary they can collect you.

Open: all year

Directions:
From the North (M53 or M56) continue around Chester on the A55 then take the A483 Wrexham Road. Turn off at signpost to Nantwich and then follow signs to Whitchurch. You will soon see sign to Bangor-on-Dee.
From the South (M6) take the M54 Telford Road and then the A41 Whitchurch Road. There join the A525 Wrexham Road until you reach the sign for Bangor-on-Dee.

Parking off street

High chairs

No smoking throughout

10% discount given to members of the Vegetarian Society and the Vegan Society.

Graianfryn

Graianfryn is on the northern edge of Snowdonia National Park between the mountains and the sea. One double and one twin at £21 per person per night and one double ensuite at £23 per person.

Breakfast is fruit juice and fresh or dried fruit salad with home made cereals or muesli, followed by veggie sausages, mushrooms, tomatoes, scrambled tofu and potato cakes with home baked organic rolls. Vegan muesli, margarine, soya milk and yoghurt available.

Dinner is £16 and could be tomatoes stuffed with flagelot beans and olives in a tomato and avocado sauce, followed by Jamaican sweet potato casserole with marinated tofu, pineapple rice and salad, and for dessert strawberry tofu ice cream. Fresh organic produce is used where possible and some of it is from the garden.

Graianfryn is set in magnificent countryside and is an ideal base for walking and exploring North Wales. It is three miles from the foot of Snowdon yet only 20 minutes drive to the nearest sandy beach. Nearby are gentle walks as well as plenty of challenging peaks for the more serious walker or climber. You could take a scenic journey on the Ffestiniog steam railway or visit one of the picturesque villages, castles, stately homes, lakes or botanical gardens.

Children over four are welcome and those under eleven are half price. Children eleven to thirteen years get 25% discount. Picnic lunches can be supplied. Secure cycle storage. There is a lounge with a fireplace, television, books and games. Tea and coffee making facilities in the rooms. Well behaved pets welcome.

Penisarwaun
Caernarfon
Gwynedd LL55 3NH

Tel: 01286 871007

www.vegwales.co.uk
info@vegwales.co.uk

Train: Bangor, 7 miles, then a bus or taxi. They can sometimes collect.

Open: all year

Directions:
From the A55 follow signs for Llanberis. Take the Bangor exit. At the roundabout at the end of the slip road, turn left then right past the Little Chef. At the next round-about, turn left along the B547. Pass Beran petrol station on your left, then take the next right to Penisarwaun. Immediately turn right again down a track. Graianfryn is on your left before the farm gates.

From A5 (South and Midlands) turn left at Capel Curig then right over the Llanberis Pass and through the village of Llanberis. After the second lake turn right down the B4547 towards Bangor. Ignore the first left turning for Penisarwaun but take the next, then immediately turn right down a track. Graianfryn is on your left before the farm gates.

Parking: available

No smoking throughout

Green Haven

Vegetarian B&B in a modern bungalow close to Pembrokeshire Coast National Park. They have a double and a twin room both costing £17.50 per person per night.

Breakfast could be dried fruit salad and soya yoghurt with vegan muesli, followed by grilled mushrooms and tomatoes, baked beans and sauteed potatoes with toast and preserves, as well as tea and coffee. Veggie sausages, vegan margarine and soya milk are available.

Dinner is offered for £9 and could be celery soup with garlic bread, followed by tomato and basil gnocci with mixed salad and green beans. For dessert, apple and apricot crumble with soy cream. All the above are home-made ensuring only vegan ingredients are used. There is also a restaurant which caters for veggies only a five minute walk away.

A major attraction throughout the year is the famous coastal path, which winds for 186 miles around bays and headlands through the Pembrokeshire Coast National Park. There are beaches within a ten minute drive and surfing is possible.

You can get a ferry to Ireland at Fishguard, half an hour's drive away. There are also plenty of museums, castles, standing stones and other places of interest. Boat trips are also possible to Skomer, Skokholm and Ramsey.

The tiny cathedral city of St. David's is a twenty minute drive. In August 2002 the National Eisteddfod will be held near here.

Tea and coffee making facilities are in the rooms and there is a TV lounge. Children are welcome.

Nolton Road
Simpson Cross
Haverfordwest
Pembrokeshire SA62 6ES
Wales

Tel : 01437 710756

Email:
Tonyreflexology@aol.com

Train station:
Haverfordwest, 4 miles,
then bus or taxi, or they
can collect.

Open: all year

Directions:
From the centrally located
market town of
Haverfordwest take the
A487 for about four miles
towards St Davids, into
the village of Simpson
Cross. Green Haven is
about fifty yards down
Nolton Road.

Parking: plenty available

Disabled access possible

No smoking throughout.

Gwalia Farm

Vegetarian
Bed & Breakfast

Gwalia is a small and remote farm with beautiful views of the Snowdonian mountains. There are two rooms; one twin and one family costing £20 per person per night.

They aim to produce as much of their own food as possible. Virtually all their fruit and vegetables are from their own organic garden. Breakfast could be muesli or porridge followed by veggie sausages, baked beans and home-made whole wheat organic bread with home-made preserves. Vegan margarine and soya milk available.

Dinner is offered for £10 and could be sweet and sour beans with brown rice and home grown freshly picked organic veggies, followed by fruit crumble made from freshly picked rhubarb.

As well as the rooms in the house, they also have a self contained caravan, or if you'd rather be out in the elements you can pitch a tent.

If you fancy a swim or a paddle in a canoe, the farm has a lake in the conservation area.

It is an excellent spot for walking and bird watching. The Centre for Alternative Technology is nearby.

There are no televisions, but they do have 'a log fire, spring water and silence'. Children are welcome and they have a high chair. Pets are also welcome. No smoking throughout.

Cemmaes
Machynlleth
Powys SY20 9PZ
Wales

Tel: 01650 511377

Email:
harry@gwalia99.fsnet.co.uk

Train station:
Machynlleth, 9 miles

Open: all year

Directions:
Take the A489 from Machynlleth, or from Newtown take the A470. Gwalia Farm is between Cemmaes and Commins Coch.

Parking: available

Heartspring

Vegan B&B
and Retreat Centre

Ecological Victorian Country House overlooking stunning coastal conservation area. One single room at £24–£28 per night and two family rooms at £26–£38 per person per night. All rooms decorated with chemical free paints, simple country furniture and natural fabric. Rooms have large south facing windows with views of the sea, village and castle.

Breakfast is an organic buffet with a large selection of fruit and cereals with plant milks and soy yoghurt as well as breads with various jams. Gluten free choices. Vegan margarine and muesli available. A vegan organic dinner is offered from £5. Special attention is paid to those with allergies. Veggie restaurants and health food shops in nearby Carmarthen.

The house is south facing and due to its elevated position receives long hours of sunshine. It's surrounded by an acre of organic gardens and is only five minutes walk to the beach. Numerous coastal paths to explore and the ruined castle is just up the lane. For the active, there is sailing, canoeing, walking, cycling and swimming.

B&B stays, self catering breaks, group courses and workshops and tailor made individual healing retreats are all possible at Heartspring. There is a therapy room, a wooden meditation sanctuary in the garden and a wood burning stove in the workshop space. Fresh spring water for drinking and bathing. Wide choice of therapies and teaching sessions such as Meditation, Profound Relaxation, Massage, Reiki and more.

Tea and coffe making in rooms. No TV's to spoil the natural environment.

Hill House
Llansteffan
Carmarthen
Carmarthenshire
SA33 5JG
Wales

Tel: 01267 241999

www.heartspring.co.uk

Email:maddie@heart spring.co.uk

Train Station: Carmarthen, 7 miles, then bus taxi or owners can collect.

Open: all year

Directions: Follow the M4 west through South Wales until it becomes the A48. Follow until you reach Carmarthen. Then follow signs for A40 (St Clears). Continue for a 1/4 mile and take the first exit signed Johnstown & Llansteffan. Turn right at the T junction for Llansteffan. Follow this B troad for 6 miles to the village of Llansteffan. Continue to the centre of the village. Go past the Sticks Hotel on your right and after four houses turn right into a narrow driveway (opposite church tower). Heartspring is the big pink house at the top.

Parking: available

Children welcome and there are cots and highchairs

No smoking throughout

Hendre Vegetarian B&B

Veggie B&B standing in one and a half acres of garden and woodland in an idyllic elevated location with views over Nantglyn Valley. There are two rooms at £22.50–£24.50 per person per night, consisting of one double ensuite room and one twin room with private shower room.

Begin your day with cereal, dried and fresh fruit and soy yoghurt, followed by a full cooked breakfast with toast and home made preserves. Wholefood ingredients are used and special dietary requirements can be catered for. Vegan margarine, soy milk, vegan muesli and veggie sausages are all available.

Dinner is generally not offered, but if required can be provided on the day of arrival. The owners will be happy to provide you with details of veggie friendly places to eat in the area.

There are loads of outdoor activities in the area like walking, mountain biking, sailing and bird watching, or just take it easy sightseeing and relaxing. Llyn Brenig, a large lake at the edge of Clocaenog Forest, is close by. Snowdonia National Park is within half an hour's drive. The coastal resorts of Colwyn Bay, Llandudno, the Conwy Valley and Isle of Anglesey are all accessible, as is the historic city of Chester.

Tea and coffee making in the rooms. Children three and above are welcome and they have a high chair. No pets. No smoking throughout.

Vegetarian
Bed and Breakfast

*Nantglyn
nr Denbigh
Denbighshire
Wales LL16 5PP*

Tel: 01745 550207

*Email:
hendre@hendreguest
house.fsnet.co.uk*

*Train Station: Rhyl,
17 miles, but no buses or
taxis. You need own
transport.*

Open: Easter–September

*Directions: they are rurally
located and directions are
complex. Detailed
instructions will be sent
to you on request.*

Parking: available on site

The Old Post Office

(In Llanigon)

Veggie B&B in an outstandingly beautiful area with the Brecon Beacons national park on the doorstep.

There are three rooms in this grade 2 listed house; one twin/double at £18 per person per night and two twin/double ensuites at £28 per person per night.

Breakfast starts with cereal or muesli with fruit, followed by potato cakes, tomatoes, mushrooms, beans, fried bread and fresh locally made bread with preserves. All washed down with fruit juice, tea and coffee of course. Vegan margarine, soya milk, vegan muesli and soya yoghurt are all available. Ask in advance if you'd like veggie/vegan sausages.

Dinner is not offered but veggie proprietor Linda will point you in the right direction. Hay is only two miles away where there are a good selection of cafes and restaurants. She'll give you an eating out guide.

Llanigon is a nice quiet town with not much night life apart from a few pubs. However, there is loads to tire you out during the day so you'll probably just fall into bed in the evenings. Being so close to the Brecon Beacons there are miles of walking and mountain bike trails. The River Wye is not far away where you can go canoeing. Paragliding is also available nearby – the best way to see the amazing scenery and it's not scary – honest!

There are tea and coffee making facilities in the rooms and a TV in the lounge.

Children are welcome depending on which rooms are available. Animals are welcome.

Vegetarian Guest House

Llanigon
Hay-on-Wye
Powys HR3 5QA
Wales

Tel: 01497 820008

www.oldpost-office.co.uk

Train station:
Hereford, 20 miles, then bus to Hay, then taxi

Open: all year

Directions:
From Hay-on-Wye take B4350 towards Brecon. After 1/2 mile, turn left signposted 'to Llanigon'. Drive another mile, turn left before school. It is the big white house on the right opposite church.

Parking: available

No smoking throughout

10% discount to members of the Vegetarian Society, Vegan Society, Viva!, PETA, Animal Aid and people presenting this book if staying three nights or more in the ensuite room or a week or more in the standard room. Please advise her when you book.

Plas Dolmelynllyn

Country hotel in a Welsh Manor house built in 1550. It is situated in Dolmelynllyn, in the southern part of Snowdonia National Park. There are ten rooms all with ensuite bathrooms; two singles at £55–£65 per night, four doubles and three twins at £97.50–£125 per room per night and one family room at £110 per night. There is a 10% discount on stays early in the season and short breaks for dinner, bed and breakfast are available all year.

A cooked veggie breakfast is offered. The award-winning chef, Joanna provides a four course dinner for £24.50. Vegetarian options are always on the menu and most dishes can be adapted to accommodate other diets. Advise them when you book if you are vegan. The menu changes daily, but expect something like deep fried red onion and corn fritters to begin, then pineapple and lime water ice, devilled field mushrooms on sweet potato mash with chilli dressing for your main course and for dessert, warm coconut crempogs with grilled mango on passion fruit sauce. They use local produce whenever possible and are open to non-residents for dinner.

The hotel is set in three acres of terraced gardens with a stream running through it and is surrounded by National Trust owned forests, mountains and meadows. There are many attractions such as gold mines and slate mines, castles and stately homes, superb beaches and little villages nestling in the grand scenery. If you're feeling adventurous why not climb Cader Idris or Snowdon just a short drive away.

Each of the bedrooms has a different decorative theme and all have a television, radio, telephone, hair dryer and tea and coffee making facilities.

Omnivorous Hotel

Ganllwyd
Dolgellau
Gwynedd LL40 2HP
Wales

Tel: 01341 440273

Fax: 01341 440640

www.dolly-hotel.co.uk

Email:
info@dolly-hotel.co.uk

Train station:
Barmouth, 10 miles

Open: March–November
(inclusive)

Directions:
5 miles north of Dolgellau
on the A470

Parking: 20 spaces

Breakfast can be served in
rooms if requested

No smoking throughout

10% discount to members
of the Vegetarian Society

Plas Madoc

Vegetarian
Guest House

60 Church Walks
Llandudno
Conwy LL30 2HL
Wales

Tel: 01492 876514

www.vegetarianguest
house.com

Email:
plasmadoc@vegetarian
guesthouse.com

Train station:
Llandudno, 1/2 mile

Open:
all year, except Christmas
and new year

Directions:
A55 along North Wales
coast, then A470 to
Llandudno. Go straight
through the town, left at
Empire Hotel and past
tram station. It's the
second hotel on the right.

Parking: off road parking
available

Well-behaved children
welcome

No smoking throughout

10% discount given to
members of the
Vegetarian Society, Vegan
Society and Viva!

Vegetarian guest house with splendid views of Llandudno, the sea and the mountains of Snowdonia. There are four bedrooms, all with ensuite bathrooms. One single £30 per night, one double £25–£30 per person, one twin £25 per person.

There is lots on offer at breakfast and all the food is organic when possible. Begin with fruit juice and a selection of cereals with fruit and soya yoghurt. Follow up with veggie sausages, tomatoes with basil, mushrooms, baked beans and potato rosti served with thick crusty toast. Tea, coffee, fruit tea and dandelion coffee are all on offer. They have vegan margarine, muesli and soya milk.

You'll never go to bed hungry after eating their three course dinner for £15, which could be pea and mint soup, Persian aubergine, and apple and almond cake with Swedish glace ice-cream.

There are miles of breathtakingly beautiful walks in the area and it is a birdwatcher's delight. A 10 minute walk from the house is Great Orme and Ski Llandudno which has a dry slope and 700m toboggan run. Take the longest cable-operated tramway in Britain to the top of Great Orme, or if you have a head for heights take a cable car. The town itself is fronted by a sweeping bay and has much to offer like ten pin bowling, an art gallery, a museum and a theatre. Watersports and bike hire available.

The mountains of Snowdonia are only fifteen minutes drive and the sandy beaches in Anglesey half an hour's drive.

Tea & coffee making facilites and TV's in rooms. Guest lounge (no TV) well stocked with books, maps, guides and games.

Trericket Mill

Vegetarian guest house, bunk house and camp site situated in the Upper Wye Valley. There are three rooms in the house; two doubles and one twin costing £21–£24 per person per night all with ensuite bathrooms and tea and coffee making facilities. The bunkhouse sleeps up to eight people at £8.50–£10.50 per person per night in two cosy rooms. In the mill, overlooking the garden, there is an ensuite bunkroom for two, a common room with games, books and a TV along with drying facilities. The terraced orchard provides a few camping pitches for tents and small camper vans with the use of the bunkhouse shower and toilet facilities.

Breakfast can be a continental or a full cooked English Breakfast, including home-made bean, tomato and basil sausages, mushrooms, tomatoes and baked beans. Breakfast can be provided for bunkhouse guests and campers if desired. Soya milk and yoghurt, vegan margarine and vegan muesli are all available.

Dinner at £12.75 could be mushroom pate with wholegrain toast, followed by chickpea stew with apricots, wild rice and veggies, finished with apple and raspberry crumble and soya ice cream for dessert.

Trericket Mill is a brilliant base for activities in the Brecon Beacons National Park. The Wye Valley walk passes the door providing riverside walks in both directions. A national cycle route also passes by and there are numerous opportunities for off road cycling. Wildlife abounds here and there are so many delights to discover such as Prince Llewellyn's cave or the fairy glen with its hidden bathing pool.

Erwood
Builth Wells
Powys LD2 3TQ
Wales

Tel: 01982 560312

Fax: 01982 560768

www.trericket.co.uk

Email:
mail@trericket.co.uk

Train station:
Builth Road, 11 miles,
then a bus.

Open:
all year, except Christmas

Directions:
Set back from the A470
Brecon to Builth Wells
road between the villages
of Llyswen and Erwood.

Parking: available

Well supervised children
are welcome. They have a
cot and high chair.

Pets are allowed in the
bunkhouse only.

Smoking is allowed in a
designated room.

5% discount to members
of the Vegetarian Society,
Vegan Society and Viva!

Ty'r Ysgol

**Vegetarian
Guest House**

Veggie guest house in an early Victorian school house situated in a large garden surrounded by field and fells. There are three double ensuite rooms priced from £25-£29 per person per night. Each room is individually designed and all have views over the garden, countryside and hills.

*Botwnnog
Pwllheli
Gwynedd LL53 8PY
Wales*

Tel: 01758 730661

www.tyr-ysgol.co.uk

*Email:
maureenlewis@botwnnog.
freeserve.co.uk*

For breakfast begin with fruit juice, fresh fruit and cereal or muesli, followed by tofu sausages, field mushrooms, tomatoes, baked beans and toast. Specials are offered some mornings. Vegan margarine, soya milk, rice milk, vegan muesli, gluten and yeast free breads are available.

Train station: Pwllheli, 10 miles, then bus or taxi or collection is possible.

Open: all year

Dinner is offered for £17.50 and could be carrot and coriander soup to begin, followed by leek and wild mushroom croustade accompanied by salad or vegetables. For dessert, apple, pear and blackberry crumble. If the weather's nice you might like to have your dinner in the garden or the summerhouse. Organic produce is used where possible. Advise when booking if you are vegan or have any food intolerances or allergies.

Directions: From the A55 along the north coast road, leave at the second Bangor exit towards and through Caernarfon following the A487. After 5 or 6 miles, there is a roundabout where the A487 goes left towards Portmadog. Take the A499 towards Pwllheli. Continue through Pwllheli to Llanbedrog. After the 30 mph signs, take the next right turn, (B4413) signposted 'Aberdaron, Botwnnog, Sarn and Archery school'. Continue for 6 miles to Botwnnog. After entering the village and passing a large health centre, take the only main road to the right, signposted Llaniestyn. Continue up the hill passing the school and church on your right. Just after the national speed limit signs you will see the entrance of Ty'r Ysgol on the right.

There are ten beaches all within a twenty minute driving radius of the schoolhouse, including the four mile sandy beach Porth Neigwl (Hell's Mouth) which is popular with surfers. It is possible to get lessons and hire equipment for both surfing and sailing at nearby Abensoch. Wildlife and flora are abundant including seals, dolphins, herons and badgers. Further afield is Snowdonia National Park, Portmeirion Italianate village, the Welsh Highland Railway and many more attractions.

Children and one dog are welcome. Tea and coffee making facilities and TV's in the rooms. Guest lounge. No smoking except in the garden. Parking available.

The West Usk Lighthouse

Beautifully converted lighthouse on the east coast of St. Brides, with the sea a stone's throw from the front door. One of the proprietors is veggie. The lighthouse has one single ensuite at £50 per night, three double ensuites and one family room at £45 per person per night (£10 for children). The single room has a sea view and a four poster bed. One of the double rooms also has a four poster bed, one has a water bed and the other an antique bed.

Begin the day with cereal, followed by a cooked breakfast. Soy milk and veggie sausages available. For added romance, order some champagne with it. If you want to sweep your partner of his or her feet, a Rolls Royce drive to a local highly acclaimed restaurant can be arranged.

Local attractions include the palatial Tredegar House, Castell Coch, the Roman city of Caerleon and the castles of Caldicot Cardiff, Caerphilly and Penhow. There are also dry ski slopes, helicopter rides and go-karting for those who need some action. Both the Usk Valley and the Brecon Beacons are an easy, scenic drive away.

Take in the 360 degree view from the lantern room, or relax in the roof garden, watching the ships go by, whilst basking in the sunset or sunrise. West Usk Lighthouse is the perfect place to come for a romantic secluded break. If you're hoping your partner will propose, you may well get your wish. The host claims that in the last seven years, they've had twenty one marriage proposals among guests.

If you need extra pampering, they have a floatation tank and provide many complimentary therapies from £35. Tea and coffee making facilities and TV's in rooms.

494

Omnivorous
Bed and Breakfast

Lighthouse Road
St. Brides
Wentloog
near Newport
Gwent NP10 8SF
(Monmouthshire)

Tel: 01633 810126

Fax: 01633 815582

www.westusklighthouse.co.uk

Email:
lighthouse1@tesco.net

Train Station: Newport Gwent, 5 miles, then taxi or collection can be arranged

Open: all year

Directions: from the M4, at junction 28, take the A48 for Newport, then B4239 St. Brides. Drive for two miles. Turn left at Cattle Bridge into a long winding bumpy road.

Parking: available

Pets accepted by arrangement

Children welcome

No smoking

Cefn Gribyn

Vegetarian B&B and Self Catering

Carmel, Llannerchymedd,
Isle of Anglesey, Wales LL71 7BU
www.corfe-castle.demon.co.uk
Email: lesh@corfe-castle.demon.co.uk
Open: all year

Tel: 01248 470606
Train Station:
Holyhead 8 miles,
Bangor 15 miles

Double and twin room in a self contained cottage. Bed and breakfast £14.30–£20 per person per night, getting cheaper the longer you stay. If you self cater, it's only £50 per person per week, based on four people sharing. Discounts for regular customers. No children or pets. No smoking throughout.

Tremeifion

Vegetarian Hotel

Soar Road, Talsarnau,
Gwynedd, Wales, LL47 6UH
Open: all year, except Christmas and New Year

Tel: 01766 770491
www.vegetarian-hotel.com
Train station:
Talsarnau, 5 minutes walk

Five double rooms £49–£62 per person per night for dinner, bed and breakfast. Cheaper rates in Autumn and Winter. Children and pets welcome. No smoking throughout.

The Old Rectory Hotel

Vegetarian Hotel

Maentwrog, Gwynedd,
Wales LL41 4HN
Open: all year

Tel: 01766 590305
Train Station: Porthmadog 6
miles, then bus or taxi

Six double ensuites £49–£59 per room per night, two twin ensuites £49 and two family rooms £69 per room. Evening meal £13.95. Special diets catered for. Children and pets welcome. No smoking throughout.

Caerleon House Hotel

Omnivorous guest house

61 Caerau Road
Newport
Gwent NP20 4HJ

Tel: 01633-264 869
www.caerleonhousehotel.com
caerleonhousehotel@hotmail.com

Omnivorous guest house, owned by the people who run Chapel House. Veggie or vegan breakfast available. £20 single with shared bathroom, £25 single ensuite, £30 ensuite double or twin used as a single, £23 per person double or twin ensuite. Near the Civic Centre, 10 minutes walk from the train station. Smoking allowed. Visa, MC. Children welcome. Pets welcome. Large garden and pleasant views. Most restaurants in Newport offer a vegetarian dish.

The Old Post Office
(in Rosebush)

Omni
guest house
& restaurant

Omnivorous small guest house, 24 seat bistro, bar and 15 seat restaurant, open to non-residents, with masses for vegetarians, half of it vegan. One double and one twin (or as family rooms with cots available), £20 per person per night. Tea/coffee making, washbasins and TV in rooms. Cooked vegan or veggie breakfast. Pets welcome (not elephants). Laundry and drying facilities.

Restaurant has Welsh and international menu and a specials board that changes two or three times a week. 4 vegan and 7 veggie entrées £2.95-3.75 like basil and tomato soup, broccoli and walnut vegan pancake. 7 vegan and 7 veggie main courses £6.45-7.00 like mushroom loaf, Brazil nut pancake, Moroccan stuffed peppers. Desserts £1.95-2.95 including vegan sorbets, always a fruit salad, vegan apple pie or treacle tart. Beer, 2 or 3 real ales each week, house wine from £6.45 bottle, £1.60 glass. Tea or coffee, soya milk and milkshakes.

Smoking in the bar only. No credit cards at time of publication. Children welcome, they have a toy box in the bistro. Best to book for meals.
Directions: from A40 take B4313 at Narberth. Rosebush is 8 miles. Head for Maenclochog.
Not to be confused with the other Old Post Office in Powys.

*Rosebush, near
Maenchlochog
Pembrokeshire SA66 7QU*

Tel: 01437 532205

*oldpo_rosebush@
hotmail.com*

*Restaurant:
Mon 19-23.00,
Tue-Sat 11-23.00,
Sun 12-15.00
or later, 17-23.00*

Tomlins

Vegetarian restaurant with a menu that changes weekly. The lunchtime menu features a different country or region each fortnight. V

Starters around £4, include cream of cauliflower soup (can be vegan), and grilled aubergine and cucumber salad in ginger marinade.

Main courses, £11.10–11.65 such as hemp seed roast made with carrot, mixed nuts, toasted hemp seed, courgette and leek, with a port gravy, braised chicory and carrot and leek tagliatelle; courgette and coriander balls with a spiced creamy sauce.

There are several desserts at £3.70, such as pear sorbet, and apple and rhubarb strudel.

All diets/allergies catered for – please give 24 hours notice if possible. Soya milk, vegan margarine and ice-cream available.

Tomlin's is open alternate Sundays with a set menu. Two courses 8.50, 3 courses 10.50.

They have joined the Taste of Wales scheme and aim to source as many ingredients locally as possible, many of them organic.

Paintings on the wall are for sale. Basement is available to rent as an artist's studio or similar. /

Vegetarian
Restaurant

46 Plassey Street
Penarth
Cardiff
South Glamorgan
CF4 8ED

Tel: 01222-706644

www.tomlinsvegetarian-
restaurant.co.uk
(no hyphen)

Train:
Valles line from Cardiff to
Penarth Dingle Road

Open:
Tue–Thu 19.00–00.30,
Fri and Sat 12–14.30 &
19.00–00.30.
Alternate Sundays 12–
14.30.
Closed Monday

Children's portions
High chairs

Fully licenced.
Organic, vegan and
vegetarian wine.

No smoking

Visa, MC, Amex, Diners

Service charge not
included

Hunky Dory Vegetarian Coffee Shop

Vegetarian cafe

17 Charles Sreet
Newport, Gwent NP20 1JU
Open: Mon–Sat 10–16.00,
occasional evening every two weeks

Tel: 01633–257 850

Vegetarian café. Main meals £4.95 such as broccoli bake, pies, pizza, pasta bake. Home made cakes, scones, flapjacks, almost all vegan. No smoking. No credit cards.

The Wall Place Vegetarian Café

Vegetarian cafe

Bishops Yard, Chapel Street
Conwy, Gwynedd LL32 8BP
Open: April–Sept, Mon–Sun 12–15.00, 18–22.00

Tel: 01492–596 326
www.wallplace.co.uk
info@wallplace.co.uk

Vegetarian café, virtually vegan, with a large outside seating area in a beautiful walled courtyard. Lunch filled pittas for £2.25 and specials with salad, such as chilli and corn chips, at £5.95. Evening meal starters, £2.95–£3.95, include tofu rissoles, and mains, £7.95–£8.95 with grilled tarine and smoked tofu and mushroom tempura. Desserts, £2.45–£3.25, with vegan puddings and ice creams. Can cater for special diets and most of the menu, and all the puddings, are gluten–free. Non smoking. Visa, MC.

The Harvest Moon Café and Healing Centre

Vegan cafe

4 Newry Street
Holyhead, Isle of Anglesey
Gwynedd LL65 1HP
Open: Tue–Sat 10.00–17.00

Tel: 01407 763670
www.holyhead.co.uk

Vegan café set in a healing centre which offers a variety of treatments and runs meditation groups and a lending library of over 500 books. Nothing over £5, with lots of healthy vegan fare like soups, garlic bread, burgers, chilli and sandwiches, £2. Homemade cakes from £1.20 and several fruit smoothies, £1. Non smoking. No credit cards.

Waverley Vegetarian Restaurant

Vegetarian & Vegan cafe

23 Lammas Street
Carmarthen
Pembrokeshire SA31 3AL
Open: Open: Mon–Sat 9–17.00

Tel: 01267 236 521

Vegetarian and vegan café. Mains £3.50–£4.50 such as potato cake with salad. Vegan desserts like apple pie. Non smoking. Visa, MC.

Beehive Café

Omnivorous cafe

Bridge Street
Newport
Pembrokeshire SA42 0TB
Open: every day 9.30–14.00;
Tue, Fri–Sat also 19.00–20.30 (last orders).
Will open other nights for a group booking.

Tel: 01239–820372

Omnivorous café with vegetarian dishes, sometimes vegan on request. £5 for a veggie big breakfast. Bring your own alcohol, £1 corkage.

Great Oak Cafe

Vegetarian cafe

12 Great Oak Street
Llanidloes
Powys SY18 6BU
Open: 10–4 Mon–Sat, closed Sun

Tel: 01686–413 211

Wholefood vegetarian café and some vegan meals including cakes.

Centre for Alternative Technology Restaurant Vegetarian

Pantperthog
Machynlleth
Powys SY20 9AZ
Open: Winter 10–16.00, Summer 9.30–17.00. Closed
Xmas, Boxing Day and two weeks in January.

Tel: 01654–705950
www.cat.org.uk

Vegetarian wholefood café in the Centre for Alternative Technology. Main course £5–6 such as chilli with rice., vegan clearly marked but not always available. Licensed for alcohol. Non smoking. Credit cards ok. High chair.
The centre itself is open all year apart from above holidays, summer 9.30–18.00, winter 10–16.00. Admission summer adult £7, children £3.60, concessions £5, family (2+2) £20, (2+3) £22.50, (+4) £26. Winter adult £5, children £2.60, concessions £4, families £14.20, £15.20, £18.80. Three miles north of Machynlleth on the A487. 10% discount if you arrive by bus (every 20–40 minutes on weekdays in the summer), bike, train and show your tickets or put your bike in their shed. Right on Sustrans 8 national bike route.

Quarry Café

Vegetarian cafe

13 Heol Maengwyn
Machynlleth
Powys SY20 8EB
Open: Winter Mon–Sat 9–16.30 (Thu –14.00), closed Sun.
Summer Mon–Sat 9–17.00, Sun 10–16.00.

Tel: 01654–702 624
Fax: 01654 702 624

Vegetarian café and take–away using some organic and fair–traded produce, part of the Centre for Alternative Technology but this café is in the town not the centre (3 miles away). Soup, hummus, various curries, nut roasts, pasta bakes, salads. Filled roll £1.30 up to a main dish £5.15. Desserts including vegan cakes and vegan fruit crumble 75p–£2.35. Teas, coffees, cappucino 60p–£1.20, soya milk ok. Prepack soya milkshakes. Bring your own booze, no corkage charge. High chairs, some children's portions, one step wheelchair access. Wholefood shop in the same street.

Crumbs

Vegetarian cafe

33 David Morgan Arcade
Cardiff
South Glamorgan CF1 2AF
Open: Mon–Fri 10–15.30, Sat 10–16.00, closed Sun

Tel: 02920 395 007

Vegetarian café. Salads £3.65, spuds from £1.70–£2.90, hot dishes like curry or pasta £4.25. Desserts include fruit salads, carrot cake and muffins. No smoking except outside in the summer. No credit cards. Children's portions.

The Chapter Arts Centre Cafe

Omnivorous cafe

Market Road, Canton
Cardiff, South Glamorgan
Open: every day 09.00–22.00

Tel: 029–2039 7999
www.chapter.org

50% vegetarian café with some vegan and gluten–free dishes. Aubergine and lentil bake £4. Lots of home–made cakes, flapjacks, including vegan. Alcohol in the daytime, but in the evening there's a bar on site. Tea 60p, cappucino £1.10, they have soya milk. 50% non smoking and there's a big outdoor patio seated area.

Cafe Naz

Omnivorous Indian

Unit 8/8c Mermaid Quay
Cardiff Bay CF10 5BZ
Open: every day 12.00–23.30 (00.30 Fri–Sat)

Tel: 029 2049 6555
www.cafenaz.co.uk

Classy omnivorous Indian restaurant with many veggie dishes. Reckon £12 per person including drinks. Thali £12.95. Bottle of house wine £7, glass £3. Smoking area. Visa, MC. Pay and park area in the complex. Reservations required evenings. Children welcome.

Govindas Vegetarian Restaurant

Vegetarian Indian

8 Cradock St
Swansea, West Glamorgan SA1 3EN
Train: Swansea Central
Open: Mon–Wed 12.00–15.00, Thu–Sat 12.00–20.00

Tel: 01792–468 469
Fax: 01792–468 469
govin_das@hotmail.com

Vegetarian restaurant 2 minutes from town centre and with three quarters of menu vegan and clearly indicated. Starters, £1.10–£1.95, include soups and salads. Mains, £3.50–£4.95, with burgers and a daily changing Govindas special which includes daal and vegetable dishes. Desserts such as vegan cake of the day at £1.85 and apple pies, also vegan friendly. Non smoking. No credit cards.

Holland & Barrett   Health food shop

Unit 2 Colwyn Centre, Sea View Road   Tel: 01492–534 336
Colwyn Bay
Denbighshire LL29 8DG

30 High Street   Tel: 01745–816 965
Denbigh
Denbighshire LL16 3RY

Natural Choice   Wholefood shop

14 Colwyn Avenue   Tel: 01492 549520
Rhos-on-Sea,
Denbighshire LL28 4RB (Conwy)
Open: Mon–Sat 9–17.00

Wholefood shop, cruelty-free toiletries, remedies, supplements, and a therapy room at the back where they offer reflexology, homoeopathy, Reiki, Indian head massage etc by appointment. There's a sandwich shop next door which they're encouraging to do more veggie options.

Holland & Barrett   Health food shop

58 High Street   Tel: 01745–355 044
Rhyl
Denbighshire LL18 1TW

27 Hope Street   Tel: 01978–262 847
Wrexham
Denbighshire LL11 1BD

73 Monmow Street   Tel: 01600–772 153
Monmouth
Gwent ND5 3EW

42a Commercial Street   Tel: 01633–264 596
Newport
Gwent NP20 1LP

51 Mostyn Street   Tel: 01492–870 814
Llandudno
Gwynedd LL30 2NN

Vegonia Wholefoods

Vegan wholefood shop

49 High St
Porthmadog
Gwynedd
Open: Mon–Sat 10–17.00

Tel: 01766 515195

Completely vegan wholefood shop. Sometimes they have pasties and of course vegan ice–cream.

Holland & Barrett

Health food shop

13 Graham Way
Merthyr Tydfil
Mid Glamorgan CF47 8ED

Tel: 01685–382 086

62 Taff Street
Pontypridd
Mid Glamorgan CF37 4TD

Tel: 01443–409 431

Aardvark Wholefoods

Wholefood shop

2 Mansel Street
Carmarthen
Pembrokeshire
Open: Mon–Wed & Fri–Sat 9–17.00, Thu 9–18.30

Tel: 01267–232 497

Omnivorous wholefood shop with vegetarian and vegan choices.

Holland & Barrett

Health food shop

Unit 8, Greyfriars
Carmarthen
Pembrokeshire SA31 3BN

Tel: 01267–237 198

Unit 16, Riverside Key
Haverfordwest
Pembrokeshire SA61 2LJ

Tel: 01437–762 723

Natural Grocer

Wholefood shop

11 Quay Street
Haverfordwest
Pembrokeshire SA61 1BG
Open: Mon–Sat 9–17.30 (17.00 Sat)

Tel: 01437 767499

Wholefood shop with a fridge containing things like tofu and vegan cheese.

Holland & Barrett

Health food shop

16 Stepney Street
Llanelli
Pembrokeshire SA15 3UP

Tel: 01554–744 131

Beanfreaks Ltd

Wholefood shop

Chartist Towers, Upper Dock Street
Newport
Pembrokeshire
Open: Mon–Sat 9–17.30

Tel: 01633 666150

Wholefood shop. No take–aways.

Quarry Shop

Health food shop

27 Heol Maengwyn
Machynlleth
Powys SY20 8EB
Open: Winter Mon–Sat 9–17.00 (Thu –14.00), closed Sun.
Summer Mon–Sat 9–17.30, Sun 10–16.00.

Tel: 01654–702 339

Vegetarian shop, mainly organic and fair trade, with wholefoods, vitamins, homeopathic remedies, toiletries.10% discount for Vegetarian and Vegan Society members.

Holland & Barrett

Health food shop

4 Queen Street
Neath
West Glamorgan SA11 1DL

Tel: 01639–645 745

10 Union Street
Swansea
West Glamorgan SA1 3EF

Tel: 01792–644 011

Northern Ireland

Ahimsa
Vegetarian bed and breakfast

243 Whitepark Road,
Bushmills, Co Antrim

Tel: 028 207 31383
Open all year

Vegetarian B&B catering for vegans, macrobiotic. Traditional cottage, tastefully modernised. It is warm and cosy inside and vegetables are mostly supplied from its own organic garden. It is very close to the Giants Causeway and the surrounding spectacular coastline. An ideal centre for walking, birdwatching, etc. Yoga and reflexology are available on request. Accommodates 4, non-smoking, children welcome. Tourist Board approved. Twin room £18, double room £15. Evening dinner available with notice £10.

Bushymead Country House
Omnivorous guest house

86 Drumaness Road,
Ballynahinch, Co Down BT24 8LT

Tel: 028 97 561171
Open all year except Dec

Non-vegetarian, catering for vegetarian and vegan diets. Large country house built in classical style. All rooms have tea/coffee facilities, TV and central heating. Separate guest lounge and children's play areas. Situated on main A24 Belfast-Newcastle road in the centre of Co Down. Close to all tourist attractions, forest parks, National Trust properties, museums, coast of Down. Nearest railway station – Lisburn. Open all year except December. £22.50 pp sharing with reduction for extended stay. Breakfast in rooms on request. Near health food shops in Newcastle and Lisburn. Buffet breakfast – fruit, cereal, yoghurt, cooked. No evening meal available. Pets welcome provided they are housetrained. Accommodates 20, non-smoking, Tourist Board approved..

Little India
Vegetarian restaurant

53 Dublin Road,
Belfast BT2 7HE
littleindia@admleisuregroup.com
Open: every day 11-14.30, 17-23.30 (Fri-Sat -24.00)

Tel: 028 9058 3040
Train: Botanic

Small and intimate vegetarian restaurant serving indian vegetarian food. Good selection with 80% or the 70 dishes vegan. Main courses £5-6. Non-vegan dishes marked on menu. Licensed and bring your own (corkage). Seats approx. 25.

Eatwell Healthfoods

Health food shop

413 Lisburn Road,
Belfast BT9

Tel: 028 9066 4362
Train: Adelaide

Excellent range of vegan/vegetarian refrigerated food and deserts; home baked savoury pastries and scones; Beauty Without Cruelty cosmetics; crueltry free toiletries. Vegetarian proprietors – friendly, family run.

Framar Health

Health food shop

595 Lisburn Road,
Belfast BT9

Tel: 028 9068 1018
Train: Adelaide

Average range of foods; emphasis on supplements and toiletries.

Framar Health

Health food shop

391 Ormeau Road,
Belfast

Tel: 028 9069 4210
Train: Botanic

The Nutmeg

Wholefood shop

Lombard Street,
Belfast BT1

Tel: 028 9024 9984
Train: Glengall St

Small city centre wholefood shop, compact and varied range of foods with vegan pastries, cakes and snacks.

Holland & Barrett

Health food shop

Unit 55–57, Tower Centre
Ballymena

Tel: 02891 478812

Bloomfield Shopping Centre
Bangor

Tel: 02890 321948

Unit 38, Park Centre
Belfast BT12

Tel: 028-6632 9879

Unit 14 Erneside Shopping Centre
Enniskillen

Tel: 0289-264 0570

Bow Street
Lisburn

Unit 4a Buttercrane Shopping Centre
Newry

14 Abbey Centre
Newtonabbey
BT37 9UH

With grateful thanks for compiling this section to Beverly Riley at Northern Ireland Animal Rights Campaign, PO Box 1115, Belfast BT1 1AT. niarc@02.co.uk

Republic of
Ireland

This chapter contains a selection of some of the best vegetarian places to stay and eat in Ireland. There are terrific places to eat out in Dublin and wonderful country retreats.

You can pick up additional information at these great Irish websites:

www.vegetarian.ie

www.ireland.travel.ie

www.visitdublin.com

www.cork-kerry.travel.ie

www.northwestireland.travel.ie

www.westireland.travel.ie

www.hostels-ireland.com

www.irelandyha.org
Phone +353-830 4555 to get free fold-out leaflets with maps and information about 36 hostels throughout Ireland.

www.ryanair.com (cheap flights)

www.swiftcall.ie (cheap overseas calls)

www.daft.ie (long term accommodation)

As with all internet listings, beware of places that have closed down and always phone first before going.

With grateful thanks to Nana Luke and friends, who compiled the Vegetarian Guide to Ireland, for all their work.

Telephone dialling code for Ireland from the UK is 00 353 then drop the first 0 of the phone number. From overseas +353.

Green Lodge

Vegetarian self catering

Pearson's Bridge
Bantry
Cork
homepage.eircom.net/~greenlodge
Bookings: greenlodge@bigfoot.com

Tel: 027-66146
Open: all year

Self catering apartments for vegans and vegetarians with private cooking facilities, bathroom and own entrance. 8km from Bantry in peaceful wooded surroundings. Ensuite single room 90 euros per week (55e for 3 days), double/twin 115e (70e). Apartment for two with dining room and kitchen 155e per week (100 for 3 days). Family flat from 165-185e for 3-5 people (110-130 for 3 days). Children welcome, babysitting by arrangement, free cot. No pets. Booking deposit 75 euros per week. No credit cards. TV's in apartments. Wheelchair access. Laundry service. Table tennis and basketball.

Shiplake Mountain Hostel

Vegetarian youth hostel

Dunmanway
Cork
www.shiplakemountainhostel.com
Email: Use link from website

Tel: 023-45750
Open: all year except two
weeks in winter, phone to
check

Vegetarian youth hostel for 20 people on the side of a mountain, about 5km from Dunmanway. Traditional gypsy caravans for two people (can also take a child) 11.50 euros per person per night in low season, 13.50 in high season. Private room 16.50 all year per person. Dorm for 6-8 people 11 euros. Camping adult 6 euros, child 4 euros. Breakfast 2.50-5.00 euros, packed lunch 4.50 euros, 2 course dinner 8.50 euros, 3 courses 10.50 euros. They can do vegan food but said they find us vegans rather fussy! Smoking only in the common room. Bicycle hire 8.50 euros, maps available. Laundry service. Courtesy pickup from town. Weekly and group discounts.

Chysalis Holistic Centre

Vegetarian b&b & holistic centre

Donard
Wicklow
Open: al year except Christmas, office 10-17.00

Tel: 045-404713
www.holistic.ie/chrysalis
chrysalis@clubi.ie

Vegetarian holistic centre in its own grounds. Bed and breakfast, lunch and dinner also available. Craft shop, sauna, therapies, meditation garden. Non smoking. Call them for a programme of events.

Cussens Cottage Vegan Guest House   Vegan guest house

Ballygrennan, Bulgaden
Kilmallock
Limerick
http://homepage.eircom.net/~cussenscottage

Tel: 063-98926
cussenscottage@eircom.net

Set in over 1.5 acres of gardens, Cussens Cottage is we believe Ireland's only vegan guest house. All rooms are ensuite with their own door opening onto the gardens. Doubles 38.50 euros (£24) per person, 54.50 euros (£34) single. Rooms have electric heaters, hairdryers and kettles with teas, coffees and milks. Breakfast is a huge affair which keeps you well fed on vegan food until the four course dinner, 19 euros. Much of the food comes from their veganic garden, i.e. organic with no animal manure. They run veganic gardening weekends and other special events. An ideal base for touring the south-west, or stay here ande take the train into Dublin. No smoking in public rooms. Not a suitable holiday venue for children.

Ceann Cursa   Vegetarian bed & breakfast

Pier Road, Murrisk
Westport
Mayo

Tel: 098-64864
ceanncursa@esatclear.ie
Open: all year

Vegetarian bed and breakfast, walking distance from Croagh Patrick mountain, five miles from Westport. Sea and mountain views. One room with a double and a single bed, 25 euros per person sharing. Advance booking essential.

The Phoenix   Vegetarian guest house & restaurant

Shanahill East, Boolteens
Near Castlemaine
Kerry
Open: Easter-Oct, rest of the year bookings only.
Restaurant all day 09.00-midnight

Tel: 066-9766284
www.kerryweb.ie/thephoenix
phoenixtyther@hotmail.com

Organic vegetarian restaurant and farmhouse accommodation resting under Slieve Mish mountains on the Dingle peninsula. Lounge with open fire, library, studio for workshops, guests' kitchen, extensive gardens. Camping, group and private facilities. Sandy beach and Kerry airport nearby. Courtesy lifts available to and from Castlemaine. Dublin Express bus stops in Castlemaine. Half an hour drive from Kerry airport.

Escape Vegetarian Restaurant

Vegetarian restaurant

1 Albert Ave
Bray
Wicklow
Open: Mon–Fri 16.00–22.30 (last orders),
Sat 12.30–22.30, Sun 12.30–20.30

Tel: 01-2866 755
www.escapeinfo.cjb.net

Vegetarian restaurant about 30 minutes from Dublin city centre by DART train. 45 euros will feed two people amply. Bring your beer and wine, 2 euros per person corkage. Vegans, coeliacs welcome. Smoking allowed. Children very welcome, two high chairs at least.

Blazing Salads

Vegetarian take–away

42 Drury Street
Dublin 2
Open: Mon–Sat 9.00–17.30 (later in summer),
Sun closed

Tel: 01 6719552
blazingsalads@eircom.net

Vegetarian take–away using mainly organic ingredients, with a regularly changing menu. Soups, self serve salad bar with cost by weight, sandwiches, samosas, tofu and veg spring rolls, apricot slices and fruit and nut bars. They cater for vegan, gluten–free and wheat–free diet and have soya milk, soya cappuccinos and soya milkshakes. Fresh juices and smoothies by the cup or litre. Visa, MC, Amex.

Blazing Salads

Vegearian cafe & take–away

25c Powerscourt Town Centre
Dublin 2
Open: Mon–Sat 12.00–16.30, Sun closed

Tel: 01 6719552

Vegetarian counter service café on Level 2 of Powerscourt Shopping Centre. Soups, salads, baked potatoes. Main dishes like kidney bean casserole with brown rice and two salads. Vegan heaven with a wide choice of desserts including apple pie with cashewnut topping, date, oat and orange square; hot apple crumble; fruit and nut bar; even vegan tofu nut cream to pour over them. Special diets no problem. There is a discount for re–using bottles.

Cornucopia

Vegetarian cafe & take–away

19 Wicklow Street
Dublin 2
Open: Mon–Sat 08.30–20.00,
Thurs late till 21.00, Sun 12–18.00

Tel: 01 6777583

Very busy vegetarian counter service café, with a great selection for vegans. There are always two soups, ten salads, four or five main dishes such as Moroccan lentil stew with rice and salad, cakes and cookies. Freshly baked bread by the slice including vegan soda bread. Breakfast menu served 09.00–12.00. Special diets no problemo with all items clearly marked which diets they are suitable for. Organic ingredients are used as much as possible. Take–away is available. Smoking is allowed, but there is a non–smoking area.

Juice

Vegetarian restaurant

78–83 South Great Georges Street
Dublin 2
Open: every day 11.30–23.00

Tel: 01 4757856

Vegetarian restaurant with a friendly atmosphere which would suit both a romantic dinner for two or a group of friends. It is also possible to sit at the front of the restaurant and just enjoy a fresh juice or a wine. Plenty for vegans, clearly marked. Start with soup, miso broth, yam wedges chilled tofu mayonnaise dip, or a selection of dips. Lots of exotic side dishes. Main courses include Asian noodles in Ponzu sauce with tofu or tempeh; vegetable fried ricewith tofu, tempeh or seitan; organic aduki Juiceburger and chips; cashew and hazelnut roast. Organic vegan wines. Soya milk, cappucinnos and milkshakes. Homemade desserts and even vegan icecream. Visa, MC.

Wagamama Dublin

Japanese omnivorous restaurant

South King Street
Dublin 2
Open: Sun–Thu 12.00–23.00,
Fri–Sat 12.00–24.00 (last orders 22.50)

Tel: 01 4782152

Omnivorous Japanese noodle bar with several branches also in London. Vegetarian dishes are clearly marked. Some are suitable for vegans. Reasonably priced. Non smoking. Licensed. MC, Visa, Amex, Diners.

Nature's Way
Health food shop

Stephen's Green Shopping Centre, Grafton Street   *Tel: 01 478 0165*
Dublin 2
Open: Mon–Sat, (except Thu) 9.00–18.00, Thu 9.00–20.00, Sun closed.

The Parnell Mall, The Ilac Centre   *Tel: 01 8728391*
Dublin 1
Open: Mon–Sat 9.00–18.00, except Thu 9.00–20.00, Sun closed

Unit 121, Blanchardstown Shopping Centre   *Tel: 01 822 2560*
Dublin 15   Train/Tube Bus 39
Open: Mon–Tue & Sat 9.00–18.00, Wed–Fri 9.00–21.00, Sun 11.00–18.00

The General Health Food Store
Health food shop

93 Marlborough Street   *Tel: 01 8743290*
Dublin 2
Open: Mon–Sat 9.00–18.00. Sun closed.

Holland & Barrett
Health food shop

U67 Donaghmede Shopping Centre   *Tel: 00353–1867 1174*
Dublin

U51 Blackrock Shopping Centre   *Tel: 00353–1288 6696*
Dublin

U236A The Square Shopping Centre   *Tel: 00353–1459 6268*
Tallaght, Dublin

U121 Blanchardstown NTC   *Tel: 00353–1822 2560*
Dublin

U115 St Stephens Green Shopping Centre   *Tel: 00353–1478 0165*
Dublin

8 Church Street
Coleraine   BT51 5QU

U20 Wilton Shopping Centre   *Tel: 00353–214544284*
Cork

UG5 Merchants Quay Shopping Centre   *Tel: 00353–214275989*
Cork

U7 Blackpool Shopping Centre   *Tel: 00353–214212041*
Cork

U5 Paul Street Shopping Centre   *Tel: 00353–214270729*
Cork

U14 Market Cross Shopping Centre   *Tel: 00353–5665896*
Kilkenny

U2 Arthurs Quay Shopping Centre   *Tel: 00353–61310466*
Limerick

Ronny's Top Tips
for restaurateurs

The vegan population is growing rapidly, faster than vegetarianism, and awareness about food allergies and cholesterol is also increasing. Therefore a very significant number of your customers will be actively avoiding eggs and dairy products as well as meat. If you make sure that many of your meals are completely animal free, you will tap into a significant market. Here are some suggestions:

1. There are numerous brands of vegetarian **sausages, burgers and bacon substitutes**. All are quite similar, but some brands contain egg. If you always buy egg-free ones, you will be able to cater for both vegetarians and vegans at the same time. For a total vegan breakfast feast, offer scrambled (mashed and lightly fried) **tofu** as an alternative to scrambled eggs.

2. Always have **soya milk.** It keeps for over a year unopened and up to 5 days when opened. **Soya dessert** and **soya cream** also keep for a long time. Soya milk makes excellent cappuccinos and is perfect for making custard and rice puddings.

3. Try serving **Tofutti** or **Swedish Glace** ice cream, either on its own or to accompany hot pies and puddings. Just try it and you won't need any further convincing!

4. **Soya cheese** can be used to create some amazing vegan dishes, yet is rarely used in catering. It is easily available pre-packed at wholefood stores, or in bulk blocks from manufacturers and wholesalers. Redwood Foods make a very popular brand called 'Cheezley'. It has a longer shelf life than dairy cheese, even after you open it. Or make your own using *The Uncheese Cookbook* by Joanne Stepaniak, from The Vegan Society, www.vrg.org, amazon.co.uk, or ask at your bookshop.

5. Vegan salads are easy to prepare. **Egg-free mayonnaise** is available in small jars from wholefood stores or buy the excellent Plamil brand in bulk tubs from wholesalers. Alternatively make your own mayonnaise-style dressing by blending vegetable oil with roughly equal quantities of vinegar and soya milk. You could also offer a **vinaigrette** made with olive oil, herbs, mustard and lemon juice or vinegar. If you make up a big batch of this, it will keep for weeks, just shake before serving.

6. **Vegan dips** are no problem. You can easily buy or make hummous, and guacamole can be made just as well without yogurt. Try roasting aubergines and liquidising with olive oil and black pepper for a very rich and creamy baba ganoush dip.

7. For an uncooked **vegan breakfast**, serve a muesli that doesn't have honey or whey in it, or offer toast, crumpets or muffins with vegan margarine. Most brands of vegetable margarine are not vegan as they contain whey powder, but virtually all supermarkets stock at last one vegan brand. Catering size tubs can be bought from wholesalers.

8. Avoid glazing **pastries** with egg, and make sure that the pastry itself as well as the contents are vegan. Bulk packs of frozen puff, filo and shortcrust pastry are widely available from wholesalers.

9. Aim to make **at least half your starters and main courses vegan**. If only one out of four or six options is vegan we don't have any choice. Cheese, cheese or cheese isn't much of a choice for veggies either.

10. It is very frustrating that so many restaurants offer a choice of vegan starters and main courses, but no **dessert**. When there is a dessert, it is often completely unimaginative. Vegans are as fed up with fruit salad and sorbet as vegetarians are with omelettes and cheese salad! Why not offer vegan ice cream (see above) with fruit salad, or better still, experiment with egg-free recipes for cakes and puddings. It is possible to make delicious trifles, flans and cheese-cakes which are completely vegan.

If you have any questions, or would like some free vegan cake recipes, write to me c/o Vegetarian Guides. You could also contact **the Vegan Society** (below) for their catering pack (which includes a list of wholesalers of vegan food and alcohol) and their merchandise catalogue full of cookbooks. Alternatively, see what's on offer in any of the restaurants listed that are particularly good for vegans. The IVU and VRG websites are also a great source of inspiration.

Ronny has been a vegan campaigner and caterer for many years, has written The Complete Scoffer *cookbook and co-authored* Campaign Against Cruelty – an activist's handbook. *She currently works as a campaigner at Animal Aid (www.animalaid.org.uk) and has published a vegan cake cookbook* **The Cake Scoffer,** *available by sending a cheque for £1.50 (£1 + 50p postage) to Animal Aid, The Old Chapel, Bradford St, Tonbridge, Kent TN9 1AW. www.animalaid.org.uk. Ronny's brand new* **The Salad Scoffer – picnic and party food recipes** *is £1.25 + 50p postage = £1.75 from Animal Aid (inflation y'know). See some Scoffer recipes at www.campaignagainstcruelty.co.uk.*

Examples of dishes which can easily be made vegan:

Stir fries, spaghetti bolognese, soups, salads, curries, stews, risottos, pizzas (simply leave off the cheese and drizzle with olive oil), pasta.

Examples of desserts which are easy to veganise:

Plum pudding with custard (soya milk), fruit salad with soya cream/soya ice cream, chocolate cornflake clusters (made with dairy-free chocolate), iced bagels, fruit crumble, summer pudding.

Top websites for recipes & cookbooks

International Vegetarian Union: www.ivu.org

www.vegan-food.net

The Vegetarian Society (UK): www.vegsoc.org
Parkdale, Dunham Rd, Altrincham, Cheshire WA14 4QG, UK
Tel (+44) 0161-925 2000, Fax 0161-926 9182. Email: info@vegsoc.org
Organisers of National Vegetarian Week, in early summer, a good time to promote your business to the local community. They run the Cordon Vert cookery school which trains professional chefs and new restaurateurs. See their advertisements near the front of this book.

Vegetarian Resource Group: www.vrg.org
PO Box 1463, Baltimore, MD 21203, USA.
Tel (+1) 410-366 8343. Fax 410-366 8804. vrg@vrg.org
Experts on vegetarian cooking and nutrition. Heaps of vegan cookbooks, some of them also available from the Vegan Society.

The Vegan Society: www.vegansociety.com, info@vegansociety.com
Donald Watson House, 7 Battle Rd, St Leonards-on-Sea, East Sussex TN37 7AA, UK. Tel (+44) 0845 45 88244. Fax 01424-717064.
Mail order catalogue contains many vegan cookbooks including American titles. Organisers of World Vegan Day (1st November) and National Vegan Week (around it), the perfect time to promote new vegan menus, see www.worldveganday.org.

Profit from Emerging Dietary Trends – Ten Steps to Success by John Hartley. The professional caterer's manual for significantly increasing turnover and profitability by offering more vegan dishes and veganizing the ones you already have, making them acceptable to virtually all diets and religions. The author is hugely experienced in mainstream catering, training and business consultancy. www.gopublish.co.uk, info@gopublish.co.uk

National Vegan Festival in central London annually at the end of the summer, has stalls by caterers. www.veganfestival.freeserve.co.uk

Be a Cake Scoffer!

If you enjoy eating vegan cakes, but are never quite sure how to make them, you'll love *The Cake Scoffer*, a 20 page laminated and illustrated booklet packed with exciting egg and dairy free cake, dessert and sweet recipes.

INDEX OF VEGAN ENTRIES

RETREAT CENTRES

ACCOMMODATION INDEX

HOSTELS AND CAMPING

RESTAURANTS INDEX

INDEX OF PLACES

527